R. Gupta's®

Popular Master Guide

NATIONAL TESTING AGENCY (NTA)

CUET-UG

Common University Entrance Test for
Under Graduate Courses/Programmes

CUET-UG
Books Series
30

SECTION-II
DOMAIN SPECIFIC SUBJECT

AGRICULTURE

Subject Code : 302

by
Sourav Bhardwaj

2026-27
EDITION

RAMESH PUBLISHING HOUSE, NEW DELHI

Published by
O.P. Gupta *for* Ramesh Publishing House

Admin. Office
12-H, New Daryaganj Road, Opp. Officers' Mess,
New Delhi-110002 ✆ 23275224, 23245124

E-mail: info@rameshpublishinghouse.com
For Online Shopping: www.rameshpublishinghouse.com

Showroom
- Balaji Market, Nai Sarak, Delhi-6 ✆ 23282525 📱 9354373464
- 4457, Nai Sarak, Delhi-6, ✆ 23918938

Book Code: R-2464

ISBN: 978-93-5477-533-8

Price: ₹ 220

Printed at: Deepak Offset, Delhi

CONTENTS

★ ★ ★ ★ ★

Previous Years' Paper

Common University Entrance Test for UG Programmes

CUET-UG—AGRICULTURE*

Entrance Exam, 2025

(Exam held on 21-05-2025)

Subject Code: 302

1. Match List-I with List-II.

List-I (Weather element)	List-II (Instrument)
A. Temperature	I. Dew gauge
B. Rainfall	II. Anemometer
C. Wind velocity	III. Rain gauge
D. Dew	IV. Thermometer

Choose the ***correct*** answer from the options given below:

1. A-IV, B-III, C-II, D-I
2. A-I, B-II, C-III, D-IV
3. A-I, B-II, C-IV, D-III
4. A-III, B-IV, C-I, D-II

2. Which among the following is greenhouse gas?

1. Methane
2. Oxygen
3. Nitrogen
4. Hydrogen

3. ____ is the major site for ATP synthesis amid oxidative metabolism and so called power house of cells.

1. Chloroplast
2. Nucleus
3. Ribosome
4. Mitochondrion

4. Match List-I with List-II.

List-I (Crop)	List-II (First hybrid variety)
A. Maize	I. CSH-1
B. Jowar	II. H-4
C. Bajra	III. HB-1
D. Cotton	IV. Ganga-1

Choose the ***correct*** answer from the options given below:

1. A-I, B-II, C-III, D-IV
2. A-IV, B-II, C-III, D-I
3. A-I, B-II, C-IV, D-III
4. A-IV, B-I, C-III, D-II

5. The inheritance of the AB blood group in humans is an example of:

1. Co-dominance
2. Incomplete dominance
3. Complete dominance
4. Over-dominance

6. Enzymes are the molecules which?

1. Provides energy to the cell
2. Catalyse biochemical reactions
3. Saves the genetic information
4. Transmits genetic information generation to generation

7. Rickets in growing children are caused due to deficiency of:

1. Vitamin A
2. Vitamin B
3. Vitamin C
4. Vitamin D

8. Which among the following is a nitrogen-fixing bacteria?

A. *Rhizobium*
B. *Azotobacter*
C. *Azospirillim*
D. *Streptococcus*

Choose the ***correct*** answer from the options given below:

1. A, B and C only
2. A, B and D only
3. A, B, C and D
4. B, C and D only

9. Development of an embryo or seed without fertilization is called:

1. Apomixis
2. Anthesis
3. Self-incompatibility
4. Male sterility

1. 1 **2.** 1 **3.** 4 **4.** 4 **5.** 1 **6.** 2 **7.** 4 **8.** 1 **9.** 1

* *40 questions to be attempted out of 50.*

10. Syngamy led to formation of a specialized cell called:

1. Polar nuclei 2. Zygote
3. Antipodal cells 4. Endosperm

11. Match List-I with List-II.

List-I (Animal)	List-II (Breed)
A. Buffalo	I. Sunandini
B. Cow	II. White Leghorn
C. Poultry	III. Toggenburg
D. Goat	IV. Nili-Ravi

Choose the ***correct*** answer from the options given below:

1. A-IV, B-I, C-II, D-III
2. A-I, B-II, C-III, D-IV
3. A-I, B-II, C-IV, D-III
4. A-III, B-IV, C-I, D-II

12. According to egg production, arrange the poultry breeds in descending order:

A. White Leghorn B. Rhode Island Red
C. Assel D. Giriraja

Choose the ***correct*** answer from the options given below:

1. A, B, D, C 2. A, B, C, D
3. B, A, D, C 4. C, B, D, A

13. Which crop produce is widely used to feed poultry birds in India?

1. Maize 2. Rice
3. Wheat 4. Oat

14. Fermented produce of green forage is called:

1. Hay 2. Green manure
3. Silage 4. Green cakes

15. The lameness, swelling over shoulders and thighs, high temperature, death in three days to a cattle are principal symptoms of:

1. Anthrax 2. Galaghotu
3. Pneumonia 4. Black quarter

16. Hisardale is a new breed of sheep resulted from cross of:

1. Bikaneri ewes and Marino rams
2. Bikaneri rams and Marino ewes
3. Bikaneri ewes and Bikaneri rams
4. Marino ewes and Marino rams

17. Arrange the dairy cattle and buffaloes with respect to average age at maturity for puberity and sexual maturity in decreasing order:

A. Purebred exotic cattle
B. Zebu cattle
C. Buffaloes
D. Crossbreed cattle

Choose the ***correct*** answer from the options given below:

1. C, D, A, B 2. D. B, C, A
3. C, B. D, A 4. C, A, D, B

18. Frozen milk products include:

A. Kulfi B. Ice-cream
C. Ghee D. Dahi

Choose the ***correct*** answer from the options given below:

1. A, and B only 2. A, B and D only
3. A, B, C and D 4. B, C and D only

19. Fat rich milk products exclude:

A. Butter B. Khoa
C. Ghee D. Kulfi

Choose the ***correct*** answer from the options given below:

1. A, B and D only 2. B, and D only
3. A, B, C and D 4. B, C and D only

20. National Fish Farmers Day is celebrated in India on:

1. 15 June 2. 10 July
3. 5 August 4. 2 September

21. The National Genebank in India was started in:

1. 1983 2. 2023
3. 1992 4. 2001

22. Covering the surface of the soil by any material is known as:

1. Green manuring 2. Conservation tillage
3. Mulching 4. Contour farming

23. The nutrient moves up only in acropetal direction though xylem found in the plant system for:

1. Nitrogen 2. Calcium
3. Sulphur 4. Potassium

24. Glyphosate is used for weed control as a _____.

1. Post-emergence selective herbicide
2. Post-emergence non-selective herbicide
3. Pre-emergence selective herbicide
4. Pre-emergence non-selective herbicide

10. 2	**11.** 1	**12.** 1	**13.** 1	**14.** 3	**15.** 4	**16.** 1	**17.** 3
18. 1	**19.** 2	**20.** 2	**21.** 1	**22.** 3	**23.** 2	**24.** 2	

25. Nagarjunasagar project was established on river ____.

1. Krishna 2. Godavari
3. Pennar 4. Mahanadi

26. Arrange the sugarcane ratoon management practices in proper sequence:

A. Emerged shoots cut at ground level.
B. Sides of ridges are broken by plough
C. First irrigation is given 3 to 4 weeks after harvesting.
D. Nutrients are given and an earthing up operation should be done.

Choose the ***correct*** answer from the options given below:

1. A, B, C, D 2. A, D, C, B
3. B, A, D, C 4. C, B, D, A

27. Gramineae family crop includes:

A. Groundnut B. Gram
C. Wheat D. Paddy

Choose the ***correct*** answer from the options given below:

1. C and D only 2. A, B and D only
3. A, B, C and D 4. B, C and D only

28. Arrange the proper steps in sequence for wheat harvesting:

A. Winnowing and storage.
B. Threshing
C. Plants are bundled and dried for a few days.
D. Cutting the plants close to ground level.

Choose the ***correct*** answer from the options given below:

1. D, C, B, A 2. A, B, C, D
3. B, A, D, C 4. C, B, D, A

29. How much percentage of earth's surface is constituted by ocean?

1. 65% 2. 71%
3. 79% 4. 81%

30. Match List-I with List-II.

List-I (Crop)	List-II (Variety)
A. Wheat	I. Virat
B. Paddy	II. CO-86032
C. Sugarcane	III. IR-8
D. Gram	IV. HD-2496

Choose the ***correct*** answer from the options given below:

1. A-IV, B-III, C-II, D-I
2. A-I, B-II, C-III, D-IV
3. A-I, B-II, C-IV, D-III
4. A-III, B-IV, C-I, D-II

31. When fruits and vegetables are brought suddenly to a very low temperature at which all the chemical reactions stop, it is known as:

1. Freezing 2. Drying
3. Fermentation 4. Pickling

32. Match List-I with List-II.

List-I (Crop)	List-II (Variety)
A. Tomato	I. Pusa Purple Long
B. Brinjal	II. Kufri Chipsona-1
C. Mango	III. Pusa Ruby
D. Potato	IV. Amrapali

Choose the ***correct*** answer from the options given below:

1. A-II, B-I, C-III, D-IV
2. A-III, B-I, C-IV, D-II
3. A-II, B-III, C-IV, D-I
4. A-III, B-I, C-II, D-IV

33. Standard, Spray or bush form, Pot-mums and Coniform are the different types of:

1. Marigold 2. Gladiolus
3. Chrysanthemum 4. Rose

34. The commercially adopted propagation method in India for Grand Naine banana is:

1. Seed
2. Sword sucker
3. Tissue culture
4. Water sucker

35. The grape variety grown for juice extraction is:

1. Bokhari
2. Dilkush
3. Sonaka
4. Banglore Blue

36. Which of the following cabbage variety is resistant to black rot disease?

1. Pusa Ageti
2. Pusa Drum Head
3. Pusa Mukta
4. September

25. 1	**26.** 1	**27.** 1	**28.** 1	**29.** 2	**30.** 1
31. 1	**32.** 2	**33.** 3	**34.** 3	**35.** 4	**36.** 3

37. Arrange proper sequence of the steps in stone grafting in Mango:

A. Top portion of the root stock is cut off leaving 7 to 8 cm stem.
B. The scion is inserted in the vertical cut of the root stock and tied with polythene strip.
C. A scion is given slanting cuts from both the ends giving it a wedge shape.
D. A vertical cut of about 2-3 cm length is given to it.

Choose the ***correct*** answer from the options given below:

1. A, D, C, B 2. A, B, C, D
3. B, A, D, C 4. C, B, D, A

38. Which of the following planting systems is generally followed on the hills for the establishment of a fruit orchard?

1. Square system 2. Rectangular system
3. Hexagonal system 4. Contour system

39. Which of the following combinations of fruits and vegetables are the richest source of vitamin-A?

A. Mango, carrot, spinach
B. Sweet orange, acid lime
C. Papaya, leafy vegetables
D. Aonla, Guava

Choose the ***correct*** answer from the options given below:

1. A, B and D only 2. A, B and C only
3. A and C only 4. B, C and D only

40. Among the following which fruit is a richest source of ascorbic acid?

1. Winter guava 2. Acid Lime
3. Sweet orange 4. Aonla

Directions (Q.No. 41-45): *Read the following passage carefully and answer the questions:*

Kisan Credit Card (KCC)

The farmers in India have to face a lot of difficulty in arranging short term funds for the planting and harvesting season and to meet other agricultural needs. They are largely dependent on credit from the unorganized sector such as money lenders who charge exorbitant rates of interest. Realizing the need for such short-term credit, the Kisan credit card scheme was launched by the Reserve Bank of India and National Bank for Agriculture and Rural Development (NABARD). The kisan credit card is a credit scheme introduced in August 1998 by Indian banks. The model scheme was prepared by the NABARD on the recommendations of the R.V. Gupta committee to provide term loans and agricultural needs. Under the Kisan credit card scheme, customers can get two types of credit, i.e. cash credit and term loans. A short-term credit limit is offered on the Kisan credit card for smaller agricultural needs. Term loans can also be taken for cultivation, buying equipment, irrigation, etc. The farmers also receive a passbook which contains all the relevant details of land holding, credit limit, validity, etc. The repayment period in kisan credit cards is up to a maximum of 12 months and card is valid for a period between 3-5 years.

41. Kisan Credit Card scheme is introduced in:

1. August 1998 2. July 2002
3. August 1993 4. June 1998

42. Full form of NABARD is:

1. National Bank of Development
2. National Bank for Agriculture and Rural Development
3. National Bank for Agriculture Development
4. National Bank for Rural Development.

43. The repayment period in Kisan Credit Card is maximum upto:

1. 9 months 2. 24 months
3. 12 months 4. 20 months

44. Kisan Credit Card is the model scheme that was prepared by NABARD on the recommendations of:

1. M.S. Swaminathan Committee
2. Philip Kotler Committee
3. Rane Committee
4. R.V. Gupta Committee

45. The Kisan Credit Card is valid for a period of:

1. 3-5 years 2. 9-12 years
3. 13-15 years 4. 20-25 years

Directions (Q.No. 46-50): *Read the following passage carefully and answer the questions:*

Coconut

Botanical name of coconut is the *Cocos nucifera* and family is Arecaceae. The coconut tree is a member of the palm tree family. The term "coconut" can refer to the whole coconut palm, the seed, or the fruit, which botanically is drupe and not a nut. Coconuts are known for their versatility of uses, ranging from food to cosmetics. The inner flesh of the mature seed forms a regular part of the diets of many people known as Khobara. Coconuts are distinct from other fruits because their endosperm contains

37. 1	**38.** 4	**39.** 3	**40.** 4	**41.** 1	**42.** 2	**43.** 3	**44.** 4	**45.** 1

a large quantity of clear liquid and when immature, may be harvested for their coconut water known as Shahale. Mature, ripe coconuts can be used as prasad or nariyal or processed for oil and coconut milk from the flesh, charcoal from the hard shell, cocopeat and coir from fibrous husk. Dried coconut flesh is called copra, and the oil derived from it is commonly used in cooking as well as in making soaps and cosmetics. Long pinnate leaves can be used as raw material to make a variety of products for furnishing and decorating, brooms, chatai, etc. The coconut fruit also has cultural and religious significance in certain societies

46. *Cocos nucifera* is the botanical name of:

1. Papaya
2. Arecanut
3. Cashew nut
4. Coconut

47. Family of coconut is:

1. *Gramineae*
2. *Arecaceae*
3. *Leguminoceae*
4. *Anacardiaceae*

48. A product prepared from coconut fibrous husk used for planting of seedlings in nursery is:

1. Cocopeat
2. Mat
3. Liquid nutrient
4. Oil

49. Immature Coconut may be harvested for their coconut water is known as:

1. Coprale
2. Mahale
3. Shahale
4. Kahale

50. Coconut leaves are used for preparation of:

1. Brooms
2. Bedsheets
3. Shoes
4. Handkerchief

EXPLANATORY ANSWERS

1. • Temperature is measured using a thermometer because it detects and displays heat levels in degrees Celsius or Fahrenheit.
• Rainfall is recorded by a rain gauge, which collects and measures precipitation over a set time.
• Wind velocity is measured using an anemometer, which records wind speed and sometimes direction.
• Dew is measured with a dew gauge, which helps determine condensation amounts, often important in agriculture.

Thus, the correct matching is A–IV, B–III, C–II, D–I.

2. A greenhouse gas is one that traps infrared radiation, warming the Earth's atmosphere. Methane (CH_4) is a strong greenhouse gas with a warming potential many times greater than carbon dioxide. The others (oxygen, nitrogen, hydrogen) are not greenhouse gases in this sense.

3. The mitochondrion is the site of oxidative phosphorylation, where nutrients are broken down and energy is released to form ATP (adenosine triphosphate). Since it produces most of the cell's usable energy, it is called the "powerhouse of the cell."

4. • **Maize:** First hybrid variety was Ganga-1.
• **Jowar (Sorghum):** First hybrid was CSH-1.
• **Bajra (Pearl millet):** First hybrid was HB-1.
• **Cotton:** First hybrid was H-4.

Correct pairing is A–IV, B–I, C–III, D–II.

5. In co-dominance, both alleles in a heterozygous individual are fully expressed without blending. In the AB blood group, both A and B antigens appear on the red blood cell surface equally, showing neither is dominant over the other.

6. Enzymes are biological catalysts—they speed up biochemical reactions without being consumed in the process. They do not provide energy directly, store genetic information, or transmit it; instead, they make metabolic processes happen faster and more efficiently.

7. Rickets is a bone-softening disease in children caused by deficiency of Vitamin D. This vitamin is essential for calcium and phosphorus absorption, which are vital for healthy bone development. Without it, bones become soft, weak, and deformed.

8. Nitrogen-fixing bacteria convert atmospheric nitrogen into forms plants can use:
• *Rhizobium* – fixes nitrogen in legume root nodules.
• *Azotobacter* – free-living nitrogen fixer in soil.
• *Azospirillum* – associates with plant roots and fixes nitrogen.

Streptococcus is not nitrogen-fixing; it's a pathogenic bacterium.

Thus, correct set is A, B, and C only.

9. Apomixis is the development of an embryo or seed without fertilization. It is a form of asexual reproduction, producing offspring genetically identical to the parent. Anthesis is flowering, self-incompatibility prevents self-fertilization, and male sterility is inability to produce viable pollen.

10. Syngamy is the fusion of male and female gametes during fertilization, resulting in the formation of a zygote—a specialized diploid cell that develops into the embryo.

11. • **Buffalo:** Nili-Ravi (famous dairy breed from Punjab region).
• **Cow:** Sunandini (crossbreed developed in Kerala for high milk yield).
• **Poultry:** White Leghorn (commercial egg-laying breed).
• **Goat:** Toggenburg (Swiss breed known for good milk production).

Thus, the correct match is A–IV, B–I, C–II, D–III.

46. 4 **47.** 2 **48.** 1 **49.** 3 **50.** 1

12. Order by egg production (highest to lowest):

- White Leghorn – very high egg layer.
- Rhode Island Red – good layer but less than Leghorn.
- Giriraja – dual-purpose breed (meat + eggs) but fewer eggs than RIR.
- Assel – poor egg layer, mainly for meat/fighting.

So, order is A, B, D, C.

13. In India's poultry industry, maize is the most widely used cereal grain in feed formulations.

- It provides high carbohydrate energy (around 60–65% starch).
- It has good palatability and digestibility for poultry.
- Though low in protein and lysine, it forms the bulk (50–60%) of poultry feed and is balanced with other protein-rich supplements like soybean meal.

14. Silage is fermented green fodder stored in airtight conditions (silos or pits).

- The process involves anaerobic fermentation, mainly producing lactic acid, which preserves the fodder.
- Common crops used: maize, sorghum, and napier grass.
- Advantage: Keeps fodder nutritious and moist for months, especially during dry seasons when green forage is scarce.

15. Black quarter (blackleg) is a bacterial disease in cattle caused by *Clostridium chauvoei*.

- Symptoms: Sudden high fever, severe lameness, painful swelling (especially over shoulders, thighs, or neck), rapid breathing, and death within 1–3 days.
- Usually affects young cattle in good condition.
- Preventable by timely vaccination, especially before monsoon season.

16. Hisardale is a synthetic breed of sheep developed in Hisar, Haryana.

- It is a cross between Bikaneri ewes (known for adaptability and hardiness) and Merino rams (famous for fine-quality wool).
- The aim was to combine hardiness with improved wool fineness.

17. Average age at puberty/sexual maturity (decreasing order = oldest first):

- **Buffaloes:** ~36 months (late maturing).
- **Zebu cattle (desi breeds):** ~30 months.
- **Crossbred cattle:** ~24 months.
- **Purebred exotic cattle:** ~15–18 months (earliest maturing).

So, order is C, B, D, A.

18. Frozen milk products are those stored and served at sub-zero temperatures:

- **Kulfi** – traditional frozen dessert.
- **Ice-cream** – commercial frozen dairy dessert.
- **Dahi** (curd) is not frozen; Ghee is clarified butter (not frozen).

So correct set is A and B only.

19. "Fat-rich milk products" in dairy classification include items with very high milk fat like butter and ghee (also cream, butter oil). Khoa is grouped under concentrated milk products, and kulfi is a frozen dairy product, not classified as fat-rich. Therefore, the items excluded from fat-rich products are Khoa (B) and Kulfi (D).

20. National Fish Farmers Day is celebrated in India on 10 July every year.

- It marks the historic achievement in 1957 when Dr. Hiralal Chaudhuri and his team successfully induced breeding of Indian major carps (*Catla catla*, *Rohu*, *Mrigal*) using hypophysation technique (injection of fish pituitary extract).
- This breakthrough laid the foundation for modern aquaculture in India, boosting fish production and farmers' income.
- The day is used to honour fish farmers, researchers, and aquaculture professionals for their contribution to the fisheries sector.

21. India's National Genebank (at ICAR-NBPGR, New Delhi) started in 1983 with the commissioning of its first cold-storage module; the facility was later expanded and in 1996 the new Genebank building was inaugurated and notified as the National Genebank.

22. Mulching is the practice of covering the soil surface with organic materials (like straw, leaves, crop residues) or synthetic materials (like plastic films).

- Purpose: Retains soil moisture, suppresses weed growth, prevents soil erosion, moderates soil temperature, and improves soil health over time.
- Widely used in horticulture and agriculture to conserve resources and improve yield quality.

23. In plants, calcium is absorbed through roots and moves only acropetally (upwards) via the xylem.

- It is immobile in the phloem, meaning it cannot be redistributed from older to younger tissues.
- Because of this, calcium deficiency symptoms (like tip burn or blossom-end rot) show up first in young, developing leaves and fruits.

24. Glyphosate is a post-emergence non-selective herbicide.

- Post-emergence = applied after weeds have emerged.
- Non-selective = kills almost all plant species it contacts.
- Mode of action: Inhibits EPSP synthase in the shikimic acid pathway, essential for amino acid synthesis.
- Commonly used to clear fields before sowing crops, and in non-crop areas to control perennial weeds.

25. The Nagarjunasagar Project is built across the Krishna River, between Andhra Pradesh and Telangana.

- Type: One of the largest masonry dams in the world.
- Functions: Irrigation for millions of acres, hydroelectric power generation, and drinking water supply.
- Historical note: Inaugurated in 1967, it is a key component in the Green Revolution's success in southern India.

26. In sugarcane ratoon management, the correct sequence of practices is:

A. Emerged shoots are cut at ground level to encourage uniform regrowth.

B. Sides of ridges are broken by plough to loosen soil and aid aeration.

C. First irrigation is given 3–4 weeks after harvesting to help sprouting.

D. Nutrients are given and earthing-up is done to support plant stability and growth.

Thus, correct sequence: A, B, C, D.

27. The Gramineae family (also called Poaceae) includes cereal and grass crops like wheat, paddy, maize, barley, etc.

- From the given list: Wheat (C) and Paddy (D) belong to Gramineae.
- Groundnut (A) belongs to Fabaceae, and Gram (B) belongs to Fabaceae as well.

28. Wheat harvesting follows a standard post-maturity process:

D. Cutting the plants close to ground level: This is done when the grains reach physiological maturity and moisture content is around 20–25%.

C. Bundling and drying: The harvested plants are tied in bundles and dried under the sun for a few days to reduce grain moisture for effective threshing.

B. Threshing: Separation of grains from the straw, done manually or by machines like threshers/combines.

A. Winnowing and storage: Grain is cleaned to remove chaff and stored under dry, pest-free conditions.

Correct sequence: D, C, B, A.

29. The Earth's surface is about 71% ocean and 29% land.

- Oceans regulate global temperature, influence climate, and are vital for the water cycle.
- The Pacific Ocean alone covers nearly one-third of the total ocean area.

30. Crop–variety matches:

- **Wheat – HD-2496:** High-yielding wheat variety suitable for irrigated conditions.
- **Paddy – IR-8:** A famous high-yield rice variety developed during the Green Revolution.
- **Sugarcane – CO-86032:** Popular for high cane yield and sugar recovery.
- **Gram – Virat:** High-yielding, disease-resistant gram variety.

Correct match: A–IV, B–III, C–II, D–I.

31. When fruits and vegetables are exposed to very low temperatures rapidly enough to halt enzymatic and microbial activity, the process is called freezing.

- This preserves texture, flavour, and nutritional value for extended storage.
- Common in food processing industries to extend shelf life.

32.
- **Tomato – Pusa Ruby (A–III):** Good color, medium fruits, widely adapted.
- **Brinjal – Pusa Purple Long (B–I):** Long purple fruits, high yield.
- **Mango – Amrapali (C–IV):** Sweet, fiberless, regular-bearing hybrid.
- **Potato – Kufri Chipsona-1 (D–II):** Ideal for chips, high dry matter.

33. Chrysanthemum has several forms based on plant habit and flower display:

- Standard – large single flowers.
- Spray or bush form – multiple small blooms per stem.
- Pot-mums – compact pot-grown plants.
- Coniform – shaped like a cone for decorative purposes.

34. For Grand Naine banana cultivation in India, tissue culture is the commercially adopted propagation method.

- Ensures disease-free, uniform, and vigorous planting material.
- Helps in large-scale multiplication in a short time.

35. Bangalore Blue is a grape variety grown mainly in Karnataka, especially around Bangalore.

- It belongs to the *Vitis labrusca* species and is known for its distinct foxy flavour.
- Primarily used for juice extraction, wine-making, and preparing jams and jellies.
- The berries are bluish-black, medium-sized, and have a slip-skin texture, making them easy to process.

36. Pusa Mukta is a tropical cabbage variety developed to resist black rot disease caused by *Xanthomonas campestris pv. campestris*.

- Produces compact, medium-sized heads.
- Adapted for growing in warm and humid climates where black rot is a serious problem.

37. Stone grafting in mango is a popular method to produce true-to-type plants quickly:

A. Cut the top of the rootstock (7–8 cm stem left) to prepare for grafting.

D. Make a vertical slit (~2–3 cm) in the stem for scion insertion.

C. Shape the scion into a wedge by giving slant cuts on both sides for better cambial contact.

B. Insert the scion into the slit and tie tightly with a polythene strip to hold in place and prevent moisture loss.

38. In hilly areas, the contour system of planting is used:

- Trees are planted along contour lines to reduce runoff and soil erosion.
- Helps conserve rainwater, maintain soil fertility, and provide uniform spacing on slopes.

39. Fruits and vegetables richest in Vitamin A (from beta-carotene) include:

A. Mango, carrot, spinach – all high in provitamin A carotenoids.

C. Papaya and leafy vegetables – also excellent beta-carotene sources.

Sweet orange, acid lime, aonla, and guava are mainly Vitamin C-rich, not Vitamin A-rich.

40. Aonla (Indian gooseberry) contains extremely high ascorbic acid (Vitamin C) levels — up to 600 mg per 100 g pulp.

- Retains Vitamin C even after processing due to presence of tannins that prevent oxidation.
- Far exceeds citrus fruits in Vitamin C content.

41. The Kisan Credit Card (KCC) scheme was launched in August 1998 by Indian banks to give farmers easy access to short-term credit for cultivation, harvesting, and other agricultural needs.

- It reduced dependence on informal moneylenders who charged high interest rates.
- It also allowed farmers to draw credit in a flexible manner, similar to a cash credit system.

42. NABARD stands for National Bank for Agriculture and Rural Development.

- It is the apex institution in India for rural development financing.
- It supports credit-related policies and provides funds to banks for agriculture and rural infra-structure projects.

43. Under the KCC scheme, the repayment period for short-term credit is up to a maximum of 12 months.

- This means farmers must repay the loan within one year, often after harvest.
- This aligns with agricultural cycles to ensure repayment after income is generated from crops.

44. The KCC model scheme was designed by NABARD on the recommendations of the R.V. Gupta Committee.

- The committee studied the problems of farmers in accessing credit and recommended a simple, flexible system to meet their production and investment needs.

45. A Kisan Credit Card remains valid for 3–5 years.

- During this period, the farmer can use the card for multiple crop cycles.
- The credit limit can also be increased if repayment is regular and satisfactory.

46. The botanical name *Cocos nucifera* refers to the coconut tree.

- It is a tropical plant belonging to the palm family and is cultivated worldwide for its fruit, oil, fiber, and other products.
- The coconut fruit is botanically classified as a drupe, not a true nut.

47. Coconut belongs to the family Arecaceae, also known as the palm family.

- This family includes many economically important palms such as date palm and arecanut.
- Members of Arecaceae are characterized by unbranched stems and large pinnate or palmate leaves.

48. Cocopeat is produced from the fibrous husk of the coconut.

- It is a byproduct of coir fiber extraction and is used as a growing medium in nurseries.
- Benefits: retains moisture, improves aeration, and supports healthy root development for seedlings.

49. The clear liquid found in immature coconuts is known as Shahale.

- It is rich in natural sugars, electrolytes, and minerals, making it a refreshing and hydrating drink.
- Shahale is consumed fresh and is valued for its health benefits.

50. Coconut leaves, especially their long pinnate fronds, are traditionally used to make brooms in rural and urban households.

- The midrib of the leaf is dried, bundled, and tied to form durable sweeping tools.
- Leaves are also used in mat-making and decorative items.

Previous Years' Paper

Common University Entrance Test for UG Programmes

CUET–UG—AGRICULTURE*

Entrance Exam, 2024

(Exam held on 19-07-2024)

Subject Code: 302

1. Arrange the following gases in descending order in terms of percentage in dry air of the lower atmosphere.

(*a*) Carbon dioxide
(*b*) Argon
(*c*) Nitrogen
(*d*) Oxygen

Choose the **correct** answer from the options given below:

A. (*d*), (*c*), (*a*), (*b*)
B. (*c*), (*a*), (*d*), (*b*)
C. (*c*), (*d*), (*a*), (*b*)
D. (*c*), (*d*), (*b*), (*a*)

2. Match List-I with List-II:

List-I (Parameter)	List-II (Instrument for measurement)
(*a*) Humidity	I. Anemometer
(*b*) Wind	II. Lysimeter
(*c*) Light intensity	III. Hygrometer
(*d*) Evapotranspiration	IV. Luxmeter

Choose the **correct** answer from the options given below:

	(*a*)	(*b*)	(*c*)	(*d*)
A.	III	I	IV	II
B.	I	III	II	IV
C.	I	II	IV	III
D.	III	IV	I	II

3. The evidence of particulate nature for the units of inheritance was first presented by ....

A. Mendel B. Correns
C. Mojica D. Morgan

4. Which of the following statements are **correct** about the genes?

(*a*) Genes are located on chromosomes.
(*b*) Split genes are composed of exons only.
(*c*) Genes move from one linkage group to another.
(*d*) Chromosomes with identical arms on which genes are located are known as isochromosomes.

Choose the **correct** answer from the options given below:

A. (*a*), (*b*) and (*d*) only
B. (*a*), (*b*) and (*c*) only
C. (*a*), (*b*), (*c*) and (*d*)
D. (*a*), (*c*) and (*d*) only

5. The term heterosis is coined by ....

A. Hull, 1945 B. Bruce, 1910
C. East, 1908 D. Shull, 1914

6. Arrange the following steps of plant breeding in **correct** sequence.

(*a*) Selection of superior variants
(*b*) Creation of variation
(*c*) Multiplication and distribution
(*d*) Evaluation of variants

Choose the **correct** answer from the options given below:

A. (*a*), (*b*), (*c*), (*d*) B. (*a*), (*c*), (*b*), (*d*)
C. (*b*), (*d*), (*a*), (*c*) D. (*c*), (*b*), (*d*), (*a*)

7. Who is the father of tissue culture?

A. Jethro Tull B. Folke Karl Skoog
C. Toshion Murashige D. Haberlandt

8. Protein is a polymer of ....

A. Amino acids B. Lipids
C. Nucleic acids D. Carbohydrates

1. C **2.** A **3.** A **4.** D **5.** D **6.** C **7.** D **8.** A

* *40 questions to be attempted out of 50.*

9. Which of the following are Cyanobacteria?

(*a*) Nucleopolyhedrovirus
(*b*) Anabaena
(*c*) Nostoc
(*d*) Oscillatoria

Choose the **correct** answer from the options given below:

A. (*a*), (*b*) and (*d*) only
B. (*a*), (*b*) and (*c*) only
C. (*a*), (*b*), (*c*) and (*d*)
D. (*b*), (*c*) and (*d*) only

10. Starch is an example of ....

A. Monosaccharides
B. Oligosaccharides
C. Disaccharides
D. Polysaccharides

11. Egg of poultry contains almost all the Vitamins with the exception of Vitamin ....

A. B
B. C
C. A
D. D

12. Match List-I with List-II:

List-I (Cattle Breed)	List-II (Place of Origin)
(*a*) Tharparkar	I. Netherland
(*b*) Holstein Friesian	II. United Kingdom
(*c*) Jersey	III. Sindh
(*d*) Gir	IV. Kathiawar

Choose the **correct** answer from the options given below:

	(*a*)	(*b*)	(*c*)	(*d*)
A.	I	II	III	IV
B.	I	III	II	IV
C.	III	I	II	IV
D.	III	IV	I	II

13. What in the name of the process required to make sperm competent for in-vitro fertilization?

A. Capacitation
B. Syngamy
C. Parturition
D. Ovulation

14. The colostrum should be fed at the rate of ....

A. 25% of calf's body weight
B. 30% of calf's body weight
C. 10% of calf's body weight
D. 40% of calf's body weight

15. Ranikhet disease is caused by ....

A. *Herpesvirus*
B. *Paramyxovirus*
C. *Avipoxvirus*
D. H1N1 influenza virus

16. Which of the following is an exotic breed of poultry?

A. Busra
B. Chittagong
C. Plymouth rock
D. Kadaknath

17. Match List-I with List-II:

List-I (Milk product)	List-II (Classification)
(*a*) Basundi	I. Fat rich milk product
(*b*) Paneer	II. Fermented milk product
(*c*) Dahi	III. Concentrated milk product
(*d*) Ghee	IV. Coagulated milk product

Choose the **correct** answer from the options given below:

	(*a*)	(*b*)	(*c*)	(*d*)
A.	III	IV	II	I
B.	I	III	II	IV
C.	I	II	IV	III
D.	III	IV	I	II

18. Jute is a ....

A. Forage crop
B. Fibre crop
C. Drug crop
D. Medicinal and aromatic crop

19. Forage crops include:

(*a*) Berseem
(*b*) Safflower
(*c*) Lucerne
(*d*) Sunflower

Choose the **correct** answer from the options given below:

A. (*a*), (*b*) and (*d*) only
B. (*a*) and (*c*) only
C. (*a*), (*b*), (*c*) and (*d*)
D. (*b*), (*c*) and (*d*) only

20. Arrange the following soil particles in descending order of their diameter.

(*a*) Clay
(*b*) Silt
(*c*) Fine sand
(*d*) Coarse sand

Choose the **correct** answer from the options given below:

A. (*a*), (*b*), (*c*), (*d*)
B. (*a*), (*c*), (*b*), (*d*)
C. (*d*), (*c*), (*b*), (*a*)
D. (*c*), (*b*), (*d*), (*a*)

9. D **10.** D **11.** B **12.** C **13.** A **14.** C **15.** B **16.** C **17.** A
18. B **19.** B **20.** C

21. Which of the following statements are correct about function of essential plant nutrients?

(*a*) Nitrogen is not a component of nucleic acids.
(*b*) Potassium plays important role in activation of enzymes.
(*c*) Sulphur is part of some amino acids and coenzymes.
(*d*) Phosphorus deficiency results in terminal bud necrosis.

Choose the **correct** answer from the options given below:

A. (*a*), (*b*) and (*d*) only
B. (*b*) and (*c*) only
C. (*a*), (*b*) and (*c*) only
D. (*b*), (*c*) and (*d*) only

22. Which of the following concentrated organic manures has the highest percentage of P_2O_5?

A. Neem cake B. Raw bone-meal
C. Poultry manure D. Fish manure

23. Volume of water required to apply 5 cm irrigation over one hectare area?

A. 500 cubic meter B. 50 cubic meter
C. 5000 cubic meter D. 50000 cubic meter

24. National Rainfed Area Authority was established in ....

A. 2000 B. 2013
C. 1998 D. 2006

25. Match List-I with List-II:

List-I (Methods of weed control)	List-II (Measures of weed control)
(*a*) Preventive method of weed control	I. Proper crop rotation
(*b*) Mechanical method of weed control	II. Control of *Lantana camera (Ghaneri) by Lantana bug*
(*c*) Cultural method of weed control	III. Use weed free crop seeds
(*d*) Biological method of weed control	IV. Hand weeding

Choose the **correct** answer from the options given below:

	(*a*)	(*b*)	(*c*)	(*d*)
A.	I	II	III	IV
B.	I	III	II	IV
C.	I	II	IV	III
D.	III	IV	I	II

26. Which of the following statements is **not** correct about the weeds?

A. Weeds compete with crop for space
B. Weeds compete with crops for light
C. Weeds compete with crops for nutrients
D. Weeds has no affect on the yield and quality of crops

27. Which of the following is **not** a pest of rapeseed-mustard crop?

A. White rust B. Stalk borer
C. Aphids D. Alternaria blight

28. Which of the following crops is NOT a legume crop?

A. Berseem B. Rapeseed-mustard
C. Soybean D. Groundnut

29. Which of the following crops requires relatively wider line to line and plant to plant spacing?

A. Maize B. Chickpea
C. Berseem D. Sugarcane

30. Match List-I with List-II:

List-I (Name of crop)	List-II (Disease of crop)
(*a*) Sugarcane	I. Red rot
(*b*) Cotton	II. Black arm
(*c*) Groundnut	III. Tikka (Leaf spot)
(*d*) Sorghum	IV. Grain smut

Choose the **correct** answer from the options given below:

	(*a*)	(*b*)	(*c*)	(*d*)
A.	I	II	III	IV
B.	I	III	II	IV
C.	I	II	IV	III
D.	III	IV	I	II

31. Gladiator and Super Star are the varieties of which crop?

A. Tuberose B. Rose
C. Marigold D. Chrysanthemum

32. Arrange the process of preparation of jelly in proper sequence.

(*a*) Judging of end point and cooling.
(*b*) Addition of sugar and cooking of jelly.
(*c*) Peeling and extraction of pectin.
(*d*) Harvesting of firm ripe fruits and washing.

Choose the **correct** answer from the options given below:

A. (*a*), (*b*), (*c*), (*d*) B. (*d*), (*c*), (*b*), (*a*)
C. (*b*), (*a*), (*d*), (*c*) D. (*c*), (*b*), (*d*), (*a*)

21. B **22.** B **23.** A **24.** D **25.** D **26.** D **27.** B **28.** B **29.** D **30.** A **31.** B **32.** B

33. Match List-I with List-II:

List-I (Vegetable)	List-II (Family)
(*a*) Onion	I. Cruciferae
(*b*) Carrot	II. Solanaceae
(*c*) Potato	III. Umbelliferae
(*d*) Cauliflower	IV. Liliaceae

Choose the **correct** answer from the options given below:

	(*a*)	(*b*)	(*c*)	(*d*)
A.	IV	III	II	I
B.	I	III	II	IV
C.	I	II	IV	III
D.	III	IV	I	II

34. Alphonso, Dasheri, Ratna and Amrapali are the varieties of ....

A. Citrus B. Pomegranate
C. Mango D. Banana

35. Brinjal belongs to the family ....

A. Solanaceae B. Malvaceae
C. Cruciferae D. Amaryllidaceae

36. Rose is commercially propagated by ....

A. Bulbs B. Seed
C. Tuber D. 'T' budding

37. Physical method of fruit juice preservation includes:

(*a*) Refrigeration (*b*) Salt addition
(*c*) Sugar addition (*d*) Pasteurization

Choose the **correct** answer from the options given below:

A. (*a*) and (*d*) only B. (*a*), (*b*) and (*c*) only
C. (*a*), (*b*), (*c*) and (*d*) D. (*b*), (*c*) and (*d*) only

38. Which of the following disease is caused by Vitamin D deficiency?

A. Rickets B. Night blindness
C. Scurvy D. Beriberi

39. Botanical name of Spinach is ....

A. *Allium cepa* B. *Spinacia oleracea*
C. *Bombax ceiba* D. *Cucumis sativus*

40. Which of the following methods are used for banana propagation?

A. Cutting and grafting
B. Rhizomes and sword suckers
C. Grafting and layering
D. Budding and cutting

Directions (Qs. No. 41-45): *Read the passage given below carefully and answer the questions that follow.*

Oilseeds scenario of India

India is next to USA, China and Brazil in vegetable oils production. Areas and production of oilseeds crops is next to food crops. India account for 14% of world's oilseeds area, 8% of world's oilseeds output and 11% of world's edible oils consumption. India grows nine field oilseeds crops of which linseed and castor are non-edible. In the edible oilseeds crops, soybean has the highest acreage followed by rapeseed-mustard, groundnut, sesame, safflower, sunflower and niger. India is not self sufficient in oilseeds production and 50% requirement of vegetables oils is met through the import. Of the total import, about 60% is palm oil. Among the states, Madhya Pradesh ranks at top in area and production of vegetables oils followed by Rajasthan, Gujarat and Andhra Pradesh. Oilseeds occupies about 13-14% of the gross cropped area and account for nearly 1.4% to gross national product and 7% of the value of all agricultural commodities.

41. India's vegetable oils import is about .... % of its total requirement of vegetables oils.

A. 40 B. 50
C. 15 D. 60

42. Arrange the following edible oilseed crops in increasing order of area under cultivation in each crop in India:

(*a*) Sesame (*b*) Soybean
(*c*) Groundnut (*d*) Rapeseed-mustard

Choose the **correct** answer from the options given below:

A. (*a*), (*d*), (*c*), (*b*) B. (*a*), (*c*), (*b*), (*d*)
C. (*b*), (*a*), (*d*), (*c*) D. (*a*), (*c*), (*d*), (*b*)

43. Which of the following statements are **correct** about the oilseed crops in India ?

(*a*) India grows nine oilseed crops
(*b*) Gujarat contribution to total oilseed production is the highest
(*c*) India is not self-sufficient in vegetable oilseeds production
(*d*) India's oilseed production ranked fourth in the world

Choose the **correct** answer from the options given below:

A. (*a*), (*b*) and (*d*) only B. (*a*), (*c*) and (*d*) only
C. (*a*), (*b*), (*c*) and (*d*) D. (*b*), (*c*) and (*d*) only

33. A **34.** C **35.** A **36.** D **37.** A **38.** A **39.** B **40.** B **41.** B **42.** D **43.** B

44. Which of the following is a non-edible oilseed crop?

A. Safflower B. Niger
C. Castor D. Sesame

45. What is the contribution of oilseed crops to Gross National Product?

A. 7% B. 1.4%
C. 10% D. 4%

Directions (Qs. No. 46-50): *Read the passage given below carefully and answer the questions that follow.*

Mandarin orange-Fruit Crop

Mandarin oranges (Botanical name - *Citrus reticulata*, Family - Rutaceae), commonly known as *Santra* are the most refreshing and health promoting juicy fruits. Besides Vitamin C, it is an excellent source of pectin and certain essential oils. The juice is advised to patients. Subtropical and tropical climate are required for growth of *santra*. The trees grow luxuriously in 1.5 m deep well-drained soils free from excess salts and having adequate content of organic matter. The important varieties are Nagpur santra (Maharashtra), Khansi mandarin (Assam), Coorg mandarin (Karnataka), Kinnow (Punjab), Emperor, Hill orange, Mudkhed seedless, Honey (for kitchen gardening). *Santra* are commercially propagated by shield or 'T' budding on rootstocks like jamberi or rangpur lime. Average yield is 80 to 160 fruits/trees.

46. What is the botanical name of *santra*?

A. *Citrus reticulata* B. *Annona squamosa*
C. *Cocus nucifera* D. *Vitis vinifera*

47. Which is the family of mandarin orange?

A. Rhamnaceae B. Myrtaceae
C. Annonaceae D. Rutaceae

48. Mandarin orange commercially propagated by ....

A. Stone grafting B. Air layering
C. 'T' budding D. Suckers

49. Which of the following is a variety of *santra*?

A. Muscat B. Gola
C. Sardar D. Kinnow

50. What is the average yield of Mandarin orange crop?

A. 80-160 fruits/trees
B. 40-50 fruits/trees
C. 200-280 fruits/trees
D. 300-600 fruits/trees

EXPLANATORY ANSWERS

1. (C): In dry air of the lower atmosphere, Nitrogen (*c*) makes up about 78%, Oxygen (*d*) about 21%, Argon (*a*) roughly 0.93%, and Carbon dioxide (*b*) about 0.04%. Therefore, the correct descending order based on percentage composition is Nitrogen, Oxygen, Argon, and Carbon dioxide.

2. (A): Humidity is measured using a Hygrometer (III), Wind speed by an Anemometer (I), Light intensity by a Luxmeter (IV), and Evapotranspiration by a Lysimeter (II). This matches correctly with the instruments listed for each parameter.

3. (A): Gregor Mendel, through his experiments on pea plants, first presented clear evidence for particulate inheritance, identifying that traits are passed from parents to offspring in discrete units or genes.

4. (D): Genes are located on chromosomes (*a*) is correct. Genes move from one linkage group to another (*c*) is inaccurate in traditional genetics as genes do not typically change linkage groups; however, translocation can occur during genetic recombination or mutations. Chromosomes with identical arms on which genes are located are known as isochromosomes (*d*) is correct. The statement that split genes are composed of exons only (*b*) is incorrect as split genes include both exons and introns.

5. (D): The term heterosis, which refers to the phenomenon where crossbred individuals exhibit superior qualities compared to their parents, was coined by George Harrison Shull in 1914. This term is synonymous with hybrid vigour, which has been extensively observed and utilized in agricultural practices.

6. (C): The correct sequence in plant breeding starts with the creation of variation (*b*) through methods like hybridization or mutation. This is followed by evaluation of variants (*d*) to assess their performance under different conditions. Next, selection of superior variants (*a*) is conducted based on desired traits.

44. C	45. B	46. A	47. D	48. C	49. D	50. A

Finally, multiplication and distribution (*c*) of the selected variants is done to reach farmers and markets.

7. **(D):** Gottlieb Haberlandt is known as the father of tissue culture for his pioneering work in the early 1900s where he conceptualized the idea of growing plant cells in vitro, setting the foundation for modern plant tissue culture techniques.

8. **(A):** Proteins are polymers of amino acids linked together by peptide bonds. Each protein is a sequence of amino acids which determines its structure and function in biological processes.

9. **(D):** Anabaena (*b*), Nostoc (*c*), and Oscillatoria (*d*) are all examples of Cyanobacteria, a group of photosynthetic bacteria found in a variety of aquatic and terrestrial environments, known for their blue-green colour due to the pigment phycocyanin.

10. **(D):** Starch is a polysaccharide consisting of a large number of glucose units joined by glycosidic bonds. It serves as a form of energy storage in plants and is broken down into glucose as needed by the organism.

11. **(B):** Poultry eggs contain almost all vitamins except for Vitamin C. Unlike most animals, birds, including poultry, do not synthesize or store significant amounts of Vitamin C, and it is generally absent in eggs.

12. **(C):** Tharparkar cattle originate from Sindh (III), Holstein Friesian from Netherland (I), Jersey from United Kingdom (II), and Gir from Kathiawar (IV). This matching reflects the correct geographical origin of each cattle breed.

13. **(A):** The process required to make sperm competent for in-vitro fertilization is known as capacitation. This biological process involves the alteration of the sperm's head membrane to allow it to penetrate and fertilize an egg, essential for successful in-vitro fertilization.

14. **(C):** The colostrum, which is the first form of milk produced immediately following the delivery of the newborn, should be fed at the rate of 10% of the calf's body weight. This is crucial for providing necessary antibodies and nutrition to the newborn calf, ensuring a strong start to its immune system.

15. **(B):** Ranikhet disease, also known as Newcastle disease, is caused by a virus belonging to the *Paramyxoviridae* family, specifically classified as a *Paramyxovirus*. It is a contagious and often severe disease affecting birds with high rates of mortality.

16. **(C):** Plymouth Rock is an exotic breed of poultry known for its distinctive appearance and utility in meat and egg production, originally bred in the United States, contrasting with native breeds like Busra, Chittagong, and Kadaknath from other regions.

17. **(A):** Basundi, a concentrated milk product (III), involves reducing milk to make it thick and creamy. Paneer is a coagulated milk product (IV) formed by curdling milk with an acid. Dahi is a fermented milk product (II), made by bacterial fermentation of milk. Ghee is a fat-rich milk product (I) derived from butter.

18. **(B):** Jute is a widely known fibre crop used for making burlap, hessian, or gunny cloth. Its fibres are sourced from the stems of jute plants and are highly valued for their length, softness, and lustrous finish, commonly used in textiles.

19. **(B):** Forage crops are primarily grown to feed animals, not for oil production as in the cases of safflower and sunflower. Berseem (*a*) and Lucerne (*c*) are typical forage crops, used commonly as animal fodder due to their high nutritional content.

20. **(C):** In terms of soil particle size, coarse sand (*d*) has the largest diameter, followed by fine sand (*c*), then silt (*b*), and clay (*a*) has the smallest diameter. This order helps in understanding soil texture and its implications on water retention and aeration.

21. **(B):** Nitrogen is a crucial component of nucleic acids, contrary to statement (*a*), making it incorrect. Potassium does play an important role in the activation of enzymes (*b*), and Sulphur is indeed a part of some amino acids and coenzymes (*c*), confirming their correctness. Phosphorus deficiency typically results in stunted growth and dark green colouring, not necessarily terminal bud necrosis as stated in (*d*), making it incorrect.

22. **(B):** Among the options given, raw bone-meal typically has the highest percentage of P_2O_5 (phosphorus pentoxide), which is a key nutrient for plant growth. It's particularly valued in organic farming for its slow-release properties of phosphorus.

23. **(A):** To apply 5 cm of irrigation over one hectare (10,000 square meters), the volume of water required is calculated as follows: 5 cm = 0.05 meters, and 0.05 meters × 10,000 square meters = 500 cubic meters.

24. **(D):** The National Rainfed Area Authority (NRAA) was established in 2006 to coordinate and manage

the development of rainfed areas in India, aiming to increase agricultural productivity and address water scarcity in non-irrigated regions.

25. (D): The Preventive method of weed control includes using weed-free crop seeds (III), Mechanical method involves hand weeding (IV), Cultural method incorporates proper crop rotation (I), and Biological method refers to the use of natural predators or control agents like the Lantana bug to control weeds such as Lantana camara (II). This matching accurately reflects the methods and their appropriate measures of weed control.

26. (D): Weeds has no affect on the yield and quality of crops: This statement is incorrect as weeds significantly affect both yield and quality of crops by competing for space, light, nutrients, and sometimes even by secreting harmful substances that inhibit crop growth.

27. (B): Stalk borer is not typically a pest of rapeseed-mustard crops. White rust and Alternaria blight are fungal diseases affecting these crops, and aphids are common insect pests, but stalk borers primarily target cereal and maize crops.

28. (B): Rapeseed-mustard is not a legume crop. Legume crops, like soybean (C) and groundnut (D), are known for their ability to fix atmospheric nitrogen through symbiotic relationships with bacteria in their root nodules. Berseem (A) is a forage crop but also belongs to the legume family.

29. (D): Sugarcane requires relatively wider line to line and plant to plant spacing compared to other listed crops. This is due to its tall, dense growth habit which necessitates more space to maximize exposure to sunlight and to support extensive root systems for water and nutrient uptake.

30. (A): This matching is correct as follows:

- Sugarcane is susceptible to Red rot (I).
- Cotton is affected by Black arm disease (II).
- Groundnut suffers from Tikka disease, also known as leaf spot (III).
- Sorghum can be affected by Grain smut (IV).

This correct matching reflects each crop's association with specific diseases.

31. (B): Gladiator and Super Star are varieties of roses, known for their distinct characteristics and popularity in horticulture and landscaping due to their aesthetic appeal and variety in colour and form.

32. (B): The correct sequence for the preparation of jelly begins with harvesting of firm ripe fruits and washing (*d*), followed by peeling and extraction of pectin which is crucial for jelly's gelatinous consistency (*c*). Next, addition of sugar and the cooking process of the jelly mixture occur (*b*), and finally, judging the end point and cooling the jelly to set properly (*a*).

33. (A): The matching of vegetables to their families is correct as follows:

- Onion belongs to the Liliaceae family (IV).
- Carrot is a member of the Umbelliferae family, known for its aromatic compounds and roots (III).
- Potato is classified under the Solanaceae family, which includes other staple crops like tomatoes and eggplants (II).
- Cauliflower is from the Cruciferae family, which includes many other leafy green vegetables (I).

34. (C): Alphonso, Dasheri, Ratna, and Amrapali are all popular varieties of mangoes, widely cultivated in India for their unique flavors, textures, and suitability to various climates and soils.

35. (A): Brinjal, also known as eggplant, belongs to the Solanaceae family. This family also includes other important agricultural crops such as tomatoes, potatoes, and bell peppers, sharing common characteristics such as the type of flowers and seed structure.

36. (D): Rose is commonly propagated commercially by 'T' budding. This method involves inserting a bud from a selected variety into the stock of another plant, typically a rootstock that provides robust roots, thereby combining desirable flower qualities with hardy growth characteristics.

37. (A): The physical methods of fruit juice preservation that do not involve chemical additives include refrigeration (*a*) and pasteurization (*d*). Refrigeration slows down microbial growth by lowering the temperature, and pasteurization involves heating the juice to kill pathogens and spoilage organisms, thereby extending its shelf life without changing its chemical composition.

38. (A): Rickets is a disease caused by a deficiency of Vitamin D, which is crucial for the absorption of calcium and phosphate in the body. This deficiency leads to softening and weakening of bones in children, often resulting in skeletal deformities.

39. (B): The botanical name of spinach is *Spinacia oleracea*. This name reflects its classification within the plant kingdom and distinguishes it from other vegetables by specifying its unique genus and species.

40. (B): Banana plants are typically propagated through rhizomes and sword suckers. Rhizomes are horizontal underground stems that produce new shoots, and sword suckers are vigorous shoots that grow from these rhizomes.

This method ensures genetic uniformity and quicker establishment compared to seed propagation, which is rarely used for commercial banana production.

41. (B): India is not self-sufficient in oilseeds production and meets approximately 50% of its vegetable oils requirement through imports, as mentioned in the passage.

42. (D): According to the passage, among the edible oilseeds crops listed, sesame has the smallest acreage followed by groundnut, rapeseed-mustard, and soybean, which has the highest acreage.

43. (B): The passage confirms that India grows nine oilseed crops (*a*), is not self-sufficient in vegetable oilseeds production (*c*), and ranks fourth in the world in oilseed production (*d*).

The statement about Gujarat having the highest contribution to total oilseed production is incorrect (*b*); Madhya Pradesh is noted as the leading state.

44. (C): Among the options listed, castor is specified in the passage as a non-edible oilseed crop grown in India.

45. (B): The passage mentions that oilseeds account for nearly 1.4% of the Gross National Product in India, highlighting their economic contribution relative to other agricultural commodities.

46. (A): The botanical name for santra is *Citrus reticulata*, as detailed in the passage. This specifies its classification within the citrus family and distinguishes it from other fruit crops.

47. (D): Mandarin orange, or santra, belongs to the Rutaceae family. This family is noted for including various citrus fruits, which share similar characteristics and growth requirements.

48. (C): The passage specifies that santra (mandarin orange) is commercially propagated by shield or 'T' budding on rootstocks like jamberi or rangpur lime. This method involves grafting a selected bud onto a rootstock to combine desirable fruit qualities with robust root systems.

49. (D): Among the listed options, Kinnow is mentioned in the passage as an important variety of santra. Kinnow is a high yield mandarin developed to thrive in specific climatic conditions.

50. (A): The passage states that the average yield of mandarin orange trees is between 80 to 160 fruits per tree, reflecting the productivity range typical for these fruit trees under good growing conditions.

PREVIOUS YEARS' PAPER (SOLVED)

Common University Entrance Test for UG Programmes

CUET-UG—AGRICULTURE

Entrance Exam, 2023

(Online exam held on 26-05-2023)

Subject Code: 302

1. Match List-I with List-II.

List-I	List-II
(*a*) Radish	I. Tuber
(*b*) Potato	II. Root
(*c*) Onion	III. Stem
(*d*) Cauliflower	IV. Bulb

Choose the correct answer from the options given below:

	(*a*)	(*b*)	(*c*)	(*d*)
A.	I	II	III	IV
B.	IV	I	III	II
C.	II	I	IV	III
D.	II	I	III	IV

2. In a dihybrid cross, if an individual heterozygous for both the characters is crossed with double recessive, which phenotype ratio would be expected?

A. 1 : 2 : 2 : 1 B. 1 : 2 : 1 : 1
C. 1 : 1 : 1 : 1 D. 9 : 3 : 3 : 1

3. Match List-I with List-II.

List-I (Weather element)	List-II (Instruments)
(*a*) Light	I. Hygrometer
(*b*) Wind Velocity	II. Thermometer
(*c*) Humidity	III. Sunshine recorder
(*d*) Temperature	IV. Anemometer

Choose the correct answer from the options given below:

	(*a*)	(*b*)	(*c*)	(*d*)
A.	I	II	III	IV
B.	III	IV	I	II
C.	II	I	IV	III
D.	IV	III	II	I

4. What are those fungi called which live in symbiotic association with roots of higher plants?

A. Saprophytes B. Parasites
C. Lichens D. Mycorrhiza

5. During collection of semen from a bull, the artificial vegina should be held at .... angle to the ground.

A. 90° B. 0°
C. 45° D. 60°

6. What is the water use efficiency, if grain yield of a crop is 6 ton/he and water requirement for growing the crop is 2000 mm?

A. 3 kg/he-mm B. 0.003 kg/he-mm
C. 3 t/he-mm D. 0.3 kg/he-mm

7. Which of the following fruits is not indigenous to India?

A. Mango B. Guava
C. Banana D. Jackfruit

8. 'Totapuri' is a variety of:

A. Litchi B. Banana
C. Papaya D. Mango

9. ICAR-Indian Veterinary Research Institute is situated at:

A. Karnal B. Izatnagar
C. Malegaon D. Kolkata

10. Which of the following crop requires 'puddling' operation?

A. Transplanted rice B. Direct seeded rice
C. Transplanted wheat D. Direct seeded wheat

11. Growing potato in the interspaces of apple trees in the first few years is an example of:

A. Crop rotation B. Inter cropping
C. Mixed cropping D. Mono cropping

12. Which country is the second largest producer of fruits and vegetables in the world?

A. India
B. China
C. United States of America
D. Brazil

13. Which of the following is an example of buffer solution?
A. A mixture of nitric acid and sodium nitrate
B. A mixture of sodium hydroxide and nitric acid
C. A mixture of acetic acid and sodium hydroxide
D. A mixture of acetic acid and sodium acetate

14. Which of the following are pressurized irrigation systems?
(*a*) Furrow irrigation (*b*) Flood irrigation
(*c*) Drip (*d*) Rainguns
(*e*) Micro-sprinklers

Choose the ***correct*** answer from the options given below:
A. (*a*) and (*b*) only
B. (*a*), (*b*) and (*c*) only
C. (*c*), (*d*) and (*e*) only
D. (*c*) and (*e*) only

15. Which of the following is known as 'power house' of the cell?
A. Mitochondrion B. Plastid
C. Lysosome D. Vacuole

16. Which is fat rich milk product?
A. Paneer B. Ghee
C. Dahi D. Kulfi

17. Which is the most cultivated species of wheat in India?
A. *Triticum aestivum*
B. *Triticum durum*
C. *Triticum dicoccum*
D. *Triticum sphaerococcum*

18. Cow and buffaloes come into heat, after a period of .... days.
A. 15-17 B. 19-21
C. 25-27 D. 30-31

19. Amoeba belongs to the kingdom:
A. Fungi B. Plantae
C. Protista D. Animalia

20. Which of the following has African and French varieties?
A. Marigold B. Chrysanthemum
C. Gladiolus D. Rose

21. When is medical examination needed, if heifer is not showing heat symptoms for breeding?
(*a*) After 3-years age
(*b*) After 300 kg body weight
(*c*) After 5-years age
(*d*) At 2-years age

Choose the correct answer from the options given below:
A. (*a*) only B. (*c*) and (*d*) only
C. (*a*) and (*b*) only D. (*a*), (*b*) and (*c*) only

22. Which of the following is known as a secondary nutrient element for plants?
A. N B. P
C. Fe D. S

23. How much single super phosphate (SSP) is needed to supply 80 kg P_2O_5 to 1 hectare area?
A. 160 kg B. 320 kg
C. 500 kg D. 80 kg

24. Arrange the soils of the following textural classes according to descending order of their clay percentage.
(*a*) Sandy clay (*b*) Clay
(*c*) Sandy loam (*d*) Sandy clay loam
(*e*) Sand

Choose the ***correct*** answer from the options given below:
A. (*b*), (*a*), (*d*), (*c*), (*e*) B. (*b*), (*c*), (*a*), (*d*), (*e*)
C. (*c*), (*a*), (*b*), (*e*), (*d*) D. (*b*), (*a*), (*c*), (*d*), (*e*)

25. Di-ammonium phosphate is a complex fertilizer and contains:
A. Nitrogen only
B. Phosphorus only
C. Nitrogen and phosphorus
D. Nitrogen, phosphorus and potash

26. A chromosome with the centromere situated close to its end forming one extremely short and one very long arm is called:
A. Telocentric B. Metacentric
C. Acrocentric D. Sub-metacentric

27. Operation Flood is associated with:
A. River protection B. Ganga basin protection
C. Milk production D. Fish production

28. Except for raspberry and strawberry jams, what should be the minimum percentage of fruit pulp in a jam?
A. 10% (w/w) B. 25% (w/w)
C. 45% (w/w) D. 60% (w/w)

29. In Artificial Insemination semen from single bull can be used for inseminating more than .... cows per year.
A. 10,000 B. 20,000
C. 30,000 D. 50,000

30. Match List-I with List-II.

List-I (Flower Crop)	**List-II (Commercial method of propagation)**
(*a*) Gladiolus	I. Seed
(*b*) Rose	II. Corm
(*c*) Marigold	III. T-Budding
(*d*) Chrysanthemum	IV. Suckers

Choose the correct answer from the options given below:

	(a)	(b)	(c)	(d)
A.	I	II	III	IV
B.	I	IV	III	II
C.	II	III	I	IV
D.	II	I	IV	III

31. The institute in India responsible for collection and conservation of plant germplasm is:

A. National Bureau of Animal Genetic Resources, Karnal
B. Indian Agricultural Statistics Research Institute, New Delhi
C. National Bureau of Plant Genetic Resources, New Delhi
D. National Bureau of Fish Genetic Resources, Lucknow

32. What is the name of the phenomenon where one plant exerts adverse effects on neighbouring plants through production and release of toxic chemicals?

A. Symbiosis B. Allelopathy
C. Parasitism D. Mutualism

33. Arrange the following phenological stages of wheat in correct order:

(*a*) Tillering (*b*) Crown root initiation
(*c*) Jointing (*d*) Dough
(*e*) Milk

Choose the ***correct*** answer from the options given below:

A. (*a*), (*b*), (*c*), (*e*), (*d*) B. (*b*), (*a*), (*c*), (*e*), (*d*)
C. (*a*), (*b*), (*c*), (*d*), (*e*) D. (*e*), (*a*), (*c*), (*b*), (*d*)

34. Deep litter and cage systems of poultry can be categorized as .... system.

A. Free range B. Semi intensive
C. Intensive D. Easy management

35. Pure line selection is an effective method of crop improvement in which of the following crops?

A. Often cross-pollinated crops
B. Self- and cross-pollinated crops
C. Self-pollinated crops
D. Cross-pollinated crops

36. If c is the speed of light; λ and ν wavelength and frequency, respectively, of an electromagnetic radiation, then which of the following is true?

A. $\lambda = c^2$ B. $\nu = c^2$
C. $\lambda = \frac{\nu}{c}$ D. $\lambda = \frac{c}{\nu}$

37. Removal of weeds through hand pulling, hoeing, mowing is considered as .... method.

A. Physical B. Cultural
C. Biological D. Chemical

38. Which is ***not*** a polysaccharide?

A. Pectin B. Lignin
C. Hemicellulose D. Glucose

39. Which of the following is ***not*** a bacterial disease?

A. Haemorrhagic septicaemia
B. Rinderpest
C. Black quarter
D. Mastitis

40. In which crop, 'crown-root initiation' is considered as the most moisture sensitive stage for irrigation?

A. Rice B. Wheat
C. Maize D. Pearl millet

Directions (Qs. No. 41-45): *Attempt items based, on the passage given below:*

In RNA, every nucleotide residue has an additional –OH group present at 2' position in the ribose. Also, in RNA the uracil is found at the place of thymine (5-methyl uracil, another chemical name for thymine).

DNA as an acidic substance present in nucleus was first identified by Friedrich Meischer is 1869. He named it as 'Nuclein'. However, due to technical limitation in isolating such a long polymer intact, the elucidation of structure of DNA remained elusive for a very long period of time. It was only in 1953 that James Watson and Francis Crick, based on the X-ray diffraction data produced by Maurice Wilkins and Rosalind Franklin, proposed a very simple but famous Double Helix model for the structure of DNA. One of the hallmarks of their proposition was base pairing between the two strands of polynucleotide chains. However, this proposition was also based on the observation of Erwin Chargaff that for a double stranded DNA, the ratios between Adenine and Thymine and Guanine and Cytosine are constant and equals one.

41. What is the common name of 5-methyl uracil?

A. Adenine B. Thymine
C. Guanine D. Cytosine

42. Which base is present in RNA, but not in DNA?

A. Adenine B. Thymine
C. Uracil D. Guanine

43. What is the ratio between Guanine and Cytosine in DNA?

A. > 1 B. < 1
C. $= 1$ D. $= \alpha$

44. Initial name of DNA was:

A. Nucleotide B. Nucleon
C. Nuclein D. Nucloid

45. Who proposed 'Double Helix' structure of DNA?

A. Wilkins and Franklin
B. Watson and Crick
C. Wilkins and Watson
D. Watson and Franklin

Directions (Qs. No. 46-50): *Attempt items based on the passage given below:*

Types of compound soil structure and their characteristics

Type	Shape and Characteristics
Blocky 	All the three dimensions of peds are of about same size providing a shape of block having flat or rounded faces. These peds are further subdivided into *angular blocky* and *sub-angular blocky*. In the former, faces are flat, and edges and corners are sharp while in the latter, face and edges are mainly rounded. The blocky structure is usually found in B-horizon and promotes good drainage, aeration and root penetration.
Prismatic 	The peds are elongated more in vertical than in horizontal direction giving a column like shape. Vertical cleavage planes are predominant. When the tops of peds are relatively angular and flat, it is called *prismatic* and when rounded, it is called *columnar*. Prismatic structure commonly occurs in subsurface horizons in arid and semiarid regions.
Platy 	Horizontal axis is longer than vertical axis resulting in a plate like appearance. Horizontal cleavage planes are predominant. When peds are thick, they are called *platy*, and when thin, are called *laminar*. Platy structure is often inherited from parent material and may also be formed due to compaction of clayey soils by heavy machinery.
Spherical 	Peds are roughly spherical or granular and sub-divided into *granular* and *crumb*. Granular structure is less porous than the crumb due to low organic matter content. Spherical structure is formed by biotic activities in surface horizon and promotes infiltration, percolation, aeration and root penetration in soils.

46. When the peds, are elongated more in vertical than in horizontal direction and tops of peds are rounded, the structure is called:
A. Sub-angular blocky B. Crumb
C. Prismatic D. Columnar

47. When all the three dimensions of peds are of about the same size and, faces and edges are mainly rounded, the soil structure is called:
A. Angular blocky B. Sub-angular blocky
C. Laminar D. Columnar

48. When the peds are longer in horizontal axis than in vertical axis the soil structure is called:
A. Prismatic B. Angular blocky
C. Platy D. Granular

49. Which of the following soil structure is roughly spherical and is formed by biotic activities in surface horizon and promotes aeration and infiltration?
A. Crumb B. Laminar
C. Columnar D. Prismatic

50. Which of the following soil structure is generally found in B-horizon, promotes aeration, good drainage and penetration?
A. Platy B. Laminar
C. Crumb D. Blocky

ANSWERS

1. (C): Radish is a root vegetable, so it's a part of the root system of the plant. Therefore, it matches with II. Root. Potato, on the other hand, is a tuber, which is a modified part of the stem that grows underground. Hence, it pairs with I. Tuber. Onion is a bulb, which is a modified, underground stem surrounded by fleshy modified leaves that store food. It correlates with IV. Bulb. Cauliflower is actually part of the plant's flower system. While it's not specifically mentioned in the options, III. Stem is the closest match given the options.

2. (C): When a heterozygous dihybrid organism (AaBb) is crossed with a double recessive (aabb), the phenotype ratio expected is 1:1:1:1. This is because the heterozygous dihybrid will produce four types of gametes in equal frequency (AB, Ab, aB, and ab) and when crossed with the double recessive which produces only one kind of gamete (ab), we get four different phenotypic combinations in equal proportions.

3. (B): For weather elements and their respective instruments:

- Light is measured by a Sunshine recorder, so (a) matches with III.
- Wind Velocity is measured using an Anemometer, hence (b) correlates with IV.

- Humidity indicates the amount of moisture present in the air. It is quantified using a Hygrometer. Therefore, (c) pairs with I.
- Temperature, which is the degree of hotness or coldness measured in terms of any of several arbitrary scales like Celsius or Fahrenheit, is measured using a Thermometer. Thus, (d) matches with II.

4. (D): Mycorrhiza refers to the symbiotic association between certain fungi and the roots of most plants. In this association, the fungi assist the plant by extending its root's nutrient absorption capability, especially for phosphorus. In return, the plant provides the fungi with carbohydrates. This relationship is vital for many plants to thrive in their respective environments. Notably, the association is so crucial that some plants can't survive without their mycorrhizal partners.

5. (C): During the collection of semen from a bull using an artificial vagina, the angle of the artificial vagina is crucial to mimic the natural process as closely as possible and ensure that the semen is collected safely and efficiently. It is generally held at a 45° angle to the ground. This angle ensures that the semen flows down into the collection container without any obstruction or spillage. Proper technique ensures the health and safety of both the bull and the individual collecting the semen, and also ensures the viability of the collected sample.

6. (A)

7. (B): While mango, banana, and jackfruit are all indigenous to India and have a long history in its culture and cuisine, guava is not. Guava is believed to have originated in Central America and was brought to India by Portuguese traders in the 17th century. Since its introduction, it has become a staple in many Indian fruit salads and dishes, highlighting the influence of global trade on the evolution of regional cuisines.

8. (D): 'Totapuri' is a variety of mango. Mango, being the national fruit of India, comes in various shapes, sizes, and flavors, and 'Totapuri' is one of the many celebrated varieties. Recognized by its parrot-beak like tip, the 'Totapuri' mango is commonly found in the southern states of India. This mango is slightly tangier and is often used in salads and pickles due to its firm flesh and unique taste.

9. (B): The ICAR-Indian Veterinary Research Institute (IVRI) is located in Izatnagar, Uttar Pradesh, India. Established in 1889, it's one of the premier veterinary research institutions in India. The institute has been pivotal in research related to livestock and poultry diseases, developing vaccines, and improving animal health throughout the country. IVRI's role has been crucial in enhancing livestock production and contributing to the economy through its research and development initiatives.

10. (A): 'Puddling' is an operation that involves the churning of soil in the presence of water to create a soft, saturated, and granular structure. This is primarily done for transplanted rice. The main objectives of puddling are to reduce percolation losses of water, control the growth of weeds by creating anaerobic conditions, and to prepare a soft bed for easy transplanting of rice seedlings. Puddling creates a hardpan below the surface layer, preventing deep-rooted weeds from growing but allowing the shallow roots of rice to spread and grow.

11. (B): Growing potato in the interspaces of apple trees in the first few years is an example of intercropping. Intercropping is a method where two or more crops are grown together in the same field during a growing season. The aim is to utilize resources efficiently that might otherwise be wasted. In the case of growing potatoes between apple trees, the potatoes can make use of the sunlight, nutrients, and water in the interspaces that the young apple trees aren't yet fully utilizing, ensuring maximum productivity from the land.

12. (A): India is the second-largest producer of fruits and vegetables in the world, following China. India boasts a diverse range of agro-climatic zones, enabling the cultivation of various fruits and vegetables throughout the year. Not only does the country produce staples like rice and wheat in vast amounts, but it also contributes significantly to the global production of fruits such as mangoes, bananas, citrus fruits, and vegetables like onions, brinjals, and cauliflowers.

13. (D): A buffer solution is a solution that can resist changes in pH when small amounts of an acid or base are added. A mixture of acetic acid and sodium acetate serves as a buffer solution. Here's why: Acetic acid is a weak acid that partially dissociates in water. Sodium acetate, its salt, can provide acetate ions, which can react with any excess H^+ ions added to the solution. Similarly, the acetic acid can react with any excess OH^- ions. This mutual compensation ensures the pH remains relatively stable.

14. (C): Pressurized irrigation systems are designed to deliver water directly to the plants in a controlled manner, often reducing water wastage. Among the options provided:

- Drip irrigation delivers water drop by drop directly to the roots of plants.
- Rainguns simulate rainfall by spraying water over crops.

- Micro-sprinklers are a type of sprinkler system that operates at lower pressures, distributing water in a controlled manner over the crop. In contrast, furrow and flood irrigation methods are gravity-driven and are not pressurized systems.

15. (A): The mitochondrion is often referred to as the "powerhouse" of the cell. This is because mitochondria produce adenosine triphosphate (ATP), the main energy currency of the cell, through a process called cellular respiration. Within the mitochondria, glucose and oxygen are used to produce ATP, carbon dioxide, and water. This ATP is then used to power various cellular activities. Structurally, mitochondria are unique in that they have two membranes and their own DNA, which is believed to be a result of an ancient symbiotic relationship between a primitive eukaryotic cell and a prokaryotic cell.

16. (B): Ghee is a fat-rich milk product. It is clarified butter, which means it is butter that has been simmered and strained to remove all water. This leaves a product that is nearly 100% fat. Ghee is used extensively in Indian cooking and also in various religious rituals. Due to its high-fat content, ghee has a rich flavour and is often used in small amounts to add depth to dishes. In comparison, paneer, dahi, and kulfi contain fats but are not predominantly fat.

17. (A): *Triticum aestivum* is the most cultivated species of wheat in India. This type of wheat is commonly referred to as bread wheat. India, being one of the largest producers of wheat globally, primarily grows this variety due to its high yield and adaptability to diverse climatic conditions. *Triticum aestivum* has a hexaploid genome, which means it contains six copies of every chromosome. This genetic makeup contributes to its robustness and versatility.

18. (B): Cows and buffaloes typically come into heat or experience estrus after a period of 19-21 days. This is known as the estrous cycle. During this time, the female is receptive to mating and shows several behavioral signs like restlessness, increased vocalization, and mounting other animals. Timely identification of the heat period is crucial in animal husbandry to ensure successful mating and optimal reproductive efficiency.

19. (C): Amoeba belongs to the kingdom Protista. Organisms in this kingdom are generally unicellular and eukaryotic, which means they have a well-defined nucleus. The amoeba is a classic example of a protist and is often studied in biology for its unique movement mechanism using pseudopods. Pseudopods, or "false feet", are temporary projections that the amoeba forms to move and capture food. The flexibility and adaptability of amoebas make them a fascinating subject in the microscopic world.

20. (A): Marigold has African and French varieties. Marigold is a popular flower known for its bright yellow and orange blooms. The African marigold, often larger with yellow or orange flowers, is scientifically known as *Tagetes erecta*. On the other hand, French marigold *(Tagetes patula)* is smaller and often displays a wider range of colours, including reds and browns. Both varieties are used for ornamental purposes, and their vibrant colours make them a favourite choice for gardens and floral decorations.

21. (C): If a heifer is not showing heat symptoms for breeding, a medical examination is generally needed after 2-years of age and after achieving a certain body weight. It is vital to recognize reproductive problems early to ensure optimal herd management and fertility. Weight, more than age, is often a significant determinant because a heifer should achieve a specific weight before coming into heat. In many cattle breeds, a weight of around 300 kg is considered a standard threshold. Therefore, a combination of age and body weight becomes essential criteria to decide when to conduct a medical examination for non-showing of heat symptoms.

22. (D): Sulphur (S) is known as a secondary nutrient element for plants. While the primary nutrients (N, P, K) are required in the largest amounts by plants, secondary nutrients like Calcium, Magnesium, and Sulphur are needed in moderate quantities. Sulphur plays a vital role in the formation of certain amino acids, vitamins, and enzymes. Moreover, it aids in the production of chlorophyll and promotes nodule formation in leguminous plants. The deficiency of Sulphur can cause plants to turn pale and exhibit stunted growth.

23. (C): To calculate the amount of single super phosphate (SSP) required, we need to consider the phosphate content in SSP. SSP generally contains around 16% P_2O_5 (Phosphorus pentoxide). If you need to supply 80 kg P_2O_5 to 1-hectare area, the calculation becomes: Required SSP = (80 kg P_2O_5) ÷ 0.16 (or 16%) = 500 kg. Thus, 500 kg of SSP is needed to supply 80 kg P_2O_5 to a hectare.

24. (A): Soil textural classes categorize soils based on the relative percentages of sand, silt, and clay. The order for clay content in descending order among the provided options is: (*b*) Clay—Comprised of over 40% clay. (*a*) Sandy clay—Has between 35% to 65% clay. (*d*) Sandy clay loam—Contains 20% to 35% clay. (*c*) Sandy loam—Comprises less than 20% clay but more than sand. (*e*) Sand—Consists mainly of sand particles with minimal clay. Thus, the correct sequence is (*b*), (*a*), (*d*), (*c*), (*e*).

25. (C): Di-ammonium phosphate (DAP) is a complex fertilizer that contains both Nitrogen and Phosphorus. DAP is widely used as a source of both these essential nutrients to enhance plant growth. The nitrogen is provided in the ammonium form, which can be quickly taken up by plants, while the phosphorus is readily available for plant uptake. DAP has the benefit of providing essential nutrients in a balanced form, ensuring optimal growth and development of crops. It does not contain potash, so if a soil requires potassium supplementation, an additional source must be added.

26. (C): Acrocentric chromosomes have a centromere situated close to one end, resulting in one very long arm and one very short arm. The positioning of the centromere dictates the chromosome's shape and how it will align and separate during cellular processes like mitosis. Other categories based on centromere positioning include metacentric (middle), sub-metacentric (between the center and the end), and telocentric (at the very end). The acrocentric chromosome plays a role in certain genetic conditions and evolutionary processes.

27. (C): Operation Flood, launched in 1970, is the world's largest dairy development program. Initiated by the National Dairy Development Board (NDDB) of India, it transformed India from a net importer of dairy products into the world's largest milk producer. This was achieved by creating a nationwide milk grid linking producers throughout India with consumers in over 700 towns and cities, emphasizing the value of milk as a source of rural income and of reasonable prices for consumers. This success was built on the foundational cooperative approach, allowing both production and demand-side measures to be integrated.

28. (C): For jams (excluding raspberry and strawberry jams), the minimum percentage of fruit pulp required is 45% (w/w). This standard ensures that the jam retains the flavor, aroma, and essential characteristics of the fruit it is made from. In many countries, legal standards mandate this minimum to prevent adulteration or dilution with excess sweeteners and water, ensuring consumers get a product that is truly representative of the fruit mentioned.

29. (B): Through the process of Artificial Insemination (AI), semen from a single bull can be used to inseminate more than 20,000 females. AI is an assisted reproduction technique where sperm is collected, processed, and stored to be used later for breeding. It has many advantages over natural mating: it prevents disease transmission, allows for genetic improvement by using semen from superior bulls, and reduces the need for maintaining bulls on the farm. Moreover, with the cryopreservation technique, semen can be stored for an extended period without losing its viability.

30. (C): Commercial propagation methods vary according to the flower crop in question, as they possess distinct biological characteristics:

(*a*) Gladiolus	II. Corm—Gladiolus is propagated mainly by corms. A corm is a swollen stem base that is modified into a mass of storage tissue.
(b) Rose	III. T-Budding—Roses are commonly propagated using the T-budding method, especially for the hybrid varieties. This method ensures true-to-type plants that maintain the characteristics of the parent.
(c) Marigold	I. Seed—Marigold is often propagated by seeds because they germinate easily and grow rapidly.
(d) Chrysanthemum	IV. Suckers—Chrysanthemums can be propagated by suckers that arise from the base of the plant. This ensures uniformity in the progeny.

31. (C): National Bureau of Plant Genetic Resources, New Delhi is the primary institution in India responsible for the collection and conservation of plant germplasm. Germplasm is living tissue from which plants can be grown. It can be a seed or another plant part – a leaf, a piece of stem, pollen or even just a few cells that can grow into a whole plant. The NBPGR conducts explorations to collect the germplasm, conserves them in gene banks, and conducts research on their genetic characterization and documentation.

32. (B): Allelopathy refers to the biological phenomenon where one plant inhibits the growth of another plant, neighboring or nearby, by producing and releasing chemical substances into the environment. These chemicals, often referred to as allelochemicals, can be beneficial (positive allelopathy) or detrimental (negative allelopathy) to the receiver organisms. Allelopathic interactions are considered important in understanding plant community structures, agricultural practices, and forest regeneration.

33. (B): The phenological stages of wheat, in their correct order, are: (b) Crown root initiation: It is the initial stage where roots start to emerge. (a) Tillering: It is the phase when the plant starts branching out. (c) Jointing: This phase witnesses the elongation of internodes above the ground. (e) Milk: At this stage, if the grain is squeezed, a milky substance comes out. (d) Dough: This is the final stage before maturity when the grain becomes hard but still has moisture. It feels doughy when squeezed. Understanding these stages is crucial for efficient crop management and achieving optimal yield.

34. (C): Deep litter and cage systems for poultry fall under the Intensive system of rearing. The intensive system is designed to raise a large number of birds in a relatively smaller space. In the deep litter system, birds are raised on the floor covered with litters like straw or husk, while in the cage system, birds are kept in cages, usually in layers. Both methods aim at maximizing production while minimizing the land required, ensuring better monitoring of birds, and providing a controlled environment for feeding, growth, and disease management.

35. **(C):** Pure line selection is an effective method of crop improvement primarily for Self-pollinated crops. In this method, genetically identical or nearly identical plants are produced over successive generations. Pure lines are essentially homozygous and show little variability, ensuring consistent characteristics over generations. This technique is beneficial for self-pollinated crops because these crops have naturally high levels of homozygosity. Using pure line selection in such crops can lead to the stabilization of desirable traits, ensuring uniformity in yield and other attributes.

36. **(D)**

37. **(A):** Removal of weeds through methods like hand pulling, hoeing, and mowing is considered a Physical method. Physical weed control involves the manual or mechanical removal of weeds. Hand pulling is self-explanatory, where weeds are uprooted by hand. Hoeing involves the use of a hoe to cut or uproot weeds, and mowing is the process of cutting off the tops of weeds. These physical methods are effective but can be labor-intensive, especially in larger areas.

38. **(D):** Glucose is not a polysaccharide. Glucose is a simple sugar or monosaccharide. It serves as an essential energy source for plants and animals. On the other hand, pectin, lignin, and hemicellulose are complex carbohydrates or polysaccharides. Polysaccharides are made up of multiple monosaccharide units linked together. While glucose serves primarily as an energy source, polysaccharides can have structural roles (like in the case of lignin in plants) or can act as food storage molecules.

39. **(B):** Rinderpest is not a bacterial disease; it's a viral disease. Rinderpest, also known as cattle plague, was caused by the rinderpest virus and was characterized by fever, oral erosions, diarrhea, and high mortality. This disease was declared eradicated in 2011 by the World Organisation for Animal Health (OIE). On the other hand, *Haemorrhagic septicaemia*, Black quarter, and Mastitis can be caused by bacteria. Specifically, Mastitis can be caused by a range of microorganisms, including bacteria, viruses, and algae.

40. **(B):** In wheat, the 'crown-root initiation' is considered the most moisture-sensitive stage for irrigation. Wheat has several growth stages, and the crown root initiation is a critical phase in its development. This is the time when secondary roots start to develop from the base of the shoot. Adequate moisture during this phase ensures healthy root development, which is essential for the plant's overall growth, nutrient uptake, and eventual grain yield. Proper irrigation management ensures that the crop gets the right amount of water at the most critical times, optimizing yield and quality.

41. **(B):** Thymine is the common name for 5-methyl uracil. Both thymine and uracil are pyrimidine bases, but thymine is specific to DNA, while uracil is found in RNA. The presence of a methyl group at the 5th position differentiates thymine from uracil. This substitution of thymine in DNA instead of uracil is critical as it adds an additional level of stability to the DNA structure.

42. **(C):** The base that is present in RNA but not in DNA is uracil. In DNA, thymine takes the place of uracil. This distinction is essential for maintaining the integrity of the genetic code. If uracil were present in DNA, it could easily be deaminated to form cytosine, leading to potential mutations. By using thymine instead of uracil, DNA minimizes the chance of this mutation occurring.

43. **(C):** The ratio between Guanine (G) and Cytosine (C) in DNA is 1:1. This is based on the observation made by Erwin Chargaff, known as Chargaff's rules. He observed that the quantity of adenine (A) always equaled the quantity of thymine (T), and the quantity of guanine (G) always equaled the quantity of cytosine (C). These observations laid the groundwork for understanding the base-pairing rules that are foundational to the structure of the DNA double helix.

44. **(C):** The initial name given to DNA was "nuclein". Friedrich Meischer identified DNA as an acidic substance present in the nucleus in 1869. The name "nuclein" derived from its location in the nucleus and its acidic nature. Over time, as our understanding of its structure and function evolved, the name was changed to deoxyribonucleic acid, or DNA.

45. **(B):** The 'Double Helix' structure of DNA was proposed by James Watson and Francis Crick. Their groundbreaking work in 1953 unveiled the molecular structure of DNA, which explained how genetic information could be stored and replicated. While Watson and Crick made this revolutionary discovery, it was based on the X-ray diffraction data produced by Maurice Wilkins and Rosalind Franklin. Franklin, in particular, played a significant role in producing the X-ray images that were key to understanding the double helix structure, but her contribution was not fully recognized until much later.

46. **(D)** **47.** **(B)** **48.** **(C)**

49. **(A)** **50.** **(D)**

• • •

PREVIOUS YEARS' PAPER (SOLVED)

Common University Entrance Test for UG Programmes

CUET-UG—AGRICULTURE*

Entrance Exam, 2022

Subject Code: 302

1. Example of quantitative inheritance is:
A. Color/Colour of skin
B. Colour Blindness
C. Klinefelter's Syndrome
D. Allaptonuria

2. Swedish geneticist H. Nilsson-Ehle discovered polygenic inheritance in ______.
A. Jowar seed
B. Wheat kernel colour/color
C. Pea seed coat
D. Maize seed colour/color

3. Short range forecasting of weather is predicted for the period of:
A. one or two days
B. three to ten days
C. four weeks
D. two months

4. Match List-I with List-II.

List-I	List-II
(*a*) Temperature	I. Anemometer
(*b*) Rainfall	II. Ordinary rain guage
(*c*) Wind Velocity	III. Thermometer
(*d*) Relative Humidity	IV. Hygrometer

Choose the correct answer from the options given below:

	(*a*)	(*b*)	(*c*)	(*d*)
A.	I	III	IV	II
B.	II	IV	III	I
C.	III	II	I	IV
D.	IV	III	II	I

5. Meiosis involves one cycle of ______.
(*a*) DNA replication
(*b*) Cytokinesis
(*c*) Karyo kinesis
(*d*) Formation of all membrane
(*e*) Combination of chromosome replicants

Choose the correct answer from the options given below:
A. (*a*) only
B. (*b*) and (*c*) only
C. (*d*) and (*e*) only
D. (*e*) only

6. Which is/are the milch purpose breeds of cattle?
(*a*) Bargur
(*b*) Sahiwal
(*c*) Nimari
(*d*) Red Sindhi
(*e*) Dangi

Choose the correct answer from the options given below:
A. (*a*) only
B. (*c*) only
C. (*a*), (*c*) and (*e*) only
D. (*b*) and (*d*) only

7. Which one of the following is a chemical property of soil?
A. Soil pH
B. Soil structure
C. Soil colour
D. Soil plasticity

8. In Papaya which method of propagation is commonly followed?
A. Sexual (By seed)
B. Budding
C. Asexual
D. Layering

9. Which of the following statements contributed Mendel's success?
(*a*) Selection of Pea plant
(*b*) His knowledge of history
(*c*) One character at one time
(*d*) His statistical knowledge
(*e*) Knowledge of geometry

Choose the correct answer from the options given below:

*40 Questions to be attempted out of 50

A. (*b*) only
B. (*a*), (*c*) and (*d*) only
C. (*b*) and (*e*) only
D. (*e*) only

10. *Tagets erecta* is the botanical name of ______.
A. African marigold
B. French marigold
C. Rose
D. Jasmine

11. What is the origin of Holstein Friesian exotic breed of cow?
A. Switzerland
B. Island Jersey
C. Friesland and Holland
D. India

12. ______ is normal pH of the bull semen.
A. 7.9 to 8.1 B. 6.4 to 6.8
C. 3.2 to 3.5 D. 4.0 to 4.5

13. What are the different system of irrigation?
(*a*) Random field ditches irrigation
(*b*) Surface irrigation
(*c*) Subsurface irrigation
(*d*) Sprinkler irrigation
(*e*) Drip irrigation

Choose the correct answer from the options given below:
A. (*a*) only
B. (*a*) and (*e*) only
C. (*b*), (*c*) and (*d*) only
D. (*b*), (*c*), (*d*) and (*e*) only

14. Which one of the following is not used in organic farming?
A. Glomus B. Earthworm
C. Snail D. Oscillation

15. ________ breed of buffalo is intermediate cross between Murrah and Surti.
A. Banni B. Mehsana
C. Jafarabadi D. Nagpuri

16. According to NASA, the gases in earth's atmosphere include ________ % of carbon dioxide.
A. 78% B. 0.93%
C. 0.03% D. 0.01%

17. Which acid is present in abundance in the gram leaves?
A. Hydrocynic acid
B. Carbonic acid
C. Acetic acid
D. Malic acid

18. ______ refers to the development of embryo from egg cell without fertilization.
A. Parthenogenesis
B. Apogamy
C. Apospory
D. Adventive embryony

19. The indigenous breed of poultry is _______.
A. Assel B. Sussex
C. Minorca D. Longshan

20. _______ means the physical condition of soil resulting from tillage operations.
A. Mulching B. Harvesting
C. Soil tilth D. Threshing

21. Di-ammonium Phosphate (DAP) is the example of ______ type of fertilizer.
A. Mixed fertilizers
B. Soil amendments
C. Straight fertilizer
D. Complex fertilizer

22. Match List-I with List-II.

List-I	List-II
(*a*) Wheat	I. CO-740
(*b*) Paddy	II. Sonalika
(*c*) Sugar cane	III. Basmati
(*d*) Soyabean	IV. Brag

Choose the correct answer from the options given below:

	(*a*)	(*b*)	(*c*)	(*d*)
A.	I	II	IV	III
B.	II	III	I	IV
C.	IV	II	III	I
D.	III	II	IV	I

23. Which one of the chemical is not used in preservation of fruit products?
A. Acetic acid
B. Potassium metabisulphate
C. Sodium benzoate
D. Nitric acid

24. Match List-I with List-II.

List-I	List-II
(*a*) Guava	I. Myrtaceae
(*b*) Custard	II. Annonaceae
(*c*) Cashewnut	III. Anacardiaceae
(*d*) Papaya	IV. Cariaceae

Choose the correct answer from the options given below:

	(*a*)	(*b*)	(*c*)	(*d*)
A.	IV	III	I	II
B.	III	I	IV	II
C.	I	II	III	IV
D.	II	III	IV	I

25. _______ is the inherent potentiality of plant cell to give rise to whole plant:
A. Mutation

B. Polyploidy
C. Embryoculture
D. Totipotency

26. In _______ cattles are arranged in head out manner and their is a common passage between two rows called central or litter alley.
A. Head to head housing system
B. Tail to tail housing system
C. Loose housing system
D. Individual housing system

27. Which is the viral disease of poultry?
A. Chronic respiratory disease
B. Coccidiosis
C. Ranikhet
D. Anthrax

28. Flower containing both stamen and pistil is a _______.
A. Staminate flower
B. Pistillate flower
C. Perfect flower
D. Unisexual flower

29. Which is not the type of watershed?
A. Milli watershed
B. Long watershed
C. Micro watershed
D. Mini watershed

30. Which of the following is an example of herbicide?
A. Thirum
B. Chloropyriphos
C. Butachlor
D. Mancozeb

31. _______ are the modified flower that develops into plants directly without formation of seeds.
A. Bulbil B. Suckers
C. Stolons D. Runners

32. Botanical name of groundnut is _______.
A. Oryza sativa
B. Cicer arietinum
C. Triticum aestivum
D. Arachis hypogaea

33. In cattle housing system the width of Manger should be:
A. 1.3 meter
B. 0.8 meter
C. 1.5 meter
D. 1.0 meter

34. Scurvy cardiac disorder pains in joints, bleeding of gums and tooth decay is caused by deficiency of _______.
A. Naicin-nicotinic acid
B. Vit-D
C. Ascorbic acid
D. Vit-E

35. Black Quarter (B.Q) disease is caused by _______.
A. *Clostridium chauvoei*
B. *Pasteurella multocida*
C. *Brucella abortys*
D. *Bacillus anthracis*

36. In _______ system of planting row to row and plant to plant distance is same.
A. Square B. Rectangular
C. Contour D. Triangular

37. Anacardiaceae is the family of which crop?
A. Papaya B. Banana
C. Santra D. Mango

38. Match List-I with List-II.

	List-I	List-II
(*a*)	American Poultry breed	I. Cochin
(*b*)	English Poultry breed	II. Ancona
(*c*)	Mediterranean Poultry breed	III. Red cap
(*d*)	Asian Poultry breed	IV. Plymothrock

Choose the correct answer from the options given below:

	(*a*)	(*b*)	(*c*)	(*d*)
A.	I	II	III	IV
B.	II	IV	I	III
C.	III	IV	I	II
D.	IV	III	II	I

39. Which one of the following is not a nitrogen fixing biofertilizers?
A. Azosprillum B. Acetobacter
C. Azotobacter D. Aspergillus

40. Pungency in onion is due to presence of the _______.
A. Lycopene
B. Allyl propyl disulphide
C. Capsanthin
D. Malic acid

Directions (Qs. No. 41-45): *Based on the passage given below answer the question that follows:*

Soybean (Glycine *max*) is an important oilseed as well as pulse crop. Average oil content is 20 p.c. and protein content is 41 p.c.

It is principally a tropical crop but also grown in subtropical and temperate region.

It is grown in *Kharif* and *Rabi* seasons and usually on light to sandy loam soils.

Most common varieties are Brag, Clark, Punjab 1, MACS-13, MACS-57, and MACS-124. etc.

Water requirement vary between 450 to 750 nn. Flowering and pod formation are most critical stages of its growth for irrigation.

Important pests are stem borer, pod borer, hairy caterpillar, white flies and aphids.

The major disease are bacterial blight, mosaic leaf spot and downy mildew.

41. Which of the following is an important oil seed and pulse crop:
A. Groundnut B. Gram
C. Paddy D. Soyabean

42. How much protein and oil content is present in Soyabean?
A. 41% and 20%
B. 20% and 41%
C. 30% and 30%
D. 50% and 10%

43. Which one of the following is not the variety of Soyabean?
A. Brag B. Clark
C. IR-8 D. MACS-57

44. Which are the important and critical growth stages of Soyabean for irrigation?
A. Tillering and Rooting
B. Flowering and Pod formation
C. Rooting and maturity
D. Maturity and Tillering

45. Which is the most important disease of Soyabean?
A. Aphid B. Jassid
C. Mosaic D. Stemborer

Directions (Qs. No. 46-50): *Based on the passage given below answer the questions that follows:*

Most of the fruits are perishable. Heavy weight, larger volume and delicacy are the threats in transport, storage and marketing of the fruits. We can overcome these problems by way to preservation.

Preservation is nothing but a technique of extending storage life of the Product without deterioration in its edible quality for its future use.

Principles involved in preservation are prevention or delay of microbil decomposition, prevention or delay of self decomposition of the product and presentation or minimizing damages by insect, pest and disease.

Physical methods, chemical methods and aspesis are the different methods of preservation. Jam, jelly and pickles are the preserved products of fruits.

46. Which principle is not involved in the preservation process?
A. Prevention or delay of microbial decomposition
B. Prevention or delay of self decomposition
C. Prevention or minimizing damage by insect
D. Prevention of market rate

47. Which one of the following is the method of preservation?
A. Physical B. Biological
C. Legal D. Curative

48. Which one of the following is not the preserved products of fruits?
A. Pickles B. Jelly
C. Jam D. Bread

49. _______ is a technique of extending storage life of product without deterioration of its quality.
A. Preservation B. Marketing
C. Spoilage D. Decomposition

50. Problem of fruits during transport storage and marketing can overcome by the way of _______.
A. Increase in Price of the product
B. Increase in quality of product
C. Increase in dose of fertilizer
D. Preservation

ANSWERS

1	2	3	4	5	6	7	8	9	10
A	B	A	C	A	D	A	A	B	A
11	**12**	**13**	**14**	**15**	**16**	**17**	**18**	**19**	**20**
C	B	D	C	B	C	D	A	A	C
21	**22**	**23**	**24**	**25**	**26**	**27**	**28**	**29**	**30**
D	B	D	C	D	B	C	D	B	C
31	**32**	**33**	**34**	**35**	**36**	**37**	**38**	**39**	**40**
A	D	C	C	A	A	D	D	D	B
41	**42**	**43**	**44**	**45**	**46**	**47**	**48**	**49**	**50**
D	A	C	B	C	D	A	D	A	D

•••

AGRICULTURE

UNIT 1

Agrometeorology, Genetics and Plant Breeding, Biochemistry and Microbiology

AGROMETEOROLOGY

Agriculture is more than just a means of livelihood. It's a passion that is deeply ingrained in the hearts of farmers around the world. The art of cultivating the land and rearing livestock is an age-old tradition that has been passed down from generation to generation.

The art of agriculture necessitates a profound comprehension of the land, the climate, and the crops or animals being raised. It involves a deft balance of intuition and experience, as well as a willingness to adjust to shifting circumstances.

In terms of business, agriculture is geared toward attaining maximum profitability while minimizing expenses. This involves the management of resources such as land, labor, water, and capital, as well as making informed decisions regarding everything from selecting crops to devising marketing strategies. Given the ever-increasing commercialization of agriculture, mechanization is playing an increasingly crucial role in maximizing efficiency and productivity.

As a science, agriculture leverages cutting-edge technologies and scientific principles to optimize production and increase yield. From crop breeding to production techniques to crop protection, agriculture is in a state of constant evolution and improvement, thanks to advancements in areas such as genetics, biotechnology, and data analysis. For many, agriculture is not just a science, but a way of life that is deeply rooted in their cultural heritage.

Farmers pour their heart and soul into the crops they grow and the animals they raise, nurturing them with care and dedication. The satisfaction they feel when they see their hard work come to fruition is immeasurable.

At its core, agriculture is about sustainability, not just for the farmers and their families, but for the entire world. It provides us with the food we eat, the clothes we wear, and the fuel we use. As the world population continues to grow, the importance of agriculture only becomes more evident.

Despite the challenges that farmers face, from weather fluctuations to market fluctuations, they continue to persevere. Agriculture is not just a job, it's a way of life, and farmers are proud to carry on the legacy of their forefathers. As we continue to rely on agriculture for our basic needs, we must never forget the hard work and dedication of the farmers who make it all possible.

BRANCHES OF AGRICULTURE

Agronomy: The word Agronomy is derived from two Greek words "Agros" meaning field and "Nomos" meaning to manage. It is defined as the agricultural science that deals with the principles and practices of crop production and field management, including soil, water, and crop management.

Horticulture: The word Horticulture is derived from two Latin words "Hortus" meaning garden and "Cultura/ Cultus" meaning cultivation. It is a branch of agriculture that deals with fruit crops; vegetable crops, ornamental plants, commercial flowers, medicinal crops, aromatic crops, spices crops, plantation crops, individual trees, shrubs, climbers, and post-harvest management and processing.

Animal husbandry: Animal husbandry is derived from "Animal" and "Husband" words, where animal means livestock and husband means one who takes care. It is the branch of agriculture concerned with animals that are raised for meat, fiber, milk, eggs, or other products, including day-to-day care, selective breeding, and the raising of livestock.

Forestry: The word Forestry is derived from the French word "Forest" meaning wooded country. It is defined as the theory and practice of all that constitutes the creation, conservation, and scientific management of forests and the utilization of their resources. This includes all thinking and all actions pertaining to the creation and management of forests, including harvesting, marketing, and utilization of all forest products and services. It includes not only the management of existing forests but also the creation of new forests.

Fishery science: Aquatic and fisheries science is the study of aquatic ecosystems to increase scientific understanding and to apply basic ecological principles to their management, thereby sustaining them for multiple uses.

Agricultural Engineering: Agricultural Engineering is the branch of engineering involved with the design of farm machinery, soil management, land development, mechanization, and automation of livestock farming, as well as the efficient planting, harvesting, storage, and processing of farm commodities.

OTHER BRANCHES

Apiculture: Apiculture is a branch of agriculture that deals with the study of beekeeping and honey production.

Sericulture: Sericulture is a branch of agriculture that deals with the study of Silkworm *(Bombyx mori)* domestication and silk production. It is an economically important insect, being a primary producer of silk. A silkworm's preferred food is white mulberry leaves, though they may eat other mulberry *(Morus nigra)* species and even osage orange.

Lac Culture: Lac culture is a branch of agriculture that deals with the study of the lac insect *(Laccifer lacca)* domestication and lac production.

METEOROLOGY

Meteorology is a branch of science that explores the characteristics and behavior of the atmosphere, including its physical, chemical, and dynamic properties, and their effects on the Earth's surface, oceans, and life in general. Climatology, on the other hand, is a scientific study that focuses on understanding, describing, and interpreting climate patterns over long periods of time. This involves analyzing the processes that generate climate conditions, including their causes and effects.

Ecology is another branch of science that investigates the relationships between living organisms and their surrounding environment. It aims to understand how living things interact with each other and with their physical and biological surroundings, including the impact of human activities on these ecosystems.

Weather refers to the atmospheric conditions of a specific location over a short period of time, including factors such as temperature, pressure, wind, humidity, precipitation, sunshine, and cloud cover. Seasons, which are caused by the tilt of the Earth's axis and its revolution around the sun, are characterized by specific sets of weather conditions.

Climate, on the other hand, refers to the average weather patterns that prevail in a region over a long period of time. It is calculated based on data collected over several decades and is considered to be relatively stable. Different regions of the world have distinct climates, such as the hot and arid climate of Rajasthan, the tropical rainy climate of Kerala, the cold desert climate of Greenland, and the temperate continental climate of Central Asia.

Difference between Weather and Climate

Weather forecast is the process of predicting the future atmospheric conditions by analyzing current and past meteorological data. Agricultural weather forecast, in particular, focuses on predicting weather elements that are

Sr. No.	Weather	Climate
1	Instantaneous physical state of atmosphere at particular place.	Normal physical state or generated condition of atmosphere or long term average condition of a place.
2	Weather changes refer to specific instant of time (day or week)	It is generalized over a longer span of time and for a longer area.
3	It is expressed in terms of numerical values of meteorological elements.	It is expressed in terms of time averages and area averages of meteorological elements.
4	Weather is measured in observatory. So the observatory must at a place for which weather is to be described.	This is derived information on regional basis. So scripts of observatories extending over a region are necessary.
5	It provides meteorological information.	It constitutes geographical information in respect of weather.
6	Weather of two places having same numerical value must be same.	Climate of the two places having the same averages of weather can not be same, because their distribution over the years may be different.
7	Weather can be categorized as fair, unfair, excellent etc.	Climate is classified as desert climate, marine climate, tropical climate etc.
8	Weather decides the success or failure of a crop in a particular season.	Climate decides the type of crop suitable for a region, while introducing new crops climate is considered.
9	Adverse weather results into crop failure or loss and warrants short term contingent planning.	Climate is considered in long terms agricultural planning.

essential for farming and agricultural operations, such as rainfall, temperature, wind, humidity, dew, and sunshine hours. The accuracy of weather forecasting plays a crucial role in the agricultural sector as it helps farmers make informed decisions and plan for adverse weather conditions that could harm crops, livestock, and farming activities.

Additionally, weather forecasts provide advance notice of any hazardous weather conditions, such as thunderstorms, hailstorms, snow, or frost, allowing farmers to take appropriate measures to mitigate their impact. Therefore, accurate weather forecasting is a vital tool for agricultural planning and decision-making, enabling farmers to manage their resources effectively and optimize crop yields.

Weather forecasting can be classified based on their time scale or validity periods as short-range, medium-range, and long-range forecasts. Short-range forecasts are typically issued twice a day and cover a period of up to 3 days or 72 hours. These forecasts are based on the current synoptic situation and are broadcasted from the local weather center.

Medium-range forecasts cover a range of 3-10 days and provide predictions for meteorological elements over different agro-climatic zones. These forecasts are issued from the Weather Forecasting Centre in Noida, Uttar Pradesh, and are helpful for farmers in planning their agricultural activities accordingly.

Long-range forecasts, on the other hand, cover a period of more than 10 days, such as a month or a season. These forecasts are broadcasted from the Indian Meteorological Department (IMD) in Pune, Maharashtra, and provide valuable information for long-term agricultural planning and decision-making.

Overall, the classification of weather forecasting based on time scale is an important tool for farmers to make informed decisions about their agricultural activities and plan for adverse weather conditions.

Factors Affecting the Climate

There are various factors that affect the temperature and climate of a region. These factors include latitude or distance from the equator, altitude or height from the mean sea level, continentality or the distance from the sea, nature of the prevailing winds, cloud cover, and ocean currents.

Latitude plays a crucial role in determining the temperature of a place. Places near the equator receive more direct sunlight and have a warmer climate compared to those that are farther away. The rays of the sun fall vertically on the equator and slant in the temperate and polar regions, which causes a concentration of heat over a smaller area in equatorial regions.

Altitude is another factor that affects temperature. The temperature decreases with increasing height above sea level. For every 165 meters of vertical rise, there is an average decrease of 1°C in temperature. Thus, higher altitudes are generally cooler than lower ones.

The distance from the sea, or continentality, also influences temperature and climate. Coastal areas experience less temperature variation due to the moderating effect of the sea. In contrast, inland areas experience more extreme temperatures with a higher range of diurnal and annual temperatures. Onshore winds bring moisture from the sea and cause rainfall, while offshore winds are dry and promote evaporation.

Cloud cover affects temperature by reducing the amount of incoming solar radiation that reaches the ground. Areas with a lot of cloud cover have lower temperatures compared to areas with clear skies. This leads to a smaller diurnal range in temperature, as is the case in areas with heavy rainfall such as Thiruvananthapuram.

Ocean currents also have a significant impact on climate. Warm ocean currents raise the temperature of the coast and can bring rainfall, while cold currents lower the temperature and create fog near the coast. The onshore winds passing over a warm current carry warm air to the interior, raising the temperature of inland areas, while winds blowing over cold currents carry cold air, causing fog and mist.

Mountain chains act as a natural barrier for the wind, causing on-shore moisture-laden winds to rise after striking against the mountains, resulting in heavy rainfall on the windward side. On the other hand, winds descending on the leeward side cause very low rainfall. The great Himalayas act as a barrier, checking the moisture-laden monsoon winds from crossing over to Tibet, and also prevent biting polar cold winds from entering into India. This is why the northern plains of India receive rains while Tibet remains a perpetual rain shadow area with a lesser amount of rainfall.

The concentration of heat is more on gentle slopes, which raises the temperature of the air above them. In contrast, its lesser concentration along steeper slopes lowers the temperature. Additionally, mountain slopes facing the sun are warmer than slopes that are away from the sun's rays. The southern slopes of the Himalayas are warmer than the northern slopes.

The nature of soil depends on its texture, structure, and composition, which can vary from one soil type to another. Stony or sandy soils are good conductors of heat, while black clay soils absorb the heat of the sun's rays quickly. The bare surface of soil also reradiates heat easily. In desert areas, temperatures are high during the day and low at night. Forested areas have a lower range of temperature throughout the year, in contrast to non-forested areas.

WEATHER COMPONENTS

Climatic factors have a significant impact on crop production, with almost 50% of crop yield being attributed to them. Among the atmospheric weather variables, precipitation plays a crucial role in crop growth and development. Precipitation refers to all forms of water that fall from the atmosphere, such as rainfall, snow, hail, fog, and dew.

The amount and distribution of precipitation greatly influence the choice of crops cultivated in a particular area. In regions with heavy and evenly distributed rainfall, crops such as rice in plains and tea, coffee, and rubber in the Western Ghats are commonly grown. Conversely, in areas with low and uneven distribution of rainfall, dryland farming is common, with drought-resistant crops such as pearl millet, sorghum, and minor millets being cultivated. In desert areas, grasses and shrubs are common due to the hot desert climate.

Although rainfall has a major influence on crop yields, the yields are not always directly proportional to the amount of precipitation. Excessive rainfall above the optimal amount can actually reduce yields. The distribution of rainfall is also critical, especially in dryland regions, to ensure a longer growing period for the crops.

Temperature is a crucial factor affecting crop production, as it influences various processes within plants. The temperature range required for the maximum growth of most agricultural plants falls between 15 and 40°C. The temperature of a place is determined mainly by its latitude and altitude, which, in turn, affects the distribution of crops and vegetation.

Temperature affects the germination, growth, and development of crops, as well as the production, expansion, and flowering of leaves. Physical and chemical processes within plants are also influenced by air temperature, and diffusion rates of gases and liquids change with temperature.

Additionally, the solubility of different substances within a plant is dependent on temperature. The minimum, maximum (above which crop growth ceases), and optimum temperature of an individual plant are called its cardinal temperature.

Crops	Minimum temp. °C	Optimum temp. °C	Maximum temp. °C
Rice	10-12	30-32	36-38
Maize	8-10	32-35	40-42
Tobacco	13-14	28-30	36-38
Sorghum	8-10	30-32	36-38
Average for Kharif	15-18	31-37	38-47
Wheat	3-4.5	25-27	30-32
Barley	3-4.5	20-25	38-40
Pea	1-2	30-32	35-37
Lentil	4-5	30-32	36-38
Average for Rabi	0-5	25-30	31-35

Atmospheric humidity, or relative humidity (RH), is a measurement of the amount of water vapour in the air compared to the amount that would completely saturate the air at a specific temperature. If RH reaches 100%, the air is fully saturated with water vapour, and no further evaporation or transpiration can occur in plants. The impact of atmospheric humidity on crop production is significant and can be summarized as follows:

- The water requirements of crops are influenced by relative humidity.
- For optimal growth, most crops thrive in relative humidity levels between 40-60%.
- However, some crops may not perform well in high relative humidity conditions above 80%.
- High relative humidity can also increase the susceptibility of crops to pest and disease outbreaks.

The role of solar radiation, an essential component for life, is vital in the growth and development of crops, starting from the germination phase and continuing throughout the entire crop cycle.

The process of photosynthesis, which is the production of biomass in crops, is entirely dependent on the availability of light.

All physical processes that occur in the soil, plants, and environment are influenced by light. The distribution of crops in a particular region is determined by the temperature distribution controlled by solar radiation.

Visible radiation, particularly the Photosynthetically Active Radiation (PAR - 0.4 – 0.7μ), is critical for the production of carbohydrates that ultimately leads to biomass production. Blue-violet and orange-red light spectrums ranging from 0.4 to 0.6 μ are highly active and essential for the process of photosynthesis, while green-yellow light of the same range has low activity in the process.

Plants exhibit different responses to the duration and intensity of light, which influences their growth and development. Photoperiodism is a term used to describe the plant's reaction to the length of the day and night cycles.

Plants can be categorized into three groups based on their photoperiodic responses: short day plants, long day plants, and day-neutral plants.

Short day plants require less than 9 hours of daylight to initiate flowering, while long day plants require more than 13 hours of daylight to do so. Day-neutral plants, on the other hand, are less influenced by day length and can flower under a wide range of photoperiods. Phototropism is another light-related phenomenon that describes the directional growth of plants in response to light. It allows plants to optimize their light exposure for photosynthesis.

Finally, photosensitive plants have a specific period during which they need to receive a certain amount of light to flower, such as certain seasonal varieties.

Wind Velocity

- Wind plays a vital role in carrying moisture and heat, as well as fresh CO_2 for photosynthesis.
- A wind speed of 4-6 km/hour is beneficial for most crops, but excessive wind can cause mechanical damage to crops, such as removing leaves and twigs.
- Wind is essential for the natural dispersal of pollen and seeds in certain crops.
- However, it can also cause soil erosion, spread pests and diseases, and increase evaporation.
- On the positive side, wind can help clean produce for farmers.

Atmospheric Gases and Their Impact on Plant Growth

- The atmosphere is composed of various gases, including CO_2 (0.03%), O_2 (20.95%), N_2 (78.09%), Argon (0.93%), and others (0.02%).
- CO_2 is crucial for photosynthesis, and plants absorb it through their leaves via stomata. CO_2 is also released back into the atmosphere during the decomposition of organic matter and respiration.
- O_2 is important for the respiration of both plants and animals, and it is produced by plants during photosynthesis.
- Nitrogen is a major plant nutrient, and atmospheric N is fixed in the soil by lightning, rainfall, and nitrogen-fixing microbes in pulse crops, making it available to plants.
- However, certain gases such as SO_2, CO, CH_4, and HF released into the atmosphere can be toxic to plants.

Climate Change, Global Warming

- Climate change, also known as global warming, is the increase in average surface temperatures on Earth.
- Temperature records dating back to the late 19th Century show that the Earth's surface temperature has increased by about 0.8C (1.4F) in the last 100 years.
- About 0.6C (1.0F) of this warming occurred in the last three decades.
- Global sea levels have increased by an average of 3 mm per year in recent decades, with thermal expansion of seawater being a major contributor to this rise.
- The melting of mountain glaciers and polar ice sheets are also important factors contributing to rising sea levels.
- Most glaciers in temperate regions and along the Antarctic Peninsula are in retreat, and the Arctic sea-ice extent has shown a dramatic decline since 1979.
- The Greenland Ice Sheet has experienced record melting, and if it were to melt entirely, it would raise sea levels by 6 m.
- Satellite data shows the West Antarctic Ice Sheet is also losing mass, and recent studies suggest that even East Antarctica may have started to lose mass.
- Climate change is affecting vegetation and land animals, causing changes in the territories occupied by animals and earlier flowering and fruiting times for plants.
- The primary cause of global warming is the increase of greenhouse gases in the Earth's atmosphere, such as carbon dioxide, methane, and nitrous oxide, due to human activities like burning fossil fuels, deforestation, and agriculture.

Greenhouse Gases

- Some gases in the Earth's atmosphere act a bit like the glass in a greenhouse. These gases trap the sun's heat and prevent it from escaping back into space, similar to a greenhouse effect.
- Human activities are increasing the concentration of these greenhouse gases in the atmosphere, including carbon dioxide (CO_2), methane, nitrous oxide, and fluorinated gases.
- CO_2 is the most commonly produced greenhouse gas by human activities, responsible for 64% of man-made global warming. Its concentration in the atmosphere has increased by 40% since industrialization began.
- Methane is responsible for 17% of man-made global warming, and nitrous oxide for 6%.
- Burning coal, oil, and gas produces carbon dioxide and nitrous oxide emissions, contributing to the rising concentrations of greenhouse gases.
- Deforestation also contributes to rising greenhouse gas concentrations, as trees absorb CO_2 from the atmosphere and release it when cut down.
- Livestock farming produces large amounts of methane emissions from cows and sheep digestion.
- Fertilizers containing nitrogen produce nitrous oxide emissions.
- Fluorinated gases are released in smaller quantities but have a very strong warming effect, up to 23,000 times greater than CO_2. EU regulations are phasing these gases down.

GENETICS & PLANT BREEDING

CELL AND ITS STRUCTURE, CELL DIVISION- MITOSIS AND MEIOSIS AND THEIR SIGNIFICANCE

- All living organisms are made up of cells.
- Some organisms have a single cell while others, like higher fungi, plants, and animals, have many cells.
- Human body is made up of about one trillion cells.
- Cells vary in size and structure based on their specialized functions.
- The basic components of a cell are common to all biological cells.
- Robert Hooke observed small compartments in a piece of cork under the microscope in 1665, which he called "cells."
- Anton Van Leeuwenhoek observed bacteria, sperms, and red blood corpuscles, which were all cells.
- In 1831, Robert Brown observed that all cells had a centrally positioned body which he termed the nucleus.

The Cell Theory

- The "cell theory" was formulated by M.J. Schleiden and Theodore Schwann in 1838.
- The theory maintains that all organisms are composed of cells, cells are the structural and functional unit of life, and cells arise from pre-existing cells.
- Cells can vary greatly in shape and size.
- Nerve cells in animals have long extensions and can be several centimeters in length.
- Muscle cells are elongated in shape.
- The ostrich egg is the largest cell, measuring 75 mm.
- Some plant cells have thick walls.
- The number of cells in different organisms can vary widely.

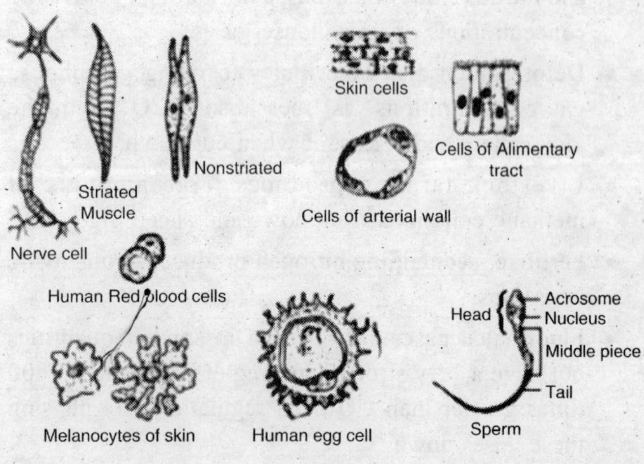

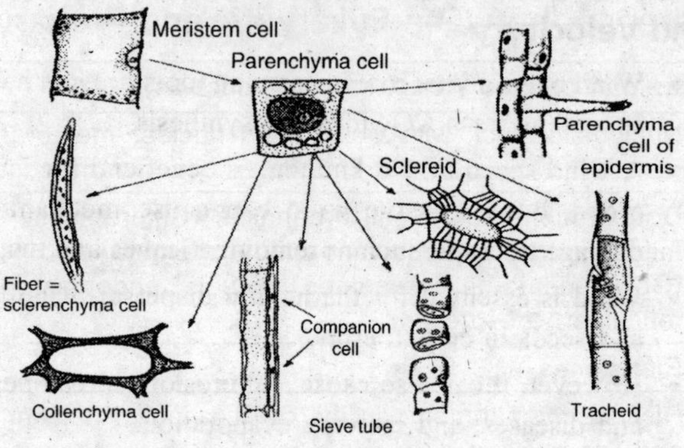

The Cell

- A cell is a unit of protoplasm surrounded by a plasma or cell membrane, and containing a nucleus.
- Protoplasm is the life-giving substance and consists of cytoplasm and nucleus.
- Cytoplasm contains organelles such as ribosomes, mitochondria, golgi bodies, plastids, lysosomes, and endoplasmic reticulum.
- Plant cells have large vacuoles in their cytoplasm that contain non-living inclusions like crystals and pigments.
- Bacteria do not have well-defined cell organelles or a well-formed nucleus.
- All cells have three major components: plasma membrane, cytoplasm, and DNA (which is naked in bacteria and enclosed by a nuclear membrane in all other organisms).

Two basic types of cells

- There are two main types of cells: prokaryotes and eukaryotes.
- Prokaryotic cells, such as bacteria, do not have a clearly defined nucleus.
- Eukaryotic cells, on the other hand, have a well-formed nucleus that is surrounded by a nuclear membrane.
- Cytologists are scientists who study cells and they distinguish between these two types of cells.
- The nucleus is an important feature of eukaryotic cells and plays a key role in their function.
- The absence of a well-formed nucleus is a defining characteristic of prokaryotic cells.

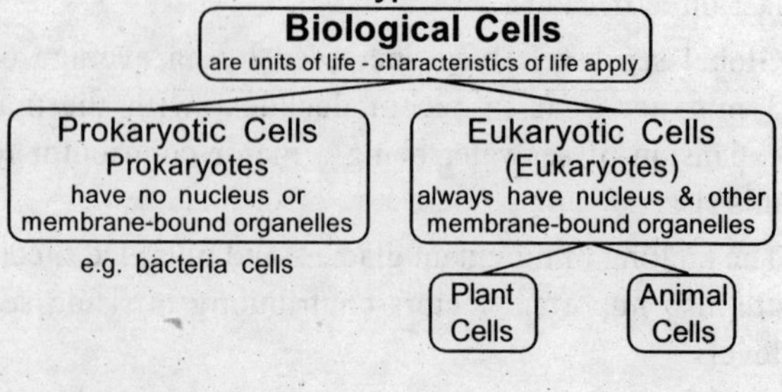

Differences between Eukaryotic and Prokaryotic cells

Eukaryotic cell (eu = true, karyon = nucleus)	**Prokaryotic cell** (Pro = early/primitive)
1. Nucleus distinct, with well-formed nuclear membrane.	1. Nucleus not distinct, it is in the form of a nuclear zone 'nucleoid'. Nuclear membrane absent.
2. Double-membraned cell organelles (Chloroplasts, mitochondria, nucleus) and single membraned (Golgi apparatus, lysosomes, vacuole, endoplasm reticulum) are present	2. Single-membraned cell bodies like mesosomes present. Endo-plasmic reticulum, plastids, mitochondria microbodies like lysosomes, and Golgi body absent.
3. Ribosomes - 80 S	3. Ribosomes - 70 S
4. Distinct compartments in the cell i.e. the cytoplasm and the nucleus	4. No compartments.
5. Depending upon the species number of chromosomes per nucleus varies from two to many.	5. There is only one chromosome per cell.
6. Each chromosome is linear with its two ends free.	6. The chromosome is circular and remains attached to cell membrane at one point.
7. Each chromosome has one linear double-stranded DNA complexed with histones	7. The chromosome has single double-stranded circular DNA molecule and is not associated with histones.
8. Each chromosome has one centromere that divides a chromosome into two arms. However, if the centromere is terminal, the chromosome would have only one arm.	8. The chromosome lacks a centromere.

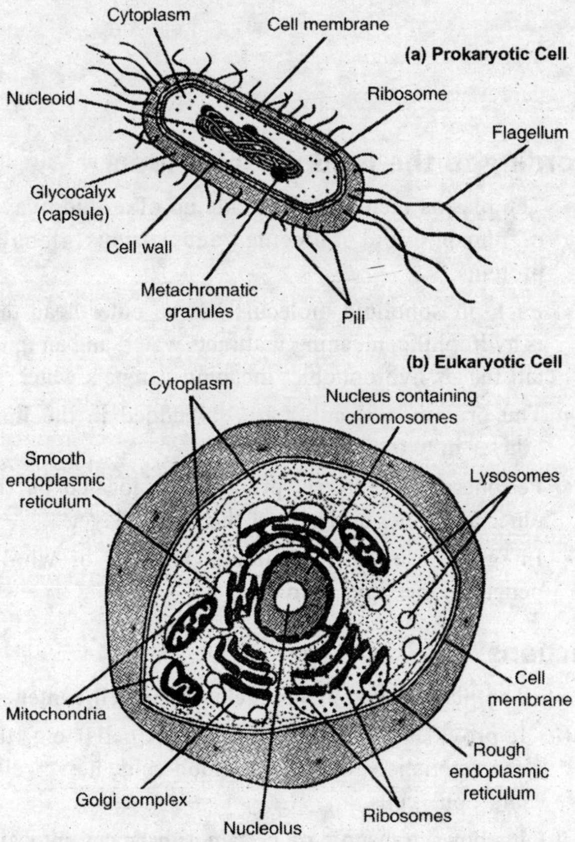

- The Svedberg unit is a measure of the sedimentation rate of particles in a solution, typically used to measure the size of macromolecules such as ribosomes.
- When a cell is broken down into its components by spinning it in an ultracentrifuge at different speeds, the ribosomes of eukaryotic and prokaryotic cells settle at different rates.
- The rate of sedimentation is represented in Svedberg units (S), which reflect the size and shape of the particle.
- The Svedberg unit is not a measure of time, but rather of relative sedimentation rate, which is influenced by factors such as mass, shape, and surface properties of the particle.
- The Svedberg unit is named after the Swedish chemist Theodor Svedberg, who developed the ultracentrifuge and pioneered the use of sedimentation analysis in the study of macromolecules.

Difference between plant and animal cell

Plant cell	Animal cell
1. Cellulose cell wall present external to cell membrane.	1. No cell wall, outermost structure is cell membrane or plasma membrane
2. Vacuoles are usually large.	2. Generally vacuoles are absent and if present, are usually small.
3. Plastids present.	3. Plastids absent.
4. Golgi body present in the form of units known as dictyosomes.	4. Golgi body well developed having 2 Cisternae
5. Centriole absent.	5. Centriole present.

Components of the Cell

The major components of the cell are

1. cell membrane,
2. cytoplasm, and
3. nucleus.

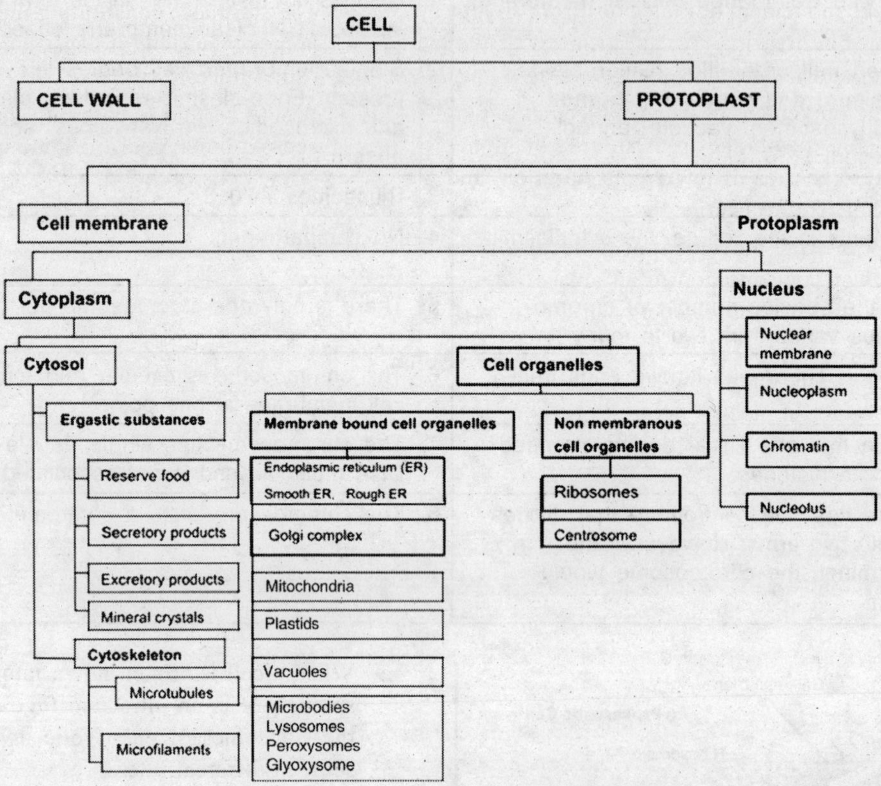

Cell membrane (Plasma membrane)

- Every cell has a boundary called the cell membrane or plasma membrane.
- In animal cells, the plasma membrane is outermost while in plant cells, it is internal to the cell wall.
- The plasma membrane is flexible and can fold in (as in food vacuoles of Amoeba) or fold out (as in the formation of pseudopodia of Amoeba).
- The plasma membrane is composed of proteins and lipids.
- Several models were proposed to describe the arrangement of proteins and lipids in the plasma membrane.
- The fluid mosaic model proposed by Singer and Nicholson (1972) is widely accepted.

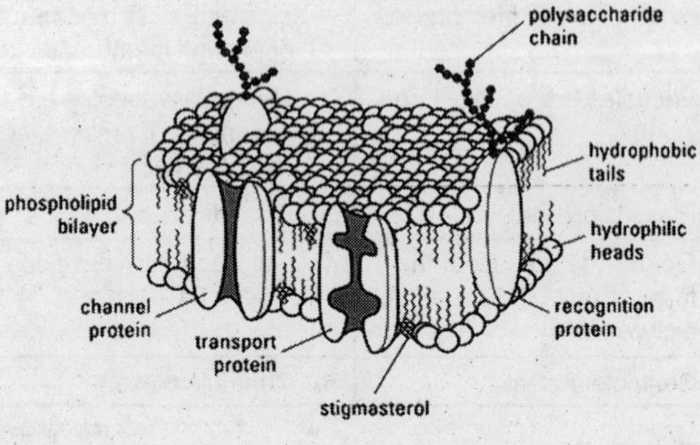

According to the fluid mosaic model

- The plasma membrane is made up of a lipid bilayer of phospholipid molecules and various globular proteins.
- Each phospholipid molecule has an outer head that is hydrophilic, meaning it attracts water, and an inner tail that is hydrophobic, meaning it repels water.
- The protein molecules are embedded in the lipid bilayer in two different ways.
- Peripheral or extrinsic proteins are located on the outer and inner surfaces of the lipid bilayer.
- Integral or intrinsic proteins partially or wholly penetrate the lipid bilayer.

Functions

(*i*) The plasma membrane encloses the cell contents.

(*ii*) It provides cell shape (in animal cells) e.g. the characteristic shape of red blood cells, nerve cells, and bone cells.

(*iii*) It allows transport of certain substances into and out of the cell but not all substances so much it is termed 'selectively permeable'.

Transport of small molecules (such as glucose, amino acids, water, mineral ions etc).

- Small molecules can be transported across the plasma membrane in three ways: diffusion, osmosis, and active transport.
- Diffusion is the movement of molecules from an area of higher concentration to an area of lower concentration, and it does not require energy.
- Osmosis is the movement of water molecules across a semipermeable membrane from an area of higher concentration to an area of lower concentration, and it also does not require energy.
- Active transport is the movement of molecules from an area of lower concentration to an area of higher concentration, and it requires energy in the form of ATP.
- Active transport can occur through a carrier molecule, which binds to the molecule being transported and changes shape to move it across the membrane.
- An example of diffusion is the absorption of glucose into a cell.
- The movement of molecules in diffusion and osmosis is along the concentration gradient, while active transport is against the concentration gradient.
- The energy required for active transport is provided by ATP, a molecule that stores and releases energy as needed by the cell.

Transport of Large Molecules (Bulk Transport)

During bulk transport the membrane changes its form and shape. It occurs in two ways:

(*i*) Endocytosis (taking the substance in)

(*ii*) Exocytosis (passing the substance out).

Endocytosis is of Two Types

Phagocytosis	Pinocytosis
1. Intake of solid particles	1. Intake of fluid droplets
2. Membrane folds out going round the particle, forming a cavity and thus engulfing the particle	2. Membrane folds in and forms a cup-like structure and sucks in the droplets.

Cell membrane regulates movement of substance into and out of the cell. If the cell membrane fails to function normally, the cell dies.

Cell Wall

In bacteria and plant cells the outermost cell cover, present outside the plasma membrane is the cell wall. Bacterial cell wall is made up of peptidoglycan.

(a) Structure

- Outermost non-living layer present in all plant cells.
- Secreted by the cell itself.
- In most plants, it is chiefly made up of cellulose but may also contain other chemical substances such as pectin and lignin.
- The substance constituting the cell wall is not simply homogeneous but it consists of fine threads or fibres called microfibrils.
- It may be thin (1 micron) and transparent as in the cells of onion peel. In some cases it is very thick as in the cells of wood.

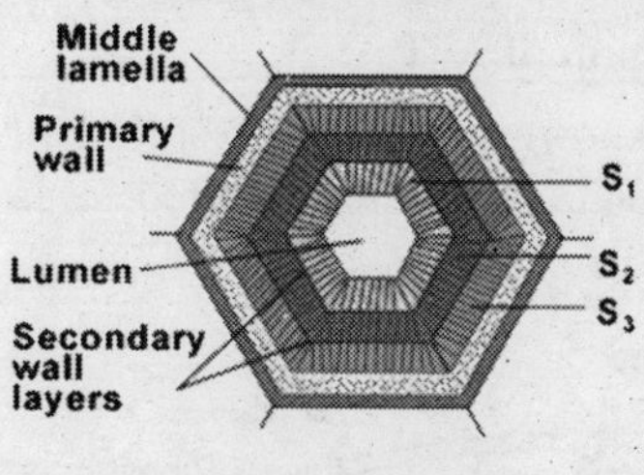

T.S. of a plant cell

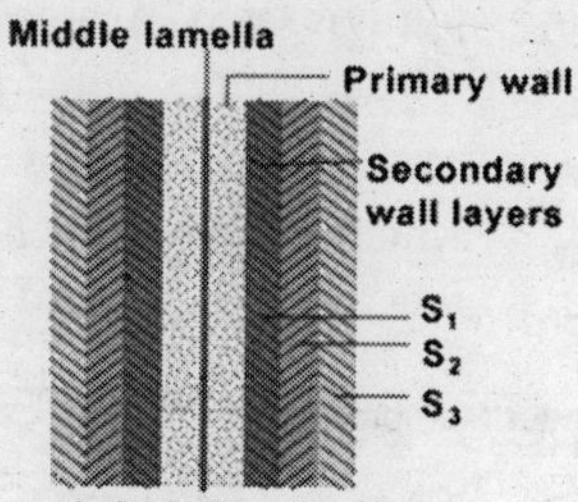

L.S. Cell walls of two adjacent cells

(b) Functions

- The cell wall serves to protect the inner parts of the cell from external damage.
- The rigidity of the cell wall gives shape to the cell and prevents it from being distended.
- The turgidity of the cell resulting from the cell wall's rigidity is useful in many ways.
- The cell wall allows water and other chemicals to pass freely into and out of the cell.
- Adjacent cells are connected by cytoplasmic strands called plasmodesmata, which pass through breaks in the primary cell wall.
- The walls of two adjacent cells are joined by a cementing material called the middle lamella, which is made of calcium pectinate.

The Cytoplasm and the Cell Organelles

The cytoplasm contains many cell organelles like:

1. Cells contain different organelles that serve specific functions.
2. Some organelles trap and release energy, such as mitochondria and chloroplasts.
3. Other organelles are involved in synthesis and transport, such as the Golgi apparatus, ribosomes, and endoplasmic reticulum.
4. Cilia and flagella are organelles involved in motility.
5. Lysosomes are organelles that contain digestive enzymes and are involved in breaking down cellular waste.
6. The nucleus is the organelle that controls all activities of the cell and contains the genetic material.
7. Mitochondria release energy, while chloroplasts trap energy, with chloroplasts only being found in green plant cells.

Mitochondria (Singular = mitochondrion)

1. Mitochondria are tiny, thread-like structures that can be observed under a light microscope.
2. They are typically 0.5-1.0 μm in size, with a few hundred to a few thousand per cell.
3. Mitochondria have a specific internal structure that can be observed using an electron microscope.
4. The primary function of mitochondria is to oxidize pyruvic acid, a breakdown product of glucose, to release energy in the form of ATP.
5. This process is also known as cellular respiration, which is why mitochondria are often referred to as the "powerhouse" of the cell.

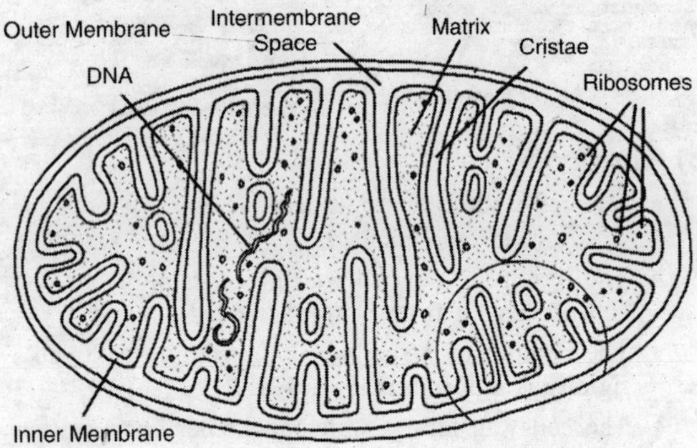

Plastids

1. Plastids are organelles found exclusively in plant cells.
2. They can be either colorless or colored, and based on this, they are classified into three types: leucoplasts, chromoplasts, and chloroplasts.
3. Leucoplasts are colorless and do not contain pigments.
4. Chromoplasts are colored and contain pigments such as blue, red, or yellow.
5. Chloroplasts are green and contain chlorophyll, which is essential for photosynthesis.
6. The different types of plastids perform various functions in plant cells, such as storage of starch, synthesis of pigments, and photosynthesis.

Chloroplast

- Chloroplasts are present in the cytoplasm of green plant cells, with a number ranging from 1 to 1000+.
- They are typically disc-shaped or laminate, but can also be ribbon-shaped (as in Spirogyra) or cup-shaped (as in Chlamydomonas).
- The chloroplast has a double membrane wall, with groups of stacked thylakoids interconnected by lamellae.
- The thylakoids are sac-like structures that are stacked on top of one another to form a granum.
- The fluid-filled region inside the chloroplast is called the stroma.
- Chloroplasts are the site of photosynthesis, the process by which plants produce sugars (glucose) from carbon dioxide and water in the presence of sunlight.

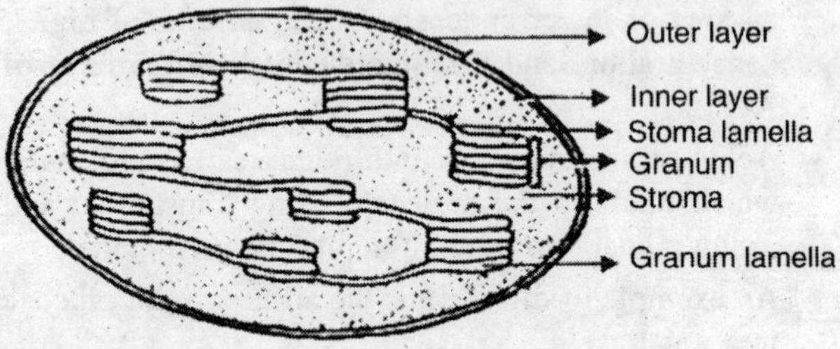

Chloroplast Versus Mitochondria

Differences and similarities between mitochondria and chloroplasts:

Differences

- Mitochondria are present in all eukaryotic cells, while chloroplasts are found only in photosynthetic cells of plants and algae.
- Mitochondria are involved in cellular respiration, while chloroplasts are involved in photosynthesis.
- Mitochondria release energy by breaking down complex molecules, while chloroplasts trap solar energy by converting it into a complex molecule.
- Mitochondria have a double membrane, while chloroplasts have a triple membrane.

Similarities

- Both organelles contain their own DNA and RNA, allowing them to self-duplicate.
- Both organelles are semi-autonomous and depend on the cell's nucleus for most of their protein synthesis.
- Both organelles are involved in energy transformation within the cell.

Endoplasmic Reticulum (ER), Golgi Body and Ribosomes

- The Endoplasmic reticulum (ER) and Golgi body are single-membrane bound organelles found in eukaryotic cells.

- The ER is involved in transporting and storing cellular products, while the Golgi body is responsible for modifying, sorting, and packaging proteins and lipids for secretion.
- Both the ER and Golgi body have a similar lipid-protein structure to the plasma membrane.
- Ribosomes are not membrane-bound and are involved in protein synthesis within the cell.
- These three organelles work together in the process of protein synthesis and secretion within the cell.

Lysosomes (Lysis = Breaking Down; Soma = Body)

Lysosomes are present in almost all animal cells and some non-green plant cells.

They perform intracellular digestion.

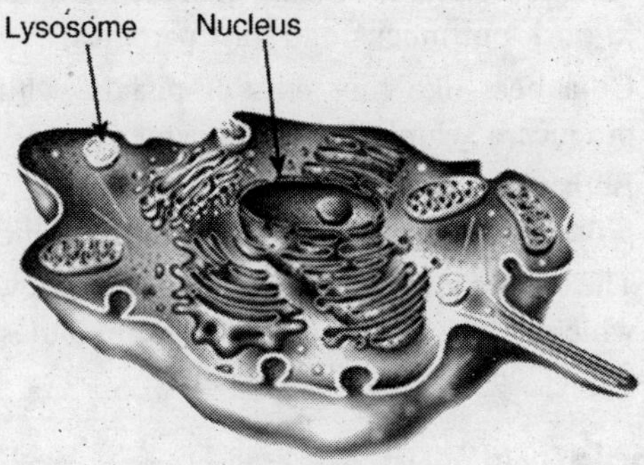

Endoplasmic Reticulum (ER)

Structure: A network of membranes with thickness between 50 – 60 Å. It is of two types—

Rough endoplasmic reticulum (RER) i.e., when ribosomes are attached to it and Smooth endoplasmic reticulum (SER) when no ribosomes are present.

Distributed throughout the cytoplasm and is in contact with the cell membrane as well as the nuclear membrane.

Function: Provides internal frame work, compartment and reaction surfaces, transports enzymes and other materials throughout the cell. RER is the site for protein synthesis and SER for steroid synthesis, stores carbohydrates.

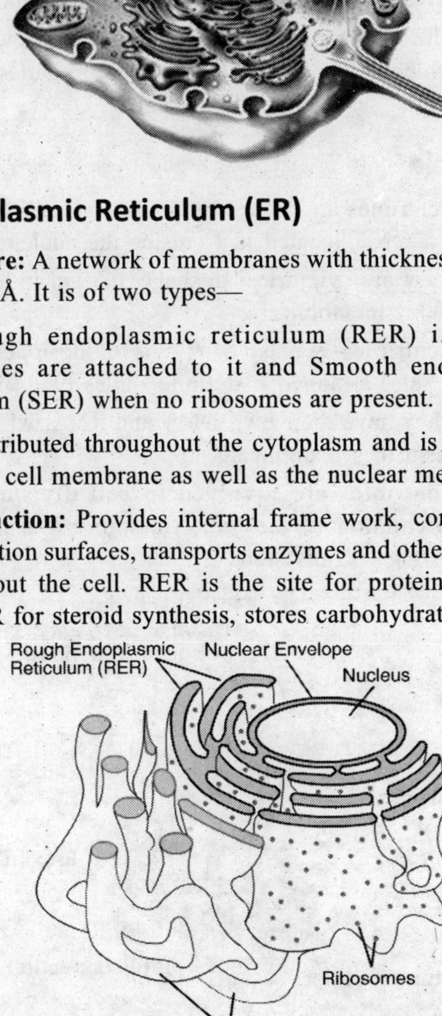

Golgi Body

Structure: Is a stack of membranous sacs of the same thickness as ER. Exhibit great diversity in size and shape.

In animal cells present around the nucleus, 3 to 7 in number.

In plant cells, many in number of and present scattered through out the cell called dictyosomes.

Function: Synthesis and secretion as enzymes, participates in transsformation of membranes to give rise to other membrane structure such as lysosome, acrosome, and dictyosomes, synthesize wall element like pectin, mucilage.

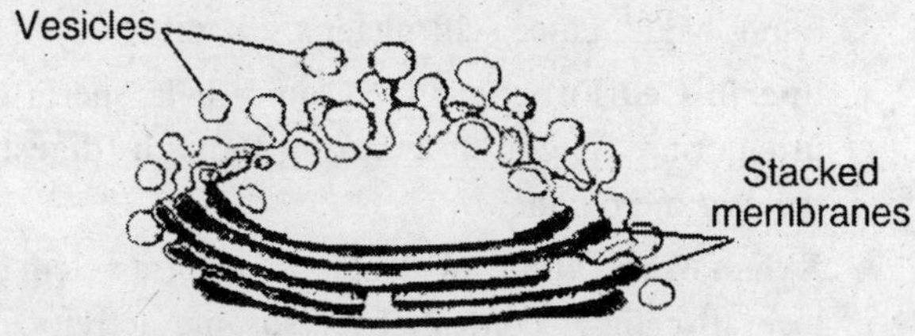

Ribosomes

Structure: Spherical about 150 – 250Å in diameter, made up of large molecules of RNA and proteins (ribonucleo proteins). Present either as free particles in cytoplasm or attached to ER. Also found stored in nucleolus inside the nucleus. 80S types found in eukaryotes and 70S in prokaryotes (S-svedberg unit of measuring ribosomes).

Function: Site for protein synthesis.

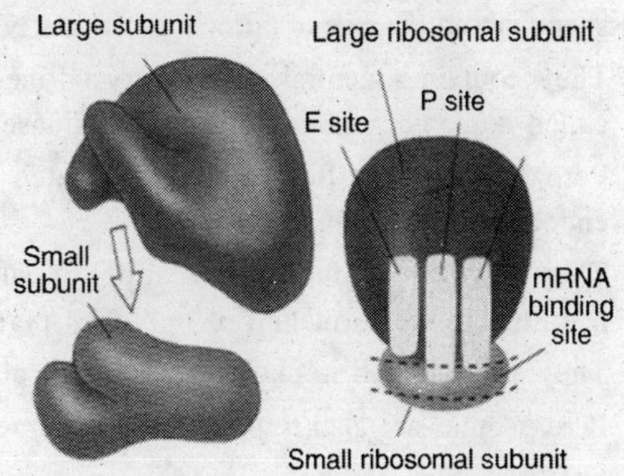

The main features of lysosomes are as follows:

- Lysosomes are membrane-bound sacs that bud off from the Golgi body.
- A single cell can have hundreds of lysosomes.
- Lysosomes contain numerous enzymes, about 40 in number.
- The materials to be acted upon by enzymes enter the lysosomes.
- Lysosomes are called "suicidal bags" as the enzymes contained in them can digest the cell's own material when it is damaged or dead.

Importance of intracellular digestion by the lysosomes

- **Nutrient Digestion:** Lysosomes help in the nutrition of the cell by digesting food, as they contain various hydrolyzing enzymes that can digest almost all major chemical constituents of the living cell.
- **Defense:** They help in defending the body by digesting germs, as seen in white blood cells.
- **Cell Cleaning:** Lysosomes help in cleaning up the cell by digesting damaged material of the cell.
- **Energy Supply:** They provide energy during cell starvation by digesting their own parts of the cells (autophagic, auto: self; phagos: eat up).
- **Sperm Cell Function:** Lysosomes help sperm cells in entering the egg by breaking through (digesting) the egg membrane.
- **Xylem Maturation:** In plant cells, mature xylem cells lose all cellular contents by lysosome activity.
- **Cell Recycling:** When cells are old, diseased, or injured, lysosomes attack their cell organelles and digest them. In other words, lysosomes are autophagic, i.e., self-devouring.

Peroxisomes

- Found in both plant and animal cells, but mainly found in the green leaves of higher plants.
- They are small organelles, spherical or ovoid in shape, about the size of mitochondria and lysosomes.
- They contain a central core of crystalline material called nucleoid, composed of urate oxidase crystals.
- Peroxisomes are often closely associated with the endoplasmic reticulum (ER).
- They participate in the oxidation of substrates, resulting in the formation of hydrogen peroxide.
- They are involved in photorespiration in plant cells.
- Peroxisomes are also responsible for fat metabolism in cells.

Glyoxysomes

- Glyoxysomes are microbodies found in plant cells and are morphologically similar to peroxisomes.
- They are also found in the cells of yeast, certain fungi, and oil-rich seeds in plants.
- They contain enzymes involved in fatty acid metabolism.
- They play a role in the conversion of lipids to carbohydrates during germination.

Cilia and flagella (the organelles for motility)

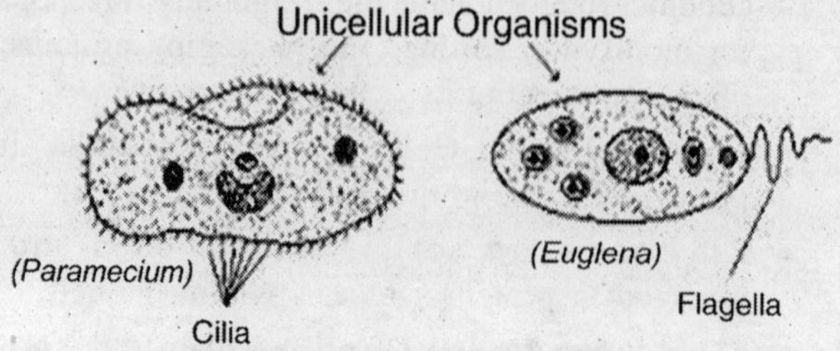

- Cilia and flagella are present in both unicellular and multicellular organisms.
- Unicellular organisms like Paramecium and Euglena use cilia and flagella, respectively, to swim in water.
- In multicellular organisms, some tissues like epithelial tissues have cilia that beat to create a current in fluid, for example, in the windpipe (trachea) to push out mucus and dust particles.
- Cilia beat like tiny oars or pedals, while flagella produce a whiplash-like movement.
- Both cilia and flagella are made up of contractile protein tubulin arranged in the form of microtubules.
- The arrangement of microtubules is known as 9+2, which refers to two central microtubules and nine duplet sets surrounding them.

Centriole

- Centrioles are present in all animal cells (except for Amoeba), located just outside the nucleus.
- They are cylindrical in shape, 0.5 μm in length, and lack a membrane.
- Centrioles consist of 9 sets of peripheral triplet tubules arranged at definite angles (9 + 0).
- They have their own DNA and RNA, which allows them to self-duplicate.
- Centrioles are involved in cell division, giving orientation to the "mitotic spindle" which forms during cell division.

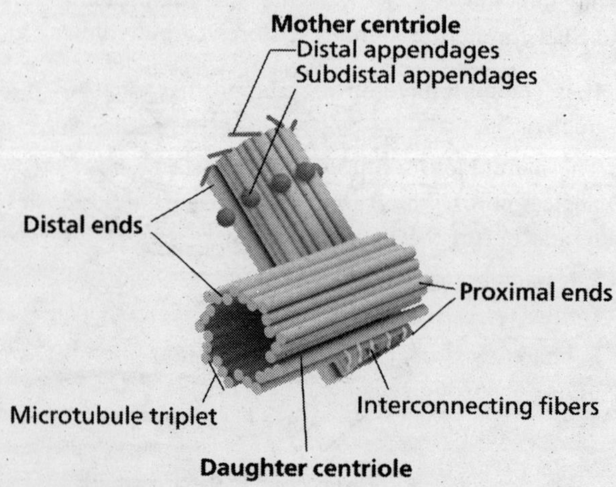

Basal bodies

- Basal bodies are structures similar to centrioles.
- They have the same organization of nine sets of triplet microtubules (9+0) as in centrioles.
- Basal bodies give rise to cilia and flagella in cells.
- They are found at the base of cilia and flagella and are involved in their movement.

Nucleus (The Hereditary Organelle)

- The nucleus is the largest organelle in the cell and is clearly visible when the cell is not dividing.
- It is mostly spherical in shape and stains deeply, although white blood cells have lobed nuclei.
- Most cells have a single nucleus (uninucleate), but some cells have many nuclei (multinucleate).
- The nucleus is enclosed by a double-layered nuclear membrane that has fine nuclear pores.
- The nucleoplasm is the fluid inside the nucleus and contains a chromatin network (DNA and protein) and a nucleolus, which is responsible for the synthesis of ribosomes.

Functions

1. **Maintenance:** The nucleus helps in maintaining the cell in a working order.
2. **Coordination:** It coordinates the activities of other cell organelles.
3. **Repair:** The nucleus takes care of repair work.
4. **Cell Division:** It participates directly in cell division to produce genetically identical daughter cells. This division is called mitotic cell division.
5. **Meiotic Cell Division:** The nucleus participates in the production of gametes and meiospores through another type of cell division called meiotic cell division.

The parts of a nucleus are given here:

Nuclear Membrane

- It is a double-layered membrane that encloses the nucleus.
- The membrane is interrupted by a large number of nuclear pores, which allow the transport of molecules in and out of the nucleus.
- The membrane is made up of lipids and proteins, similar to the plasma membrane of the cell.
- Ribosomes are attached to the outer membrane, giving it a rough appearance.
- The membrane keeps the hereditary material in contact with the rest of the cell.

Chromatin

- Karyolymph or nucleoplasm is a jelly-like substance present within the nuclear membrane that is rich in proteins.
- Chromatin fibrils form a network in the karyolymph which gets condensed to form chromosomes during cell division.
- On staining, two regions can be identified in the chromatin material: heterochromatin, which is dark, and euchromatin, which is light.
- Heterochromatin has highly coiled DNA and is genetically less active than euchromatin, which has highly uncoiled DNA and is genetically more active.
- The number of chromosomes is fixed in an organism, and during mitotic cell division, chromosomes divide in a manner that the daughter cells receive identical amounts of hereditary material.

Nucleolus

- Membraneless, spheroidal bodies present in all eukaryotic cells except in sperms and some algae.
- Their number varies from one to a few, they stain uniformly and deeply.
- Contains DNA, RNA, and proteins.
- It is a storehouse for RNA and proteins.
- Disappears during the early phase of the cell cycle and reappears after telophase in the newly formed daughter nuclei.
- Regulates the synthetic activity of the nucleus.
- Nucleus and cytoplasm are interdependent, and this process is called nucleo-cytoplasmic interaction.

Cell Division

1. Cell division is essential for growth in shape, size, and number of all living beings, including plants, and is the basis for reproduction.
2. Rudolf Virchow first proposed the concept of cell division, stating that new cells arise from pre-existing cells by division and are thus called daughter cells.
3. Continuity of life depends on cell division.
4. Unicellular plants reproduce asexually by binary fission, resulting in the production of two identical daughter cells.
5. Multicellular plants begin as a single cell, the zygote, which is formed by the fusion of two haploid gametes (male and female).
6. The zygote divides and redivides to produce different types of cells, which are specialized for different functions in multicellular plants.

- **Haploid (n):** Refers to plants or cells with only one set of chromosomes, denoted as N.

- **Diploid (2n):** Results from the fusion of two haploid gametes (male gamete N + female gamete N = zygote 2N), resulting in a diploid zygote. Plants with two (di) sets of chromosomes are known as diploid and denoted as 2N. Ploidy is a term denoting the number of sets of chromosomes.
- **Polyploid:** Refers to plants with more than two sets of chromosomes.
- **Homologous chromosomes:** Refers to chromosomes that carry the same genes. They are paired during meiosis and can exchange genetic material through crossing over.

Types of cell division

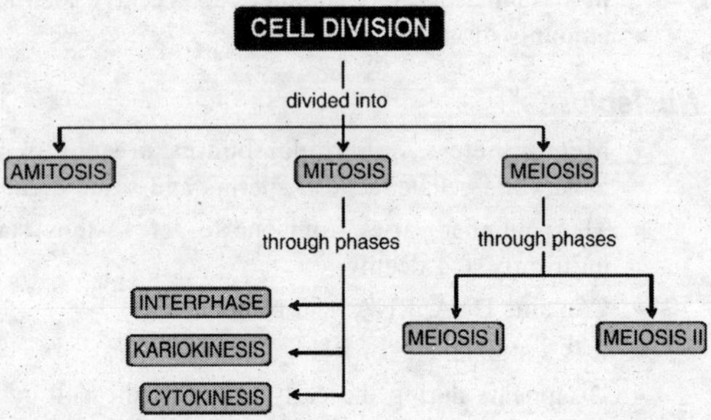

Three types of cell division occur in plants. These are:

1. Amitosis or direct cell division (Robert Remak -1855)
2. Mitosis or indirect cell division (Flemming -1882)
3. Meiosis or reduction division (Farmer and Moore - 1905)

Amitosis

1. Amitosis is a type of cell division that occurs in some specialized cells in unicellular, prokaryotic plants, and in transitory or degenerating structures.
2. The process involves simple cleavage of the nucleus without any change in its structure such as the formation of chromosomes, followed by the division of cytoplasm.
3. Amitosis is not the usual mode of division. It occurs mainly in highly specialized cells which are incapable of long-continued multiplication, in transitory structures, and in those in early stages of degeneration.
4. Examples of cells that undergo amitosis include cynobacteria, bacteria, yeast, internodal cells of *Chara zeylanica* and *Chara contraria*, and endosperm cells of developing seed.

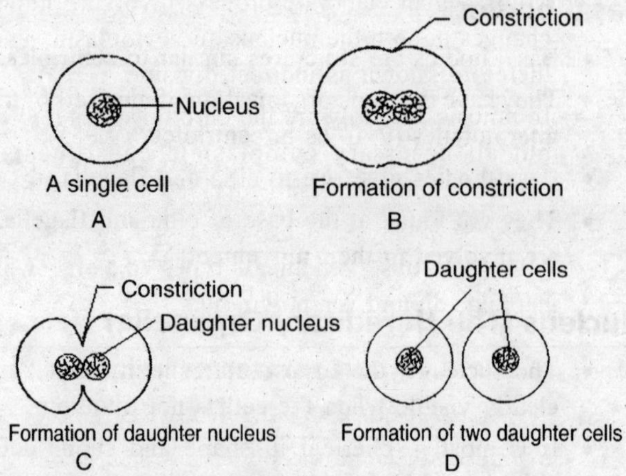

Cell in various stages of amitotic cell division

Amitosis occurs in two stages

- Amitosis occurs in two stages: nuclear division (karyokinesis) and cytoplasmic division (cytokinesis).
- During nuclear division, the nucleus elongates and a constriction appears in the center, resulting in a dumbbell-shaped structure. The constriction deepens and the nucleus is divided into two daughter nuclei.
- There is no spindle formation and no formation of chromosomes during amitosis.
- During cytoplasmic division, the cell is divided into two daughter cells.
- The two daughter nuclei resulting from amitosis are always similar in shape and size.
- Amitosis is a quantitative division and does not result in the production of genetically different daughter cells like in mitosis or meiosis.

Mitosis

- Mitosis is a common method of nuclear division, followed by cytokinesis. It occurs in vegetative or somatic cells and is known as somatic division.
- It occurs in meristematic tissues such as the shoot and root tip. It leads to an increase in size, shape, and volume of plant parts, causing growth.
- Mitosis results in the production of two genetically identical daughter cells. The pattern of mitosis is the same in all cells.
- The daughter cells resemble each other and the parent cell both qualitatively and quantitatively.
- Mitosis involves the separation of sister chromatids into two new cells with the same number of chromosomes and half the amount of nuclear DNA.
- It is also known as equational division because the resulting daughter cells have the same number of chromosomes as the parent cell.

- Mitosis is an elaborate process involving important changes in both the nucleus and cytoplasm, and it is therefore known as indirect division.
- In mitosis, not only are the chromosomes replicated, but all necessary cytoplasmic constituents and organelles are precisely divided between the two daughter cells.
- Mitosis is observed in all types of cells, whether haploid, diploid, or polyploid.

Some important terms related to cell division include

- **Chromosome:** A chromosome is a structure composed of DNA and proteins, carrying genetic information in the form of genes. Chromosomes are located in the nucleus of eukaryotic cells and are visible during cell division.
- **Chromatid:** A chromatid is one of the two identical DNA helices that are formed after DNA replication in preparation for cell division. The two chromatids are connected by a structure called the centromere, and are known as sister chromatids. During cell division, the sister chromatids separate and are distributed to two daughter cells.

Cell Cycle

The cell cycle is a sequence of events that occurs between the formation of a cell and its division into two daughter cells. It consists of four distinct phases: G1, S, G2, and M phase, with the first three phases collectively known as interphase, and the M phase involving mitosis and the C phase involving cytokinesis. In simple terms, a cell duplicates its contents and then divides into two. The cell cycle includes interphase, nuclear division (mitosis), and cytokinesis.

Interphase + Nuclear division (mitosis) + Cytokinesis = Cell cycle

Interphase

- Interphase is a phase in the cell cycle that occurs before mitosis (M phase).
- During interphase, the cell is actively growing and preparing for cell division by accumulating nutrients and replicating DNA.
- Interphase is the longest phase in the cell cycle, accounting for about 90% of the total cycle time.
- Although it is sometimes called the "resting stage," interphase is actually the most active phase of the cell cycle, during which many metabolic processes occur.

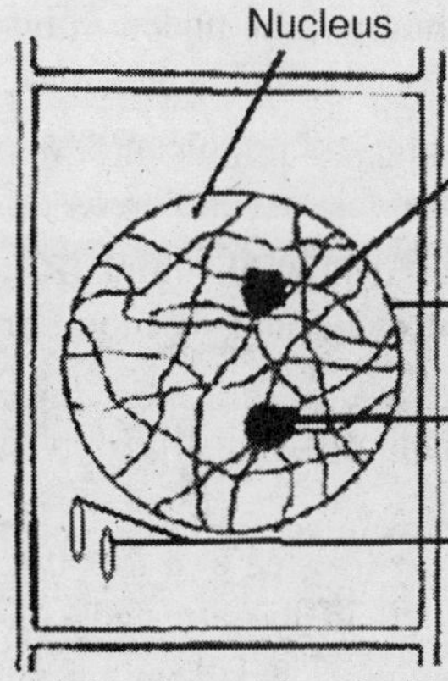

Interphase of a plant cell

G1 Phase

- G1 phase occurs between the end of mitosis and the start of S phase.
- The length of G1 phase varies between different cell types and can range from 8 hours to 100 days or more.
- Differences in cell cycle times are mainly due to the variations in the length of G1 phase.
- Cells in rapidly developing tissues have a short G1 phase, while slowly dividing cells can stay in G1 phase for days or even longer.
- After cytokinesis, the daughter cells are small and low on ATP, but they acquire ATP and increase in size during G1 phase.
- In G1 phase, the cell undergoes cytoplasmic growth and prepares its enzymatic machinery for the next stage, S phase.
- Chromosomes are thread-like and invisible in the dispersed state, and there is no change in DNA amount or chromatin.
- Each chromosome contains only a single molecule of DNA and is called an unduplicated or unreplicated chromosome.
- G1 (first gap) is a phase in the cell cycle that separates the end of mitosis and the start of the S phase.
- During G1 phase, the cell undergoes intensive formation of biochemicals and cellular synthesis.
- In this phase, there is production of various organelles including mitochondria, plastids, endoplasmic reticulum, lysosomes, golgi apparatus, and vacuoles.
- Nucleolus produces ribosomal RNA (rRNA) and there is also synthesis of messenger RNA (mRNA) and ribosomes.
- Structural and functional proteins, amino acids for histone formation, nucleotides, and energy-rich substance ATP are synthesized.

- The cell metabolic rate is high and is controlled by enzymes.

During G1 phase, a cell may follow one of the three options:

- If it has reached the restriction point (R point), it will continue on the cycle and divide after a short rest.
- The cell may permanently stop division and enter G0 or quiescent stage.
- The cell cycle may be arrested at a specific point in G1 phase, and the cell in the arrested condition is said to be in the G0 state. The G0 state is considered as the withdrawal from the cell cycle. When conditions change and growth is resumed, the cell re-enters the G1 phase.

S (synthetic phase) Synthesis of DNA and histones phase:

- S phase is the phase of the cell cycle in which DNA synthesis or replication occurs.
- It is sandwiched between G1 and G2 phases.
- During S phase, each chromosome is duplicated resulting in two identical copies of DNA molecules, and the DNA content of the nucleus is doubled.
- Proteins are also synthesized during this phase.
- DNA replication starts at specific sites called origins of replication, and proceeds bidirectionally until the entire genome is replicated.
- The double helical DNA molecule is unwound by helicase enzymes at the origin of replication, and each strand acts as a template for the synthesis of new complementary strands by DNA polymerase enzymes.
- As the DNA breaks apart at different points along the strands, new single strands join the two halves of original strands.
- Two new DNA strands are formed, which are attached together by specific proteins at a short sequence of DNA called a centromere.
- The two DNA copies resulting from S phase are not visible through a light microscope because they have not yet condensed to form chromosomes, remaining as chromatin.
- Each chromosome becomes two chromatids during S phase.
- Histone proteins are synthesized after DNA duplication, covering each DNA strand in a process called chromatin synthesis.
- The number of chromosomes remains the same as in the newly formed cell (1n or 2n), but each chromosome changes from a single stranded form to a two stranded form during S phase.

G2 Phase

- The G2 phase is a growth and energy acquisition stage that follows the S phase.
- The cell acquires energy during this phase, which is used in cell division (mitosis).
- During G2 phase, RNA and protein synthesis continues, but DNA synthesis stops.
- The mitotic spindle proteins, which are involved in the movement of chromosomes during mitosis, are formed during this phase.
- Chloroplasts and mitochondria multiply through binary fission during G2 phase.
- Materials needed for mitosis, a nuclear event, are produced during G2 phase.
- During the G2 phase, the cell continues to grow and acquire energy necessary for cell division (mitosis), following the energy-draining process of DNA synthesis during S phase.
- RNA and protein synthesis continues during G2, while DNA synthesis stops. The cell produces mitotic spindle proteins, which are involved in the movement of chromosomes during mitosis.
- Chromatin begins to condense into compact structures called chromosomes, which become visible under a light microscope. The chromosomes remain attached through their centromeres.
- The cell prepares for chromosomal segregation during G2, but the actual segregation does not yet occur. The nuclear membrane remains intact.
- The durations of the S phase, G2 phase, and mitosis are generally constant across most cell types.

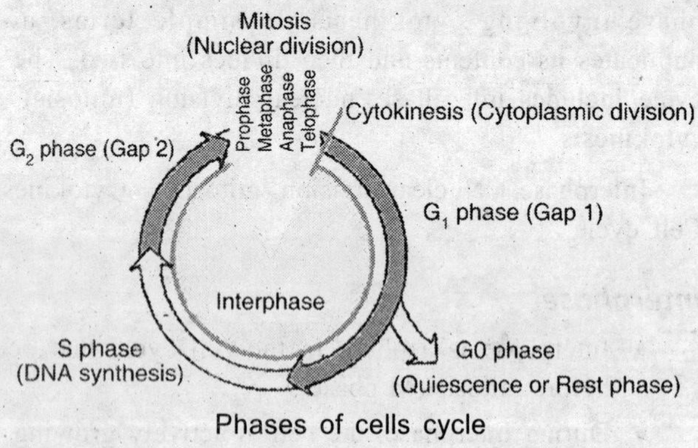

Phases of cells cycle

Mitosis

Mitosis is a phase of the cell cycle that involves the division of the cell nucleus.

Mitosis phase is the shortest phase in cell cycle.

Although mitosis is a continuous process, the mitosis itself involves the condensation and separation of the replicated chromosomes.

Mitosis has been subdivided into five phases:

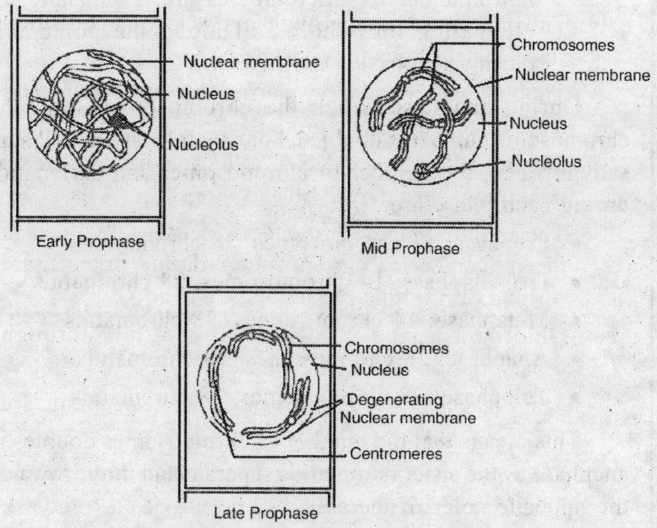

Stages in mitosis of a plant cell (different stages of prophase)

A. Prophase (condensation): A stage of chromosome condensation.

- Prophase is a stage of chromosome condensation during mitosis.
- Initially, the chromosomes appear as thin, filamentous and uncoiled structures.
- As prophase progresses, chromosomes become coiled, shortened and more distinct, making this stage much longer than other stages of mitosis.
- Nucleoli disappear during prophase.
- Each chromosome longitudinally splits into two identical sister chromatids, and the double structure of each chromosome becomes visible in late prophase.
- The duplicated chromosome subunits (chromatids) join together at the centromeres.
- Two chromatids are attached to spindle tubules (chromosomal fibers) with the help of protein plates called kinetochores, which are specialized structures that develop on either surface of the centromere of each chromosome.
- The kinetochore is the actual site of the insertion of the spindle fibers and is a permanent part of the chromosome.

B. Prometaphase

- The nuclear membrane dissolves, resulting in no differentiation between cytoplasm and nucleoplasm.
- The chromosomes become attached to the spindle fibers through their centromeres.
- This type of mitosis is called extranuclear mitosis or eumitosis, and it takes place outside the nuclear membrane in many protozoans and some animal cells.
- The chromosomes move freely and proceed towards the equator.
- The nuclear membrane disintegrates, and the chromosomes become free in the cytoplasm. The chromosomes are attached to the spindle fibers through their centromeres.
- A system of microtubules called spindle fibers, needed to move the chromosomes, begins to form during prophase. These spindle fibers form from an area of the cell called the centrosome, which duplicates just before prophase, producing a second centrosome. During prophase, microtubules radiate from each centrosome, some of which extend from one centrosome toward the other.
- Spindle fibers extend from the poles to the equator, forming the spindle apparatus. The entire complex of centrosomes and spindle fibers is called the spindle apparatus.
- The two centrosomes move to opposite poles of the cell, elongating their "+" ends. At the end of prometaphase, the two centrosomes are at opposite poles of the cell, and some of the spindle microtubules are attached to the chromosome at the kinetochore.
- The microtubule from one pole may attach to the kinetochore first, and the chromosome begins to move toward the other pole, aligning the chromosomes at the equatorial plane.
- For microtubules to remain attached to a kinetochore, there must be a force exerted on the chromosome from the opposite end of the cell.
- Kinetochore microtubules are spindle fibers that attach to the kinetochores and move the chromosomes to the center of the cell.
- The next phase (Metaphase) begins when the chromosomes become aligned in the center of the cell.

C. Metaphase

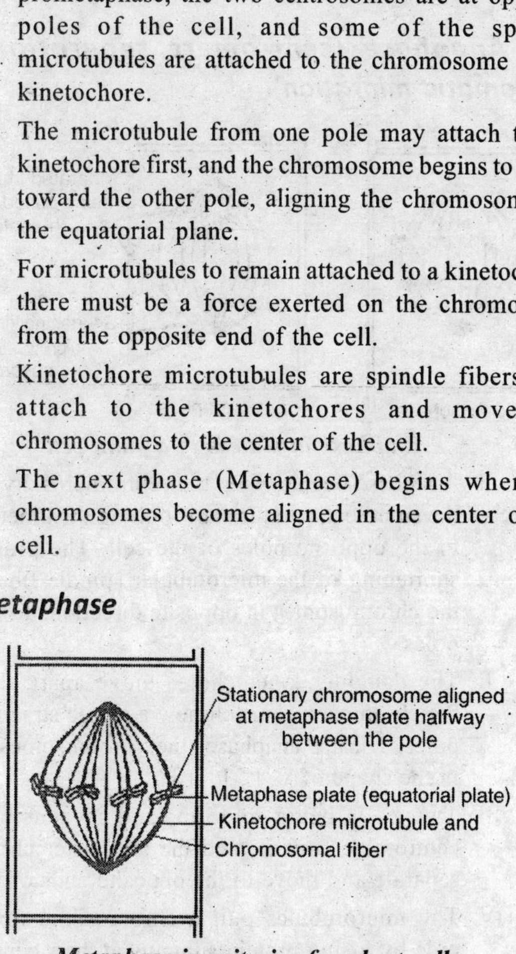

Metaphase in mitosis of a plant cell

- During metaphase, the chromosomes align along a plane known as the metaphase plate or equatorial plate.
- Each chromosome's centromere lies on the metaphase plate, while the arms of the chromatids extend outwards.
- The chromosomes are perpendicular to the axis of the spindle apparatus.
- Smaller chromosomes usually position themselves towards the center of the cell while larger chromosomes are more peripheral.
- Around 15-35 microtubules are attached to each kinetochore by kinetochore microtubules.

There are also two types of non-kinetochore microtubules:

- Some microtubules radiate from the centrosome toward the metaphase plate but do not attach to chromosomes.
- Other microtubules are too short to reach the metaphase plate.
- Still others extend across the plate and overlap with non-kinetochore microtubules from the opposite pole of the cell.

D. Anaphase (centromere separation and chromatid migration)

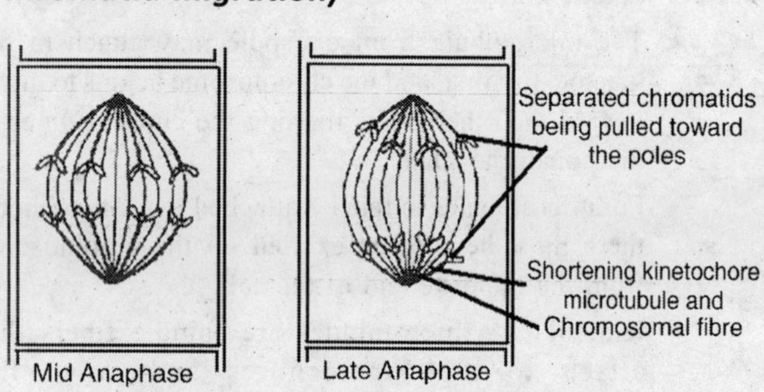

Anaphase in mitosis of a plant cell

I. Anaphase begins when the centromeres divide, and the spindle apparatus starts pulling the kinetochores to the opposite poles of the cell. The progressive shortening of the microtubular spindle fibers pulls the chromosomes in opposite directions toward the poles.

II. The daughter kinetochores move apart, dragging the chromosomes (each now a single strand) to the poles. During anaphase, the chromosomes appear in the shape of V, L, J, or I.

III. Two cells begin to form, and in anaphase, the centromeres divide, and the two sister chromatids separate and move to the opposite ends of the cell.

IV. The microtubules pull a chromosome towards a pole by losing protein subunits at their centrosome and at the end attached to the kinetochore. The non-kinetochore microtubules are responsible for elongating the whole cell along the polar axis during anaphase.

During anaphase, when the chromosomes split, the chromosome number is doubled. For example, in a pea (Pisum sativum) cell, the number of chromosomes and chromatids during each phase are:

- Prophase: 14 chromosomes, 28 chromatids
- Prometaphase: 14 chromosomes, 28 chromatids
- Metaphase: 14 chromosomes, 28 chromatids
- Anaphase: 28 chromosomes, 28 chromatids
- Telophase: 28 chromosomes, 28 chromatids

This means that the number of chromosomes doubles in anaphase as the sister chromatids separate and move towards the opposite poles of the cell.

- Cytokinesis, the division of the cytoplasm, begins in anaphase.
- Two cells will be produced as cytokinesis continues.

E. Telophase (recovery of nuclear envelope and decondensation).

Telophase marks the end of mitosis and begins when the chromosomes reach the poles of the daughter cells. Many events in telophase are the reverse of prophase, but now there are two nuclei instead of one:

I. Chromosomes decondense and uncoil.

II. Nuclear membranes reappear around the daughter nuclei.

III. The spindle fibers become disorganized and break down.

IV. The nucleolus reappears.

V. The cell membrane pinches in the middle, beginning the formation of two cells. The new cell plate expands centrifugally.

Each daughter cell receives the same complement of chromosomes and nucleoli as the mother cell. During division, cell organelles such as mitochondria, plastids, golgi complex, lysosomes, and the cytoplasmic matrix are distributed into the two daughter cells.

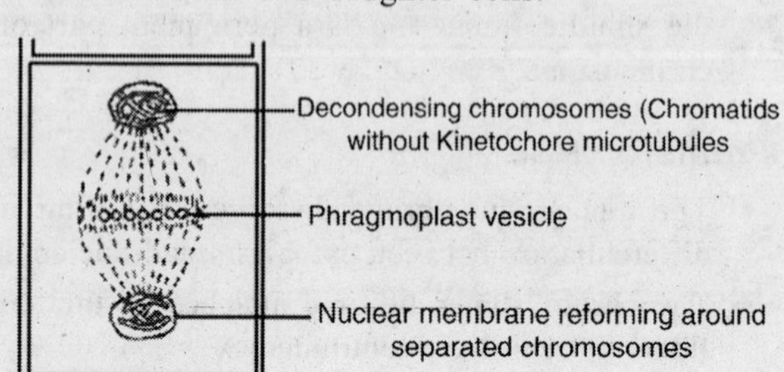

Telophase stages of mitosis

Cytoplasmic division (Cytokinesis)

Cytoplasmic division (Cytokinesis) in plant cells involves the following steps:

- Formation of a new cell wall (cell plate) between daughter nuclei at the end of telophase.
- Spindle fragments gather at the equator region and form a barrel-shaped structure called phragmoplast.
- Vacuoles of the golgi complex enter the phragmoplast and release pectins into it.
- Golgi-derived secretory vesicles carrying cell wall materials are transported to the equator of a dividing cell at the end of anaphase.
- Fusion of these vesicles gives rise to a membrane-bound compartment, the cell plate.
- The cell plate expands from the middle outwards (centrifugally) until it reaches the "zone of attachment" or division site on the mother cell wall.
- Cell plate undergoes physical and chemical changes to form the middle lamella, which divides the cytoplasm into two parts.
- On both sides of the middle lamella, primary wall materials such as cellulose and hemicellulose are deposited.
- As a result of these processes, two daughter cells are formed.
- In places where the vesicles of the cell plate fail to fuse, the cytoplasmic contact between the daughter cells is maintained.
- These cytoplasmic channels are lined by plasma membrane to form plasmodesmata.

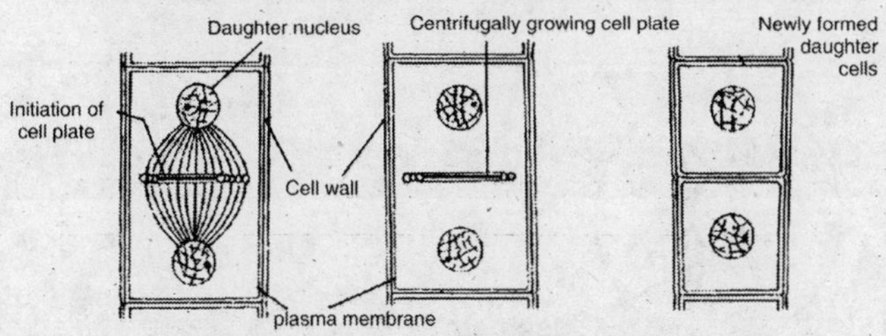

Stages of cytokinesis through cell plate formation in a plant cell

Function of Mitosis

- Mitosis is a fundamental process in plant cell division, contributing to growth, asexual reproduction, regeneration, and cell replacement.
- *Growth:* The number of cells in a plant increases due to mitosis, which leads to growth.
- *Asexual reproduction, regeneration, and cell replacement:* Many plants propagate vegetatively through mitotic divisions of cells. Regeneration of lost parts and tissue repair occurs through mitosis in multicellular plants.
- Mitosis results in the formation of two nuclei, each with the same number of chromosomes as the parent cell.
- *Endomitosis*: Replication of chromosomes without division of the nucleus is called endomitosis, which leads to the formation of polyploids. Endomitosis without separation of chromatids leads to polyteny.

Meiosis

- Meiosis is the process by which gametes (sex cells) are formed.
- During meiosis, the mother cell produces four daughter cells called gametes in which the chromosome number is reduced to half.
- Meiosis is known as reductional division.
- The gametes carry genetic recombination and are therefore not identical to the mother cell.
- Meiosis is known as heterotypic division due to the genetic recombination process.
- If the parental cell has 14 chromosomes, each daughter cell will have 7 chromosomes.

Sexual reproduction involves the processes of meiosis and fertilization.

- In meiosis, the diploid chromosome number is reduced to the haploid number.
- In fertilization, two haploid gametes fuse their nuclei to form a diploid zygote.
- In most plants, meiosis and fertilization create two distinct phases or "generations" in the life cycle of the organism.

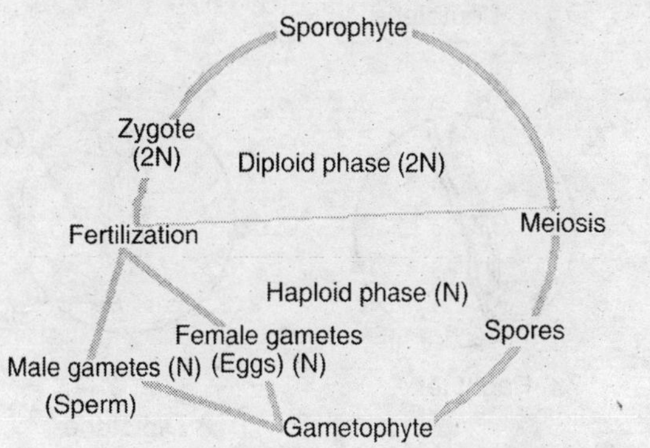

Life cycle of plant (alternation of generation)

- The gametophyte generation begins with a haploid spore produced by meiosis.
- All cells produced from the spore by mitosis are also haploid.
- The gametophyte produces gametes by mitosis.
- Sexual reproduction occurs, resulting in the production of a diploid sporophyte generation.
- The sporophyte generation starts with a diploid zygote containing the diploid number of chromosomes.

- Some reproductive cells of the sporophyte undergo meiosis, forming haploid spores.
- The haploid spores then start a new gametophyte generation.

Farmer and Moore (1905) proposed the name "meiosis" to the whole process of the two successive nuclear divisions.

Meiosis is a type of cell division that results in each daughter cell having half the number of chromosomes as the parent.

This division maintains the chromosome number constant in all sexually reproducing plants.

Meiosis occurs in diploid or polyploid cells but is absent in haploid cells.

In lower plants, meiosis takes place in the zygote, and this type of meiosis is known as zygotic meiosis (or initial meiosis), e.g., Chlamydomonas.

Premeiotic Interphase

- Premeiotic interphase is the interphase that precedes meiosis and is similar to that of mitosis.
- Premeiotic interphase consists of three phases: G1, S, and G2.
- During meiosis, the G2 phase is usually short or absent.
- Meiotic division begins after DNA synthesis is complete.
- Meiosis involves two nuclear divisions but only one round of chromosome replication.
- The first division is called meiosis I and the second one is called meiosis II, as named by Gregoire in 1904.

Phases of Meiosis

- Meiosis results in four cells with half the number of chromosomes as the parent cell.
- There are two successive divisions in meiosis that occur without a pause in plants.
- Meiosis I, also known as Reduction division, reduces the chromosome number to half the parent cell chromosome number, resulting in two haploid cells from one diploid cell.
- Meiosis I comprises four phases, including:

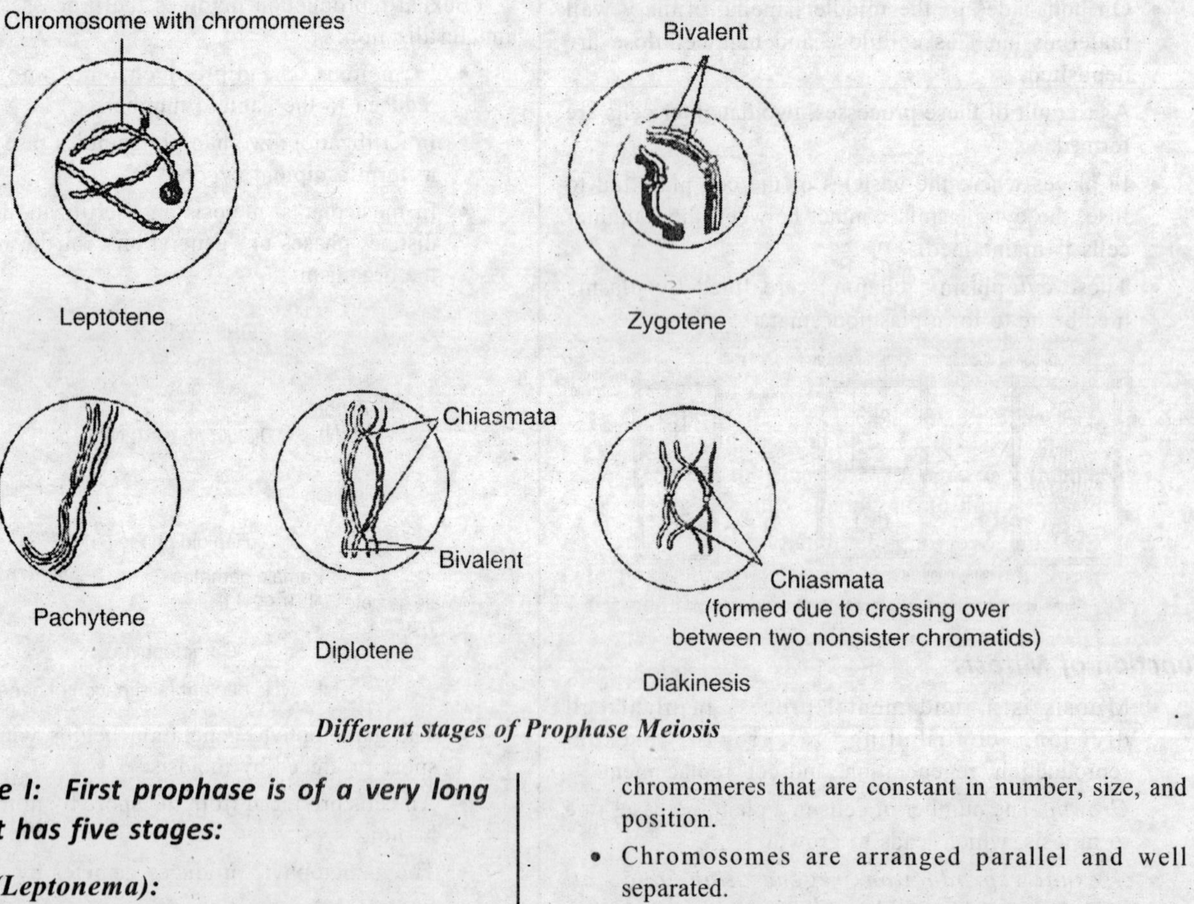

Different stages of Prophase Meiosis

1. Prophase I: First prophase is of a very long duration. It has five stages:

Leptotene (Leptonema):

- Chromatin condenses into long thin thread-like chromosomes.
- Chromosomes have bead-like thickening called chromomeres that are constant in number, size, and position.
- Chromosomes are arranged parallel and well separated.
- At the end of leptotene, homologous paternal and maternal chromosomes come close together at a point known as the bouquet stage.

Zygotene (Zygonema):

- Homologous chromosomes (each derived from one parental gamete nucleus) come together to form pairs.
- The process of pairing is called synapsis, and the resulting structure is called a synaptic complex.
- Synapsis starts at one or many points and extends in a zipper-like manner across the whole length of homologous chromosomes.
- Synapsis can be procentric (starting at the centromere), proterminal (starting at the end), or localized/random (starting at various points).

Pachytene (Pachynema):

- The paired chromosomes from the previous stage are now called bivalents.
- Bivalents become shorter and thicker.
- Each homologous chromosome in meiotic prophase-I consists of two closely apposed sister chromatids, so each bivalent contains four chromatids, also called a tetrad.
- At this stage, large recombination nodules appear at intervals on the synaptonemal complex, which is believed to mediate for chromosomal recombination or crossing over.
- Two non-sister chromatids of each tetrad get coiled around each other and exchange segments through crossing over.
- This is facilitated by transverse breaks that occur at the same level of non-sister chromatids of the homologous chromosomes. Such points where the chromatids physically contact each other are called chiasmata. At this stage, the chromosomes appear as X-shaped structures.
- The formation of chiasmata is a result of the action of an enzyme called endonuclease, which breaks the chromatid segments. The broken chromatid segments mutually exchange with each other and get united by the action of an enzyme called ligase.
- Crossing over or recombination occurs due to the formation of chiasmata. It leads to the exchange of genetic material and results in the recombination of characters. This process is responsible for the origin of new species and thus leads to evolution.

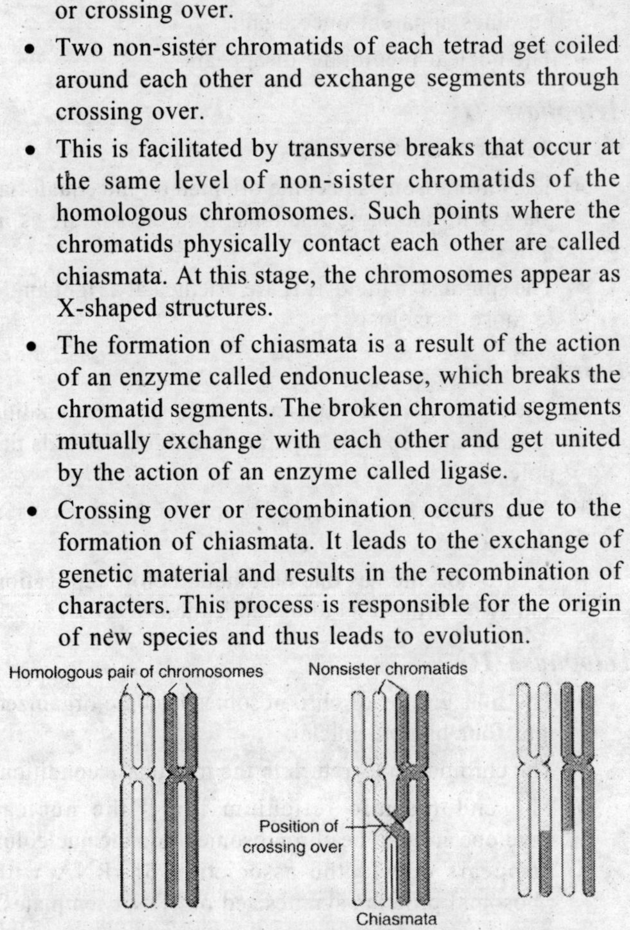

Crossing Over and result of Crossing Over

Diplotene (Diplonema):

- The synaptonemal complex dissolves, allowing the two homologous chromosomes of the bivalent to pull away from each other.
- The homologous chromosomes remain attached at one or more points where crossing over has occurred.
- These points of attachment are called chiasmata by Janssens (1909).
- This state is marked by the formation of cross-like structures, single or multiple loops.
- The chromosomes decondense and engage in RNA synthesis.
- Due to crossing over, genes from one chromosome (parental) get exchanged with genes of other chromosomes, resulting in the formation of new gene combinations.
- This process is extremely important for creating genetic diversity.

Diakinesis:

- The chiasmata start moving towards the ends of the chromosomes, leading to the terminalization of chiasmata.
- RNA synthesis stops, and the chromosomes condense and thicken, detaching from the nuclear envelope.
- Each bivalent has four chromatids and a centromere holding them together.
- Homologous chromosomes' non-sister chromatids are linked by chiasmata.
- A single chiasma forms a cross, while two and three chiasmata produce rings and loops, respectively.
- The nucleolus disassociates, and the nuclear envelope dissolves.
- Some spindle fibers start forming, and some attach to the chromosomes' centromeres.
- The fibers extend from each pole of the cell.

2. Metaphase I:

- The bivalents, which consist of homologous chromosomes, become arranged in the plane of the equator forming the equatorial plate.
- The centromere of each chromosome is directed towards the opposite poles, and the arms of chromosomes face the equatorial plate.
- The two chromatids, from each chromosome, function as a single unit at this stage.

3. Anaphase I:

- During Anaphase I, one entire chromosome, consisting of two chromatids, migrates from the equator to a pole.

- From each tetrad, two chromatids joined by their centromere move as a unit (dyad) to one pole of a spindle, while remaining two chromatids bound by their centromere migrate to the opposite pole.
- Each pole receives half the number of chromosomes or the haploid set of the chromosomes, leading to actual reduction in the number of chromosomes.
- The movement of chromosomes is brought about by the shortening of spindle fibers, similar to that during mitosis.
- When sister chromatids go to the same pole, it is called reductional or disjunctional division.
- When they separate and go to two poles, it is an equational division as in mitosis.

4. Telophase I:

- Nuclear membranes reform around the groups of daughter chromosomes.
- Each nucleus contains one nucleolus.
- Two daughter cells are formed, each with a haploid number of chromosomes, which is half the amount of DNA compared to the parent cell.

Cytokinesis:

- In plants, cytokinesis occurs by cell wall formation.
- In some plants, cytokinesis does not take place and the cell directly enters meiosis II.

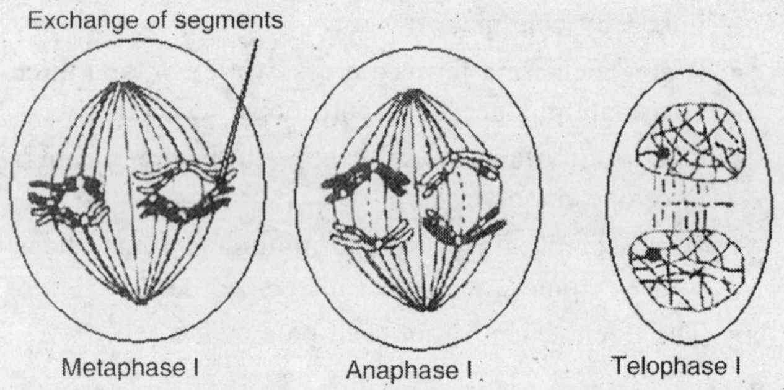

Different stages of Meiosis I

Meiosis II- equational division

- Meiosis II is the second stage of meiosis, which follows the first meiotic division.
- Meiosis II may occur with or without an intervening interphase.
- Meiosis II is necessary because during the first meiotic division, homologous chromosomes exchange genetic material through a process called crossing over. As a result, the chromatids that are produced are not identical and need to be separated.
- Meiosis II is also known as equational division because it is similar to mitosis, in which the chromatids are separated to produce two identical daughter cells.
- Meiosis II begins with a transient interphase II, which does not include the S phase of the cell cycle, meaning that no DNA replication occurs during this stage.

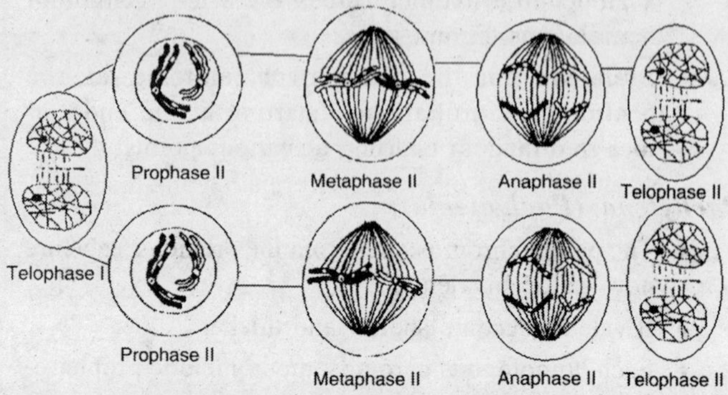

Different stages of Meiosis II

Prophase II:

- Chromosomes in both nuclei become shorter and thicker.
- The two-stranded nature of the chromosomes becomes apparent once again.
- The nuclear membrane disappears.

Metaphase II:

- Spindle formation occurs.
- The chromosomes become oriented on the equatorial plate, with the same relationship to the spindle as in mitosis.
- The spindles in meiosis II are oriented at a right angle to those in meiosis I.

Anaphase II:

- The centromeres divide, and the two sister chromatids of each chromosome separate and move towards the poles.
- After separation, each chromatid behaves as a chromosome.
- A chromosome has one chromatid before replication and two chromatids after replication.

Telophase II:

- The four groups of chromosomes become organized into four haploid nuclei.
- The chromosomes return to the interphase condition.
- The endoplasmic reticulum forms the nuclear envelope around the chromosomes, and the nucleolus reappears due to the association of rRNA with ribosomal proteins synthesized on rDNA templates.
- Each nucleus at this stage contains the haploid number of chromosomes and forms four cells.

- Cytokinesis occurs, and the two nuclei are separated, as in mitosis.

Significance of Meiosis

- Meiosis is significant for sexually reproducing organisms because it maintains a definite and constant number of chromosomes by producing haploid gametes.
- During synapsis of homologous chromosomes, pieces of chromosomes can exchange with one another through a process called crossing over. This allows for an exchange of genetic information and increases genetic variability.
- Meiosis provides an opportunity for genetic variation through crossing over and the random distribution of maternal and paternal chromosomes.
- Variation is necessary for natural selection, as it favors individuals with characteristics that are best adapted to their environments.
- Variation enables species to become adapted to their environment and allows them to change when the environment changes.

Karyotype

- Chromosomes are most clearly visible during metaphase, a stage of cell division.
- During metaphase, chromosomes are photographed, cut, and arranged in pairs based on their size.
- The arrangement of homologous chromosomes in an individual, in descending order of size, is called a karyotype.

Difference between Mitosis and Meiosis

Mitosis	Meiosis
1. Cell divides only once.	There are two cell divisions — First meiotic division and the second meiotic division.
2. Takes place in somatic cells as well as in reproductive cells which may be haploid or diploid or polyploid.	Takes place only in diploid germ cells.
3. Duration of prophase is short (few hours).	Prophase-I, is comparatively longer (takes many days).
4. Prophase simple.	Prophase I is complicated having five sub- stages namely leptotene, zygotene, pachytene, diplotene and diakinesis.
5. Synapsis does not occur.	Synapsis of homologous chromosomes takes place during prophase-I.
6. No exchange of segments during prophase between two non-sister chromatids of chromosomes.	Exchange of segments during crossing over between non-sister chromatids of two homologous chromosomes takes place.
7. Each chromosome consists of two chromatids united by a centromere.	Each bivalent has four chromatids and two centromeres.
8. Chromosomes are duplicated at the beginning of prophase.	In prophase I, chromosomes appear single although DNA replication has taken place in interphase I.
9. In metaphase all the centromeres line up in the same plane.	In metaphase I, the centromeres are lined up in two planes which are parallel to one another.
10. The metaphasic plate is made up of duplicated chromosome.	The metaphasic plate is made up of paired chromosomes.
11. Centromere division takes place during anaphase.	No centromere divisions during Anaphase I, centromeres divide only during Anaphase II.
12. Spindle fibres disappear completely in telophase.	Spindle fibres do not disappear completely during telophase I.
13. Reappearance of nucleoli attelophase.	Nucleoli do not appear in telophase I.
14. The chromosome number does not change at the end of mitosis.	There is reduction in the chromosome number from diploid to haploid.
15. The genetic constitution of chromosomes daughter cells is absolutely identical to that of parent cells.	The genetic constitution of chromosomes indaughter cells is different as compared to the parentcells. The daughter cell chromosomes contain a mixture of maternal andaternalgenes.
16. Mitosis is of shorter duration.	Meiosis is of longer duration.
17. It is the basis of growth and repair and reproduction in vegetatively orasexually reproducing organisms.	It is basis of maintaining same chromosome number in different generations of a speciesre producting sexually as well as for providing genetic variation in the progeny.

ORGANISATION OF THE GENETIC MATERIALS IN CHROMOSOMES, DNA AND RNA

- Nucleic acids were first isolated in 1868 by F. Miescher and were called nuclein. In 1889, Altman renamed them nucleic acids.
- Nucleic acids are linear, unbranched polymers made up of purine and pyrimidine nucleotides linked together through phosphodiester bonds.
- The backbone of a nucleic acid consists of alternating sugar and phosphate molecules bonded together in a long chain.
- Each sugar group in the backbone is attached to a third type of molecule called a nucleotide base.
- Long chains of nucleotides are called polynucleotides, and short chains of nucleotides are called oligonucleotides.
- The whole nucleic acid chain is usually synthesized by RNA polymerase or DNA polymerase.

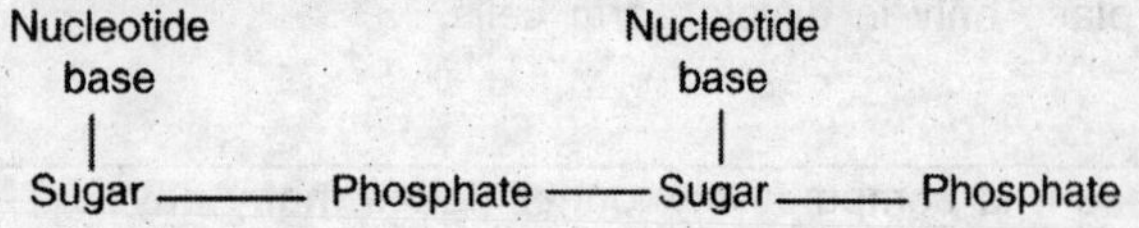

- Nucleic acids have two distinctive ends: the 5′ (5-prime) end bears a phosphate group, and the 3′ (3-prime) end bears a hydroxyl group.
- The nucleic acid chain has a direction, called polarity, which runs from 5′ to 3′ (left to right) unless otherwise indicated.
- Synthesis of a nucleic acid chain always proceeds from the 5′ end to the 3′ end.
- The arrangement or order of specific nucleotides along the chain is called the sequence.
- The sequence of nucleotides carries genetic information.

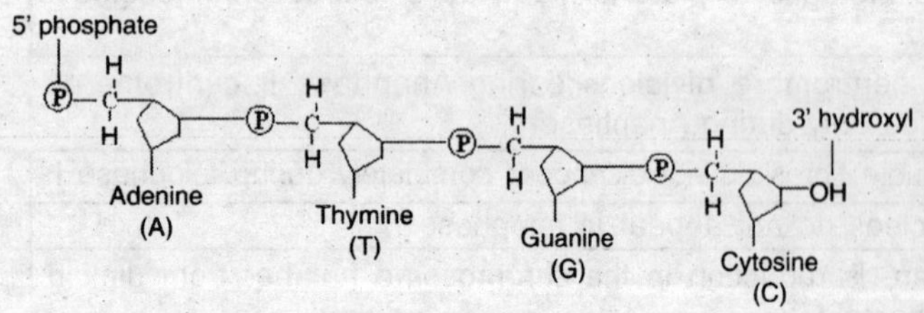

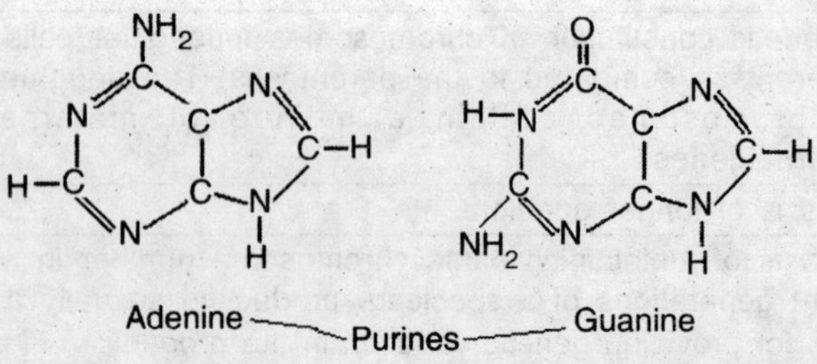

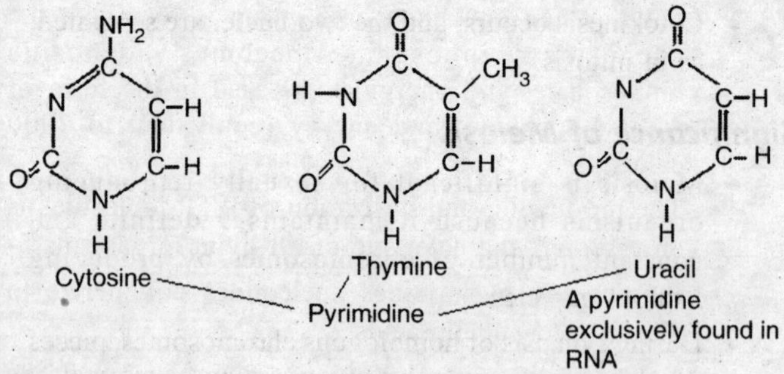

Molecular structures of purines and pyrimidines found in DNA and RNA

- Nucleotides are complex molecules made up of C, H, O, N, and P.
- Each nucleotide is composed of a 5-carbon sugar (pentose), a nitrogenous base, and phosphoric acid. The acidic character of the nucleic acids is due to the presence of the phosphoric acid.
- The pentose sugar is either ribose or deoxyribose. Ribose sugar occurs in nucleotides of RNA as well as nucleotides present free in the cytoplasm or inside coenzymes. Deoxyribonucleotides, which are the monomers of DNA, have deoxyribose as their sugar component.
- The two major purines are Adenine (A) and Guanine (G), which are bicyclic (two-ring) bases. The three major pyrimidines are Thymine (T) and Cytosine (C), which are monocyclic (single-ring) bases, and Uracil (U), which is exclusively found in RNA.
- Erwin Chargaff discovered that in any DNA molecule, the amount of purines (A and G) is equal to the amount of pyrimidines (T and C). Additionally, the amount of adenine (A) is always equal to the amount of thymine (T), and the amount of guanine (G) is always equal to the amount of cytosine (C).
- Nucleotides are a crucial component of the information transfer system and participate in the energy transfer system.
- In cells, free nucleotides may contain one (mono), two (di), or three (tri) phosphate groups. Adenosine monophosphate (AMP) has one phosphate group, adenosine diphosphate (ADP) has two, and adenosine triphosphate (ATP) has three phosphate groups.
- When nucleotides contain more than one phosphate group, they are referred to as higher nucleotides (e.g., ATP and ADP).
- Individual nucleotides play important roles in the cellular activity of a cell. In a molecule of ATP, the two terminal chemical bonds that link the O and P atoms are known as high-energy phosphate bonds. The replacement of one of these bonds by H-O bonds liberates two or three times as much energy as most chemical bonds. In living cells, the energy is made available by the hydrolytic splitting of the ATP molecule at the outermost high-energy phosphate

bond. When one phosphate group is removed, the adenosine triphosphate becomes adenosine diphosphate, and energy is released in the form of ADP, phosphate, and energy (equivalent to 7000 calories).

- The production and utilization of ATP molecules is an essential characteristic of all living organisms.
- Purines and pyrimidines nucleotides polymerize to give rise to nucleic acids.
- Nucleotides of vitamins nicotinamide - Nicotinamide adenine dinucleotide (NAD+) and Nicotinamide adenine dinucleotide phosphate (NADP+) and the nucleotides of riboflavin - Flavin mononucleotide (FMN) and Flavin adenine dinucleotide (FAD) play a role in oxidation reactions occurring in the cell.
- When all phosphate groups of a nucleotide are removed, a nucleotide becomes a nucleoside.
- The combination of a base and a pentose is called a nucleoside. For example, adenosine is made up of ribose + adenine.
- The following table lists various nucleosides and their mono- NMP (nucleoside monophosphate) or dNMP (deoxynucleoside monophosphate), di- NDP (nucleoside diphosphate) or dNDP (deoxynucleoside diphosphate), and triphosphates-NTP (nucleoside triphosphate) or dNTP (deoxynucleoside triphosphate).
- For DNA, these are dATP, dCTP, dGTP, and dTTP.
- For RNA, these are ATP, CTP, GTP, and UTP.

Types of Nucleic Acids

- There are two main types of nucleic acids: Deoxyribonucleic acid (DNA) and Ribonucleic acid (RNA).

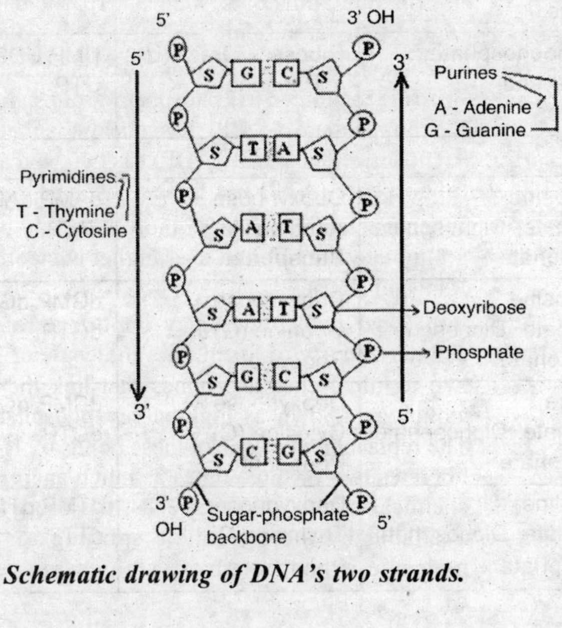

Schematic drawing of DNA's two strands.

- DNA is mainly found in the nucleus but is also present in chloroplasts, while RNA is stored in the nucleolus and moves out into the cytoplasm.
- In DNA or RNA, a nucleic acid chain is also called a strand.
- DNA is the repository of genetic information, while RNA molecules may be regarded as vectors and translators of information.
- A DNA molecule typically contains two strands, while most RNA molecules contain a single strand.
- The length of a nucleic acid chain is represented by the number of bases.
- In a double-stranded nucleic acid, bases are paired between the two strands.

DNA or Deoxyribonucleic Acid

- DNA stands for Deoxyribonucleic acid.
- The double helix structure of DNA was determined by J. Watson & S. Crick in 1953, based on X-ray diffraction works by Wilkins, R. Franklin and Astbury.
- The DNA molecule consists of two polynucleotide chains (strands) held together by hydrogen bonding between their bases.
- The two strands are wrapped plectonemically (spirally) to form a double helix.
- Each strand forms a right-handed helix with ten base pairs per spiral turn.
- The two strands of the DNA double helix run in opposite directions, one in the 5' to 3' direction and the other in the 3' to 5' direction. This is known as antiparallel.

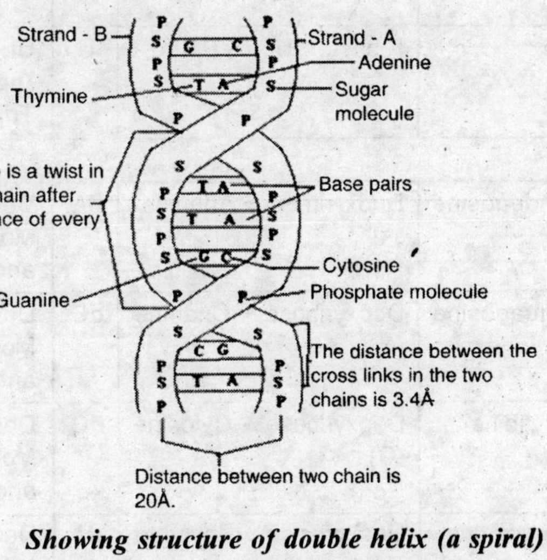

Showing structure of double helix (a spiral) DNA molecule (Watson and Crick)

- The sugar-phosphate backbone of each strand is on the outside of the helix, while the bases are on the inside, stacked on top of each other like the steps of a spiral staircase.
- The rungs of the ladder are composed of two base pairs, with either an adenine-thymine pair (two hydrogen bonds) or a cytosine-guanine pair (three hydrogen bonds).
- The base pairing is therefore restricted, with dA-dT and dG-dC base pairs occurring in specific pairs.
- During DNA replication, the DNA helix is "unzipped" to reveal two long stretches of sugar-phosphate backbone, with a line of free bases sticking up from it, like the teeth of a comb.
- Each half of the DNA molecule serves as the template for the synthesis of a new, complementary strand.
- dA-dT and dG-dC base pairs are of the same length and occupy the same space within a DNA double helix, giving the DNA molecule a uniform diameter.
- dA-dT and dG-dC base pairs can occur in any order within DNA molecules.
- The N-glycosidic bonds between the sugar and the base are not directly opposite to each other, resulting in two alternating grooves in the DNA molecule.
- These grooves are the major groove (wide and deep) and minor groove (shallow and narrow) located between the ribose-phosphate chains on the surface of the molecule.
- The major and minor grooves may facilitate binding with specific proteins, which recognize the unique chemical and structural features of DNA in each groove.
- The diameter of the DNA double helix is 2.0 nanometers.
- The distance between two neighboring base pairs in the DNA molecule is 0.34 nanometers.
- The helix makes a complete turn every 3.4 nanometers along its axis.
- Denaturation (also called melting) is the process of converting double-stranded DNA into single strands by heating or exposing to an alkali.
- Renaturation or annealing is the process of converting single-stranded DNA back to double-stranded structure.
- There are three natural forms of DNA: A, B, and Z.
- The different forms of DNA are related to the conformation of the sugar (C2′-endo or C3′-endo) and the orientation of the base relative to the sugar (syn or anti).

Adenosine	Ribose + Adenine (A)	A	Adenosine Monophosphate, Diphosphate and Triphosphate	Ribose + Adenine (A) + Phosphate	AMP, ADP, ATP
Guanosine	Ribose + Guanine (G)	G	Guanosine Monophosphate, Diphosphate and Triphosphate	Ribose + Guanine (G) + Phosphate	GMP, GDP, GTP
Cytidine	Ribose + Cytosine (C)	C	Cytidine Monophosphate, Diphosphate and Triphosphate	Ribose + Cytosine (C) + Phosphate	CMP, CDP, CTP
Uridine	Ribose + Uracil (U)	U	Uridine Monophosphate, Diphosphate and Triphosphate	Ribose + Uracil (U) + Phosphate	UMP, UDP, UTP
DNA					
Deoxyadenosine	Deoxyribose + Adenine (A)	dA	Deoxyadenosine Monophosphate, Diphosphate and Triphosphate	Deoxyribose + Adenine (A) + Phosphate	dAMP, dADP, dATP
Deoxyguanosine	Deoxyribose + Guanine (G)	dG	Deoxyguanosine Monophosphate, Diphosphate and Triphosphate	Deoxyribose + Guanine (G) + Phosphate	dGMP, dGDP, dGTP
Deoxycytidine	Deoxyribose + Cytosine (C)	dC	Deoxycytidine Monophosphate, Diphosphate and Triphosphate	Deoxyribose + Cytosine (C) + Phosphate	dCMP, dCDP, dCTP
Deoxythymidine	Deoxyribose + Thymine (T)	dT	Deoxythymidine Monophosphate, Diphosphate and Triphosphate	Deoxyribose + Thymine (T) + Phosphate	dTMP, dTDP, dTTP

- B-form is the most common natural form of DNA, found at high hydration and low ionic strength. It arranges 10 nucleotides per helix turn, all in the C2′-endo/anti conformation. The bases are nearly perpendicular to the helix axis and the helix surface exhibits two prominent grooves (major and minor).
- A-form is sometimes found in some parts of natural DNA in the presence of high cation concentration or at lower hydration (< 65%). A-DNA possesses 11 nucleotides per turn (all in the C3′-endo/anti conformation) and two grooves (a narrow deep major and a wide shallow minor).
- C-form and D-form are unusual sub-classes of the B-type. C-DNA is sometimes observed at 45% hydration while D-DNA is only found in artificial DNA.
- Z-form (Zigzag chain) is observed in DNA G-C rich local region. Z-DNA is longer, thinner and possesses an unusual left-handed helix (of 12 base pairs per turn) with a single narrow deep groove. The zigzag form results mainly from the alternation of purines (C3′-endo/syn) and pyrimidines (C2′-endo/anti).

Difference between DNA and RNA

DNA	RNA
1. It is mainly confined to the nucleus. A small quantity occurs in mitochondria and chloroplasts.	1. It mainly occurs in the cytoplasm. A small quantity is found in the nucleus.
2. Its quantity is constant in each cell of a species.	2. Its quantity varies in different cells.
3. It contains deoxyribose sugar.	3. It contains ribose sugar.
4. Its pyrimidines are adenine and thymine.	4. Its pyrimidines are adenine and uracil.
5. The amount of adenine is equal to the amount of thymine, also the amount of cytosine is equal to the amount of guanine.	5. Adenine and uracil arc not necessarily in equal amounts, nor are cytosine and guanine necessarily in equal amounts.
6. It consists of 2 polynucleotide chains held together by hydrogen bonds, and coiled into a double helix. Some viruses ($\phi \times 174$) have single-stranded DNA.	6. It consists of a single polynucleotide chain. It may fold on itself and get hydrogen-bonded and coiled into a pseudohelix. Some viruses (rheovirus) have double-stranded RNA.
7. Its molecular weight varies from 2 to 6 million.	7. Its molecular weight varies from 25,000 to 2 million.
8. It is of 2 types : linear intranuclear and circular extranuclear.	8. It is of 3 types ; mRNA, tRNA, rRNA. Each type is further of many subtypes.
9. It can replicate itself.	9. It cannot replicate itself. It is formed by DNA. Some RNA viruses (paramyxo virus) can produce RNA from RNA template.
10. It controls structure, metabolism, heredity, differentiation and evolution.	10. It brings about protein synthesis. It also starts replication.
11. It is a component of chromosomes.	11. It is a component of ribosomes.
12. It is a genetic material in all organisms.	12. It is a genetic material in certain viruses.
13. It does not contain unusual bases.	13. It may contain unusual bases in addition to the normal ones.
14. A primer is needed for replication.	14. No primer is needed for transcription.
15. Its renaturation after melting is slow.	15. Its renaturation after melting is quick.
16. It transfers its information to mRNA (transcription).	16. mRNA transfers its information to polypeptide (translation).
17. DNA is hydrolysed by the enzyme DNA-ase.	17. RNA is hydrolysed by the enzyme RNA-ase.

DNA Replication:

- DNA replication occurs before a cell divides into two daughter cells, and in eukaryotes, it occurs during the S phase of the cell cycle.
- Replication is the process of duplicating an old DNA molecule into two new DNA molecules.
- During replication, the hydrogen bonds between nucleotide bases break, and the two single strands of DNA separate.
- Each DNA strand serves as a template for the synthesis of a new complementary strand.
- New complementary bases are brought in by the cell and paired up with each of the two separate strands,

thus forming two new, identical, double-stranded DNA molecules.

- Each daughter DNA molecule is an identical copy of its parent molecule, consisting of one old and one new DNA strand.
- Therefore, replication is semi-conservative.

RNA or Ribonucleic Acid:

- RNA is usually composed of a single strand of ribonucleotides, making it shorter than DNA. However, it can be double-stranded in some viruses like Reovirus and Rice dwarf virus.
- RNA is a linear polymer made up of nucleotides linked by phosphodiester bonds between the 3′ and 5′ carbon atoms in the ribose sugar.
- RNA can form hairpin loops and adopts a helical structure in the base-paired region similar to DNA.
- RNA has four different bases: adenine, guanine, cytosine, and uracil.
- In RNA, guanine and cytosine pair (GC) by forming a triple hydrogen bond, while adenine and uracil pair (AU) by a double hydrogen bond. Guanine and uracil can also form a single hydrogen bond base pair.
- The sugar in RNA is ribose, while DNA uses 2-deoxyribose. RNA also replaces thymine with uracil in its bases.
- Ribose sugar is more reactive than 2-deoxyribose, making RNA less stable in alkaline conditions. The larger grooves in RNA also make it easier to be attacked by enzymes.
- RNA does not follow Chargaff's rules of base pairing, which state that there is a 1:1 ratio between purines and pyrimidines, due to its single-stranded nature and lack of complementarity.

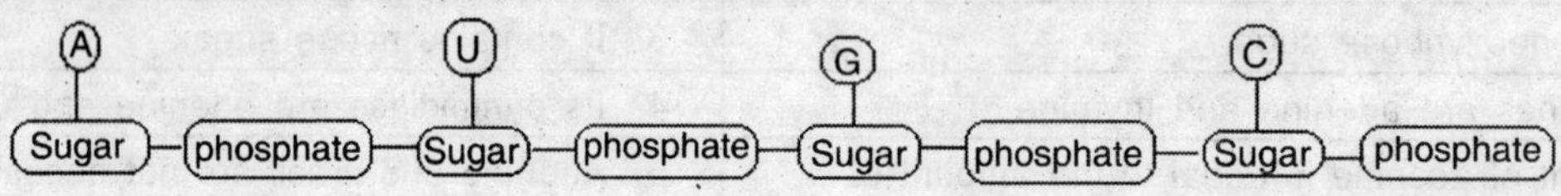

Structure of RNA molecule

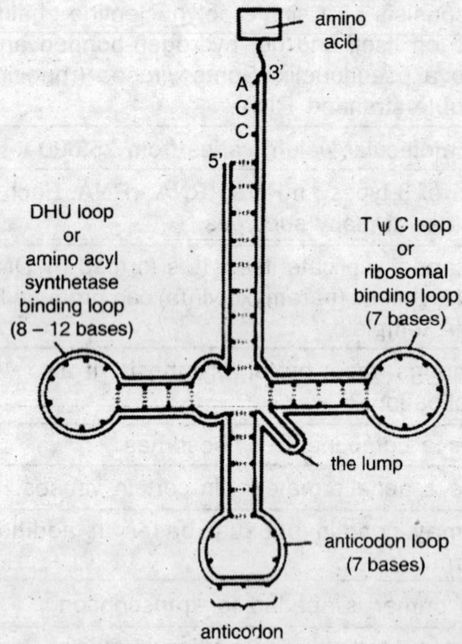

Non-genetic RNA is synthesized on DNA template and is of three types: messenger RNA, transfer RNA, and ribosomal RNA.

- Messenger RNA (mRNA) carries genetic information from the DNA in the nucleus to the ribosome, where it is translated into protein.
- Transfer RNA (tRNA) is the smallest type of RNA, constituting about 10-15% of total cellular RNA. It has on average 80 nucleotides per molecule and carries amino acids to the ribosome, where they are added to the growing protein chain.
- Each amino acid has its own specific tRNA molecule, which recognizes and binds to the corresponding codon on the mRNA through its anticodon region.
- The 5′-end of the tRNA always ends in the base guanine, while the 3′-end always ends in the base sequence CCA.
- The triplet base sequence at the anticodon is directly related to the amino acid carried by that tRNA by its own form of the enzyme amino-acyl-tRNA synthetase.
- Ribosomal RNA (rRNA) is the largest and most stable type of RNA.
- rRNA constitutes about 80% of total cellular RNA and is a major structural component of ribosomes, which are the sites of protein synthesis.
- In prokaryotes, rRNA has three types: 23S, 5S, and 16S, while eukaryotic ribosomes contain four different rRNA molecules: 18S, 5.8S, 28S, and 5S rRNA.
- Three of the eukaryotic rRNA molecules are synthesized in the nucleolus, while one is synthesized elsewhere.
- The unit "S" stands for Svedberg, which is a measure of the sedimentation rate.
- After rRNA molecules are produced in the nucleus, they combine with specific proteins to form ribosomes in the cytoplasm.
- Prokaryotic ribosomes have a size of 70S and consist of two subunits: 50S and 30S, while eukaryotic ribosomes have a size of 80S and comprise a 60S and a 40S subunit.

- Transfer RNA (tRNA) molecules are folded to form a cloverleaf-like structure.

snRNA:

- Small nuclear RNA (snRNA) is a type of small RNA molecule found in the nucleus.
- snRNA plays a crucial role in RNA splicing, which involves the removal of introns from hnRNA.
- snRNA also helps in the maintenance of telomeres, which are the protective ends of chromosomes.
- snRNA always associates with specific proteins, forming small nuclear ribonucleoproteins (SNRNP) or snurps.
- SNRNP or snurps are essential in the process of RNA splicing.
- The role of snRNA in telomere maintenance is not fully understood.

Protein Synthesis and Proteins:

1. Proteins are made up of linear polymers of amino acids, which are linked together by peptide bonds between the amino and carboxyl groups of successive amino acids.
2. Proteins are formed by one or several polypeptide chains, where polypeptides refer to long peptides and oligopeptides refer to short peptides ($<$ 10 amino acids). Proteins consist of one or more polypeptides with more than 50 amino acids.
3. The sequence of the polypeptide chain is determined by the genetic code of a gene.
4. While all proteins are polypeptides, not all polypeptides are proteins.
5. Living organisms have only 20 standard amino acids, which consist of carbon, hydrogen, nitrogen, oxygen, and two containing sulfur.
6. Ten of these amino acids have side groups that are attracted to water, while the other ten do not. In a water-based environment, hydrophobic amino acids fold inwards while hydrophilic ones remain on the outside. The backbone of amino acids forms strong covalent bonds, and the actual amino acids form temporary weak bonds. These weak bonds allow the amino acids to change shape, remain mobile, and attain flexibility.

Protein Synthesis:

- Protein synthesis occurs in the cytoplasm and involves ribosomes.
- mRNA, tRNA, and rRNA are three non-genetic RNAs involved in protein synthesis.
- All three types of RNA are synthesized directly on DNA templates.
- Proteins have a variety of functions in cells such as providing structure, storing energy, providing movement, transporting other substances, catalyzing biological reactions, and protecting against disease.
- Proteins make up more than 50% of a cell's dry weight.
- The amount of RNA in each cell is directly proportional to the amount of protein synthesis.
- In eukaryotes, three different RNA polymerases (I, II, III) catalyze the synthesis of rRNA, mRNA, and tRNA, respectively.
- In prokaryotes, a single RNA polymerase performs the function of synthesizing all types of RNA.

Two Major Steps are Involved in Protein Synthesis:

1. **Transcription:** Francis Crick proposed that genetic information flows from DNA to RNA in a process called transcription. During transcription, RNA polymerase reads the DNA sequence and synthesizes a complementary RNA molecule. This RNA molecule is called messenger RNA (mRNA) and is used to synthesize polypeptides during the next step, translation.
2. **Translation:** Translation is the mechanism by which the triplet base sequences of mRNA molecules are converted into a specific sequence of amino acids in a polypeptide chain. During translation, ribosomes bind to mRNA and decode its sequence to synthesize a polypeptide chain. Several ribosomes may bind to a single mRNA molecule, forming a structure called a polysome. Translation occurs at ribosomes located on the surface of the rough endoplasmic reticulum and as groups of ribosomes (polysomes) found free-floating in the cytoplasm.

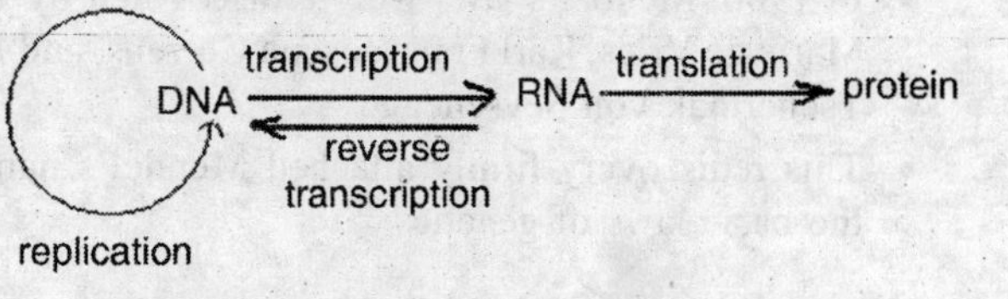

DNA makes messenger RNA makes protein

MENDEL'S LAWS OF INHERITANCE

- Genetics is the branch of science that studies heredity and variation.
- Heredity refers to the transmission of characters from parents to offspring across generations.
- Variation refers to the differences that exist between individuals, including differences between parents and offspring, between siblings, and between members of a population.
- Heritable variations arise due to mutations and recombination during reproduction.

- Variation is important for the survival of a population, as individuals with certain traits may be better adapted to new environmental conditions.
- Variation arises due to mutations, which cause sudden changes in genes, and recombination during meiosis, which leads to new gene combinations.
- Genetic recombination is a common source of variation, resulting from the random mixing of paternal and maternal chromosomes during fertilization.
- Gregor Johann Mendel is known as the father of genetics for his contributions to understanding inheritance patterns.
- Mendel was born on July 22, 1822, in Heinzendorf, which is present-day Czechoslovakia.
- He came from a family of Moravian peasants and showed talent from a young age.
- Fr. Matthaeus Klacel, a botanist who was an expert in natural sciences, was Mendel's mentor.
- Mendel conducted numerous experiments on plant hybridization between 1856 and 1863.
- He studied nearly 28,000 plants during this time period.
- In 1865, he reported on his plant hybrid experiments to the Brunn Natural Science Society with the title of "Hybridization in Plants".
- His paper on this topic was published a year later.
- In 1868, Mendel was elected abbot of the monastery and vice president of the Natural Science Society.
- He conducted more experiments with different plant species the following year and reported his findings to the Society.
- Mendel died on January 6, 1884, at the age of 61.
- In 1900, Mendel's laws were rediscovered by Hugo Marie de Vries, Karl Franz Joseph Correns, and Erich Tschermak von Seysenegg.
- This rediscovery firmly attached Mendel's name to the basic laws of genetics.

Mendel's Experiments

Monohybrid

- A monohybrid cross involves mating between two individuals with different alleles at one genetic locus.
- The character(s) being studied are governed by two or multiple alleles for a single locus.
- Law of Dominance: Each character is controlled by distinct units called factors, which occur in pairs. If the pairs are heterozygous, one will always dominate the other.
- The law of dominance explains that in a monohybrid cross between a pair of contrasting traits, only one parental character will be expressed in F_1 generation and both are expressed in F_2 generation in the ratio 3:1.
- The dominant trait is the one expressed in the F_1 generation, while the recessive trait is suppressed or masked.
- Law of Segregation: The pair of alleles segregates from each other during meiosis (gamete formation) so that only one allele will be present in each gamete.
- In a monohybrid cross, both alleles are expressed in the F_2 generation without blending.
- The law of segregation is based on the fact that each gamete contains only one allele.

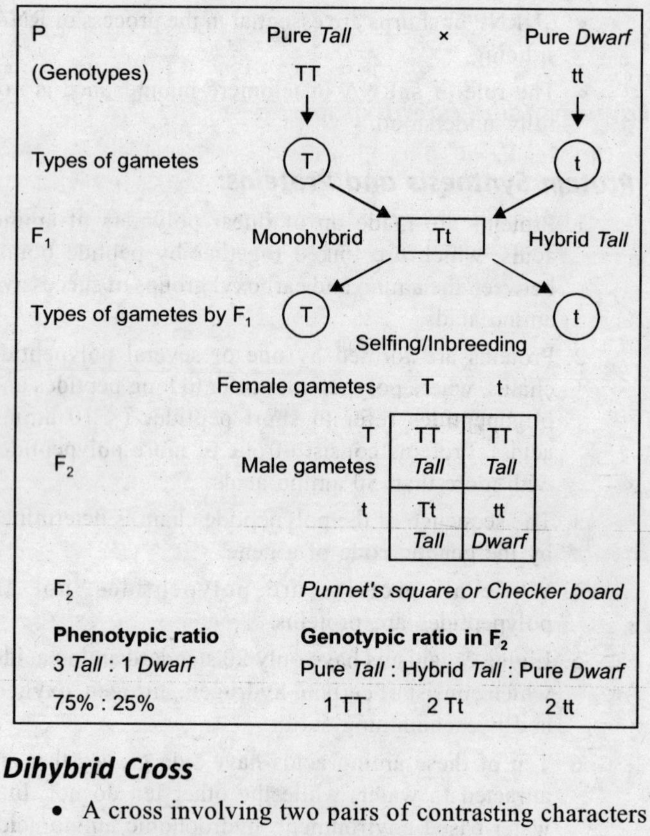

Dihybrid Cross

- A cross involving two pairs of contrasting characters
- Mendel selected seed coat and cotyledon characteristics for his dihybrid cross experiment
- He crossed a pure breeding plant with round seed coat and yellow cotyledons with a pure breeding plant with wrinkled seed coat and green cotyledons
- In the F_1 generation, all resulting plants had round seed coat and yellow cotyledons
- In the F_2 generation, four types of plants were obtained in the ratio of 9 : 3 : 3 : 1, with round yellow, round green, wrinkled yellow and wrinkled green seeds
- The genotype ratio of the F_2 generation was 1(YYRR) : 2(YYRr) : 2(YyRR) : 4(YyRr) : 1(YYrr) : 2(Yyrr) : 1(yyRR) : 2(yyRr) : 1(yyrr)

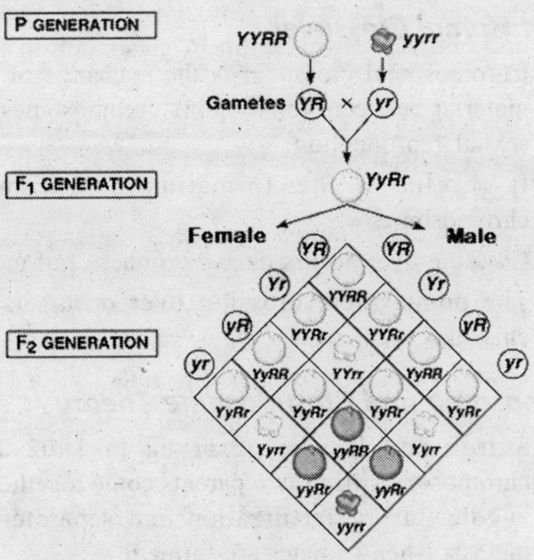

Law of Independent Assortment

- Mendel observed that the combinations of traits in progeny were always different from the parental traits, leading to the formulation of the Law of Independent Assortment.
- The Law of Independent Assortment states that during a dihybrid cross, the assortment of each pair of traits is independent of the other.
- During gamete formation, one pair of traits segregates independently of another pair of traits.
- This provides each pair of characters an opportunity to express themselves.

Incomplete Dominance

- Incomplete dominance is a form of intermediate inheritance, where one allele for a specific trait is not completely expressed over its paired allele.
- This results in a third phenotype that is a combination of both alleles.

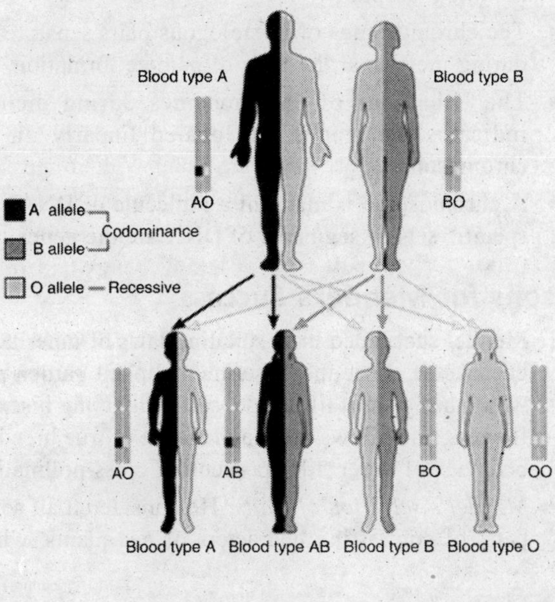

- One allele does not dominate or mask the other allele in incomplete dominance.
- The discovery of incomplete dominance is usually credited to German Botanist Carl Correns who studied four o'clock plants.
- Incomplete dominance is seen in the cross-pollination experiments between red and white snapdragon plants, resulting in pink offspring.
- The genotypes are: Red (RR) × White (rr) = Pink (Rr).

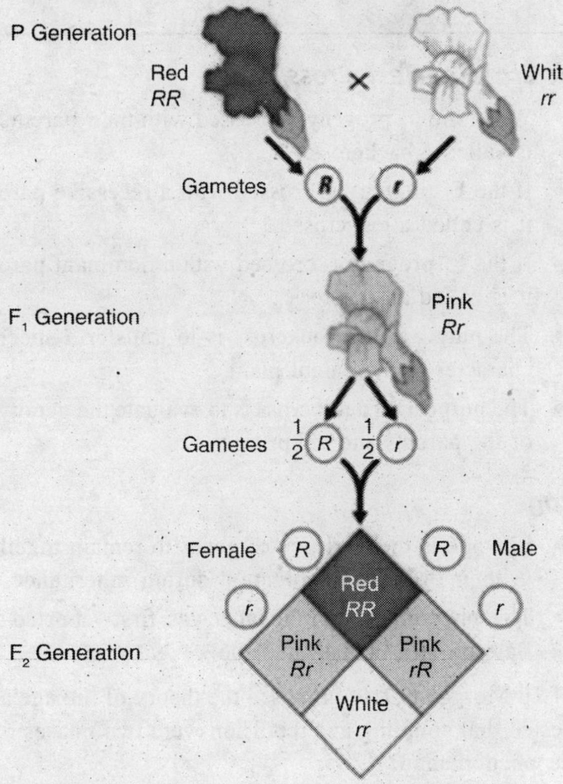

Codominance

- Codominance is a type of gene expression in which both alleles in a heterozygote are fully expressed, resulting in a unique phenotype that is different from both dominant and recessive traits.
- An example of codominance is the ABO blood group system, where people with the AB blood type have both A and B proteins in their blood at the same time.
- The ABO gene is responsible for determining a person's blood type, and each person has two copies of this gene, one from each parent.
- When a person inherits both an A and a B allele, they will have a blood type that is visible in the blood as AB.
- Codominance is different from incomplete dominance, where the two alleles blend together to

create a third phenotype, and complete dominance, where one allele dominates over the other.

Genes from Mom and Dad		Genes of	Blood Type
Mom	Dad	Offspring	Result
A	A	AA	A
A	O	AO	A
A	B	AB	AB
B	B	BB	B
O	B	BO	B
O	O	OO	O

Back Cross or Test Cross

- When the F_1 progeny is crossed with their parents, it is called a backcross.
- If the F_1 progeny is crossed with a recessive parent, it is called a test cross.
- If the F_1 progeny is crossed with a dominant parent, it is called an outcross.
- The purpose of a backcross is to transfer a specific character to the parent plant.
- The purpose of a test cross is to evaluate the genotype of the parents and offspring.

Linkage

- Linkage is the tendency of genes to remain together in their original combination during inheritance.
- The phenomenon of linkage was first reported by Bateson and Punnett in 1906.

T.H. Morgan (1910) proposed the theory of linkage and suggested that coupling and repulsion were two phases of a single phenomenon.

- Linkage refers to the tendency of two or more genes to be inherited together because they are located close to each other on the same chromosome in a linear fashion.
- Linkage reduces variability as linked genes tend to be inherited together and do not undergo independent assortment.
- Linkage can involve either dominant or recessive alleles (coupling phase) or some dominant and some recessive alleles (repulsion phase).
- Linked genes are usually located close to each other on the same chromosome.
- The strength of linkage depends on the distance between the linked genes; the closer the genes are to each other, the stronger the linkage.
- Linkage can be determined from the progeny data obtained from a test cross.

Chromosomal Crossover

- Chromosomal crossover is the exchange of genetic material between homologous chromosomes during sexual reproduction.
- It results in the formation of recombinant chromosomes.
- Crossing over occurs during prophase I of meiosis I.
- The point where crossing over occurs is called chiasma.

Chromosome and Chromosome Theory

- Sutton and Boveri observed in 1902-03 that chromosomes from two parents come together in the zygote during fertilization and separate during meiosis when gametes are formed.
- Gametes have half the number of chromosomes (n) compared to the diploid zygote (2n).
- This proves that there is a similarity between the behavior of Mendelian factors (genes) during inheritance and chromosomes during meiosis.
- This led to the development of the Chromosome Theory of Inheritance, which states that genes are located on chromosomes and the behavior of chromosomes during meiosis explains Mendel's laws of segregation and independent assortment.

This led Sutton and Boveri to propose 'chromosomal theory of inheritance' and its salient features are as follows.

- The cells of an organism, which are derived by the repeated division of zygote, have two identical sets of chromosomes and are diploid. One set is received from the mother (maternal chromosomes) and one set from the father (paternal chromosomes).
- Two chromosomes of one type (carrying genes controlling the same set of characters) constitute a homologous pair.
- The chromosomes of homologous pairs separate out during meiosis at the time of gamete formation.
- The behaviour of chromosomes during meiosis indicates that genes are located linearly on the chromosomes.
- A chromosome is made of a molecule of DNA, and specific sets of segments of DNA are the genes.

Reasons for Mendel's Success

1. Mendel succeeded in postulating laws of inheritance because he chose the experimental plant garden pea, which has a short life cycle, self-pollinating bisexual flowers, and allows the maintenance of true breeding behavior of parents by preventing cross-pollination.
2. *Mendel's selection of traits:* He considered all seven pairs of contrasting characters of pea plants, which

showed complete dominance, thus allowing him to postulate the law of dominance and the law of segregation.

3. The factors for all seven traits were either present on separate homologous chromosomes or, if present on the same chromosome, were far apart, leading to independent segregation and not being inherited together.
4. *Mendel's methodology:* His technique of experimentation helped him in discovering the Laws of Heredity, which includes:
   (*i*) Crossed homozygous pure line plants with contrasting characters.
   (*ii*) Prevented self-pollination by removing stamens for cross-pollination between desired parents.
   (*iii*) Dusting female plants with pollen grains from another plant with the contrasting feature and tying them in a bag to prevent further pollination.
   (*iv*) Collected seeds from different generations and sowed them in time.
   (*v*) Maintained and statistically analyzed the results of different generations by counting individuals exhibiting different traits.
   (*vi*) Considered the inheritance of one character at a time and then considered inheritance involving individuals differing in two contrasting characters.
   (*vii*) Performed reciprocal crosses and test crosses to confirm the results and formulated the basic laws of heredity.

Seven Traits of Pea Selected by Mendel

Mendel considered all seven pairs of contrasting characters in pea plants:

1. Seed color: yellow vs. green
2. Seed shape: round vs. wrinkled
3. Pod color: yellow vs. green
4. Pod shape: inflated vs. constricted
5. Flower position: axial vs. terminal
6. Flower color: purple vs. white
7. Stem length: long vs. short

S.No.	Characteristic	Contrasting Traits	
		Dominant	Recessive
1.	Stem Height	Tall	Dwarf
2.	Flower Colour	Violet	White
3.	Flower Position	Axial	Terminal
4.	Pod Shape	Swelled	Shrinkage
5.	Pod Colour	Green	Yellow
6.	Seed Shape	Round	Wrinkled
7.	Seed Colour	Yellow	Green

Absence of linkage in Mendel's experiments

In Mendel's experiments on the inheritance of traits in pea plants, he observed that certain traits, such as flower color, seed texture, and plant height, were inherited independently of each other. This phenomenon is known as the absence of linkage.

Mendel's work laid the foundation for the study of genetics, and his findings on the absence of linkage were significant because they contradicted the prevailing theory of blending inheritance.

The theory of blending inheritance suggested that offspring inherited a blend of traits from both parents, resulting in traits that were intermediate between those of the parents.

Mendel's experiments showed that this was not the case. Instead, he found that each trait was controlled by a pair of factors, which we now call genes. These genes were inherited independently of each other, meaning that the presence or absence of one trait did not affect the inheritance of another trait.

This absence of linkage is due to the fact that genes are located on different chromosomes. Chromosomes are structures within the cell that contain DNA, which carries the genetic information for an organism. Each chromosome contains many genes, and the location of each gene on the chromosome is known as its locus.

During sexual reproduction, chromosomes from each parent are paired and then separated into different gametes (sperm and egg cells). This means that the genes on different chromosomes are randomly assorted into different gametes, leading to independent inheritance of different traits.

The absence of linkage has important implications for agriculture and industry. Livestock breeders, for example, can selectively breed animals for desired traits, knowing that these traits will be inherited independently of each other. This has allowed for the development of specialized breeds of animals that are optimized for specific purposes, such as dairy production, meat production, or wool production.

In industry, the absence of linkage has allowed for the development of genetically modified crops that have multiple desirable traits. For example, scientists have developed crops that are resistant to pests, drought, and herbicides, while also increasing yield and nutritional content. This has the potential to improve food security and reduce the environmental impact of agriculture.

The absence of linkage in Mendel's experiments was a significant finding that helped to establish the field of genetics. This phenomenon has important implications for agriculture and industry, allowing for the selective breeding of animals and the development of genetically modified crops with multiple desirable traits.

Important Terms in Genetics

1. **Factor:** The unit of inheritance and expression of a particular character is controlled by inheritable units called factor (gene) which are present in pairs in parental cells and singly in the gametes.
2. **Gene:** A segment of DNA molecule which determines the unit of inheritance and expression of a particular character.
3. **Alleles or Allelomorphs:** Two or more alternative forms of a gene are called alleles. For example in pea plant, the gene for producing seed shape may occur in two alternative forms: smooth (S) and wrinkled (s). Genes for smooth wrinkled seeds are alleles of each other, and occupy same locus on homologous chromosomes.
4. **Trait:** It is the morphologically or physiologically visible character, e.g. colour of flower, and shape of seed.
5. **Dominant trait:** Out of the two alleles or allelomorphs of a trait, the one which expresses itself in a heterogygous organism in the F_1 hybrid is called the dominant trait (dominant allele) and the one that remains masked in F_1 individual but gets expressed in the next generation (F_2), is called recessive. Thus, if the allelic combination in an organism is Tt, and T (tallness) expresses itself but t (dwarfness) cannot, so T is the dominant allele, and tallness is dominant on dwarfness represented by 't'.
6. **Recessive trait:** Out of the two alleles for a trait, the one which is suppressed (does not express) in the F_1 hybrid is called the recessive trait (recessive allele). But the Recessive allele does express itself only in the homozygous state (e.g. tt).
7. **Genotype:** A class of individuals recognised based on its genetic constitution and breeding behaviour is called the genotype, e.g., the genotype of pure smooth seeded parent pea plant is SS and it will always breed true for smooth-seeded character, but plants having Ss on selfing would give rise to a population represented by 3 : 1 ratio for smooth seeded plants and wrinkled seeded plants.
8. **Phenotype:** A class of individuals recognised based on outward appearance of a trait in an individual is the phenotype, e.g. Smooth-seeded shape or wrinkled shape of seeds represent two different phenotypes.
9. **Homozygous:** An individual possessing identical alleles for a trait is termed homozygous e.g. TT is homozygous condition for smooth seeded character in garden-pea.
10. **Heterozygous:** An individual with dissimilar alleles for a trait is termed heterozygous for e.g. Tt represents the heterozygous condition for smooth seeded character in garden pea.
11. **Parent generations:** The parents used for the first cross represent the parent (or P_1) generation.
12. **F_1 generation:** The progeny produced from a cross between two parents (P_1) is called First filial or F_1 generation.
13. **F_2 generation:** The progeny resulting from self pollination or inbreeding of F_1 individuals is called Second Filial or F_2 generation.

QUANTITATIVE INHERITANCE, CONTINUOUS AND DISCONTINUOUS VARIATION IN PLANTS

Quantitative inheritance and continuous/discontinuous variation are important concepts in agriculture as they help in understanding the inheritance patterns of plant traits and their implications for breeding programs. Here are some important details about these concepts:

Quantitative Inheritance

Quantitative inheritance refers to the inheritance of traits that are controlled by multiple genes and are influenced by environmental factors. In quantitative inheritance, the expression of a trait is controlled by many genes, each of which contributes a small additive effect. The more genes that contribute to a trait, the more continuous and complex the variation in that trait becomes. The factors that influence quantitative inheritance include the number of genes involved in controlling a trait, the degree of dominance/recessiveness of each gene, and the environment in which the plant grows.

Significance: Understanding quantitative inheritance is important for plant breeding programs, as breeders often aim to develop cultivars that exhibit specific quantitative traits such as yield, disease resistance, or drought tolerance.

Continuous Variation

Continuous variation refers to the range of variation seen in a trait that is controlled by multiple genes and influenced by environmental factors.

In continuous variation, the expression of a trait is influenced by many genes, each of which has a small effect. This results in a range of values for the trait rather than discrete categories.

The factors that influence continuous variation include the number of genes involved in controlling a trait, the degree of dominance/recessiveness of each gene, and the environment in which the plant grows.

Understanding continuous variation is important for plant breeding programs, as it allows breeders to select for specific values of quantitative traits within a population.

Discontinuous Variation

Discontinuous variation refers to the range of variation seen in a trait that is controlled by a small number of genes and not influenced by environmental factors.

In discontinuous variation, the expression of a trait is controlled by a small number of genes, each of which has a large effect. This results in distinct categories or phenotypes for the trait.

The factors that influence discontinuous variation include the number of genes involved in controlling a trait and the degree of dominance/recessiveness of each gene.

Understanding discontinuous variation is important for plant breeding programs, as it allows breeders to select for specific traits that exhibit distinct phenotypes.

Quantitative inheritance, continuous variation, and discontinuous variation are important concepts in agriculture as they help in understanding the inheritance patterns of plant traits and their implications for breeding programs. By understanding these concepts, plant breeders can develop cultivars that exhibit specific quantitative and qualitative traits, leading to increased yield, disease resistance, and other desirable characteristics in crops.

MONOGENIC & POLYGENIC INHERITANCE

Monogenic and polygenic inheritance are two important types of genetic inheritance that play a significant role in shaping the characteristics and traits of plants in agriculture.

Monogenic inheritance refers to the inheritance of traits that are determined by a single gene, which is responsible for the expression of the trait. This type of inheritance follows Mendelian principles, where a single gene determines a single trait, and the offspring will inherit one allele from each parent. Examples of monogenic inheritance in plants include flower color, seed shape, and leaf shape.

Polygenic inheritance, on the other hand, refers to the inheritance of traits that are determined by multiple genes. This type of inheritance is more complex than monogenic inheritance, as the expression of the trait is influenced by multiple genes, each with a small effect. Polygenic inheritance can result in continuous variation of traits, rather than discrete traits as seen in monogenic inheritance. Examples of polygenic inheritance in plants include plant height, yield, and disease resistance.

Factors that influence monogenic and polygenic inheritance include the genetic makeup of the parents, environmental factors, and gene interactions. The expression of the trait can be influenced by both genetic and environmental factors, and it can vary from individual to individual.

The significance of understanding monogenic and polygenic inheritance in agriculture is immense. Farmers can use this knowledge to breed plants with desirable traits, such as high yield or disease resistance, by selecting individuals with the desired traits and crossing them to produce offspring with improved traits. This process is known as selective breeding or artificial selection.

Monogenic and polygenic inheritance are two important types of genetic inheritance that shape the traits and characteristics of plants in agriculture. Understanding these types of inheritance can help farmers improve crop yield, disease resistance, and other desirable traits through selective breeding.

ROLE OF GENETICS IN PLANT BREEDING

Plant Breeding

- Plant breeding is an applied branch of botany focused on improving agricultural crops.
- It has played a significant role in increasing food production worldwide and is of increasing importance in the field of agriculture.
- According to Riley (1978), plant breeding is a technology used to develop superior crop plants/ varieties for various purposes.
- Frankel (1958) defined plant breeding as the genetic adjustment of plants to serve humans.
- Plant breeding involves changing the genotype of plants to make them more useful.
- It is both an art and a science and has been practiced since humans began cultivating plants.

Genetics in Relation to Plant Breeding

- Plant breeding is based on genetic principles applied to improve plants.
- Variation is an important genetic principle used to improve plants.
- Variations may be due to genotype or environment.
- For example, rice and wheat plants grown on fertile soil will show more vigor and productivity than those grown on infertile soil.
- These variations in growth and development are caused by the specific environment in which the plants are grown.
- Genotypic variation in plants results from different genetic characters and remains unchanged by environmental conditions.
- Environmental variation may be observed by growing plants with similar genotypes in different environments, while genotypic variation can be

observed by growing different varieties or species in similar environments.

- Heritable variation in plants originates from gene recombination after hybridization, spontaneous mutations, and polyploidy.
- These processes have allowed plant species to evolve in nature and reach their present stage of development.
- Genotypic and environmental variations are not independent of each other, but they interact and affect the plant.
- The mechanism of heredity is dependent upon the behavior of chromosomes and the genes they carry.
- Chromosomes carry genes that determine the expression of various traits or characteristics in plants.
- The inheritance of genes and traits follows the laws of Mendelian genetics, which involve the segregation and independent assortment of genes during meiosis.

Plant breeders use a mixed population of plant species with hereditary variations to select plants with desirable traits such as seed color, size, plant height, leaf size and shape, disease resistance, etc.

Genes located on chromosomes determine the traits of a plant, and each gene has a specific position on the chromosome. Genes have alternative forms called alleles, which determine the contrasting forms of traits. Genes may be dominant (R) or recessive (r).

Plants with identical genes at a given locus on homologous chromosomes are homozygous, while those with unlike genes are heterozygous. The appearance of a plant is called its phenotype, while its genetic makeup is called its genotype.

Chromosomes are rod-shaped structures present in the nucleus of a cell that carry genes and play an important role in heredity.

Chromosomes occur singly (haploid) in spores and in pairs (diploid) in body cells. The chromosome number is constant within a species, and they divide longitudinally during mitosis, while homologous chromosomes separate during meiosis.

The mechanism of heredity can be explained with a single-gene character.

Linkage

- Genes tend to be inherited in groups due to their location on the same chromosome, known as linkage.
- A string of genes on a chromosome is called a linkage group, with the number of linkage groups being equal to the number of chromosome pairs.
- Completely linked genes on a chromosome do not allow for new combinations within the same linkage group, but recombination can occur through crossing over.
- A breeder can select plants with recombination of linked genes for desirable traits.
- Linkage can be in coupling phase (two dominant genes linked with a recessive gene) or repulsion phase (one dominant and recessive gene linked with one recessive and dominant gene).

Gene Interaction

- Gene interaction is the phenomenon in which two or more genes affect the expression of each other in various ways to develop a single character in an organism.
- Two dominant genes coming together can produce a different phenotype than their own, leading to modification of the normal F_2 phenotypic ratio.
- Gene interaction affects the expression of one character and adds variability by producing new phenotypes:

Heterosis or Hybrid Vigour

- Hybrid vigor or heterosis is the increased productivity or superiority of the hybrid offspring over its parents.
- It occurs when two homozygous inbred plants of genetically unlike constitution are crossed together.
- The resulting hybrid plants are usually more vigorous, productive, taller and sturdier than either of the parents.
- The term heterosis was coined by G.H. Shull in 1914 and it means "a different condition" in Greek.

Polyploidy and Plant Breeding

- Polyploidy is the condition in which an organism has more than two sets of chromosomes or genomes in their somatic cells.
- Polyploids may be Euploids (having exact multiple of the basic chromosome number in $3n$, $4n$, etc) or Aneuploids (having an unequal number of chromosomes i.e., Monosomic ($2n - 1$), Nullisomic ($2n - 2$), Trisomic ($2n + 1$), Tetrasomic ($2n + 2$), etc.).
- Polyploidy has played a significant role in plant breeding as it results in larger and stronger plants with bigger fruits, flowers, and seeds.
- Polyploids also tend to have greater genetic variation which allows breeders to select for desirable traits in the offspring.

Pollination

- Pollination is the transfer of pollen from anthers to stigmas.

- Self-pollination or autogamy occurs when pollen from an anther falls on the stigma of the same flower.
- Cross-pollination or allogamy occurs when pollen from an anther falls on the stigma of another flower of a different plant.
- Geitonogamy occurs when pollen from an anther falls on the stigma of another flower of the same plant.

Self Pollination

- Self-pollination is the transfer of pollen from and to the stigma within the same flower and is found in bisexual flowers.
- In most species, self-pollination is not complete and cross-pollination may occur up to 5%.
- There are various mechanisms or contrivances that promote or facilitate self-pollination.
- Bisexuality: male and female sexual organs are present in the same flower, e.g. wheat, rice, groundnut, etc.
- *Homogamy:* male and female sexual organs mature at the same time, e.g. wheat, groundnut, etc.
- *Cleistogamy:* flowers do not open at all and ensure complete self-pollination, e.g. oat, barley, wheat, grasses, etc.
- *Chasmogamy:* in some species, flowers open only after pollination has taken place, e.g. barley, wheat, oat, and many cereals.
- In crops like tomato and brinjal, the stigma is closely surrounded by anthers, ensuring self-pollination after the flower opens.
- In crops like pea, bean, and soybean, the flower opens but the stigma and anther are hidden by floral organs, ensuring self-pollination.
- In a few species, stigmas become receptive and elongate through the staminal column, ensuring self-pollination.

Genetic Consequences of Self-Pollination

- Self-pollination leads to a rapid increase in homozygosity, making self-pollinated species highly homozygous in nature.
- Self-pollinated species do not show inbreeding depression and exhibit considerable heterosis.

Cross-Pollination

- Cross-pollination is the transfer of pollen from a flower to the stigma of another flower or plant.
- Cross-pollination may be brought about by wind, water, insects, or animals.
- Anemophily refers to pollination by wind, hydrophily by water, entomophily by insects, and zoophily by animals.
- In most cross-pollinated species, such as bajra, maize, sunflower, alfalfa, and castor, cross-pollination is not complete and self-pollination may occur up to 5-10%.

Mechanisms that Facilitate Cross Pollination

- **Dicliny (Unisexuality):** Condition where flower is either staminate or pistilate.
  - (*a*) **Monoecy:** Staminate and pistilate flowers occur in the same plant, either in the same inflorescence. E.g. Maize, Cucurbit, Aonla, etc.
  - (*b*) **Dioecy:** Male and female flowers are present on different plants. E.g. Papaya, hemp, date, palm, etc.
- **Dichogamy:** Anther and stigma of hermaphrodite flower mature at different times, facilitating cross pollination.
  - (*a*) **Protogyny:** Gynoecium matures earlier than the androecium. E.g. Bajara.
  - (*b*) **Protandry:** Androecium matures earlier than gynoecium. E.g. marigold, maize, cotton, etc.
- **Heterostyly:** Different lengths of style and filaments. E.g. Linseed.
- **Herkogamy:** Presence of physical barriers or mechanical obstacles between the anther and stigma ensures cross pollination. E.g. Rui *(Calotropic gigantia)*.
- In lucerne or alfalfa, the stigma is covered by a waxy film and does not become receptive unless this film is broken by honeybees.
- A combination of two or more of the above mechanisms may occur in some species, e.g. Maize - Monoecy and Protandry.
- **Self-Incompatibility:** Refers to the failure of pollen from a flower to fertilize the same flower or other flowers on the same plant. It may be saprophytic or gametophilic. E.g. Mustard, tobacco, sunflowers, reddish.
- **Male Sterility:** Refers to the absence of functional pollen grains in a hermaphrodite flower.

Methods of Breeding in Field Crops-Introduction, Selection, Hybridization, Mutation and Polyploidy

Methods of breeding in field crops involve various techniques to develop new plant varieties with desirable traits such as high yield, disease resistance, drought tolerance, and better quality. Some of the important methods of breeding in field crops are:

Plant Introduction

- Plant introduction refers to acquiring superior varieties by importing them from other areas.

- It involves taking or introducing plants, genotypes, or groups of genotypes into new environments where they were not previously grown.
- Introduction can include new varieties of crops already grown in the area, wild relatives of crop species, or entirely new crop species.
- Plant introduction can occur within a country, between countries, or between states or regions within a country.
- The plants may be introduced from countries of other continents.
- An example of plant introduction is the introduction of Ridley wheat varieties from Australia.

Introduction may be Classified into Two Categories

- Primary introduction occurs when the introduced variety is well-suited to the new environment and is directly released for commercial cultivation without any changes to the original genotype.
- An example of primary introduction is the introduction of semi-dwarf wheat varieties Sonora, Lerma Rojo and semi-dwarf rice varieties TN-1, IR-8, IR-28, and IR-36.
- Secondary introduction occurs when the introduced variety is subjected to selection to isolate a superior variety or is hybridized with a local variety to transfer one or a few desirable characters to the local variety.
- Secondary introduction is more common than primary introduction, especially in countries with well-organized crop improvement programs.
- An example of secondary introduction is the selection of Kalyan Sona and Sonalika varieties from the material introduced from CIMMYT (Centro International de Mejoramieno de maize 'Y' Trigo), commonly known as the International Centre for Maize and Wheat Research.

Selection

One of the oldest method of breeding and is the basis for all crop improvement, practised by farmer in ancient times. Selection is essentially based on the phenotype of plants. Consequently the effectiveness of selection primarily depends upon the degree to which the phenotypes of plants reflect their genotype.

- Selection is one of the oldest breeding methods and is the basis for all crop improvement. Farmers have practiced selection since ancient times.
- Selection is primarily based on the phenotype of plants. The effectiveness of selection depends on how well the phenotypes of plants reflect their genotype.
- Selection can be natural or artificial, and it involves isolating individual or groups of plants from a mixed population.
- Before domestication, crop species were subjected to natural selection, resulting in the evolution of several local varieties of crops.
- After domestication, humans knowingly or unknowingly practiced artificial selection, which involves deliberate selection of plants with desired traits.
- For a long time under domestication, natural selection may have been more valuable, but currently, breeding methods entirely depend on artificial selection.
- Selection has two basic characteristics or limitations: (i) it is effective for heritable differences and (ii) it does not create variation; it only utilizes the variation already present in the population.
- Therefore, the two basic requirements of selection are: (a) variation must be present in the population and (b) variation must be heritable.

Hybridization

- Hybridization is the process that results in the formation of a hybrid, which is an individual produced as a result of a cross between two genetically different parents.
- Hybridization can occur naturally or artificially.
- The production of a hybrid by crossing two individuals of unlike genetic constitution is known as hybridization.
- Hybridization is an important method for combining the desirable traits of different plants.
- Hybridization does not change the genetic contents of organisms, but it produces new combinations of genes.
- The first recorded instance of natural hybridization was in corn by Cotton Mather in 1716. The first artificial interspecific plant hybrid was produced by Thomas Fairchild in 1717, commonly known as the 'Fairchild Mule'.
- The practical use of hybridization in crop improvement began with German botanist Joseph Koerauter in 1760.
- Since Mendel's time, hybridization has become the key method of crop improvement, and today it is the most common method used in crop improvement.
- The vast majority of crop varieties have resulted from hybridization.

Objectives of Hybridization

- To artificially create a variable population for the selection of types with desired combinations of characters.

- To combine the desired characters into a single individual.
- To exploit and utilize the hybrid varieties.

Types of Hybridization

Hybridization may be of following types:

1. **Intra-varietal hybridization:** The crosses are made between the plants of the same variety.
2. **Inter-varietal or Intraspecific hybridization:** The crosses are made between the plants belonging to two different varieties.
3. **Interspecific hybridization or intragenic hybridization:** The crosses are made between two different species of the same genus.
4. **Introgressive hybridization:** Transfer of some genes from one species into the genome of the other species is known as introgressive hybridization.
5. **Distant hybridization or wide crossing:** The crosses between different species of the same genus or different genera of the same family are also known as distant hybridization or wide crossing.

Procedure of Hybridization

(*i*) **Selection of parents:** The selection of parents depends upon the aims and objectives of breeding. Parental plants must be selected from the local areas and are supposed to be the best suited to the existing conditions.

(*ii*) **Selfing of parents or artificial self-pollination:** It is essential for inducing homozygosity for eliminating the undesirable characters and obtaining inbreeds.

(*iii*) **Emasculation:** It is the third step in hybridization. Inbreeds are grown under normal conditions and are emasculated. Emasculation is the removal of stamens from female parent before they burst and shed their pollens.

It can be defined as the removal of stamens or anthers or the killing of the pollen grains of a flower without affecting in any way the female reproductive organs. Emasculation is not required in unisexual plants but it is essential in bisexual or self-pollinated plants.

(*iv*) **Bagging:**

- The emasculated flower or inflorescence is immediately bagged to prevent pollination by foreign pollen.
- Bags made of paper, butter paper, glassine, or fine cloth are used.
- Butter paper or vegetable parchment bags are commonly used.
- The bags are tied to the base of the inflorescence or to the stalk of the flower using thread, wire, or pins.
- Bagging is done with emasculation in bisexual plants and before stigma receptivity and anther dehiscence in unisexual plants.
- Male and female flowers are bagged separately to prevent contamination in male flowers and cross-pollination in female flowers.

(*v*) **Tagging:**

- Emasculated flowers are tagged just after bagging.
- Circular tags of about 3 cm or rectangular tags of about 3 × 2 cm are used.
- Tags are attached to the base of the flower or inflorescence using thread.
- The information on the tag should be brief but complete, including the following:
  1. Number referring to the field record.
  2. Date of emasculation.
  3. Date of crossing.
  4. Name of the female parent is written first followed by a cross sign (x) and then the male parent, e.g., C x D denotes that C is the female parent and D is the male parent.

(*vi*) **Crossing:**

- Artificial cross-pollination between genetically dissimilar plants.
- Pollen grains collected in petri dishes or paper bags.
- Pollen grains applied to receptive stigma of emasculated flowers using brush, paper, toothpick or forceps.
- In some crops, inflorescences of both parents are enclosed in the same bag.

(*vii*) **Harvesting and storing the F1 seeds:**

- Crossed heads or pods of desirable plants harvested.
- Harvested material is dried completely and threshed.
- Seeds stored properly with original tags.

(*viii*) **Raising the F1 generation:**

- Stored seeds sown separately in the following season to raise F1 generation.
- Plants of F1 generation are the offspring of cross seeds and hence are hybrids.

Mutation

- A mutation is a sudden heritable change in a characteristic of an organism caused by changes in the base sequences of genes.
- Mutations are classified into two types: spontaneous and induced mutations.

- Spontaneous mutations occur naturally in populations without any treatment, and their frequency is generally low, around one in ten lacs.
- Induced mutations are artificially induced by exposure to certain physical or chemical agents known as mutagens.
- Mutation breeding is the use of induced mutations for crop improvement.
- Induced mutations have a significant advantage over spontaneous mutations because they occur at a relatively higher frequency, making them more practical to work with.

Characteristics of Mutations

1. Mutations can be recessive or dominant.
2. Most mutations are harmful, but a small percentage (0.1%) can be beneficial.
3. Mutations are random and can occur in any gene, although some genes may have a higher mutation rate than others.
4. Mutations can be recurrent, meaning the same mutation can occur multiple times.
5. Induced mutations often result in pleiotropy, which is caused by mutations in closely linked genes.

Mutagen

Agents used for induction of mutations are known as mutagens. The mutagens are classified into two groups, physical and chemical mutagens.

Type of Mutagen

1. Physical mutagen:

(*a*) **Ionizing radiation:** Alpha, Beta, and gamma rays of radioactive substances, Neutrons, and X rays are examples of ionizing radiation. These radiations cause ionization in atoms, leading to chemical changes in the molecules they are part of. If the molecule is a gene and it duplicates its new pattern, the result of the change is a mutation.

(*b*) **Non-ionizing radiation:** Ultra violet (UV) light is the only non-ionizing radiation capable of inducing mutations. UV radiation can be obtained from a mercury vapor lamp. When compounds absorb energy from non-ionizing radiation, their electrons are raised to higher energy levels (excitation). It results in increased reactivity of the affected molecules leading to mutations.

2. Chemical mutagens:

(*i*) Alkylating agents - e.g., EMS (Ethyl Methane Sulphonate) MMS (Methyl Methane Sulphonate).

(*ii*) Acridine dyes - e.g., Ethidium Bromide, acriflavine, proflavine.

(*iii*) Base analogs - e.g., 5 Bromouracil, 5 - Chlorouracil.

(*iv*) Others - e.g., Nitrous acid, hydroxylamine, sodium azide.

Mutagenesis: Treating a biological material with a mutagen to induce mutations is known as mutagenesis. Exposure of a biological material to radiation (x-rays, gamma rays, etc.) is known as irradiation.

Tissue and Cell Culture

Tissue and cell culture techniques have revolutionized the field of agriculture by enabling the production of large numbers of genetically identical plants with desirable traits. These techniques involve growing plants from small pieces of plant tissue or single cells in a laboratory setting. Tissue and cell culture can be used for various purposes in agriculture, including micropropagation of plants, conservation of rare or endangered plant species, production of genetically modified plants, and production of secondary metabolites.

Techniques Used

Tissue culture techniques involve several steps, including explant selection and preparation, sterilization of explants, nutrient media preparation, and plant regeneration. Explants are small pieces of plant tissue, such as leaves, stems, or embryos, which are selected based on the desired purpose. The selected explants are then sterilized using chemical agents or heat to eliminate any potential contaminants. Nutrient media, which contains all the necessary nutrients for plant growth, is then prepared and used to support the growth of the explants. Finally, the regenerated plantlets are transferred to soil and acclimatized to their natural environment.

Applications in Agriculture

Tissue and cell culture techniques have several applications in agriculture, including:

Micropropagation of Plants: Tissue culture techniques can be used to produce large numbers of genetically identical plants with desirable traits, which is known as micropropagation. This technique is particularly useful for crops that are difficult to propagate using traditional methods, such as clonally propagated crops like bananas and grapes.

Conservation of Rare or Endangered Plant Species: Tissue culture techniques can be used to preserve rare or endangered plant species by storing their cells in vitro. This technique, known as cryopreservation, can help to maintain genetic diversity and prevent the extinction of plant species.

Production of Genetically Modified Plants: Tissue culture techniques can be used to produce genetically modified plants with specific traits, such as increased resistance to pests or environmental stresses. This is achieved by introducing foreign genes into the plant cells using various methods, such as biolistics or Agrobacterium-mediated transformation.

Production of Secondary Metabolites: Tissue culture techniques can be used to produce secondary metabolites, such as alkaloids, flavonoids, and terpenoids, which are used in the pharmaceutical, cosmetic, and food industries. This is achieved by manipulating the growth conditions of the plant cells, such as changing the nutrient media or adding plant hormones.

Plant Breeding and Genetic Improvement: Tissue culture techniques can be used to accelerate the process of plant breeding and genetic improvement. This is achieved by selecting and propagating plants with desirable traits, such as disease resistance or high yield, and then using tissue culture techniques to produce large numbers of genetically identical plants with those traits.

Tissue and cell culture techniques have revolutionized agriculture by providing efficient and reliable methods for the propagation of plants, preservation of genetic diversity, production of genetically modified plants, production of secondary metabolites, and plant breeding and genetic improvement.

These techniques have enabled the production of high-quality, disease-free planting material, the preservation of rare and endangered plant species, and the development of crops with improved resistance to pests and diseases, increased tolerance to abiotic stresses, and enhanced nutritional value. The application of tissue and cell culture techniques in agriculture is likely to continue to grow in the future, as they provide sustainable and eco-friendly methods for plant propagation and genetic improvement.

PLANT BIOTECHNOLOGY-DEFINITION AND SCOPE IN CROP PRODUCTION

Plant biotechnology is an interdisciplinary field of science that uses living organisms, cells, and molecules to improve crop production. It is an emerging field that combines principles of genetics, molecular biology, microbiology, biochemistry, and engineering to develop better crop varieties, enhance crop productivity, and improve food security. Plant biotechnology involves the use of various tools and techniques to manipulate the genetic makeup of plants and improve their traits.

One of the most important techniques used in plant biotechnology is genetic engineering or recombinant DNA technology. This involves the insertion or deletion of genes into the genome of a plant to modify its characteristics. Genetic engineering has been used to develop crop plants that are resistant to pests and diseases, have improved nutritional value, and can grow under adverse environmental conditions.

Another important tool used in plant biotechnology is tissue culture. Tissue culture involves the growth of plant cells, tissues, or organs in vitro under controlled conditions. This technique has been used to produce disease-free plants, develop new crop varieties, and regenerate plants from cells.

Plant biotechnology also includes the use of molecular markers to identify and characterize specific genes or traits in plants. Molecular markers can be used to select plants with desirable traits, such as disease resistance, high yield, or improved quality, and to identify genes associated with specific traits.

The scope of plant biotechnology in crop production is vast. It can be used to develop crops that are resistant to pests and diseases, have improved nutritional value, and can grow under adverse environmental conditions. Plant biotechnology can also be used to improve the efficiency of plant breeding programs, reducing the time required to develop new crop varieties. It has also been used to develop crops that produce pharmaceuticals or industrial products, such as biofuels or bioplastics.

Plant biotechnology is an emerging field that has the potential to revolutionize crop production. By using tools and techniques such as genetic engineering, tissue culture, and molecular markers, plant biotechnology can be used to develop crops that are more productive, more nutritious, and more resilient to environmental stresses. As such, it has become an important tool for ensuring food security in a world with a growing population and changing climate.

BIOCHEMISTRY

The term Biochemistry was first introduced by, German scientist/chemist CARL NEUBERG in 1903.

Biochemistry may be defined as a science concerned with chemical nature and chemical behaviour of the living matter. Biochemistry may be treated as a discipline in which biological phenomenon are analyzed in terms of chemistry. Hence termed as Biological Chemistry or Chemical Biology

Biochemistry deals with study of:

- The nature of the chemical constituents of the living matter and the chemical substances produced by living things.
- The functions and transformations of their chemical entities in biological systems.
- The chemical and energetic changes associated with the transformation in the course of the activity of living matter.

Scope and Importance of Biochemistry in Agriculture

- To evaluate nutritive value of cereals, pulses, poultry and cattle feed.

- Development and exploitation of better genotypes.
- Removal and inactivation of toxic or anti nutritional factors present in food grains in general and grain legumes in particular by breeding and chemical treatments, *e.g.* BOAA in Lakh dal, Trypsin inhibitors of soybean, Aflatoxins of groundnut.
- Food preservation and processing technology and post-harvest physiology of fruit crops and vegetables and their nutritional quality.
- Biochemistry of disease and pest resistance.
- Biochemistry of drought resistance, proline and hydroxyproline imparts drought resistance to Jowar.
- Formulation of balanced diet
- Use of nonconventional sources of protein foods viz., single cell proteins, fish protein concentrates, mushrooms and leaf proteins.
- Developments in the field of inter mediatory metabolism *i.e.*, synthesis and degradation of constituents of living tissues.

Biomolecule

An organic compound normally present as an essential component of living organism.

Characteristics of Biomolecules:

- Most of them are organic compounds.
- They have specific shapes and dimensions.
- Functional group determines their chemical properties.
- Many of them are asymmetric.
- Macromolecules are large molecules and are constructed from small building block molecules.
- Building block molecules have simple structure.
- Biomolecules first gorse by chemical evolution.

Important Biomolecules of life:

- **Water:** Being the universal solvent and major constituents (60%) of any living body without which life is impossible. It acts as a media for the physiological and biochemical reactions in the body itself. Maintain the body in the required turgid condition.
- **Carbohydrates:** It is very important for source of energy for any physical body function.
- **Proteins:** These are very important from body maintenance point of view, helps in tissue, cell formation.
- **Lipids:** These are very important from energy source as well as human nutrition point of view.
- **Nucleic Acids:** Nucleic acids are very important as DNA carries the hereditary information and RNA helps in protein formation for the body.
- **Enzymes:** Enzymes are simple or combined proteins acting as specific catalysts and activates the various biochemical and metabolic processes within the body.

Table: Fundamental Biological Molecules (Biomolecules)

Sr. No.	Small Molecule	Atomic Constituents	Derived Macro-Molecule
1.	Amino Acid	C, H, O, N (S)	Proteins
2.	Sugars	C, H, O	Starch, Glycogen
3.	Fatty Acids	C, H, O	Fats, Oils
4.	Purines and Pyrimidine	C, H, O, N	Nucleic Acids
5.	Nucleotide	C, H, O, N, P	Nucleic Acids (DNA and RNA)

TEST FOR SOIL pH

The pH is the negative logarithm of the hydrogen ion activity or the logarithm of the reciprocal of the H ion concentration.

$$pH = -\log_{10} [H^+]$$

The pH of pure water at 25°C is 7 while that of acid is below 7 and that of base is above 7.

Significance of Soil pH Measurement

Plant can grow on different types of soils with wide varieties of properties and wide ranges of pH. However, plants do have a preference for a specific range of soil reactions or soil pH. In above figure we have seen different ranges of soil pH like from slightly acidic to very strong acid from slightly alkaline to very strongly alkaline and intermediate of both, neutral.

This soil reaction does have its effects on availability of nutrients and thus on growth of plants. Soil pH has influence on various soil properties like chemical, physical and biological.

Rating Chart for Soil pH:

Less than 6.0	: Acidic
7.0 – 8.5	: Normal
8.6 – 9.0	: Tendency to become alkaline.
Above 9.0	: Alkali

Methods of pH Measurement

- **Glass Electrode pH Meter:** The glass electrode generally used for the pH measurement employes a glass membrane of special, chemically pure, soft glass paired with a calomel reference electrode are used for measuring the soil pH.
- **Hydrogen Electrode:** In order to measure hydrogen ion concentrations of pH of a solution use of hydrogen gas as a metal electrode and dip in a

solution under test and measure the electrode potential.

- **Quinhydrone Electrode:** It consists of equimolecular mixture of quinone and hydroquinone added directly to the solution under test. This electrode does not give correct reading in alkaline solution for pH greater than 9.0.

Factors Affecting pH Measurement

- **Soil Solution Ratio:** Condition being the same, the more water added to the soil sample the higher the soil pH.
- **Salt and Electrolyte Content:** A salt also increases the hydrolysis of Al and Fe ions, increasing the H^+ in solution. The salts lower the pH. The use of 0.01 M $CaCl_2$ has been recommend as a solution which masks small differences in salt contents without displacing a large fractions of the hydrogen ions.
- **Degree of Dissociations of Hydrogen Ions:** Soil colloids differ in the amounts of discrete hydroxyl groups capable of ionizing the hydrogen ions.
- **Type of the Acidity:** Hydrogen ions adsorbed to electrostatic bands that have great tendency to dissociate than those from the OH^- groups.
- **CO_2 Content:** The CO_2 dissolved in water forming H_2CO_3 lowers the pH markedly.
- **Liquid Junction Potential:** Appreciable liquid junction potential (Ej) may occur at the liquid junction particularly into very concentrated colloidal electro suspension. Liquid junction potential kept low by the use of a saturated KCl solution.
- **Equipment and Procedure:** Major difference in the pH appears due to inadequate standardization of the equipment rather than a limitation of the equipment.

Method of Soil pH Measurement—Glass Electrode pH Meter

The glass electrode generally used for the pH measurement employes a glass membrane of special, chemically pure, soft glass paired with a calomel reference electrode are used for measuring the soil pH.

Composition of corning glass electrode: 72% SiO_2, 6.0% CaO and 22.0% Na_2O.

1. Vacuum tube volt meter
2. Hg, Hg_2Cl_2 Half cell
3. Saturated KCl.
4. Glass membrane
5. KCl crystals
6. HCl
7. Test solution

Glass electrode system for measurement of pH.

Across the glass membrane develops an electrical potential that is proportional to the difference in pH, between the two slide in accord with concentration cell in which the glass membrane and liquid junction. A systematical potential E develops across the glass membrane even, when solution of the same H^+ ion activity is on the two sides. For this reason the meter must be calibrated with the standards buffer solution.

Advantages of the Glass Electrode pH Meter:

1. It does not expel dissolved gases such as CO_2 from the system under measurement.
2. It is adaptable to thick fluid, paste and coloured solution.
3. It is not affected by oxidizing and reducing solution in contrast to quinhydrone or hydrogen electrode.
4. It does not require H_2 gas or catalytic surface required by H electrode.
5. It has relatively low salt error.
6. After standardization give accuracy within 0.1 pH unit with care within 0.02 pH unit.
7. Rapid convenient in expansive and adaptable for long term recording.

Precaution in the Use of Glass Electrode:

1. Electrode is not allowed to remain in the test solution or suspension longer than necessary especially if more alkaline than pH 9.0.
2. Immediately after testing, the electrode is washed off with a strong stream of distilled water from a wash bottle. If the system was alkaline, the electrode should be dipped for a few second in the acid pH buffer or dilute HCl to remove the film of $CaCO_3$ that some time forms.
3. For storage after cleaning the electrode is suspended in distilled water and the system is protected from to evaporation. Drying out of the electrode is avoided.
4. Failure of the glass electrode pH meter is indicated, when, after standardization it gives slow response to large pH changes.

CARBOHYDRATES

Carbohydrates are defined as polyhydroxy aldehydes or polyhydroxy ketones and the substances which yield these derivatives on hydrolysis.

Functions of Carbohydrates:

- Supply energy
- Stored energy for future use
- Structural constituents
- Proteins sparing action

- Necessary for oxidation of protein and fat
- Necessary for synthesis of nonessential amino acids
- Conserve water and electrolyte
- Beneficial effect on micro flora.

Classification of Carbohydrates

Carbohydrates are classified into three major classes on the basis of complexity and behaviour on hydrolysis

1. Monosaccharides
2. Oligosaccharides
3. Polysaccharides

1. Monosaccharides: Simple sugars are cannot be hydrolyzed into smaller units. Depending upon no. of carbon in a unit, monosaccharides are subdivided into a dioses to decoses. More common subclasses of monosaccharides are:

Aldoses:

Aldotrioses *e.g.* Glycerose,
Aldotertroses *e.g.* Erythrose,
Aldopentoses *e.g.* Ribose,
Aldohexoses *e.g.* Glucose, Galatose
Aldoheptose *e.g.* Glucoheptose.

Ketoses:

Ketotrioses *e.g.*, Dihydroxyacetone,
Ketotetroses *e.g.*, Erythrulose,
Ketopentoses *e.g.*, Ribulose,
Ketohexoses *e.g.*, Fructose,
Ketoheptose *e.g.*, Sedoheptulose.

Properties of Monosaccharides:

(*a*) Muta-rotation
(*b*) Glycoside Formation
(*c*) Reducing Power
(*d*) Reduction
(*e*) Oxidation with mild and strong oxidizing agent
(*f*) Methylation/Esterification
(*g*) Dehydration
(*h*) Form osazone with phenyl hydrazine.

2. Oligosaccharide: Oligosaccharides are polymers of monosaccharides containing two to ten residues accumulate in vacuole while polysaccharides in plastids, they are classified as

(*a*) **Disaccharides:** Yield two mono saccharides on hydrolysis.

(*i*) **Reducing Disaccharides:** *e.g.* Maltose (Glucose + Glucose), Lactose (Galactose + Glucose), other examples are Isomaltose, Cellobiose.

(*ii*) **Non Reducing Disaccharides:** Sucrose (Glucose + Fructose)

(*b*) **Trisaccharides:** *e.g.* Raffinose (Glucose + Fructose + Galactose) found in cotton seed and sugar beet.

(*c*) **Tetrasaccharides:** Yield 4 mono saccharides on hydrolysis *e.g.* stachyose (Glucose + Fructose + Galactose + Galactose) (only tetrasaccharide known to exist in plant).

3. Polysaccharides: Polysaccharides are polymeric anhydrides of monosaccharides. The long chain polymers are either straight chain or branched. They are also called glycanes.

Classification of Polysaccharides:

1. On the Basis of Function:
   (*a*) Storage *e.g.* Starch, Glycogen
   (*b*) Structural *e.g.* Cellulose, Pectin
2. On the Basis of Composition:
   (*a*) Homo polysaccharides
   (*b*) Hetero polysaccharides

(*a*) Homo Polysaccharides:

On hydrolysis gives single monosaccharide units:

(*i*) **Pentosan:** Contains pentoses ($C_5H_8O_4$).

(*ii*) **Hexosans:** Contains hexoses ($C_6H_{10}O_5$) subdivided in to

(A) **Glucosans:** Polymer or glucose *e.g.* Starch, Glycogen
(B) **Fructosans:** Polymer or fructose *e.g.* Inulin
(C) **Galactans:** Polymer of galactose *e.g.* Galactan
(D) **Mannans:** Polymer of mannose *e.g.* Mananas.

(*b*) Hetero Polysaccharide: *e.g.* Hyaluronic acid, Chondroitin sulphates.

(A) **Gum:** Consist of arabinose, rhamnose, galactose and glucoronic acid.

(B) **Agar:** The sulphuric acid esters of galactans consists of galactose, galactouronic acid.

(C) **Pectins:** Fundamental unit is pectic acid, consist of arabinose, galactose, galactouronic acid.

Functions of Polysaccharides:

1. They serve as structural components of the cells
2. They serve as stored form of energy
3. They serve as nutrient.

Structure and Properties of Starch: Consist of two components, Amyloses and Amylopectin. Amylose is a long chain polysaccharides containing α-D glucose molecules linked by 1-4 glycosidic linkages, produce blue colour with iodine. Amylopectin is a branched chain polysaccharides consisting α-D-glucose molecules linked by 1-4 glycosidic linkage and branches by 1-6, linkage produce purplish colour with iodine and forms a gel with hot water.

Cellulose: It is structural polysaccharide found in cell walls of plants, made up of long chains of α-D-Glucose molecules linked by 1-4 linkages, no branching, yield on hydrolysis crystalline D-glucose.

Pectin: Present in apple, lemon, form gel with sugar sole, contains galactouronic acid, galactose and arabinose.

Plant Proteins and their Quality, Essential Amino Acids and Limiting Amino Acids

- Between 10 and 30% of the protein in forage is converted into human food by ruminants, whereas 40 to 60% of the protein can be extracted. The approximate consequences of fractionating forage crop rather than using it as fodder.
- Leaves are the main site of protein synthesis and there are losses during translocation to other parts of a plant.
- When LP is made, the crop is harvested when less mature than when silage is made, and much less mature than when hay is made or a conventional crap is taken, the cost of harvesting is greater but an immature crop is not at risk for so long from diseases and pests.
- Crops that regrow several times after being cut young, or perennial crops, maintain cover on the ground, this enables fuller use to be made of sunlight and protects the ground from erosion.
- The fibrous residue contains the protein that was not extracted. Depending on the processing conditions, it can have two to five times as great a percentage of dry matter as the original crop and can therefore be dried to produce conserved ruminant feed economically.

Crops: Species and varieties selected for seed production or for a use other than LP extraction have been the source of most of the LP made in bulk. If varieties, possibly of species not at present used in agriculture, were investigated, yields would probably be greater than those so far attained.

Cowpea *(Vigna unguiculata)* gave 895 kg/ha in 80 days i.e., more than 4 tons if that rate could have been maintained for a year. In short term experiments yields as great as 17 kg of extracted protein per ha per day have been claimed.

Separation of Extract from Fiber: The yields given above were measured on 4 to 5 kg samples of leaf taken from within a crop, pulping them in the unit designed for IBP (Davys & Pixie, 1969), pressing a sample in the unit similarly designed and measuring the amount of protein perceptible from the extract with trichloroacetic acid. In large-scale work it is usually advantageous to re-extract the fiber, this can give half as much protein again as a single extraction, but it would be difficult in the laboratory to get quantitative and repeatable results from a double extraction. The manner in which increasing skill in agronomy and processing have increased yields at Rothamsted.

Separation of Protein from Extract: Heat coagulation is generally accepted as the most satisfactory method for making a protein curd. Green, predominantly 'chloroplastic', protein coagulates at 50 to 60°C, if that is separated; colourless 'cytoplasmic' protein separates at 70°C. No more protein coagulates on further heating, but heating to 100°C is probably advantageous in other ways it ensures a more nearly sterile product and it inactivates leaf enzymes more completely. When steam is injected into a stream of juice, heating takes place in 1 or 2 seconds; this produces had, easily filtered cured, and there is less enzyme action before inactivation. Chlorophyllase rich plants such as lucerne and wheat show the importance of this; the chlorophyll in LPs made by heating to 80 °C was almost completely hydrolysed to chlorophyllide, whereas there was little hydrolysis during quick heating to 100°C.

Phaseolus Group: Moong beans, urd beans and moth bean are considered to be native to India, having been originated from *Phaseolus sublobatus* which grows wild in India.

Moong Bean or Green Gram *(Phaseolus aureus)*: The research work on the improvement of moong beans was started in India in 1925 with large collections of seed samples from different districts of the country and also from Burma. Pure line selection from the local materials resulted in some promising varieties, *e.g.*, GG-127, GG-188, Krishna-11, Khargone-1, Co. 1, Kopergaon, NP-23 and Jalgaon 781.

Urd Bean or Black Gram *(Phaseolus mungo)*: The earliest attempts to improve urd bean started in 1925, when 125 strains were isolated from the local bulks. Systematic improvement of urd was started in 1943. These efforts resulted in a number of promising varieties, both for dry areas, *e.g.* BG-379, B.R. 61, Mash-48, Mash 35-5, Khargone-3, T-27, T-65 and Sindh Kheda 1-1, and also for wetlands, *e.g.*, ADT-1.

Moth Bean *(Phaseolus acontifolius)*: A breeding program on this crop was started in 1943 and 150 collections were made from the cultivated areas of the country. From single plant selections, two types, namely B-15 and B-18, were identified as good grain types and T-3 as a good fodder variety. Another variety No. 88, was identified as a better grain type, maturing in 120 days. These lines showed some improvement in yield, by 10-15 %, but no varieties resistant to diseases have been identified. Disease resistance and quality aspects are being considered in future breeding program.

Dolichos Beans: Two major species of Dolichos, are commonly cultivated in India. One is *Dolichos lablab*, commonly known as walve or avare and the other *Dolichos biflorus*, known as horse gram or kulthi.

Walve or avare *(Dolichos lablab)*: Research work on improvement of avare has been carried out with the object of developing drought resistant, high yielding types with good quality pods. Some of the varieties *e.g.* Co. 1, Co. 5 and Co. 6, have shown wide adaptability and are being popularized in rotation with late paddy in areas where winters are mild.

Horse Gram or Kulthi *(Dolichos biflorus)*: Very little work has been done on the improvement of horse gram; however, as a result of single plant selections from the local bulks, a number of varieties recording 15-20% more yield than local bulks have been developed. Some of the varieties *e.g.* BGM 1-1, No. 35, D.B. 7 have been found promising. Variety BGM-1 exhibited a high degree of virus resistance.

Cowpea: A breeding program for improvement of this crop *(Vigna sinensis)* has been in progress since 1940. A number of grain, fodder and vegetable varieties have been identified from time to time largely from collections made within the country or from abroad of the grain types, N.P. 2, N.P. 7, C-32, T-I, K-11, K-14; of the fodder varieties.

Pea or Matar: There are two main types of cultivated pea *(Pisum sativum)*, namely the large, smooth or wrinkled seeded garden pea and the small, round or dimpled seeded field peas. While the former type is used as a table variety, the latter is used as pulse, whole or split.

Garden Pea: A breeding program on the garden pea was initiated at the Indian Agricultural Research Institute in the thirties. Through single plant selection, the medium-tall, wrinkled-seeded variety NP-29 was developed which is still popular in the country for its quality. During the same period, green-seeded Hara Bauna and white round seeded Lucknow Poniya were popularized for general cultivation in northern India. In central India, where the winters are comparatively short, the variety Khapar Kheda became more popular. In the warm-temperate zone around the Himalayas, a smooth, white-seeded variety was popularized under the name Kala Nagini or Kanawari. In recent years, a few more varieties, *e.g.*, Early Badger, Boneville and Perfection with very attractive pod size have been introduced for general cultivation.

Lentil: Varietal improvement programs for this species *(Lens esculntus)*, were initiated in India in 1924 by collecting mixed samples bought in bazaars all over the country. Single plant selections were picked up from the bulk population and sixty-six types were isolated. Some of these varieties *e.g.*, N.P. 11, N.P. 47 (IARI), T-36, T-8 (UP), L-9-12 (Punjab) and B.R. 25 (Bihar).

Khesari or Teora: The consumption of this pulse *(Lathyrus satiyus)*, in large quantities leads to lathyrism because of the presence of, *l*-N-oxalyl amino alanire (β-OAA). It is a very hardy crop and comes up well even under water logging and extreme drought conditions. Therefore in areas which are completely dependent on the monsoon, farmers insist on growing it.

LIPIDS

The term lipid was first used by the German biochemist Bloor in 1943. Chemically lipids are defined as esters of glycerol and fatty acids or as the triglycerides of fatty acids.

General formula of lipid = Glycerol + Fatty acid = Triglycerides

$$\underset{\text{(Glycerol)}}{(HOCH_2)_2\,CHOH} + 3C_{15}H_{31}COOH \rightarrow$$

$$CH(C_{15}H_{31}\,COOCH_2)_2 + 3\,H_2O$$

Palmitic Acid — Tripalmitic Water

Classification of Lipid

(A) On the basic of Reaction with NaOH/KOH:

(*i*) Saponifiable

(*ii*) Non saponifiable

(B) On the basis to Products of Hydrolysis:

(1) **Simple Lipids:** On hydrolysis gives fatty acids and alcohol (trihydric or monohydric)

Oils: Unsaturated fatty acid + glycerol.

Fats: Saturated fatty acids + glycerol.

Waxes: Fatty acids + mono or dihydric alcohol.

Simple glyceride: Contains same fatty acids.

Mixed glyceride: Contains different fatty acids.

(2) **Compound lipids: (Complex lipids):** On hydrolysis gives phosphoric acid, various sugars, sphingosine, ethanolamine and serine in addition to fatty acids and glycerol.

(*a*) **Phospholipid:** Fatty acids + glycerol + phosphoric acid + nitrogenous base.

e.g. Lecithin: Fatty acids + glycerol + phosphoric acid + choline.

Cephalin: Fatty acids + glycerol + phosphoric acid + ethanolamine.

(*b*) **Glycolipids:** Glycerol + fatty acid + carbohydrates (on hydrolysis).

They are sub classified as galactosyl diglyceride, cerebrosides and sulpholipids.

(*c*) **Sphingophospholipids:** Fatty acids + sphingosine + phosphoric acid + choline.

(3) **Derived Lipids:** Hydrolytic products of simple and compound lipids

(*a*) **Alcohols:** Glycerol and other sterol

(*b*) Fatty acids

(*c*) Terpenoids

Chemical Properties of Lipids:

(*a*) Hydrolysis

(*b*) Hydrogenation

(*c*) Halogenation

(*d*) Saponification
(*e*) Oxidation
(*f*) Rancidity (oxidative and hydrolytic)

ENZYMES

Catalytically active protein of biological origin or organic catalyst produced by living cells.

Substrate: Substance upon which an enzyme acts.

Classification of Enzyme: Based on Type of Reaction Enzyme is classified as below:

1. Oxidoreductase (Dehydrogenases): Reaction catalyzed - Biological oxidation - Reduction- *e.g.*, Pyruvic oxireductase, Ascorbic oxidase, Succinic dehydrogenase, Cytochrome oxidase.

2. Transferases (Transaminase): Ex. Transketolase, Transmethylase, Reaction catalyzed: Transfer of groups.

3. Hydrolases: Ex. Lipases, urease, pepsin, amylase, cholinesterase. Reaction catalyzed - Hydrolysis.

4. Lyases (Decarboxylases): Ex. Carboxylases, aldolases, fumarase. Reaction catalyzed - catalyzed removal of groups.

5. Isomerases: Ex. Triose phosphate isomerase, epimerase, alanine racemase. Reaction catalyzed - Catalyse conversion to other isomeric form.

6. Ligases or synthetases: Ex. Succinic thiokinase, Glutamine synthetase. Reaction catalyzed - catalyse linking together of two compounds.

Mechanism of Enzyme Action: The enzyme combines with the substance on which it acts (substrate) to form an enzyme substrate complex called Michaelis complex

$E + S \rightarrow ES$

Enzyme is liberated and the substrate is broken into the products of the reaction

$ES \rightarrow E + P$ (products)

Active Site: The region of an enzyme surface that binds the substrate molecule and catalytically transforms it.

Functional Groups Present at the Active Site: Amino acids such as aspartic acid, glutamic acid, lysine, serine etc. the side chain groups $-COOH$, $-NH_2$, $-CH_2OH$ etc. serve as catalytic groups at active site.

Factors Affecting Enzyme Activity:

1. pH
2. Temperature
3. Substrate Concentration
4. Enzyme Concentration
5. Concentration of any Activator Present
6. Concentration of any Inhibitor Present
7. Ionic Strength
8. Redox Potential
9. Concentration or Reaction Products

Properties of Enzymes:

1. Catalytic Property
2. Specificity
3. Heat Destruction
4. Enzyme Inhibitors
5. High Molecular Weight
6. Colloidal
7. Water Soluble
8. Reversibility of Action

Functions of Enzyme:

1. To accelerate or retard or bring about reaction
2. Regulate reaction
3. To make possible the metabolic reactions
4. To facilitate reaction
5. To break down larger molecule to small molecule
6. To carry out flow of reaction smoothly

Uses of Enzymes in Solution

Enzymes have a wide variety of applications in industry, medicine research etc. Some of the important applications are briefly discussed under the following headings:

(*i*) Uses of enzymes in solution,
(*ii*) Use of bi-phasic systems,
(*iii*) Uses of immobilized enzymes, and
(*iv*) Biosensors

The various uses of enzymes in solution are briefly described below.

I. Detergents: Detergents represent the largest industrial application of enzymes amounting to 25-30% of the total sales of enzymes. The enzymes used in detergents must be cost effective, safe to use and be able to perform the task in the presence of anionic and non-ionic detergents, soaps, oxidants etc. at pH between 8 and 10.5. Enzymes constitute only 0.4-0.8% crude enzyme by weight (about 1% by cost) of detergents. The chief enzymes used are proteases, α-amylase and, sometimes, cellulase.

1. **Proteases:** Proteases are used to digest away proteins present in blood stains, milk, grass etc. and also in association with dirt; therefore, they help in removal of dirt as well. Only serine proteases are suitable for use in detergents. These enzymes are produced by *Bacillus licheniformis* and *Bacillus amyloliquefaciens*. Proteases are packed inside dust-free granules coated with wax materials made from Paraffin oil or PEG plus hydrophilic binders; the granules disperse in wash releasing the enzyme. This strategy protects uses from hypersensitivity to the enzymes.
2. **α-Amylase:** Amylase is used to digest away starch present in association with dirt and stains; they are produced by *B. licheniformis.*

3. **Celluloses:** Celluloses, produced by fungi, are used for washing cotton fabrics. The enzyme digests away the small fibers raised from the fabric without damaging the major fibers of the fabric. This restores the fabric to 'as new' condition, and also removes soil particles by digesting the associated cellulose.

4. **Lipases:** Lipases suitable for detergent use have been identified and are used for digestion lipids present in stains and/or dirt.

II. Leather Industry: Alkaline proteases (0.1-1% w/w) are used to remove hair from hides; this is safer and more pleasant than the traditional method using sodium sulphide. De-haired hides are processed or bated often using pancreatic enzymes to increase their suppleness and softness in appearance. Bating is necessary for the production of soft leather clothing.

III. Wool Industries: Wool fibers are covered with overlapping scales pointing towards the tip this favours problem is successfully overcome by a partial digestion of the scales by papain (protease); this process also gives the wool a silky appearance and adds to its value. However, the process is no more in use due to economic reasons (mainly high cost of papain), but is likely to be initiated again with the availability of cheaper enzymes.

IV. Food, Dairy, Juice and Beverages Industries: Several processes in the production of food, beverages etc. utilize enzymes *e.g.* production of glucose syrup, maltose syrup and sucrose industry for preparation of invert syrup.

V. Use in Medicine: Enzyme applications in medicine are as extensive as in industry. Pancreatic enzymes have been used in digestive disorders since nineteenth century. Most enzymes are used extra cellularly for

(*i*) Topical applications, *e.g.* collagenase,

(*ii*) Removal of toxic substances, *e.g.* rhodonase,

(*iii*) Disorders within blood circulation system, *e.g.*, streptokinase, urokinase etc.

The enzyme preparations must be of high purity and free from unwanted contamination; therefore, they are generally from animal sources and very costly. For example, urokinase is isolated from human urine and costs nearly $ 200/mg; the annual market for this enzyme is nearly $150 million. Enzymes have a major potential application in treatment of cancer, *e.g.* asparagenase in the treatment of lymphocytic leukemia. Tumor cells are unable to synthesize L-asparagine due to an enzyme deficiency, and obtain this amino acid from body fluids. Asparaginase drastically reduces the levels of free L-asparagine in the food stream, creating starvation in tumor cells for this amino acid; normal cell are not affected since they can synthesize L-asparagene. Asparaginase is injected intravenously, slows half-life of about 1 day (in dog), and may lead to complete recovery in 60% of the cases.

VI. Aspartame Synthesis: Aspartame is a dipeptide containing one residue each of L-aspartic acid and methyl ester of L-phenylalanine. It is 180 times sweeter than sucrose, and is used as low level amino group is protected by a reaction with, usually, benzyl chloroformate and methyl ester of L-phenylalanine by the protease thermolysin. D-phenylalanine methyl ester is also added in a quantity equal to that of the L-isomer; the D-isomer forms an addition complex with aspartame which forms a precipitate. This removes aspartame from the reaction mixture and gives high yields at concentrations above 1 M. Later, aspartate is recovered from the precipitate by suitably changing the pH, and finally the benzyl chloroformate (attached to the amino group of L-aspartic acid) is removed by a simple hydrogenation process.

VITAMINS

Vitamins are defined as organic compounds required in minute amounts for catalytic and regulatory functions in cell metabolism in absence of which certain deficiency diseases occur.

Classification of Vitamins:

1. Fat soluble Vitamin A, D, E, K
2. Water Soluble Vitamin B complex and Vitamin C

Role as Co-enzymes in Different Biochemical Reactions:

1. Oxidation Reduction
2. Transfer of Group
3. Crboxylation
4. Transamination
5. Decarboxylation

Table: Co-enzyme Derivatives of Water soluble Vitamins and their Function

Sr. No.	Vitamin	Coenzyme Derivatives	Functions Performed
1.	Vit B1 Thiamin	TPP	Aldehyde group transfer
2.	Vit B2 Riboflavin	FMN, FAD	Hydrogen group transfer, Electron transfer in Redox Reaction
3.	Vit B3 Pantothenic acid	CoA	Acyl group transfer
4.	Vit B5 Niacin	NAD, NADP	Hydrogen group transfer
5.	Vit B6 Pyridoxine	PP	Amino group transfer
6.	Vit B7 Biotin	Biocytin	Carboxyl group transfer i.e. CO_2 fixing
7.	Vit B9 Folic acid	THFA	One carbon group transfer
8.	Vit. B12 Cynocobalamin	Deoxyadenosyl cobalamin	Cofactor in hydroxylations

MICROBIOLOGY

It is branch of science/microbiology which deals with study of soil microorganisms and their activities in the soil.

BACTERIAL CELL STRUCTURE

Bacterial cells are much smaller than plant or animal cells. They were first seen under a microscope by Anton van Leeuwenhoek in 1676. As microscopes have improved, scientists have come to understand bacterial cell structure better.

Using electron microscopes we know that bacteria have a cell wall. This is similar to a plant cell wall but is more flexible. Bacteria do not have a nucleus. They do have two types of DNA—plasmid and chromosomal. The chromosomal DNA carries most of the genetic information. Plasmid DNA forms small loops and carries extra information. Some bacteria have a flagellum—a whip like tail. This helps the bacteria to move itself along. When we talk about these flagellum tails in multiple bacteria, we call them flagella.

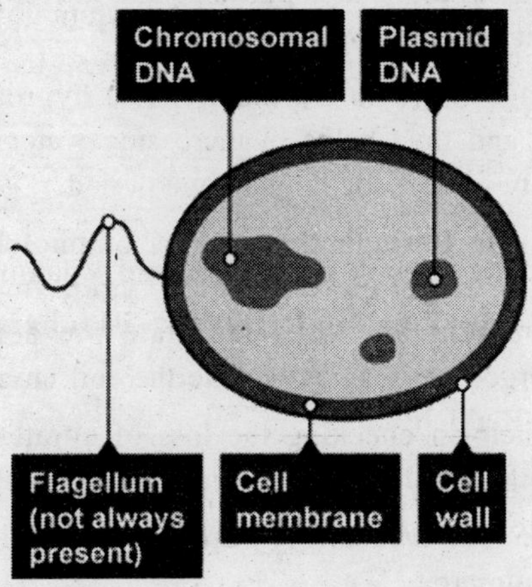

Structure of a bacteria cell

Types of Microorganisms in Soil

Living organisms both plants and animals, constitute an important component of soil. The pioneering investigations of a number of early microbiologists showed for the first time that the soil was not an inert static material but a medium pulsating with life. The soil is now believed to be a dynamic or rather a living system, containing a dynamic population of organisms/microorganisms. Cultivated soil has relatively more population of microorganisms than the fallow land, and the soil rich in organic matter contain much more population than sandy and eroded soils. Microbes in the soil are important to us in maintaining soil fertility/ productivity, cycling of nutrient elements in the biosphere and sources of industrial products such as enzymes, antibiotics, vitamins, hormones, organic acids etc. At the same time certain soil microbes are the causal agents of human and plant diseases.

The soil organisms are broadly classified in to two groups viz. soil flora and soil fauna, the detailed classification of which is as follows.

SOIL ORGANISMS

A. Soil Flora

(*a*) **Microflora:** 1. Bacteria 2. Fungi, Molds, Yeast, Mushroom 3. Actinomycetes, Stretomyces 4. Algae *e.g.*, BGA, Yellow Green Algae, Golden Brown Algae.

1. Bacteria is again classified in (*i*) Heterotrophic *e.g.*, symbiotic & non-symbiotic N_2 fixers, Ammonifier, Cellulose Decomposers, Denitrifiers. (*ii*) Autrotrophic *e.g.*, Nitrosomonas, Nitrobacter, Sulphur oxidizers, etc.

(*b*) **Macroflora:** Roots of higher plants

B. Soil Fauna

(*a*) **Microfauna:** Protozoa, Namatodes

(*b*) **Macrofauna:** Earthworms, moles, ants & others.

As soil inhabit several diverse groups of microorganisms, but the most important amongst them are: bacteria, actinomycetes, fungi, algae and protozoa.

FUNCTIONS/ROLE OF BACTERIA

Bacteria bring about a number of changes and biochemical transformations in the soil and thereby directly or indirectly help in the nutrition of higher plants growing in the soil. The important transformations and processes in which soil bacteria play vital role are: decomposition of cellulose and other carbohydrates, ammonification (proteins ammonia), nitrification (ammonia-nitrites-nitrates), denitrification (release of free elemental nitrogen), biological fixation of atmospheric nitrogen (symbiotic and non-symbiotic) oxidation and reduction of sulphur and iron compounds. All these processes play a significant role in plant nutrition.

Process/reaction	Bacterial genera
Cellulose decomposition (celluloytic bacteria) most cellulose decomposers are mesophilic	(a) **Aerobic:** *Angiococcus, Cytophaga, Polyangium, Sporocytophyga, Bacillus, Achromobacter, Cellulomonas*
	(b) **Anaerobic:** *Clostridium methanosarcina, Methanococcus*
Ammonification (Ammonifiers)	*Bacillus, Pseudomonas*
Nitrification (Nitrifying bacteria)	*Nitrosomonas, Nitrobacter nitrosococcus*
Denitrification (Denitrifies)	*Achromobacter, Pseudomonas, Bacillus, Micrococcus*
Nitrogen fixing bacteria	(a) **Symbiotic:** Rhizobium, *Bradyrrhizobium*
	(b) **Non-Symbiotic:** aerobic-Azotobacter *Beijerinckia* (acidic soils), anaerobic-*Clostridium.*

Bacteria capable of degrading various plant residues in soil are:

Cellulose	Hemicelluloses	Lignin	Pectin	Proteins
Pseudomonas	Bacillus	Pseudomonas	Erwinia	Clostridium
Cytophaga	Vibrio	Micrococcus		Proteus
Spirillum	Pseudomonas	Flavobacterium		Pseudomonas
Actinomycetes	Erwinia	Xanthomonas		Bacillus
Cellulomonas		Streptomyces		

FUNCTION/ROLE OF ACTINOMYCETES

- Degrade/decompose all sorts of organic substances like cellulose, polysaccharides, protein, fats, organic acids etc.
- Organic residues/substances added soil are first attacked by bacteria and fungi and later by actinomycetes, because they are slow in activity and growth than bacteria and fungi.
- They decompose/degrade the more resistant and indecomposable organic substance/matter and produce a number of dark black to brown pigments which contribute to the dark colour of soil humus.
- They are also responsible for subsequent further decomposition of humus (resistant material) in soil.
- They are responsible for earthy/musty odor/smell of freshly ploughed soils.
- Many genera species and strains (*e.g.*, Streptomyces if actinomycetes produce/synthesize number of antibiotics like Streptomycin, Tetramycin, Aureomycin etc.
- One of the species of actinomycetes *Streptomyces scabies* causes disease "Potato scab" in potato.

FUNCTIONS/ROLE OF FUNGI

- Fungi plays significant role in soils and plant nutrition.
- They plays important role in the degradation/ decomposition of cellulose, hemi cellulose, starch, pectin, lignin in the organic matter added to the soil.
- Lignin which is resistant to decomposition by bacteria is mainly decomposed by fungi.
- They also serve as food for bacteria.
- Certain fungi belonging to sub-division Zygomycotina and Deuteromycotina are predaceous in nature and attack on protozoa & nematodes in soil and thus, maintain biological equilibrium in soil.
- They also plays important role in soil aggregation and in the formation of humus.
- Some soil fungi are parasitic and causes number of plant diseases such as wilts, root rots, damping-off and seedling blights *e.g.*, *Pythium*, *Fusarium*, *Verticillium* etc.
- Number of soil fungi forms mycorrhizal association with the roots of higher plants (symbiotic association of a fungus with the roots of a higher plant) and helps in mobilization of soil phosphorus and nitrogen *e.g.*, Glomus, *Gigaspora*, *Aculospora*, (Endomycorrhiza) and *Amanita, Boletus, Entoloma, Lactarius* (Ectomycorrhiza).

FUNCTIONS/ROLE OF ALGAE OR BGA

- Plays important role in the maintenance of soil fertility especially in tropical soils.
- Add organic matter to soil when die and thus increase the amount of organic carbon in soil.
- Most of soil algae (especially BGA) act as cementing agent in binding soil particles and thereby reduce/ prevent soil erosion.
- Mucilage secreted by the BGA is hygroscopic in nature and thus helps in increasing water retention capacity of soil for longer time/period.
- Soil algae through the process of photosynthesis liberate large quantity of oxygen in the soil environment and thus facilitate the aeration in submerged soils or oxygenate the soil environment.
- They help in checking the loss of nitrates through leaching and drainage especially in un-cropped soils.
- They help in weathering of rocks and building up of soil structure.

FUNCTIONS/ROLE OF PROTOZOA

- Most of protozoans derive their nutrition by feeding or ingesting soil bacteria belonging to the genera *Enterobacter*, *Agrobacterium*, *Bacillus*, *Escherichia*, *Micrococcus*, and *Pseudomonas* and thus, they play important role in maintaining microbial/bacterial equilibrium in the soil.
- Some protozoa have been recently used as biological control agents against phytopathogens.
- Species of the bacterial genera viz. *Enterobacter* and *Aerobacter* are commonly used as the food base for isolation and enumeration of soil protozoans.
- Several soil protozoa cause diseases in human beings which are carried through water and other vectors, *e.g.*, Amoebic dysentery caused by *Entomobea histolytica*.

MULTIPLE CHOICE QUESTIONS

1. Match the following weather parameters with their measuring instruments:

List-I	List-II
(a) Solar irradiance	I. Pyranometer
(b) Temperature	II. Thermometer
(c) Humidity	III. Hygrometer
(d) Wind speed	IV. Anemometer

Choose the correct answer from the options given below:

	(a)	(b)	(c)	(d)
A.	III	II	IV	I
B.	I	IV	II	III
C.	I	II	III	IV
D.	III	IV	II	I

2. What do you call the prediction of the state of the atmosphere for a specific location and time?
A. Atmospheric disturbances
B. Wind forecasting
C. Rain forecasting
D. Weather forecasting

3. Match the atmosphere gas constituent with its percentage by volume:

List-I	List-II
(a) Nitrogen (N_2)	I. 20.95%
(b) Oxygen (O_2)	II. 78.08%
(c) Carbon dioxide (CO_2)	III. 0.0005%
(d) Helium (He)	IV. 0.03%

Choose the correct answer from the options given below:

	(a)	(b)	(c)	(d)
A.	I	II	III	IV
B.	I	II	IV	III
C.	II	I	IV	III
D.	II	I	III	IV

4. Match the weather parameter with its measuring instrument:

List-I	List-II
(a) Light	I. Hygrometer
(b) Wind Direction	II. Raingauge
(c) Humidity	III. Wind Vane
(d) Rainfall	IV. Pyranometer

	(a)	(b)	(c)	(d)
A.	I	III	II	IV
B.	II	I	IV	III
C.	IV	III	I	II
D.	III	IV	II	I

5. What is the thick layer of air surrounding the earth called?
A. Atmosphere B. Climate
C. Forecasting D. Weather

6. Which of the following is NOT a unit of wind velocity?
A. Knots B. Miles per hour
C. Kilometers per hour D. Centimeter

7. Medium-range weather forecasting provides information for a period of how many days?
A. One or two days
B. Three to ten days
C. Twenty to thirty days
D. Forty to sixty days

8. Match the items in List-I with the corresponding items in List-II:

List-I	List-II
(a) Kelvin	I. Temperature
(b) Millimetre	II. Rainfall/precipitation
(c) Knots	III. Air velocity
(d) Percentage (%)	IV. Relative humidity

Choose the correct answer from the options given below:

	(a)	(b)	(c)	(d)
A.	III	IV	I	II
B.	I	II	III	IV
C.	IV	III	II	I
D.	II	III	IV	I

9. Where is the headquarters of the Indian Meteorological Department (IMD) located?
A. Pune B. Delhi
C. Chennai D. Patna

10. Which of the following is the unit of measurement for water speed?
A. Cusec B. Kilogram
C. Hectare D. Sigma

11. The medium range weather forecast is for a period of:
A. 1-2 days B. 3-4 days to 2 weeks
C. More than four weeks D. Less than four weeks

12. The long range weather forecast is for a period of:
A. 1-2 days
B. 3-4 days to 2 weeks
C. More than four weeks
D. Less than four weeks

13. Which of the following is not a method of weather forecast:
A. Synoptic method B. Statistical method
C. Numerical method D. Asynoptic method

14. The technique of cloud seeding aims at correcting the:
A. Deficiencies of nuclei
B. Excess of nuclei
C. Deficiencies of neutrons
D. All of these

15. Silver iodide is used for:
A. Warm cloud seeding B. Cold cloud seeding
C. Both (A) and (B) D. None of these

16. What is the name of the mutation that causes an existing amino acid to be changed to a stop codon?
A. Missense mutation B. Non-sense mutation
C. Neutral mutation D. Silent mutation

17. Which of the following is NOT a mechanism of apomixis?
A. Apospory
B. Diplospory
C. Adventitious embryony
D. Parthenocarpy

18. Which of the following is the source of 'neutrons' used as physical mutagen?
A. Cobalt-60 B. Caesium-137
C. Uranium-235 D. Phosphorous-32

19. Which of the following vectors can clone large fragments (in megabase range)?
A. Plasmid
B. Cosmid
C. Yeast artificial chromosome (YAC)
D. Bacterial artificial chromosomes (BAC)

20. Identify the palindromic sequence in the following DNA segments.
A. 5′-CGGATCC-3′, 3′-CGGTACC-5′
B. 5′-TGGATCCA-3′, 3′-ACCTAGGT-5′
C. 5′-CGCCTCG-3′, 3′-GCGGAGC-5′
D. 5′-ATGTATAC-3′, 3′-TACATATG-5′

21. Match List-I with List II.

List-I	List-II
(*a*) Monosomy	I. $2n + 1$
(*b*) Nullisomy	II. $2n - 1$
(*c*) Pentasomy	III. $2n - 2$
(*d*) Trisomy	IV. $2n + 3$

Choose the correct answer from the options given below:

	(*a*)	(*b*)	(*c*)	(*d*)
A.	II	III	IV	I
B.	IV	III	II	I
C.	II	I	IV	III
D.	III	IV	I	II

22. India has been divided into:
A. 12 agro climatic zones
B. 15 agro climatic zones
C. 18 agro climatic zones
D. None of these

23. Radiation harmful to the plants comes in the spectral region:
A. < 0.4 μm B. 0.4 μm – 0.7 μm
C. 0.7 μm – 1.0 μm D. > 0.4 μm

24. Photosynthetically active radiation comes in the spectral region:
A. < 0.4 μm B. 0.4 μm – 0.7 μm
C. 0.7 μm – 1.0 μm D. > 0.4 μm

25. Which of the following statements is correct regarding autogamy in a chasmogamous flower?
A. Both anther and stigma mature simultaneously
B. Pollen release and stigma receptivity are not synchronized
C. Stigma becomes receptive much before the release of pollen
D. Anther and stigma are placed at different positions

26. The development of embryo directly from diploid cells of ovule outside the embryo sac belonging to either nucleus or integuments is referred to as:
A. apospory B. adventive embryony
C. Opogamy D. Micropropagation

27. Which are the causes of parthenogenesis:
(*a*) Very long style
(*b*) Early degeneration of sperm
(*c*) Short pollen tube
(*d*) Apogamy
(*e*) Apospory

Choose the correct answer from the options given below:
A. (*a*) only B. (*a*) and (*b*) only
C. (*a*), (*b*), and (*c*) only D. (*d*) and (*e*) only

28. If an individual wants to see diakinesis stage, which of these would be required:
A. Hair B. Leaf
C. Onion root D. Flower bud

29. Mitosis can be observed in:
(*a*) Polyploid individual
(*b*) Diploid individual
(*c*) Haploid individual
(*d*) Tetraploid individual
(*e*) Hexaploid individual

Choose the correct answer from the options given below:
A. (*a*) only B. (*b*) only
C. (*a*), (*b*), and (*c*) only D. (*d*) and (*e*) only

30. Extrachromosomal single circular coiled DNA in a prokaryotic cell is called:
A. Mesosomes B. Nucleoid
C. Plasmid D. Inclusion bodies

31. Breeding of crops to increase the levels of essential nutrients is called:
A. biofertification B. biomagnification
C. bioinformatics D. biotechnology

32. The plant material used for culturing is called as:
A. Totipotency B. TM-plant
C. Transgenic plant D. Explant

33. Fusion of male and female gametes to form a zygote which develops into an embryo is known as:
A. Asexual reproduction
B. Sexual reproduction
C. Vegetative reproduction
D. Commercial reproduction

34. Match List-I with List-II:

List-I (Types of protozoans)	List-II (Example)
(*a*) Flagellated protozoans	I. Entamoeba
(*b*) Ciliated protozoans	II. Trypanosoma
(*c*) Sporozoans	III. Paramoecium
(*d*) Amoeboid protozoans	IV. Plasmodium

Choose the correct answer from the options given below:

	(*a*)	(*b*)	(*c*)	(*d*)
A.	IV	III	II	I
B.	II	IV	III	I
C.	II	III	IV	I
D.	IV	II	III	I

35. Chlorophyll formation is promoted by light in the spectral region:
A. < 0.25 µm B. 0.3 µm – 0.338 µm
C. 0.4 µm – 1.0 µm D. > 1.0 µm

36. Match List-I with List-II:

List I (Pesticides)	List-II (Example)
(*a*) Rodenticide	I. MCPA
(*b*) Nematicide	II. Menab
(*c*) Herbicide	III. Coumarin
(*d*) Fungicide	IV. Phenaniponos

Choose the correct answer from the options given below:

	(*a*)	(*b*)	(*c*)	(*d*)
A.	II	I	III	IV
B.	III	IV	I	II
C.	IV	I	II	III
D.	I	II	III	IV

37. Phytochrome is excited by:
A. Green light B. Red light
C. White light D. All of these

38. Sewage purification is done by:
A. Microbes B. Fertilizers
C. Antibiotics D. Antiseptics

39. The controlled use of biological agents, such as living ganisms or enzymes from organisms to make the products useful for human is called as
A. Biochemistry B. Bioinformatics
C. Biotechnology D. Microbiology

40. The symbiotic association of fungi with the roots of higher plants is referred to as
A. Eubacteria B. Actinomycetes
C. Mycorrhiza D. Lichen

41. Which one following pair is wrongly matched?
A. Methanogens – Gobargas
B. Yeast – Ethanaol
C. Streptomycetes – Antibiotics
D. Califorms – Vinegar

42. Trichoderma is used as
A. Nitrogen fixing bacteria
B. Phosphate absorber bacteria
C. Phosphate solubilizer bacteria
D. Decomposer bacteria

43. The technology of bio-gas production from cow dung was developed in India largely due to efforts of
(*a*) Indian Agricultural Research Institute
(*b*) Indian Oil Corporation
(*c*) Oil and Natural Gas Commission
(*d*) Gas Authority of India
(*e*) Khadi & Village Industries Commission

Choose the correct answer from the options given below:
A. (*b*) only B. (*d*) only
C. (*a*) and (*e*) D. (*b*) and (*d*)

44. What is Agrometeorology?
A. The study of plants and animals
B. The study of soil science
C. The study of atmospheric processes and their effects on agriculture
D. The study of agricultural economics

45. What is the process of transfer of pollen grains from anther to stigma called?
A. Fertilization B. Germination
C. Pollination D. Reproduction

46. Which type of plant breeding method involves crossing two different varieties to produce a hybrid?
A. Inbreeding B. Mutation breeding
C. Hybridization D. Polyploidy

47. What is the process by which plants use sunlight to synthesize food from carbon dioxide and water?
A. Respiration B. Photosynthesis
C. Transpiration D. Chlorophyll synthesis

48. Which of the following is a type of soil microbiology?
A. Rhizosphere microbiology
B. Plant physiology
C. Plant pathology
D. Horticulture

49. Which of the following is a soil microorganism that helps in the fixation of nitrogen?
A. Rhizobium B. Fusarium
C. Phytophthora D. Botrytis

50. Which of the following is a type of weather phenomenon that can have a negative impact on agriculture?
A. Drought B. Mildew
C. Harvesting D. Irrigation

51. What is the process of selecting and combining genes from different varieties of plants to create new, improved varieties called?
A. Mutation breeding B. Polyploidy
C. Inbreeding D. Genetic engineering

52. What is the process of breaking down organic matter into simpler compounds called?
A. Fermentation B. Transpiration
C. Nitrogen fixation D. Decomposition

53. Which of the following is a type of genetic variation that arises due to a change in a single nucleotide in DNA?
A. Mutation B. Hybridization
C. Polyploidy D. Inbreeding

54. The photosynthetic electron transport chain is formed during subsequent development of chloroplast under:
A. Green light B. Red light
C. White light D. All of these

55. The amount of solar radiation present in any layer of the crop can be calculated by:
A. $I = I_0e^{-KLAI}$ B. $I = I_0e^{-K}$
C. $I_0 = Ie^{-KLAI}$ D. $I = I_0e^{-LAI}$

56. The effect of light on plants is known as:
A. Thermoperiodism B. Photoperiodism
C. Both (A) and (B) D. None of these

57. Long day plants flower when the length of light is:
A. <14 hrs B. >14 hrs
C. <10 hrs D. >10 hrs

58. Short day plants flower when the length of light is:
A. <14 hrs B. >14 hrs
C. <10 hrs D. >10 hrs

59. The rate of increase in reaction for every 10°C in temperature is called:
A. Q_{10} B. K_{10}
C. C_{10} D. T_{10}

60. The relationship between growth duration and temperature is termed as:
A. Base temperature B. Growing degree days
C. Photothermal unit D. None the these

61. Essential fatty acids are:
A. Linoleic acid B. Arachidonic acid
C. Linolenic acid D. All of these

62. The following is not a phospholipid:
A. Sphingomyelin B. Lecithin
C. Cephalin D. Cerebroside

63. Examples of monounsaturated fatty acids are:
A. Oleic acid B. Arachidonic acid
C. Palmitic acid D. Linolenic acid

64. High content of Triglycerides are seen in:
A. LDL B. HDL
C. VLDL D. Chylomicrons

65. The most abundant bio molecule on the earth:
A. Nucleic acids B. Proteins
C. Lipids D. Carbohydrates

66. The lowest temperature below which there is no growth is called as:
A. Q_{10} B. Base temperature
C. Photothermal unit D. T_{10}

67. Coefficient of variation is given by:
A. $\frac{SD}{Mean \times 100}$ B. $\frac{SD + Mean}{100}$
C. $\frac{SD \times Mean}{100}$ D. None of these

68. Q_{10} can be calculated by:
A. $Q_{10} = \frac{\text{Rate of reaction at } (t + 10)°C}{\text{Rate of reaction at } t°C}$
B. $Q_{10} = \frac{\text{Rate of reaction at } t°C}{\text{Rate of reaction at } (t + 10)°C}$
C. $Q_{10} = \frac{\text{Rate of reaction at } (t - 10)°C}{\text{Rate of reaction at } t°C}$
D. $Q_{10} = \frac{\text{Rate of reaction at } t°C}{\text{Rate of reaction at } (t - 10)°C}$

69. Sclerophyllus natural vegetation is found in:
A. Mediterranean regions
B. Equatorial regions
C. Monsoon regions
D. Tundra regions

70. Zerophytes represent the class of vegetation found in:
A. Tropical rain forest
B. Humid microthermal climates
C. Semi-arid steppes
D. Tundra

71. In the tropical hot deserts:
A. Precipitation exceeds evaporation
B. Evaporation exceeds precipitation
C. Precipitation equals evaporation
D. Precipitation is abundant

72. Tundra climate is characterized by:
A. Abundant precipitation
B. Meager precipitation
C. Moderate precipitation
D. Droughts

73. Extreme continentality is the characteristic feature of the:

A. Continental steppe climate
B. Middle-latitude desert climate
C. Tropical monsoon climate
D. Savanna climate

74. Fats are abundantly found in:
A. Reproductive tissue B. Vegetative tissue
C. Both A and B D. None of these

75. Which of the following is/are unsaturated fatty acids?
A. Linoleic acid B. Oleic acid
C. Palmitoleic acid D. All of these

76. Fats can be stored in the cell without disturbing their:
A. Hygroxyl bond B. Aleurone layer
C. Osmotic relations D. None of these

77. Liquid form of triglycerides at ordinary room temperature are called:
A. Oils B. Solid
C. Fats D. None of these

78. The synthesis of glucose from fat is called:
A. Glycolysis B. Krebs cycle
C. Saponification D. Gluconeogenesis

79. Hydrolysis of fats by alkalies into fatty acids and glycerol is called:
A. Coagulation B. Saponification
C. Suspension D. Colloidal

80. The fats and oils are respectively rich in:
A. Unsaturated fatty acids
B. Saturated fatty acids
C. Saturated and unsaturated fatty acids
D. None of these

81. β-oxidation takes place in:
A. Mitochondria B. Cytoplasm
C. Chloroplasts D. Nucleus

82. Which is a phospholipid:
A. Lecithin B. Cholesterol
C. Sterol D. Steroid

83. The number of double bonds in Arachidonic acid:
A. 1 B. 2
C. 3 D. 4

84. The general formula of carbohydrate is:
A. $(CH_2O)n$ B. $(C_4H_2O)n$
C. $(C_6H_2O)n$ D. $(C_2H_2O)n$ COOH

85. Carbohydrates are:
A. polyhydroxy aldehydes and phenols
B. polyhydroxy aldehydes and ketones
C. polyhydroxy ketones and phenols
D. polyhydroxy phenols and alcohols

86. Structural polysaccharides include:
A. cellulose, hemicellulose and chitin
B. cellulose, starch and chitin
C. cellulose, starch and glycogen
D. cellulose, glycogen and chitin

87. Nutritional polysaccharides are:
A. starch and glycogen B. starch and chitin
C. starch and cellulose D. starch and glucose

88. Glycogen in animals are stored in:
A. liver and spleen
B. liver and muscles
C. liver and bile
D. liver and adipose tissue

89. Carbohydrates accounts:
A. 30% in plants and 20% in animals
B. 30% in plants and 10% in animals
C. 30% in plants and 1% in animals
D. 50% in plants and 50% in animals

90. Which of the following pairs is inter converted in the process of mutarotation?
A. D-glucose and D-fructose
B. D-glucose and D-galactose
C. D-glucose and D-glucosamine
D. α-D-glucose and β-D-glucose

91. Protein separation techniques are often based on the following properties except
A. solubility of the protein
B. viscosity of the protein
C. charge of protein
D. specific binding affinity of the protein

92. Which of the following separation method is suited for a protein sample with large differences in molecular mass?
A. dialysis
B. salting out process
C. density gradient centrifugation
D. rate zonal centrifugation

93. Peptide bond is
A. rigid with partial double bond character
B. planar, covalent
C. covalent
D. All of the above

94. The first protein sequenced by Frederick Sanger is
A. haemoglobin B. myoglobin
C. insulin D. myosin

95. A dipeptide has
A. 2 amino acids and 1 peptide bond
B. 2 amino acids and 2 peptide bonds
C. 2 amino acids and 3 peptide bonds
D. 2 amino acids and 4 peptide bonds

96. The most common secondary structure is
A. α-helix
B. β-pleated sheet
C. β-pleated sheet parallel
D. β-pleated sheet non parallel

97. Myoglobin is a
A. protein with primary structure
B. protein with secondary structure
C. protein with tertiary structure
D. protein with quaternary structure

98. Disulphide bonds are formed between
A. cysteine residues that are close together
B. cystine residues that are close together
C. proline residues that are close together
D. histidine residues that are close together

99. The 3-D structure of protein can be determined by
A. Nuclear magnetic resonance
B. X-ray crystallography
C. Both A and B
D. Spectroscopy

100. Cobalt containing vitamin is
A. Vitamin B_2 B. Vitamin B_6
C. Vitamin B_{12} D. Vitamin B_1

101. Which of the following pairs is not correctly matched?
A. Vitamin B_4 - Pellagra
B. Vitamin B_{12} - Pernicious anaemia
C. Vitamin C - Scurvy
D. Vitamin B_6 - Beriberi

102. Vitamin E prevents
A. Formation of Vitamin D in Skin
B. Secretion of Superfluous enzymes
C. Keratinisation of epidermal cells
D. Absorption of harmful enzymes

103. Folic acid and panthothenic acid are vitamin belonging to group
A. K B. A
C. B-complex D. D

104. Megaloblastic anaemia is caused due to the deficiency of
A. Vitamin B_9 B. Vitamin B_6
C. Vitamin B_2 D. Vitamin B_{12}

105. The term enzymes are coined by
A. Pasteur B. Buchner
C. Urey Miller D. Kuhne

ANSWERS

1	2	3	4	5	6	7	8	9	10
C	D	C	C	A	D	B	B	B	A
11	**12**	**13**	**14**	**15**	**16**	**17**	**18**	**19**	**20**
B	C	D	A	B	B	D	C	C	B
21	**22**	**23**	**24**	**25**	**26**	**27**	**28**	**29**	**30**
A	B	A	B	A	B	D	D	C	C
31	**32**	**33**	**34**	**35**	**36**	**37**	**38**	**39**	**40**
A	B	B	C	B	B	A	A	C	C
41	**42**	**43**	**44**	**45**	**46**	**47**	**48**	**49**	**50**
D	D	C	C	C	C	B	A	A	A
51	**52**	**53**	**54**	**55**	**56**	**57**	**58**	**59**	**60**
D	D	A	C	A	B	B	C	A	B
61	**62**	**63**	**64**	**65**	**66**	**67**	**68**	**69**	**70**
D	D	A	D	D	B	A	A	A	C
71	**72**	**73**	**74**	**75**	**76**	**77**	**78**	**79**	**80**
B	B	A	A	D	C	A	D	B	C
81	**82**	**83**	**84**	**85**	**86**	**87**	**88**	**89**	**90**
A	A	D	A	B	A	A	A	C	D
91	**92**	**93**	**94**	**95**	**96**	**97**	**98**	**99**	**100**
B	D	D	C	A	A	C	A	C	C
101	**102**	**103**	**104**	**105**					
D	C	C	A	D					

UNIT 2

Livestock Production

SCOPE AND IMPORTANCE

IMPORTANCE OF LIVESTOCK IN AGRICULTURE AND INDUSTRY

Livestock has played an essential role in agriculture and industry since the beginning of human civilization. From providing food and fiber to powering machines, livestock has become an integral part of human life. The importance of livestock in agriculture and industry cannot be overstated. The significance of livestock in agriculture and industry is as follows:

Firstly, livestock is a vital source of food for human consumption. Livestock provides us with meat, milk, and eggs, which are essential sources of protein, vitamins, and minerals. Without livestock, it would be challenging to meet the growing demand for food as the world population continues to increase. Livestock also provides a variety of other by-products, such as leather, wool, and manure, which are valuable to the agricultural and industrial sectors.

Secondly, livestock has a significant impact on the economy. Livestock farming creates employment opportunities for millions of people worldwide, from small-scale farmers to large-scale commercial operations. Livestock farming also provides a source of income for many rural communities, contributing to their livelihoods and improving their quality of life. The livestock industry generates billions of dollars in revenue each year, making it an essential sector of the global economy.

Thirdly, livestock plays a crucial role in sustainable agriculture. Livestock helps to maintain the fertility of the soil by providing manure, which is a natural fertilizer. Livestock also helps to control pests and weeds, reducing the need for chemical pesticides and herbicides. Livestock can also be used for land management, as they can graze on land that is unsuitable for crop production.

Fourthly, livestock is a valuable source of energy. Livestock can be used to power machines and vehicles, providing an alternative to fossil fuels. Animal power has been used for centuries in agriculture, from plowing fields to transporting goods. In many parts of the world, animal power is still the primary source of energy for agricultural and industrial activities.

Finally, livestock plays an essential role in cultural traditions and practices. Livestock is a symbol of wealth, status, and prosperity in many cultures. In some societies, livestock is used in religious ceremonies and festivals, and its consumption is associated with celebrations and feasts. Livestock has become a part of our cultural identity, and its importance cannot be understated.

Livestock is an essential component of agriculture and industry. From providing food and fiber to powering machines, livestock plays a crucial role in sustaining human life. Livestock farming creates employment opportunities, contributes to the economy, and plays a vital role in sustainable agriculture. It is an essential source of energy and a significant cultural symbol. The importance of livestock in agriculture and industry cannot be overstated, and it will continue to be a vital component of our lives.

WHITE REVOLUTION IN INDIA

The white revolution, also known as the Operation Flood, was a dairy development program implemented in India in the 1970s to increase milk production and make India self-sufficient in milk and milk products. Here are some important details and their brief explanation regarding the White Revolution in India:

Background: Before the white revolution, India's milk production was low, and the country was heavily dependent on imported milk products. The situation was alarming, and there was a need to increase milk production to meet the demand for milk and milk products.

Launch: The white revolution was launched in 1970 by the National Dairy Development Board (NDDB), with the aim of increasing milk production and improving the socio-economic status of milk producers in rural areas.

Operation Flood: The white revolution was implemented in three phases, collectively known as Operation Flood. Operation Flood I was launched in 1970, Operation Flood II in 1981, and Operation Flood III in 1996. The program was implemented in 26 states across the country.

Objectives: The main objectives of the white revolution were to increase milk production, create a national milk grid, increase the income of milk producers, and provide nutritious food to the masses.

Methodology: The white revolution focused on creating dairy cooperatives at the village level, which would collect and process milk and market it. The cooperatives were given technical and financial support by NDDB.

Impact: The white revolution was a huge success and led to a significant increase in milk production in India. It helped in creating a national milk grid, which facilitated the movement of surplus milk from one region to another. The program also provided a steady source of income to milk producers and helped in improving their socio-economic status.

Significance: The white revolution played a significant role in making India self-sufficient in milk and milk products. It also helped in reducing poverty in rural areas and improving the overall socio-economic status of milk producers. The program has been recognized as one of the most successful rural development programs in the world.

The white revolution was a crucial program that helped in transforming the dairy sector in India. The program's success can be attributed to its focus on creating dairy cooperatives at the village level and providing technical and financial support to them. The white revolution has set an example for other countries to follow in improving their dairy sectors and achieving self-sufficiency in milk and milk products.

Importance of Livestock in Agriculture, National Economy and Food Security

- Livestock is a crucial component of the Indian economy.
- Approximately 20.5 million individuals depend on livestock for their livelihood.
- Livestock contributes 16% to the income of small farm households, compared to the average of 14% for all rural households.
- Two-thirds of the rural community derive their livelihood from the livestock sector.
- Livestock provides employment to approximately 8.8% of the population in India.
- India possesses abundant livestock resources.
- The livestock sector contributes 4.11% to the country's Gross Domestic Product (GDP) and 25.6% to the total Agriculture GDP.

Contribution of Livestock in Indian Economy

1. **Food:** Livestock provides food items such as milk, meat, and eggs for human consumption. India is the world's largest milk producer.
2. **Fibre and Skins:** Livestock contributes to the production of wool, hair, hides, and pelts. Leather is the most important product which has a very high export potential. India produces about 47.9 million kg of wool per annum.
3. **Draft:** Bullocks are the backbone of Indian agriculture. They are used for various agricultural operations, saving a lot on fuel which is a necessary input for using mechanical power like tractors, combine harvesters, etc. Pack animals like camels, horses, donkeys, ponies, and mules are being extensively used to transport goods in different parts of the country, especially in hilly terrains where mules and ponies serve as the only alternative to transport goods.
4. **Dung and Other Animal Waste Materials:** Dung and other animal wastes serve as very good farmyard manure, and the value of it is worth several crores of rupees. In addition, it is also used as fuel (biogas, dung cakes), and for construction as poor man's cement (dung).
5. **Storage:** Livestock is considered as "moving banks" because of their potentiality to dispose of during emergencies. They serve as capital and in cases of landless agricultural labourers many times it is the only capital resource they possess. Livestock serve as an asset, and in case of emergencies, they serve as a guarantee for availing loans from the local sources such as money lenders in the villages.
6. **Weed Control:** Livestock is also used as Biological control of brush, plants, and weeds.
7. **Cultural:** Livestock offers security to the owners and also adds to their self-esteem, especially when they are owning prized animals such as pedigreed bulls, dogs, and high yielding cows/buffaloes, etc.
8. **Sports/Recreation:** People also use the animals like cocks, rams, bulls, etc. for competition and sports. Despite the ban on these animal competitions, the cockfights, ram fights and bull fights (jalli kattu) are quite common during festive seasons.
9. **Companion Animals:** Dogs are known for their faithfulness and are being used as companions since time immemorial. When the nuclear families are increasing in number and the old parents are forced to lead solitary life the dogs, cats are providing the needed company to the latter thus making them lead a comfortable life.

Role of Livestock in Agriculture

1. Livestock is an essential part of mixed farming systems, where the output of one enterprise becomes the input of another.

2. Livestock provides income to farmers, especially those who are resource-poor and maintain few animals. Milk from cows and buffaloes is sold regularly for income, while animals like sheep and goats can be sold during emergencies.
3. Livestock products such as milk, meat, and eggs are an important source of animal protein for farmers and their families.
4. Livestock offers social security to owners and their families, as owning animals is highly valued in Indian society. Animals are often used for socio-religious functions and gifting animals during marriages is common.
5. Bullocks are essential for agriculture in India, providing draft power for ploughing, carting, and transportation of inputs and outputs.
6. Dung is used in rural areas for fuel (dung cakes), fertilizer (farm yard manure), and as a plastering material (poor man's cement).

Overall, livestock plays a vital role in the agriculture-based economy of India, providing income, employment, and social and cultural significance to farmers and their families.

Role of Livestock in Food Security

- Livestock can make a major contribution to food security, which is defined as access to enough food for an active healthy life.
- Animals are an important source of food, particularly high quality protein, minerals, vitamins, and micronutrients.
- Dietary animal protein is valuable because it contains essential amino acids that are deficient in cereals.
- Eating even a small amount of animal products corrects amino acid deficiencies in cereal-based diets and allows more total protein to be utilized.
- Animal proteins are more digestible and metabolized more efficiently than plant proteins.

IMPORTANT BREEDS INDIAN AND EXOTIC, DISTRIBUTION OF COWS, BUFFALOES AND POULTRY IN INDIA

India is known for its diverse livestock population, including cows, buffaloes, and poultry. The country is home to many indigenous as well as exotic breeds of livestock. Here are the important details about breeds and distribution in India:

Cows: India has a large population of cows, and they are considered sacred by many Hindus. The major indigenous breeds of cows in India are Gir, Sahiwal, Red Sindhi, Tharparkar, and Hariana. The exotic breeds of cows that are reared in India are Holstein Friesian, Jersey, and Brown Swiss.

Buffaloes: India has the largest buffalo population in the world, and buffaloes are reared primarily for their milk. The major indigenous breeds of buffaloes in India are Murrah, Nili Ravi, Bhadawari, and Jaffarabadi. The exotic breeds of buffaloes that are reared in India are Mediterranean, Egyptian, and Bulgarian.

Poultry: Poultry farming is a major contributor to the Indian economy. The major breeds of poultry in India are desi (indigenous) and commercial (exotic). The desi breeds of poultry include Aseel, Kadaknath, Chittagong, and Busra. The exotic breeds of poultry include White Leghorn, Rhode Island Red, and Plymouth Rock.

Distribution: The distribution of cows, buffaloes, and poultry varies across different regions in India. The northern and western parts of the country have a higher population of cows and buffaloes, while the eastern and southern parts of the country have a higher population of poultry. The state of Uttar Pradesh has the highest population of cows and buffaloes, while Andhra Pradesh has the highest population of poultry.

India has a diverse population of livestock, including cows, buffaloes, and poultry. The indigenous breeds of cows and buffaloes are popular among farmers, while the exotic breeds are used for commercial purposes. The distribution of livestock varies across different regions in India, with some states having a higher population than others.

Important animal based food products and their role in our diet

- Animal source foods (ASF) include meat, milk, eggs, cheese, and yogurt.
- Some people may not consume or have limited access to ASF due to personal choice or accessibility issues.
- Meat products belong to one of the six major food groups and can come from poultry, red meat (beef, lamb, and pork), game, and fish.
- These products provide essential nutrients, minerals, and vitamins needed for maintaining good health.

Meat is a high source of minerals including magnesium, zinc, and iron.

- Magnesium helps in bone strength and preventing osteoporosis.
- Zinc is important for the immune system and muscle growth and repair.
- Iron maintains energy levels and maximizes oxygen transport throughout the body. Lack of iron can lead to anemia and fatigue.
- Red meat and turkey are particularly rich in iron.
- Meat is an excellent source of protein, which is essential for a healthy diet.

- Protein in meat has a high biological value (HBV) and is easily digested and absorbed quickly by the body.
- Red meat, chicken, and turkey are extremely high in protein.

Meat is a good source of vitamins, particularly vitamin E and B vitamins (B2, B6, and B12).

- Vitamin E has strong antioxidant properties, which help reduce damage to cells caused by oxygen and support muscle repair and recovery.
- B vitamins work together to convert food into energy and also have individual functions.
- B2 is essential for the production of red blood cells, which transport oxygen throughout the body.
- B6 is necessary for protein synthesis.
- B12 is critical for good nerve function.
- Meat, especially fish, is a good source of essential unsaturated fats like Omega-3 fatty acids, which can help reduce cholesterol levels, blood pressure, and the risk of developing cardiovascular diseases.
- Eggs have a biological value of 93.79%, which is comparable to 84.5% for milk, 76% for fish, and 74.3% for beef. They are a very good source of inexpensive, high-quality protein, with 33% protein content.
    - More than half of the protein in an egg is found in the egg white, which also contains vitamin B2 and lower amounts of fat and cholesterol than the yolk.
    - Egg whites are rich in selenium, vitamin D, B6, B12, and minerals such as zinc, iron, and copper.
    - Egg yolks contain more calories and fat, and are the source of cholesterol, fat-soluble vitamins A, D, E, and K, and lecithin, which enables emulsification in recipes such as hollandaise or mayonnaise.
- Milk is a valuable source of calcium, riboflavin, and protein in our diet. For vegetarians, it can also be a valuable source of vitamin A (carotene) and B12. However, they should not rely on sterilized or UHT milks for vitamin B12, as they don't contain as much as pasteurized milk.
- Dairy and milk products are commodities that are produced by primary or secondary processing of milk. All mammals produce milk that contains the correct balance of nutrients with which to feed their young. This milk can also be produced and used commercially, for example, sheep, goat, and cow's milk.

Different Dairy Products

Cheese

- Made from cows, ewes or goats milk
- Takes approximately 5 litres of milk to produce ½ kg of cheese
- Highly concentrated form of food with fat, protein, mineral salts and vitamins
- Excellent bodybuilding, energy-producing, protective food

Butter

- Natural product made from cow's and buffalo's milk
- Contains 81 % fat, like hard and soft margarine's and spreads, so all have the same number of calories
- No preservatives or colourings added, but salt may be added for extra flavour
- Made simply by churning fresh cream

Yogurt

- Cultured product made from whole or skimmed milk, with skimmed milk solids or cream sometimes added for flavour and texture
- Highly nutritious and an excellent source of protein, calcium and potassium
- Provides numerous vitamins and minerals and is relatively low in calories

Cream

- Yellowish substance created when milk is heated and a layer of high content butter rises to the surface
- Good source of fat, protein and carotene

Curd

- Dairy product obtained by coagulating milk in a process called curdling, which can be caused by adding rennet or any edible acidic substance such as lemon juice or vinegar
- Low in Saturated Fat and Cholesterol
- Good source of Protein, Vitamin B12, Pantothenic Acid, Potassium and Zinc
- Very good source of Riboflavin, Calcium and Phosphorus

Buttermilk

- Refers to a number of dairy drinks, with traditional buttermilk being the liquid left behind after churning butter out of cream
- Buttermilk content less saturated fat, good source of protein, calcium, potassium, sodium, Vitamin B12.

CARE AND MANAGEMENT

SYSTEMS OF CATTLE AND POULTRY HOUSING

Cattle and poultry housing is an important aspect of livestock management. The housing system should be designed in a way that provides a comfortable and safe environment for the animals to live in. There are several types of housing systems for cattle and poultry, including:

1. **Open Sheds:** Open sheds are the simplest type of housing system for cattle and poultry. They consist of a roof supported by pillars or posts, and the animals are free to move in and out of the shed as they please. This system is suitable for areas with mild climate and less rainfall.
2. **Closed Sheds:** Closed sheds are enclosed structures with a roof and walls that provide better protection to the animals from harsh weather conditions. They are usually well-ventilated and have enough natural light to keep the animals healthy. These are preferred for extreme climates.
3. **Deep Litter System:** In the deep litter system, a thick layer of bedding material like sawdust, straw, or husk is laid on the floor of the shed. The animals can move around freely and their droppings and urine are absorbed by the bedding material. This system provides warmth and comfort to the animals and also serves as a natural composting system.
4. **Battery Cage System:** The battery cage system is commonly used for poultry farming. The system consists of cages stacked on top of each other, with each cage housing a few birds. The cages are small and do not allow the birds to move around freely. This system is considered less humane and has been banned in many countries.

In addition to the type of housing system, proper ventilation, lighting, and temperature control are also important factors to consider. Good sanitation practices, such as regular cleaning and disinfection of the housing area, are also important to prevent the spread of diseases.

The housing system should be designed based on the specific needs of the animals and the local climatic conditions. Proper care and management of cattle and poultry housing is crucial for the health and productivity of the animals, as well as the profitability of the farm.

PRINCIPLES OF FEEDING, FEEDING PRACTICES

The care and management of livestock, particularly cattle and poultry, is crucial to their health and productivity. One of the most important aspects of care and management is feeding, as this directly affects the growth, reproduction, and overall health of the animals. Here are some important details and principles related to feeding and feeding practices:

1. **Nutrient requirements:** Cattle and poultry require a balanced diet that provides them with all the essential nutrients they need to grow and maintain their health. These nutrients include proteins, carbohydrates, fats, vitamins, and minerals. The specific nutrient requirements vary depending on the age, weight, and stage of production (such as growth, lactation, or egg production) of the animals.
2. **Feed ingredients:** Feeds for cattle and poultry can come from a variety of sources, including grains, oilseeds, forages, and protein supplements. The type and quality of feed ingredients can affect the palatability, digestibility, and nutrient content of the feed.
3. **Feeding practices:** Feeding practices include the timing, amount, and frequency of feedings, as well as the use of feed additives, such as antibiotics or growth promoters. It is important to follow recommended feeding guidelines to avoid overfeeding or underfeeding, which can lead to health problems or reduced productivity.
4. **Water:** Access to clean and fresh water is also essential for the health and productivity of cattle and poultry. Animals should have access to water at all times, and the water source should be regularly monitored and maintained.
5. **Management of feed and feeding equipment:** Proper storage, handling, and maintenance of feed and feeding equipment can help ensure the quality and safety of the feed and prevent the spread of diseases. Feed storage areas should be kept clean and dry, and feeders and waterers should be cleaned and disinfected regularly.

Effective feeding and feeding practices are essential for the health and productivity of livestock, and can play a key role in ensuring the profitability of a livestock operation.

BALANCED RATION-DEFINITION AND INGREDIENTS

Balanced ration is a term used in animal husbandry to describe a diet that contains all the necessary nutrients in the correct proportions to meet the animal's nutritional requirements for maintenance, growth, reproduction, and production. The ingredients of a balanced ration depend on the species, age, weight, and physiological state of the animal, as well as the availability and cost of feedstuffs.

A balanced ration should contain the following nutrients in appropriate proportions:

1. **Energy:** It is needed for maintenance, growth, and production. The main sources of energy are carbohydrates and fats.
2. **Protein:** It is required for the growth and repair of tissues, as well as for the production of milk and eggs. The sources of protein include soybean meal, cottonseed meal, fish meal, and other protein-rich feedstuffs.
3. **Minerals:** They are essential for the formation of bones and teeth, regulation of body fluids, and other physiological functions. The major minerals include calcium, phosphorus, sodium, and potassium.
4. **Vitamins:** They are required in small amounts for various physiological processes, such as metabolism, immunity, and reproduction. The main sources of vitamins are green fodder, bran, and oilseeds.
5. **Water:** It is essential for the maintenance of body temperature, digestion, and excretion.

The balanced ration can be prepared using the following methods:

1. **Pearson's square method:** It is a simple and convenient method of calculating the proportions of different feedstuffs required to prepare a balanced ration.
2. **Computerized ration balancing:** It is a more sophisticated method that involves the use of software programs that take into account the nutritional requirements of the animal and the nutrient content of different feedstuffs.
3. **Trial and error method:** It involves formulating a ration and adjusting it based on the animal's response and performance.

The balanced ration should be fed in the right quantity and at the right time to ensure maximum utilization of the nutrients and prevent wastage. Overfeeding or underfeeding can lead to health problems and reduced productivity. It is important to monitor the animal's body condition score and adjust the ration accordingly to maintain optimal body condition and health.

MANAGEMENT OF CALVES, BULLOCKS, PREGNANT, MILCH ANIMALS, CHICKS COCKERELS AND LAYERS, POULTRY

Management of calves, bullocks, pregnant and milch animals as well as chicks, cockerels, and layers in poultry includes the following points:

1. **Calves:** Calves require special attention as they are vulnerable to diseases and infections. They should be kept in a clean and hygienic environment, and their housing should be adequately ventilated. They should be fed with colostrum, which is the first milk produced by the mother cow, as it contains essential nutrients and antibodies that help in building the calf's immune system.
2. **Bullocks:** Bullocks are used for plowing fields and other agricultural activities. They should be given a balanced diet that provides them with the necessary nutrients and energy. Regular exercise is also essential for their health and well-being.
3. **Pregnant and milch animals:** Pregnant and milch animals require special care as they are vulnerable to various health issues. They should be kept in clean and well-ventilated housing, and their diet should be balanced and nutritious. Pregnant animals should be monitored regularly to ensure a safe and healthy delivery.
4. **Chicks, cockerels, and layers in poultry:** Proper housing and management practices are essential for the growth and health of poultry. Chicks and cockerels should be kept in a brooder house with adequate warmth, light, and ventilation. Layers should be housed in a clean and hygienic environment with proper feeding practices that provide them with the necessary nutrients for egg production.

The proper care and management of livestock, whether it be calves, bullocks, pregnant or milch animals, or poultry, involves providing a clean and hygienic environment, a balanced and nutritious diet, and regular monitoring for any health issues. By following these principles, farmers can ensure the health and well-being of their animals, which can lead to improved productivity and profitability.

SIGNS OF SICK ANIMALS, SYMPTOMS OF COMMON DISEASES IN CATTLE AND POULTRY

Care and management of livestock and poultry involves monitoring their health and well-being to ensure they are productive and free from diseases.

Signs of Sick Animals

1. **Decreased appetite:** Sick animals may lose their appetite and refuse to eat or drink as much as they normally would.
2. **Lethargy:** Animals may become weak and lethargic, showing little interest in their surroundings or usual activities.
3. **Reduced milk production:** In the case of dairy animals, sick animals may produce less milk or even stop producing milk altogether.
4. **Abnormal behavior:** Sick animals may exhibit abnormal behavior such as restlessness, aggression, or isolation from the herd or flock.

5. **Weight loss:** Animals may lose weight due to decreased appetite or changes in metabolism caused by illness.
6. **Reduced activity level:** Sick animals may show reduced activity levels, moving around less than usual and seeming to lack energy.
7. **Fever:** Animals with infections or other illnesses may have a fever, which can be detected by measuring their body temperature.
8. **Abnormal feces:** Sick animals may have diarrhea or constipation, or their feces may have an abnormal color, consistency, or smell.

It is important for livestock farmers to closely monitor their animals and be aware of any changes in behavior, appetite, or physical condition. Sick animals should be separated from the rest of the herd or flock to prevent the spread of disease and given proper treatment and care to help them recover.

Common Diseases in Cattle

1. **Bovine respiratory disease:** Bovine respiratory disease (BRD) is a common bacterial infection that affects the respiratory system of cattle. It is caused by a variety of pathogens, including bacteria, viruses, and mycoplasma. BRD can cause severe respiratory distress, pneumonia, and even death if not treated promptly.
2. **Mastitis:** Mastitis is an infection of the udder that can cause inflammation, pain, and a decrease in milk production. It is caused by bacteria that enter the udder through the teat canal. Mastitis can be acute or chronic and can lead to significant economic losses for dairy farmers.
3. **Foot-and-mouth disease:** Foot-and-mouth disease (FMD) is a highly contagious viral disease that affects cloven-hoofed animals, including cattle. FMD can cause fever, blisters on the feet and mouth, and lameness. It can also cause a decrease in milk production and weight loss. FMD is a significant concern for farmers because of its potential to spread rapidly and cause economic losses.
4. **Johne's disease:** Johne's disease is a chronic bacterial infection that affects the small intestine of cattle. It can cause diarrhea, weight loss, and reduced milk production. Johne's disease is difficult to diagnose and control, and infected animals often remain asymptomatic for several years.
5. **Brucellosis:** Brucellosis is a bacterial infection that can affect both humans and animals. In cattle, brucellosis can cause abortion, stillbirths, and infertility. It is spread through contaminated bodily fluids and can have significant economic impacts on the livestock industry.

Common Diseases in Poultry

1. **Newcastle Disease:** Newcastle disease is a highly contagious viral disease that affects all types of poultry. The virus is spread through direct contact with infected birds, their feces, or contaminated surfaces. Symptoms of the disease include respiratory distress, nervous signs, and a decrease in egg production. There is no cure for Newcastle disease, and infected birds are often euthanized to prevent the spread of the virus.
2. **Avian Influenza:** Avian influenza, also known as bird flu, is caused by influenza viruses that affect birds. The virus can be spread through contact with infected birds, their feces, or contaminated surfaces. Symptoms of avian influenza include respiratory distress, nervous signs, and a decrease in egg production. There is no cure for avian influenza, and infected birds are often euthanized to prevent the spread of the virus.
3. **Coccidiosis:** Coccidiosis is a parasitic disease caused by protozoa that affect the intestinal tract of poultry. The disease is spread through contact with infected birds, their feces, or contaminated surfaces. Symptoms of coccidiosis include diarrhea, weight loss, and decreased activity. The disease can be treated with medications, but prevention is key to controlling its spread.
4. **Infectious Bronchitis:** Infectious bronchitis is a highly contagious viral disease that affects the respiratory tract of poultry. The virus is spread through contact with infected birds, their feces, or contaminated surfaces. Symptoms of the disease include respiratory distress, nervous signs, and a decrease in egg production. The disease can be treated with medications, but prevention is key to controlling its spread.
5. **Marek's Disease:** Marek's disease is a viral disease that affects chickens and can cause tumors to develop in the nervous system, skin, and other organs. The virus is spread through contact with infected birds, their dander, or contaminated surfaces. Symptoms of the disease include paralysis, weight loss, and blindness. Vaccines are available to prevent the disease, but infected birds cannot be cured and are often euthanized to prevent the spread of the virus.

Preventive measures for livestock and poultry diseases include maintaining proper hygiene, regular vaccinations, timely deworming, and isolation of sick animals. Early detection and treatment of sick animals are crucial in controlling the spread of diseases.

Proper nutrition is also essential for the well-being of animals. Balanced rations should contain all the essential nutrients required for growth, maintenance, and production.

50. Which of the following fruits is a climacteric fruit?
A. Guava B. Citrus
C. Mango D. Papaya

51. Which of the following fruits requires a dry climate during ripening?
A. Banana B. Grapes
C. Mango D. Papaya

52. Which of the following fruits is a rich source of vitamin C?
A. Mango B. Papaya
C. Banana D. Citrus

53. Which of the following fruits requires ethylene treatment to induce ripening?
A. Grapes B. Citrus
C. Guava D. Banana

54. Which of the following fruits has the highest sugar content?
A. Mango B. Papaya
C. Banana D. Grapes

55. Which vegetable crop is considered as a good source of vitamin C?
A. Carrot B. Onion
C. Cabbage D. Tomato

56. Which of the following vegetable crops is not a root vegetable?
A. Radish B. Carrot
C. Onion D. Potato

57. Which vegetable crop is known for its high content of beta-carotene?
A. Cauliflower B. Spinach
C. Tomato D. Carrot

58. Which of the following vegetables is a good source of dietary fiber?
A. Radish B. Potato
C. Cabbage D. Spinach

59. Which vegetable crop is often used as a natural dye?
A. Radish B. Spinach
C. Onion D. Cabbage

60. Which of the following is a flower crop?
A. Mango B. Papaya
C. Marigold D. Guava

61. Which flower crop is commonly used for making garlands?
A. Gladiolus B. Canna
C. Chrysanthemums D. Roses

62. Which of the following vegetables is a root vegetable?
A. Tomato B. Onion
C. Cabbage D. Potato

63. Which vegetable crop is commonly used for making pickles?
A. Radish B. Carrot
C. Potato D. Onion

64. Which of the following is a leafy vegetable?
A. Radish B. Carrot
C. Spinach D. Cauliflower

65. Which method of fruit preservation involves heating the fruit in a sealed can or jar?
A. Dehydration B. Canning
C. Freezing D. Pickling

66. What is the process of removing air from packaging and sealing it to prevent spoilage?
A. Blanching
B. Canning
C. Vacuum packing
D. Fermentation

67. Which of the following is a chemical preservative commonly used in fruit preservation?
A. Salt B. Sugar
C. Vinegar D. Sulfur dioxide

68. What is the process of preserving food by exposing it to high pressure and temperature?
A. Dehydration B. Pasteurization
C. Irradiation D. Salting

69. Which method of vegetable preservation involves removing the water content through heat or air?
A. Canning B. Freezing
C. Dehydration D. Pickling

70. Which of the following is NOT a product prepared from fruits and vegetables?
A. Jellies B. Chips
C. Cheese D. Ketchup

71. Which preservation method involves removing water from the fruits and vegetables?
A. Canning
B. Pickling
C. Drying
D. Fermenting

72. Which of the following is NOT an ingredient used in preparing jams and jellies?
A. Sugar B. Pectin
C. Vinegar D. Fruit juice

73. Which of the following is a type of packaging used for preserving fruits and vegetables?
A. Aluminum foil
B. Plastic bags
C. Glass jars
D. All of the above

74. Which of the following is NOT a product made from potatoes?
A. Ketchup B. Chips
C. French fries D. Potato salad

be printed with the brand name, product information, and nutritional facts. However, they provide less protection against moisture and contamination compared to plastic and aluminum foil bags.

Cans are also used for packing chips. They are durable, provide excellent protection against moisture and light, and are stackable, making them easy to store and transport. Cans can be printed with the brand name, product information, and nutritional facts. However, they are more expensive than other packaging materials, and they are not as convenient for consumers to carry around.

The packing of chips involves the use of various packaging materials such as plastic bags, aluminum foil bags, paper bags, and cans. The packaging material chosen depends on factors such as cost, level of protection required, and environmental concerns. The packaging is usually printed with the brand name, product information, and nutritional facts to help consumers make informed choices.

MULTIPLE CHOICE QUESTIONS

1. Arrange the steps of making cucumber pickle in the proper sequence.
(*a*) Washing and peeling.
(*b*) Cut into small pieces and mix with salt.
(*c*) Keep in sun for a week.
(*d*) Add spices and vinegar.
(*e*) Keep in a jar for 8 hours and remove excess water.

Choose the correct answer from the options given below
A. $(d) \rightarrow (a) \rightarrow (b) \rightarrow (e) \rightarrow (c)$
B. $(d) \rightarrow (b) \rightarrow (e) \rightarrow (a) \rightarrow (c)$
C. $(d) \rightarrow (e) \rightarrow (b) \rightarrow (a) \rightarrow (c)$
D. $(d) \rightarrow (a) \rightarrow (c) \rightarrow (b) \rightarrow (e)$

2. Identify the incorrect concepts with respect to traditional storage method of fruits and vegetables?
(*a*) Sand and coir storage
(*b*) High altitude storage
(*c*) Cold storage
(*d*) Pit storage
(*e*) Modified atmospheric storage

Choose the correct answer from the options given below:
A. (*c*) and (*e*) only B. (*a*) and (*c*) only
C. (*b*) and (*d*) only D. (*d*) and (*e*) only

3. The extent of food processing percentage in India is approximately:
A. 80% B. 20%
C. 40% D. 2%

4. The methods of preservation of fruit juices include:
(*a*) Carbonation
(*b*) Flash pasteurization
(*c*) Over flow method
(*d*) Holding pasteurization
(*e*) Fermentation

Choose the correct answer from the options given below:
A. (*a*), (*b*), (*c*) only B. (*b*), (*c*), (*d*) only
C. (*c*); (*e*) only D. (*a*), (*d*) only

5. Addition of sugar at minimum is required to pressure any food product. This also improves the taste and calorific value of the preserved products.
A. 50% B. 65%
C. 60% D. 75%

6. Which one of the following variety belongs to Rose flower?
A. Ruby red B. Gladiator
C. Cracker jack D. Butter scotch

7. Gerbera is commercially propagated through:
A. Suckers B. Cutting
C. Budding D. Layering

8. While preparing pickles, preservation is primarily achieved through the addition of:
A. Salt B. Colour
C. Water D. Pectin powder

9. Keeping micro-organisms out from entering into the food is termed as:
A. Spoilage B. Asepsis
C. Decomposition D. Deterioration

10. Rose is commercially propagated by:
A. Seed B. Layering
C. Grafting D. Budding

11. Desuckering and mattocking is practiced in which crop?
(*a*) Mango
(*b*) Citrus
(*c*) Banana
(*d*) Sugarcane
(*e*) Pomegranate

Choose the correct answer from the options given below:
A. (*a*) and (*c*) Only
B. (*b*) and (*e*) Only
C. (*c*) Only
D. (*c*) and (*d*) only

12. Lychee (Litchi chinensis) is typically propagated by which method?
A. Grafting
B. Cutting
C. Seed
D. Marcotting or gootee

including egg yolk, milk, glycerol, and antibiotics. The dilution process also helps to increase the number of doses that can be obtained from a single ejaculate.

After dilution, the semen is preserved through various methods, including cooling, freezing, or a combination of both. Cooling of semen is the most common preservation method used in artificial insemination. The semen is cooled to a temperature between 0°C and 5°C and can be stored for up to 72 hours before use. This method allows the semen to be transported easily to remote locations for insemination.

Freezing of semen is another method of preserving semen. Semen can be frozen and stored at temperatures below –196°C in liquid nitrogen. This method allows semen to be stored for an extended period, usually several years, and transported over long distances. Semen that is frozen and thawed has a shorter lifespan and is less motile than fresh semen, but it is still capable of producing viable pregnancies.

Proper collection, dilution, and preservation of semen are crucial to the success of artificial insemination. They help ensure that the semen maintains its quality, and that the sperm remain viable for insemination.

Artificial Insemination in Cattle Improvement

Artificial insemination (AI) is a reproductive technology that involves the transfer of semen from a male animal to a female animal to achieve fertilization without natural mating. AI has become a popular tool for cattle breeders worldwide because of its numerous advantages over natural mating. The process involves selecting superior bulls for semen collection, processing and storage of semen, and insemination of the female with the processed semen.

The use of AI in cattle breeding has several benefits:

1. **Increased genetic progress:** AI allows breeders to use semen from superior bulls, which increases the rate of genetic progress in the herd. It enables breeders to access sires with desirable traits such as high milk yield, good temperament, and disease resistance. Breeders can also use semen from bulls that are not available locally, leading to a wider gene pool and increased genetic diversity.
2. **Reduced risk of disease transmission:** AI helps to minimize the risk of disease transmission among cattle. Natural breeding requires physical contact between animals, which increases the risk of transmitting diseases such as bovine viral diarrhea (BVD), bovine leukemia virus (BLV), and trichomoniasis. AI allows breeders to use semen from bulls that have been tested and certified free from diseases, which helps to maintain herd health.
3. **Improved reproductive efficiency:** AI allows breeders to synchronize the estrous cycle of cows, leading to more efficient breeding. With natural breeding, cows come into heat at different times, making it difficult to breed the entire herd efficiently. AI can be used to breed a large number of cows in a short period, increasing the chances of pregnancy.
4. **Increased profitability:** AI can lead to increased profitability in cattle breeding. By using superior genetics, breeders can produce offspring that are more productive and have a higher market value. AI can also reduce the costs associated with natural breeding, such as maintaining a bull and the risks of injury to both cows and bulls during breeding.

To carry out AI, a technician collects semen from a bull and then processes it to ensure that it is of high quality and suitable for use in artificial insemination. The semen is then stored in liquid nitrogen at a temperature of -196°C. When the female animal is in heat, the semen is thawed and inserted into her reproductive tract using a special insemination gun.

AI is particularly useful in selective breeding programs where superior genetics are desired to produce the next generation of animals with desirable traits such as high milk production, improved meat quality, or disease resistance. Through AI, breeders can increase the number of offspring produced by superior bulls, which can accelerate genetic progress in the herd.

Artificial insemination is a vital tool in modern cattle breeding programs, and its use continues to grow worldwide. It offers several benefits to breeders, including genetic improvement, disease control, increased safety, and efficiency.

LIVESTOCK PRODUCTS: PROCESSING AND MARKETING OF MILK AND MILK PRODUCTS

Livestock products, particularly milk and milk products, are an essential component of the human diet and are consumed worldwide. Processing and marketing of milk and milk products are important for ensuring the availability of quality products for consumers and also for generating income for farmers.

Milk is processed to make various milk products such as butter, cheese, yogurt, and condensed milk. Milk processing involves various stages, including pasteurization, homogenization, and separation of milk components such as cream. Pasteurization is a process in which milk is heated to a specific temperature for a specific time to destroy harmful bacteria and pathogens. Homogenization is a process that breaks down milk fat globules to make the milk uniform and prevent separation. Separation of milk components is done to obtain cream, which can be further processed to make butter and ghee.

Marketing of milk and milk products involves various channels, including direct sales to consumers, sales to retailers and wholesalers, and exports. The marketing of milk and milk products is regulated by various laws and regulations to ensure the safety and quality of products. Milk and milk products must meet specific standards for quality, safety, and composition before they can be marketed.

In many countries, dairy cooperatives play an important role in the marketing of milk and milk products. Dairy cooperatives are organizations owned and controlled by dairy farmers, and they provide various services such as milk collection, processing, marketing, and distribution of milk and milk products. Dairy cooperatives help farmers get a fair price for their milk and also ensure the availability of quality milk products for consumers.

Processing and marketing of milk and milk products are critical for ensuring the availability of quality products for consumers and also for generating income for farmers. The dairy industry plays a significant role in the economy of many countries, and it is essential to regulate the industry to ensure the safety and quality of products.

Pasteurization

Pasteurization is a process in which milk and other dairy products are heated to a specific temperature for a specific time to kill harmful bacteria and pathogens. The process is named after Louis Pasteur, a French scientist who developed the technique in the 19th century.

There are two types of pasteurization used in the dairy industry: high-temperature short-time (HTST) pasteurization and ultra-high-temperature (UHT) pasteurization.

1. **High-Temperature Short-Time (HTST) pasteurization:** In HTST pasteurization, the milk is heated to a temperature of 72°C for 15 seconds. The milk is then cooled to below 4°C. This process destroys most harmful bacteria, including Listeria, Salmonella, and E. coli.
2. **Ultra-High-Temperature (UHT) pasteurization:** In UHT pasteurization, the milk is heated to a temperature of 135°C for a few seconds. This process kills all harmful bacteria and extends the shelf life of the milk to several months when stored in a sterile container. UHT pasteurization is used for producing long-life milk products.

Benefits of Pasteurization

1. **Food safety:** Pasteurization reduces the risk of foodborne illnesses by killing harmful bacteria and pathogens present in milk.
2. **Extended shelf life:** Pasteurized milk has a longer shelf life than raw milk.
3. **Consistency:** Pasteurization helps to standardize the quality and consistency of milk.
4. **Improved digestibility:** Pasteurization helps to break down enzymes in milk, which can make it easier to digest.
5. **Elimination of bacterial growth:** Pasteurization reduces the bacterial growth in milk and other dairy products.

However, some argue that pasteurization also destroys beneficial enzymes and vitamins present in milk, which can affect its nutritional value.

Homogenization

Homogenization is a process used in milk processing to reduce the size of fat globules in milk and make the milk uniform in texture and appearance. The process involves forcing milk through a small opening or a set of fine pores under high pressure, which breaks down the fat globules into smaller droplets. This process helps prevent the cream from separating and settling on top of the milk, which improves the shelf life and visual appeal of the milk.

Homogenization is a mechanical process that involves two main stages: pre-homogenization and final homogenization. In the pre-homogenization stage, milk is first heated to around 60-65°C to denature the whey proteins and partially melt the fat globules, which makes them easier to break down. The heated milk is then pumped into a homogenizing valve or a series of valves where it is subjected to high pressure. The pressure causes the milk to flow through a narrow gap, which creates turbulence and shearing forces that break down the fat globules into smaller droplets.

After pre-homogenization, the milk is cooled down to around 4-5°C to solidify the fat globules and prevent them from re-coalescing. The cooled milk is then subjected to final homogenization, where it is pumped through a second set of valves at high pressure to further break down any remaining fat globules. The final homogenization is usually done at a higher pressure than the pre-homogenization stage, which ensures that the milk is fully homogenized and has a uniform texture.

The degree of homogenization can vary depending on the type of milk and the desired final product. For example, whole milk is typically homogenized to a greater degree than skimmed milk because it contains more fat globules. Similarly, some milk products, such as heavy cream, may not be homogenized at all to preserve their unique texture and flavor.

Homogenization is an important step in milk processing that helps improve the texture, appearance, and shelf life of milk products.

Separation of Milk Components

Separation of milk components is the process of separating milk into its various components, such as cream, skim milk,

C. The inheritance of one trait is not affected by the inheritance of another trait
D. The dominant allele masks the expression of the recessive allele

PASSAGE 5

pH is a measure of the acidity or basicity of a solution, with values ranging from 0 to 14. A pH of 7 is considered neutral, while values below 7 are acidic and values above 7 are basic. Buffers are solutions that can resist changes in pH when small amounts of acid or base are added. They are important in maintaining the pH of biological systems, such as blood, within a narrow range.

Carbohydrates, proteins, lipids, vitamins, and enzymes are all important biomolecules in living organisms. Carbohydrates are classified based on their size into monosaccharides, disaccharides, and polysaccharides. Proteins are composed of amino acids, and their functions include structural support, enzymatic catalysis, and regulation of gene expression. Lipids are hydrophobic molecules that include fats, oils, and steroids. Vitamins are essential organic compounds that cannot be synthesized by the body and must be obtained through diet. Enzymes are proteins that catalyze biochemical reactions, increasing the rate of chemical reactions in cells.

1. What is a pH?
   A. A measure of the acidity or basicity of a solution
   B. A measure of the concentration of protons in a solution
   C. A measure of the concentration of hydroxide ions in a solution
   D. A measure of the concentration of water in a solution
2. What are buffers?
   A. Solutions that can resist changes in pH when small amounts of acid or base are added
   B. Solutions that increase the pH of a solution
   C. Solutions that decrease the pH of a solution
   D. Solutions that are only found in acidic environments
3. What are lipids?
   A. Hydrophobic molecules that include fats, oils, and steroids
   B. Molecules composed of amino acids
   C. Essential organic compounds that cannot be synthesized by the body
   D. Proteins that catalyze biochemical reactions
4. What are enzymes?
   A. Proteins that catalyze biochemical reactions
   B. Carbohydrates that are important for energy storage
   C. Lipids that are important for membrane structure
   D. Vitamins that are important for bone growth
5. How are carbohydrates classified?
   A. Based on their color
   B. Based on their solubility in water
   C. Based on their size into monosaccharides, disaccharides, and polysaccharides
   D. Based on their ability to form double bonds

PASSAGE 6

Livestock plays a crucial role in agriculture and industry. They provide a variety of products such as meat, milk, eggs, wool, and leather. Livestock also provides non-food products like manure, which is an important source of nutrients for crops. In addition, livestock also play an important role in the cultural and social practices of many societies.

The livestock industry also provides employment opportunities for many people in different sectors, such as meat processing, veterinary medicine, and transportation. The livestock industry has a significant impact on the economy, both in terms of employment and the value of its products.

Livestock farming also has environmental impacts, such as greenhouse gas emissions and land use. Sustainable livestock management practices are important in reducing these impacts while still maintaining the production of livestock products.

1. What are some products provided by livestock?
   A. Vegetables and fruits
   B. Meat, milk, eggs, wool, and leather
   C. Fish and seafood
   D. Grains and cereals
2. What is the role of livestock in agriculture?
   A. Livestock provides an important source of nutrients for crops
   B. Livestock provides a source of renewable energy
   C. Livestock helps to control pests and weeds in fields
   D. Livestock is not important in agriculture
3. What is the economic impact of the livestock industry?
   A. It has no impact on the economy
   B. It provides employment opportunities for many people in different sectors
   C. It only benefits large corporations
   D. It is not a profitable industry
4. What are some environmental impacts of livestock farming?
   A. Reduced greenhouse gas emissions
   B. Reduced land use
   C. Increased air quality
   D. Increased greenhouse gas emissions and land use
5. Why is sustainable livestock management important?
   A. To increase greenhouse gas emissions
   B. To reduce the environmental impacts of livestock farming

ANSWERS

1	2	3	4	5	6	7	8	9	10
B	A	D	B	B	B	A	A	B	D
11	**12**	**13**	**14**	**15**	**16**	**17**	**18**	**19**	**20**
C	D	B	A	C	D	A	B	D	B
21	**22**	**23**	**24**	**25**	**26**	**27**	**28**	**29**	**30**
D	C	D	B	D	D	A	B	D	B
31	**32**	**33**	**34**	**35**	**36**	**37**	**38**	**39**	**40**
D	C	A	D	C	D	C	C	D	D
41	**42**	**43**	**44**	**45**	**46**	**47**	**48**	**49**	**50**
A	A	D	D	C	B	C	A	D	C
51	**52**	**53**	**54**	**55**	**56**	**57**	**58**	**59**	**60**
B	D	D	A	D	C	D	C	D	C
61	**62**	**63**	**64**	**65**	**66**	**67**	**68**	**69**	**70**
D	D	D	C	B	C	D	B	C	C
71	**72**	**73**	**74**						
C	C	D	A						

● ● ●

(*a*) Alignment of the shelter in east-west direction and width in north-south direction
(*b*) Separation of unproductive animals from the lot to save costs
(*c*) Durability and attractiveness of the shelter
(*d*) Keeping troughs and vessels for water clean
(*e*) Providing adequate ventilation arrangements

Choose the correct answer from the options given below:

A. (*a*), (*b*) and (*c*) only B. (*b*), (*c*) and (*d*) only
C. (*a*), (*c*) and (*e*) only D. (*c*), (*d*) and (*e*) only

6. Arrange the following steps involved in the sterilization of milk in the correct sequence:
(*a*) Cleaning and filtering of milk
(*b*) Treatment of milk at 100°F to 120°F for clarification
(*c*) Heating of milk at 150°F to 160°F to make it uniform
(*d*) Passing milk through a homogenous mixture machine after filtration
(*e*) Filling milk in sterilized vessels, sealing and dipping in a tank at 212°F to 230°F

Choose the correct answer from the options given below:

A. (*c*), (*a*), (*d*), (*b*) and (*e*)
B. (*c*), (*d*), (*a*), (*e*) and (*b*)
C. (*c*), (*b*), (*e*), (*d*) and (*a*)
D. (*c*), (*b*), (*a*), (*e*) and (*d*)

7. If an animal's temperature goes up (106°F) due to nutritional deficiency, which disorder might follow constipation?
A. Bloat B. Anemia
C. Enterotoxemia D. Coccidiosis

8. What is the cause of Marek's disease in poultry?
A. Avian Reovirus B. Paramyxovirus
C. Herpesvirus D. Avipoxvirus

9. Tuberculosis is considered a ______ type of disease.
A. Chronic B. Sub-acute
C. Acute D. Pre-acute

10. What is the recommended width of a manger in cattle housing system?
A. 1.0 meter B. 0.8 meter
C. 1.5 meter D. 1.8 meter

11. What is the daily dry fodder requirement for an adult cow?
A. 20 – 25 kg B. 5 – 7 kg
C. 1.5 – 2.5kg D. 10 – 12 kg

12. What is the term for inflammation and infection of the udder or mammary glands?
A. Foot & Mouth disease
B. Mastitis
C. Brucellosis
D. Black quarter

13. What causes black quarter disease?
A. Pasteurella multocida
B. Brucella abortus
C. Picorma vinus
D. Clostridium chanvoei

14. In what housing system are animals arranged in a face-to-face manner?
A. Head to Head B. Tail to Tail
C. Loose housing D. Open housing

15. What percentage of a calf's body weight should colostrum be fed at?
A. 20 B. 40
C. 10 D. 60

16. Which disease is caused by the Picorna virus?
A. Sheep & goat Pox
B. Paste des petits ruminants
C. Foot & mouth disease
D. Rabies

17. Which of the following is a chronic disease of animals?
A. Black quarter B. Anthrax
C. Mastitis D. Tuberculosis

18. Which of the following points is not considered while developing a housing system for a dairy farm?
A. Shed design
B. Housing of young stock
C. Milking parlour
D. Size of animal

19. What is the range of weeks of age for grower birds to be fed grower mash?
A. 9 – 19 B. 0 – 8
C. After 20 D. 0 – 4

20. Exotic breeds of cattle are:
(*a*) Holstein Friesian
(*b*) Deoni
(*c*) Jersey
(*d*) Gaolao
(*e*) Brown Swiss

Choose the correct answer from the options given below:

A. (*a*) only B. (*a*) and (*b*) only
C. (*d*) only D. (*a*), (*c*), and (*e*) only

21. What is the normal pH range of bull semen?
A. 8.5 to 8.8 B. 7.6 to 7.8
C. 6.4 to 6.8 D. 5.2 to 5.6

22. Mehsana breed of buffalo is intermediate cross between:
A. Jersey and Holstein Friesian
B. Murrah and Surti

C. Brown Swiss and Surti
D. Jersey and Murrah

23. Indian milch breeds are:
(*a*) Sahiwal (*b*) Kankrej
(*c*) Gir (*d*) Kapila
(*e*) Dangi

Choose the correct answer from the options given below:
A. (*a*) only B. (*a*) and (*c*) only
C. (*d*) and (*e*) only D. (*e*) only

24. Which of the following is NOT a benefit of livestock in agriculture?
A. Production of manure for soil fertility
B. Diversification of income sources for farmers
C. Contribution to the economy through the sale of livestock products
D. Destruction of crops due to overgrazing

25. The White Revolution in India refers to the significant increase in the production of which livestock product?
A. Milk B. Meat
C. Eggs D. Wool

26. Which of the following is NOT a reason for the importance of livestock in agriculture and industry?
A. Livestock can be used for transportation and labor
B. Livestock provide a source of food and nutrition for humans
C. Livestock can be used as a source of renewable energy
D. Livestock can help reduce greenhouse gas emissions

27. The National Dairy Development Board (NDDB) was established in India to promote which of the following industries?
A. Poultry B. Fishery
C. Dairy D. Wool

28. Which of the following is a negative impact of the White Revolution in India?
A. Increased production of milk and milk products
B. Overreliance on imported genetics for dairy cattle
C. Improved livelihoods for small-scale dairy farmers
D. Decreased consumption of dairy products among the Indian population

29. Which is an important Indian breed of cow known for its high milk yield?
A. Holstein Friesian B. Jersey
C. Sahiwal D. Ayrshire

30. Which breed of buffalo is commonly found in India?
A. Murrah B. Swiss
C. Nubian D. Alpine

31. Which state in India is known for its high population of cows?
A. Gujarat B. Punjab
C. Tamil Nadu D. Maharashtra

32. Which breed of chicken is known for its high egg-laying capacity?
A. Rhode Island Red B. Leghorn
C. Brahma D. Cochin

33. Which is an exotic breed of cow commonly found in India?
A. Gir B. Rathi
C. Tharparkar D. Holstein Friesian

34. What is the normal volume of semen per ejaculate in a buffalo bull?
A. 8-10 ml B. 5-8 ml
C. 3-4 ml D. 1-2 ml

35. What is semen preserved at –196°C in liquid nitrogen called?
A. liquid semen B. Frozen semen
C. Hot semen D. Solid semen

36. What is the most commonly used method of semen collection in animals?
A. Electro-ejaculation method
B. Artificial vagina method
C. Massage method
D. Electrical method

37. What is the specific gravity of semen in bull?
A. 1.035 B. 2.01
C. 3.01 D. 4.35

38. Approximate quantity of wool produced in India per annum is
A. 47.9 million kg B. 120.90 million kg
C. 155.5 million kg D. 7020 million kg

39. What is the primary advantage of open housing system for cattle?
A. High stocking density
B. Lower investment cost
C. Better climate control
D. Increased labour efficiency

40. Which of the following is not a type of deep litter system for poultry housing?
A. Straw-based B. Sawdust-based
C. Rice husk-based D. Wire mesh-based

41. Which type of housing system for cattle provides the greatest level of control over the animal's environment?
A. Open housing B. Semi-open housing
C. Closed housing D. Partially-closed housing

42. What is the primary disadvantage of battery cages for poultry housing?
A. Low egg production
B. High labour cost
C. Increased susceptibility to disease
D. Poor animal welfare

method is drying, where fruits and vegetables are dehydrated to remove moisture and inhibit bacterial growth. Freezing is also a popular preservation method that involves storing fruits and vegetables at very low temperatures to maintain their quality and freshness.

Other methods of preservation include pickling, where fruits and vegetables are soaked in vinegar or brine, and fermenting, where fruits and vegetables are soaked in a salt solution to encourage the growth of beneficial bacteria.

1. What is canning?
A. Storing fruits and vegetables at low temperatures
B. Sealing fruits and vegetables in airtight containers and heating to high temperatures
C. Soaking fruits and vegetables in vinegar or brine
D. Dehydrating fruits and vegetables

2. What is drying?
A. Storing fruits and vegetables at low temperatures
B. Sealing fruits and vegetables in airtight containers and heating to high temperatures
C. Soaking fruits and vegetables in vinegar or brine
D. Dehydrating fruits and vegetables

3. What is freezing?
A. Storing fruits and vegetables at low temperatures
B. Sealing fruits and vegetables in airtight containers and heating to high temperatures
C. Soaking fruits and vegetables in vinegar or brine
D. Dehydrating fruits and vegetables

4. What is pickling?
A. Storing fruits and vegetables at low temperatures
B. Sealing fruits and vegetables in airtight containers and heating to high temperatures
C. Soaking fruits and vegetables in vinegar or brine
D. Dehydrating fruits and vegetables

5. What is fermenting?
A. Storing fruits and vegetables at low temperatures
B. Sealing fruits and vegetables in airtight containers and heating to high temperatures
C. Soaking fruits and vegetables in vinegar or brine
D. Soaking fruits and vegetables in a salt solution

PASSAGE 14

Trees, shrubs, climbers, annuals, and perennials are all different types of plants based on their life cycles and growth habits. Trees are perennial woody plants that have a single stem or trunk with a well-defined crown. Shrubs are also woody plants, but they have multiple stems and usually grow to a shorter height than trees. Climbers are plants that climb on other plants or structures for support. Annuals complete their life cycle within a year, and their seeds need to be replanted each year for continuous growth. Perennials live for multiple years and regrow each season from the same roots.

Plants can be propagated by various methods, including seeds, cuttings, budding, layering, and grafting. Seeds are the most common method of propagation for annuals and some perennials. Cuttings are used to propagate shrubs and climbers, while budding and grafting are used to propagate fruit trees and other woody plants. Layering is a method of propagation where a branch is allowed to grow roots while still attached to the parent plant before being separated and replanted.

1. Which type of plant completes its life cycle within a year?
A. Trees B. Shrubs
C. Climbers D. Annuals

2. What is the primary method of propagation for annuals and some perennials?
A. Seeds B. Cuttings
C. Budding D. Grafting

3. Which method of propagation is used to propagate fruit trees and other woody plants?
A. Seeds B. Cuttings
C. Budding D. Grafting

4. Which type of plant regrows each season from the same roots?
A. Trees B. Shrubs
C. Climbers D. Perennials

5. Which method of propagation involves allowing a branch to grow roots while still attached to the parent plant before being separated and replanted?
A. Seeds B. Cuttings
C. Budding D. Layering

PASSAGE 15

Post-harvest technology plays a crucial role in maintaining the quality of agricultural produce and increasing the shelf life of crops. Storage, processing, and marketing of major field crops are essential to meet the food and nutritional requirements of a growing population.

Rice, wheat, maize, sorghum, pearl millet, groundnut, mustard, pigeon-pea, gram, sugarcane, cotton, and berseem are some of the major field crops in India. Proper storage techniques like fumigation, drying, and storage in airtight containers can prevent pest infestation and spoilage. Processing techniques like milling, threshing, and grading can improve the quality of the produce and increase its value.

Marketing of the crops involves the process of transportation, packaging, and selling to the consumers. Proper packaging techniques like vacuum packaging, modified atmosphere packaging, and use of preservatives can increase the shelf life of the crops and reduce wastage.

1. Which of the following is a major field crop in India?
A. Mango B. Banana
C. Wheat D. Papaya

C. To reduce the production of livestock products
D. To decrease employment opportunities in the livestock industry

PASSAGE 7

Since independence, India has made significant progress in foodgrain production. From a situation of food shortage and dependence on imports, India is now self-sufficient in foodgrains, producing enough to meet the needs of its population. The Green Revolution, which began in the 1960s, played a significant role in increasing foodgrain production, especially wheat and rice.

In recent years, there has been a focus on sustainable crop production, with an emphasis on reducing the use of chemical fertilizers and pesticides and promoting organic farming practices. This approach aims to improve soil health, reduce the environmental impact of agriculture, and promote the production of healthier food.

The commercialization of agriculture is also gaining importance in India. There is a growing demand for high-value crops, such as fruits and vegetables, and for processed food products. The growth of the food processing industry offers opportunities for farmers to add value to their products and increase their income.

1. What is the status of India's foodgrain production since independence?
A. India is still dependent on food imports
B. India is self-sufficient in foodgrains
C. India produces enough food for export
D. India's food production has remained stagnant

2. What was the Green Revolution in India?
A. A movement to promote organic farming
B. A campaign to reduce the use of chemical fertilizers
C. A program to increase foodgrain production, especially wheat and rice
D. A campaign to reduce the use of water in agriculture

3. What is sustainable crop production?
A. A focus on reducing the use of chemical fertilizers and pesticides
B. A focus on increasing foodgrain production at all costs
C. A focus on using genetically modified crops
D. A focus on maximizing profits for farmers

4. What is the commercialization of agriculture?
A. A focus on promoting organic farming practices
B. A focus on increasing the production of food for domestic consumption
C. A focus on promoting the growth of the food processing industry
D. A focus on reducing the use of water in agriculture

5. What are the benefits of sustainable crop production?
A. Improved soil health and reduced environmental impact
B. Increased use of chemical fertilizers and pesticides
C. Reduced food production and increased food prices
D. Increased profits for farmers

PASSAGE 8

Soil is a complex mixture of organic and inorganic materials that support plant growth. One important characteristic of soil is pH, which is a measure of the soil's acidity or alkalinity. Most plants grow best in soil with a pH between 6 and 7. Soil texture refers to the size of the mineral particles that make up the soil, which can affect water and nutrient retention.

Soil structure refers to how those particles are arranged, which can affect the soil's ability to hold water and air. Soil organisms, such as bacteria, fungi, and earthworms, play important roles in decomposing organic matter and making nutrients available to plants. Soil tilth refers to the physical condition of the soil, including its texture, structure, and water-holding capacity. Soil fertility is a measure of the soil's ability to provide essential nutrients to plants. Soil health refers to the overall condition of the soil, including its physical, chemical, and biological properties.

1. What is soil pH?
A. A measure of the soil's acidity or alkalinity
B. The size of the mineral particles in the soil
C. The arrangement of the soil particles
D. The physical condition of the soil

2. What is soil texture?
A. The size of the mineral particles in the soil
B. The arrangement of the soil particles
C. The physical condition of the soil
D. The measure of the soil's ability to provide essential nutrients to plants

3. What is soil structure?
A. The size of the mineral particles in the soil
B. The arrangement of the soil particles
C. The measure of the soil's ability to provide essential nutrients to plants
D. The measure of the soil's acidity or alkalinity

4. What are soil organisms?
A. Plants that grow in soil
B. Animals that live in soil
C. Bacteria, fungi, and earthworms
D. Rocks and minerals in the soil

5. What is soil health?
A. The physical condition of the soil
B. The measure of the soil's ability to provide essential nutrients to plants
C. The overall condition of the soil, including its physical, chemical, and biological properties
D. The size of the mineral particles in the soil

UNIT 3

Crop Production

TARGETS AND ACHIEVEMENTS IN FOODGRAIN PRODUCTION IN INDIA SINCE INDEPENDENCE

Since India gained independence in 1947, there has been a significant growth in foodgrain production. India's foodgrain production has increased from 50.8 million tonnes in 1950-51 to 296.65 million tonnes in 2019-20. In the early years after independence, the government focused on increasing the production of foodgrains, particularly wheat and rice, through the introduction of high-yielding varieties (HYVs), better irrigation facilities, and increased fertilizer usage. The Green Revolution in the 1960s and 70s played a crucial role in increasing food production, particularly in wheat and rice.

The following are some of the key targets and achievements in foodgrain production in India:

- The first Green Revolution in the 1960s and 70s helped increase the production of wheat and rice in India. As a result, the country became self-sufficient in food production and even started exporting foodgrains.
- The government launched the National Food Security Mission (NFSM) in 2007 with the aim of increasing foodgrain production by 10 million tonnes annually. The mission focused on rice, wheat, and pulses and provided farmers with improved seeds, fertilizers, and other inputs.
- The government launched the Pradhan Mantri Fasal Bima Yojana (PMFBY) in 2016 to provide insurance coverage to farmers against crop loss due to natural calamities, pests, and diseases. This scheme helped in stabilizing the income of farmers and increasing foodgrain production.
- The government introduced the Pradhan Mantri Krishi Sinchai Yojana (PMKSY) in 2015 to promote irrigation facilities and improve water-use efficiency. The scheme aimed to provide water to every farm and improve the productivity of crops.
- The government launched the Soil Health Card Scheme in 2015 to assess the nutrient status of soil and provide recommendations for appropriate fertilizer use. This scheme helped in improving soil health and increasing crop yields.

SUSTAINABLE CROP PRODUCTION

Sustainable crop production is the practice of producing food in a way that preserves the environment, conserves natural resources, and ensures the long-term viability of agriculture. Sustainable crop production focuses on improving soil health, conserving water, reducing the use of pesticides and fertilizers, and minimizing greenhouse gas emissions.

The following are some of the practices that promote sustainable crop production:

- **Crop rotation:** The practice of growing different crops in a specific sequence on the same land is known as crop rotation. It helps in improving soil health, reducing pests and diseases, and improving crop yields.
- **Integrated Pest Management (IPM):** IPM is an approach that combines different pest management strategies to minimize the use of pesticides. This approach includes the use of natural enemies of pests, crop rotation, and the use of resistant varieties.
- **Conservation agriculture:** Conservation agriculture is a farming system that involves minimal soil disturbance, crop residue retention, and crop rotation. This practice helps in improving soil health, conserving water, and reducing greenhouse gas emissions.
- **Organic farming:** Organic farming is a farming system that relies on natural inputs such as compost, crop rotation, and natural pest control methods. It helps in improving soil health, reducing the use of synthetic inputs, and producing healthier food.

COMMERCIALIZATION OF AGRICULTURE AND ITS SCOPE IN INDIA

Commercialization of agriculture refers to the shift from subsistence farming to a more commercial approach to farming. In this approach, farmers focus on producing crops and livestock for sale in the market rather than just for their own consumption. Commercialization of agriculture has the potential to increase farmers' income, improve rural livelihoods, and promote economic growth.

The following are some of the factors that have contributed to the commercialization of agriculture and its scope in India:

1. **Government Policies:** The government has implemented policies and schemes to promote commercialization of agriculture, such as setting up of agricultural marketing infrastructure, price support systems, and credit facilities for farmers. These policies have encouraged farmers to invest in modern inputs and technology, leading to higher yields and better quality crops.
2. **Technological Advancements:** The development of high-yielding crop varieties, mechanization, precision farming, and adoption of modern irrigation techniques have increased productivity and efficiency in agriculture. This has led to the production of surplus crops, which can be sold in the market.
3. **Access to Finance:** Access to finance has been made easier for farmers, enabling them to invest in agriculture on a commercial scale. Banks, financial institutions, and government schemes provide credit and loans for farmers to invest in agriculture.
4. **Market Integration:** Integration of agricultural markets across the country through the introduction of electronic trading platforms and the removal of inter-state trade barriers has led to better price discovery and market access for farmers. This has also enabled them to participate in national and global value chains.
5. **Private Sector Participation:** Private sector participation in agriculture has increased, leading to the growth of contract farming, supply chain management, and value addition. This has provided farmers with access to better inputs, technology, and markets, leading to higher profits.

The commercialization of agriculture in India has immense scope, and it is important to sustain it through appropriate policies and investments. Commercialization can lead to increased productivity, better quality produce, and higher incomes for farmers, thus contributing to the overall growth of the agricultural sector and the economy.

CLASSIFICATION OF FIELD CROPS BASED ON THEIR UTILITY-CEREALS, PULSES, OILS SEEDS, FIBRE, SUGAR AND FORAGE CROPS

Classification of field crops based on their utility is an important aspect of agriculture. Here are some important details about each category:

Cereals: Cereals are one of the major categories of field crops and are primarily grown for their edible grains, which are rich in carbohydrates and provide a major source of energy to humans and livestock. Here are some important details about cereals:

- **Rice:** Rice is a staple food crop in India and is grown in almost all parts of the country. It is a major source of carbohydrates and provides a significant amount of protein as well. India is one of the largest producers of rice in the world.
- **Wheat:** Wheat is another important cereal crop grown in India, primarily in the northern and northwestern parts of the country. It is a rich source of protein and carbohydrates and is used to make a variety of food products, such as bread, pasta, and baked goods.
- **Maize:** Maize, also known as corn, is a widely grown cereal crop in India and is used for both human consumption and animal feed. It is a rich source of carbohydrates and provides a significant amount of protein as well.
- **Sorghum:** Sorghum is a hardy cereal crop that can be grown in dry and arid regions. It is primarily used as animal feed but can also be used for human consumption, such as in the production of sorghum flour.
- **Millets:** Millets are a group of small-seeded cereal crops that are grown in various parts of India. They are hardy and can be grown in dry and arid regions. Millets are a rich source of carbohydrates and provide a significant amount of protein as well.

Cereals are an important category of field crops in India and provide a major source of energy to humans and livestock. The various cereal crops grown in India have different characteristics and are suited to different agro-climatic conditions.

Pulses: Pulses are leguminous crops. They are an important category of field crops that are grown primarily for their seeds. They are rich in protein, fiber, and other essential nutrients and are an important source of nutrition for humans and livestock. Some of the important pulse crops grown in India include chickpea, pigeon pea, lentil, and mung bean. Here are some important details about pulses:

PASSAGE 15

1	2	3	4	5
C	B	B	C	A

PASSAGE 16

1	2	3	4	5
C	B	D	A	D

PASSAGE 17

1	2	3	4	5
C	A	C	D	A

PASSAGE 18

1	2	3	4	5
C	C	B	D	C

PASSAGE 19

1	2	3	4	5
C	C	B	C	A

PASSAGE 20

1	2	3	4	5
B	D	D	B	A

2. Which of the following storage techniques can prevent pest infestation in crops?
A. Open storage B. Airtight containers
C. Direct sunlight D. High humidity

3. Which of the following processing techniques can improve the quality of the produce?
A. Over-ripening B. Milling
C. Delayed harvesting D. Improper grading

4. What is the process of transportation, packaging, and selling of crops called?
A. Cultivation B. Irrigation
C. Marketing D. Harvesting

5. Which of the following packaging techniques can increase the shelf life of crops?
A. Use of preservatives
B. Open packaging
C. Exposure to direct sunlight
D. Use of paper bags

PASSAGE 16

Weeds are unwanted plants that grow in crop fields and compete with crops for water, nutrients and sunlight. They reduce crop yield and quality. Effective weed control is essential for successful crop production. The principles of weed control include prevention, suppression and eradication of weeds.

Weed control can be achieved through cultural, mechanical, chemical, biological and integrated weed management methods. Cultural weed control involves practices like crop rotation, intercropping and use of cover crops to prevent weed growth. Mechanical weed control methods involve physical removal of weeds through hand weeding, hoeing, plowing, and use of weeders.

Chemical weed control involves the use of herbicides to kill weeds. Biological weed control involves the use of natural enemies of weeds like insects and pathogens to control weed growth. Integrated weed management involves the use of a combination of cultural, mechanical, chemical and biological weed control methods for effective weed control.

1. Which method of weed control involves the use of herbicides?
A. Cultural B. Mechanical
C. Chemical D. Biological

2. Which method of weed control involves physical removal of weeds?
A. Cultural B. Mechanical
C. Chemical D. Biological

3. Which method of weed control involves the use of natural enemies of weeds?
A. Cultural B. Mechanical
C. Chemical D. Biological

4. Which weed control method involves the use of crop rotation and intercropping?
A. Cultural B. Mechanical
C. Chemical D. Biological

5. Which method of weed control involves the use of a combination of cultural, mechanical, chemical and biological weed control methods?
A. Cultural
B. Mechanical
C. Chemical
D. Integrated weed management

PASSAGE 17

Plants require a variety of nutrients for their growth and development. There are 16 essential plant nutrients, including macronutrients and micronutrients. Macronutrients are required in large amounts, while micronutrients are needed in smaller quantities. The macronutrients include nitrogen, phosphorus, potassium, calcium, magnesium, and sulfur, while micronutrients include iron, manganese, zinc, copper, boron, molybdenum, chlorine, nickel, and cobalt.

Each nutrient has a specific function in the plant. Nitrogen is necessary for the growth of leaves and stems, phosphorus is important for root development and flower formation, potassium helps in the formation of strong stems and resistance to diseases, calcium is essential for cell wall formation, magnesium is required for chlorophyll synthesis, and sulfur is needed for protein synthesis.

Deficiency symptoms vary for each nutrient. Nitrogen deficiency leads to stunted growth and yellowing of leaves, while phosphorus deficiency causes slow growth and dark green leaves. Potassium deficiency results in yellowing and scorching of leaf margins, and calcium deficiency causes tip burn in fruits and leaves. Magnesium deficiency leads to yellowing of leaves between veins, and sulfur deficiency causes yellowing of young leaves.

1. How many essential plant nutrients are there?
A. 10 B. 12
C. 16 D. 20

2. Which nutrient is necessary for the growth of leaves and stems?
A. Nitrogen B. Phosphorus
C. Potassium D. Calcium

3. What does phosphorus deficiency cause in plants?
A. Yellowing of leaves
B. Stunted growth
C. Slow growth and dark green leaves
D. Yellowing and scorching of leaf margins

An acidic soil has a higher concentration of H^+ ions, while an alkaline soil has more hydroxyl (OH^-) ions. A neutral pH occurs when the concentrations of H^+ and OH^- ions are equal.

Slightly acidic soils with a pH ranging from 6.5 to 7 are generally considered best for plant growth as they provide the maximum availability of nutrients. Soil pH can be measured using a pH meter, pH paper method, or pH scale, which ranges from 0 to 14. A pH of 7 is neutral, while lower values indicate higher H^+ ion concentration and more acidic soil. Higher values indicate an alkaline reaction with more OH^- ions.

The effects of soil pH on plant growth are significant, including:

- An optimum soil pH of 6.5 to 7.5 provides maximum availability of nutrients for plant growth.
- Low pH levels (<6.0) can lead to an increase in aluminum content in the soil, which may become toxic to plants.
- Acidic soils generally have higher levels of toxic metals that can negatively impact soil microorganisms' activity, affecting plant growth.

Monitoring and managing soil pH is essential for ensuring optimal plant growth and productivity. Regular soil testing and appropriate corrective actions, such as liming or acidifying, can help maintain a healthy soil pH and maximize plant nutrient uptake.

SOIL TEXTURE

Soil texture refers to the physical composition of soil particles, which includes sand, silt, and clay. Understanding soil texture is important because it affects various soil properties such as water-holding capacity, nutrient availability, and soil structure, which in turn affects plant growth and productivity.

Sand particles are the largest and are generally between 0.05 and 2.0 mm in diameter. They are relatively coarse and feel gritty to the touch. Sandy soils have large pore spaces between particles, which allow for good drainage but can also lead to rapid leaching of nutrients. Because sandy soils do not hold water well, they are often low in fertility and require frequent irrigation and fertilization.

Silt particles are smaller than sand particles and range in size from 0.002 to 0.05 mm in diameter. Silt feels smooth to the touch, and soils with high silt content tend to be more fertile than sandy soils. Silt particles have intermediate pore space, which allows for good water and air movement through the soil. Soils with high silt content are often well-structured and can be easily tilled.

Clay particles are the smallest, with diameters of less than 0.002 mm. They are very fine and feel sticky and smooth to the touch. Clay soils have very small pore spaces between particles, which can cause poor drainage and waterlogging. However, they have a high capacity to hold water and nutrients, making them highly fertile. Clay soils are often prone to compaction, which can reduce plant growth and yield.

Soil texture is determined by the relative proportion of sand, silt, and clay particles in the soil. The proportion of each particle type determines the soil's texture class. The USDA soil texture triangle is a widely used tool that helps to determine soil texture based on the proportion of sand, silt, and clay in a soil sample.

In addition to sand, silt, and clay, organic matter also plays an important role in soil texture. Organic matter can help to improve soil structure and water-holding capacity, as well as provide nutrients for plant growth.

SOIL STRUCTURE

Soil structure refers to the arrangement of soil particles into aggregates, which can vary in size, shape, and stability. Soil structure is an important characteristic because it affects various soil properties, such as water infiltration, soil aeration, nutrient availability, and plant root development.

Soil aggregates can be classified into different types based on their size, shape, and stability. These include:

1. **Macroaggregates:** These are larger aggregates that range in size from 0.25 to 10 mm in diameter. Macroaggregates are stable and are held together by organic matter, roots, and fungal hyphae. They provide large pore spaces that allow for good water infiltration and soil aeration.
2. **Microaggregates:** These are smaller aggregates that range in size from 0.002 to 0.25 mm in diameter. Microaggregates are less stable than macroaggregates and are held together by clay particles and organic matter. They provide small pore spaces that can hold onto water and nutrients.
3. **Single particles:** These are individual soil particles that are not aggregated. Single particles can be sand, silt, or clay, and they determine soil texture.

Soil structure can be improved through various management practices, including:

1. **Organic matter addition:** Organic matter can act as a cementing agent, holding soil particles together and forming stable aggregates. Adding organic matter to soil can improve soil structure, increase water-holding capacity, and promote nutrient availability.
2. **Reduced tillage:** Excessive tillage can break down soil aggregates, leading to soil compaction and reduced soil structure. Reduced tillage practices, such as no-till or minimum tillage, can help to maintain soil structure and promote soil health.

3. **Crop rotation:** Growing a diverse range of crops can improve soil structure by promoting different types of root systems and organic matter inputs. Crop rotation can also help to reduce soil-borne diseases and pest pressure.
4. **Cover crops:** Growing cover crops can help to protect soil from erosion, improve soil structure, and add organic matter to the soil.

Soil structure is an essential factor in the health and productivity of soils. Farmers and soil scientists need to understand the different types of soil structure and their impacts to manage soil properly. Maintaining healthy soil structure ensures that soil can support plant growth, filter water, and store carbon.

SOIL ORGANISMS

Soil organisms are living organisms that inhibit the soil and play important roles in soil fertility, nutrient cycling, and plant growth. These organisms include microorganisms, such as bacteria, fungi, and protozoa, as well as larger organisms, such as earthworms, nematodes, and arthropods.

Microorganisms are the most numerous and diverse group of soil organisms. They are involved in various processes in the soil, such as decomposition of organic matter, nutrient cycling, and plant-microbe interactions. Bacteria and fungi are the most abundant and play crucial roles in these processes. Bacteria are important in the cycling of nutrients, such as nitrogen and phosphorus, while fungi are important in the decomposition of complex organic matter, such as lignin.

Protozoa are single-celled organisms that play important roles in nutrient cycling and plant-microbe interactions. They are predators of bacteria and other microorganisms, and their grazing can affect microbial populations and nutrient availability in the soil.

Larger soil organisms, such as earthworms, nematodes, and arthropods, also play important roles in soil health. Earthworms help to improve soil structure and nutrient cycling by burrowing through the soil and creating channels for water and air movement. Nematodes are important in the decomposition of organic matter and nutrient cycling, while some species are also plant pathogens. Arthropods, such as insects and mites, can be both beneficial and harmful to soil health, depending on the species and their interactions with other soil organisms.

Soil organisms can be affected by various environmental factors, such as temperature, moisture, and pH. Changes in these factors can affect the abundance and diversity of soil organisms, which in turn can affect soil health and plant growth. For example, high temperatures can reduce microbial activity and nutrient cycling, while low moisture levels can limit the growth of soil organisms.

Soil management practices can also affect soil organisms. Practices such as tillage, fertilization, and pesticide use can have both positive and negative effects on soil organisms. For example, tillage can disrupt soil structure and reduce microbial activity, while organic matter addition can promote microbial growth and nutrient cycling.

Soil organisms play important roles in soil health and plant growth. Understanding the diversity and functions of soil organisms can help farmers and gardeners make informed decisions about soil management practices that promote soil health and sustainable agriculture.

SOIL TILTH

Soil tilth refers to the physical condition of soil, particularly its ability to support plant growth. It is determined by various factors, such as soil structure, soil texture, soil organic matter content, and soil moisture.

Good soil tilth is important for plant growth because it affects various soil properties, such as water infiltration, soil aeration, nutrient availability, and root development. Soil with good tilth has a crumbly, well-aggregated structure that allows for good water infiltration and soil aeration, while also providing enough pore space to hold onto water and nutrients. Good soil tilth also promotes the growth of beneficial soil organisms, such as bacteria, fungi, and earthworms, which help to maintain soil fertility and nutrient cycling.

Factors that can affect soil tilth include:

1. **Soil texture:** Soil texture refers to the relative proportions of sand, silt, and clay in soil. Soil with a balanced texture, such as loam, tends to have good tilth because it provides a good balance of pore space and water-holding capacity.
2. **Soil organic matter:** Soil organic matter is an important component of soil that helps to maintain good tilth. Organic matter acts as a cementing agent, holding soil particles together and forming stable soil aggregates. It also provides a source of nutrients for plants and beneficial soil organisms.
3. **Soil compaction:** Soil compaction can reduce soil tilth by reducing pore space and limiting water infiltration and soil aeration. Compaction can be caused by heavy machinery, foot traffic, or other factors that compress soil particles.
4. **Soil erosion:** Soil erosion can also reduce soil tilth by removing topsoil and exposing subsoil, which may have a different texture or structure. Erosion can be caused by water, wind, or other factors that remove soil particles.

Improving soil tilth can be achieved through various management practices, including:

1. **Organic matter addition:** Adding organic matter to soil can help to improve soil structure and promote good tilth. Organic matter can be added through practices such as cover cropping, composting, and manure application.
2. **Reduced tillage:** Reduced tillage practices, such as no-till or minimum tillage, can help to maintain good soil structure and reduce soil compaction, which in turn promotes good tilth.
3. **Crop rotation:** Crop rotation can help to maintain soil fertility and promote good tilth by promoting diverse root systems and adding organic matter to the soil.
4. **Mulching:** Mulching can help to improve soil tilth by protecting soil from erosion, maintaining soil moisture, and adding organic matter to the soil.

Soil tilth is an important characteristic of healthy soil that affects various soil properties that are important for plant growth and productivity. Improving soil tilth through management practices such as organic matter addition, reduced tillage, crop rotation, and mulching can help to maintain soil health and promote sustainable agriculture.

SOIL FERTILITY

Soil fertility refers to the ability of soil to support plant growth and productivity. It is influenced by various factors, such as soil structure, soil texture, soil organic matter content, soil nutrients, and soil pH.

Soil nutrients are essential for plant growth, and their availability is a critical factor in determining soil fertility. There are 17 essential plant nutrients, including macronutrients such as nitrogen, phosphorus, and potassium, and micronutrients such as iron, zinc, and manganese. Plants absorb these nutrients from the soil through their roots, and deficiencies or imbalances of these nutrients can limit plant growth and productivity.

Soil organic matter is also an important factor in soil fertility. Organic matter is composed of decomposing plant and animal material and can influence soil fertility through its effect on soil structure, water-holding capacity, nutrient availability, and soil microorganisms. Organic matter can also provide a source of nutrients for plants as it decomposes.

Soil pH is another important factor in soil fertility. Soil pH is a measure of the acidity or alkalinity of the soil and can affect plant nutrient availability. Most plants grow best in slightly acidic soil with a pH range between 6.0 and 7.5.

Soil management practices can also affect soil fertility. Practices such as tillage, fertilization, irrigation, and crop rotation can all affect soil fertility. Overuse of fertilizers can lead to nutrient imbalances and environmental problems, while underuse of fertilizers can lead to nutrient deficiencies and reduced plant growth. Irrigation can affect soil fertility by affecting soil moisture levels and nutrient availability. Crop rotation can help to maintain soil fertility by promoting diverse root systems and adding organic matter to the soil.

In addition to these factors, soil fertility can also be influenced by external factors, such as climate and weather patterns, topography, and land use.

SOIL HEALTH

Soil health is a term used to describe the overall quality and function of soil as a living ecosystem. It refers to the ability of soil to support plant growth, maintain environmental quality, and provide other benefits such as biodiversity, carbon sequestration, and water filtration. Soil health is influenced by a complex interplay of physical, chemical, and biological factors, and is an important consideration for sustainable agriculture and environmental management.

Physical factors that affect soil health include soil structure, texture, and water-holding capacity. Soil structure refers to the arrangement of soil particles into aggregates, which can affect water infiltration, root penetration, and nutrient availability. Soil texture refers to the relative proportions of sand, silt, and clay particles in the soil, which can affect soil water-holding capacity, nutrient retention, and aeration. Water-holding capacity is another important factor in soil health, as it affects plant growth and can impact soil erosion and runoff.

Chemical factors that affect soil health include soil pH, nutrient availability, and the presence of contaminants. Soil pH is a measure of the acidity or alkalinity of the soil, and can impact the availability of plant nutrients and the activity of soil microorganisms. Nutrient availability is influenced by factors such as soil organic matter content, nutrient cycling, and the use of fertilizers and other amendments. The presence of contaminants such as heavy metals or pesticides can also impact soil health and environmental quality.

Biological factors that affect soil health include microbial activity, plant roots, and the presence of soil fauna such as earthworms and insects. Microbial activity is a key component of soil health, as it supports nutrient cycling, improves soil structure, and can protect plants from diseases and pests. Plant roots play a role in nutrient uptake and can improve soil structure through their growth and decay. Soil fauna such as earthworms and insects can also contribute to nutrient cycling and soil structure.

Improving soil health involves a range of management practices that aim to support soil structure, nutrient cycling, and microbial activity. Practices such as cover cropping, reduced tillage, composting, and crop rotation can help to increase soil organic matter content, reduce soil compaction, and support beneficial soil microorganisms. Integrated pest management and the use of natural fertilizers such as compost can also help to maintain soil health and reduce the use of synthetic chemicals.

Assessing soil health involves monitoring key indicators such as soil structure, texture, organic matter content, pH, nutrient availability, microbial activity, and water-holding capacity. Soil tests can be used to measure these indicators and guide soil management decisions. Regular soil testing and monitoring can help farmers and gardeners maintain healthy soil ecosystems that support sustainable agriculture and other ecosystem services.

ESSENTIAL PLANT NUTRIENTS, THEIR FUNCTIONS AND DEFICIENCY SYMPTOMS

Arnon and Stout (1939) established criteria for determining the essentiality of elements in plant growth, and based on these criteria, a total of 17 elements have been identified as essential for higher green plants. These essential plant nutrients can be classified into two groups based on the relative amounts required by plants: macronutrients and micronutrients.

Macronutrients are required by plants in large amounts, and include carbon (C), hydrogen (H), oxygen (O), nitrogen (N), phosphorus (P), potassium (K), calcium (Ca), and magnesium (Mg). These nutrients are required for the synthesis of organic compounds such as carbohydrates, proteins, and nucleic acids, which are essential for plant growth and development.

Micronutrients, also known as trace elements, are required by plants in smaller amounts, and include iron (Fe), chlorine (Cl), manganese (Mn), boron (B), zinc (Zn), copper (Cu), nickel (Ni), and molybdenum (Mo). These nutrients are essential components of enzymes and co-factors involved in various metabolic processes.

Deficiency of any of these essential plant nutrients can lead to stunted growth, reduced yield, and ultimately death of the plant. Deficiency symptoms vary depending on the nutrient, but common symptoms include yellowing of leaves (chlorosis), necrosis, and abnormal growth patterns.

Some examples of the functions of essential plant nutrients and their associated deficiency symptoms include:

- **Nitrogen (N):** Required for the synthesis of proteins and nucleic acids. Deficiency symptoms include yellowing of leaves and stunted growth.
- **Phosphorus (P):** Required for energy transfer, nucleic acid synthesis, and root development. Deficiency symptoms include stunted growth and purplish leaves.
- **Potassium (K):** Required for water balance, enzyme activation, and protein synthesis. Deficiency symptoms include yellowing and scorching of leaf margins.
- **Calcium (Ca):** Required for cell wall development, enzyme activation, and ion balance. Deficiency symptoms include leaf necrosis and deformation.
- **Iron (Fe):** Required for chlorophyll synthesis and electron transfer in photosynthesis. Deficiency symptoms include chlorosis of young leaves.

In addition to these essential plant nutrients, there are other elements that may have beneficial effects on plant growth, but are not considered essential. These elements are referred to as beneficial elements or plant growth-promoting elements, and include silicon (Si), sodium (Na), cobalt (Co), and selenium (Se), among others.

Classification of Plant Nutrients based on Quantity

Classification of plant nutrients based on quantity is a common way to categorize different types of nutrients essential for plant growth and development. The following are the various categories of plant nutrients based on quantity:

1. **Framework Nutrients/Structural Nutrients:** These are plant nutrients that participate in structural development and are essential for the formation of plant tissues. Examples of framework nutrients include carbon, oxygen, and hydrogen.
2. **Macro Nutrient:** Macro nutrients are essential plant nutrients that are required in relatively large amounts. They must be present in plant tissue in concentrations greater than 1 mg per gram of dry weight. Macro nutrients can be further divided into two categories:
   (*i*) **Primary Nutrients:** The three primary nutrients are nitrogen (N), phosphorus (P), and potassium (K). These nutrients are required in large quantities by plants and are crucial for successful crop growth.
   (*ii*) **Secondary Nutrients:** The secondary nutrients include calcium (Ca), magnesium (Mg), and sulfur (S). They are required in smaller quantities than primary nutrients but are still important for plant growth and development.
3. **Micro Nutrients/Trace Nutrients:** These are plant nutrients that are present in plant tissue in concentrations of ≤ 1 mg/gram. They are also known as trace elements or micronutrients. Examples of micro nutrients include iron (Fe), zinc (Zn), manganese (Mn), copper (Cu), boron (B), and chlorine (Cl).
4. **Ultra-Micro Nutrients:** These are plant nutrients that are present in plant tissue in concentrations of < 1 ppb. They are also known as ultra-trace elements or ultra-micronutrients. Examples of ultra-micronutrients include molybdenum (Mo) and cobalt (Co).

5. **Beneficial Plant Nutrients:** These are plant nutrients that are not required by all plants but can promote plant growth and development. They may be essential for several plant species. Examples of beneficial plant nutrients include sodium (Na), vanadium (V), silicon (Si), and cobalt (Co).
6. **Quasi-Essential Elements:** Quasi-essential elements are plant nutrients that are not considered essential in the traditional sense. However, their deficiency can cause various abnormalities with respect to plant growth and development. Silicon (Si) is considered a quasi-essential element for plants. Its deficiency can affect the structural integrity of plants, especially those with high silica demands such as grasses.

Classification on the basis of Mobility of Nutrient in the Soil

Plant nutrients can also be classified based on their mobility within the plant. This classification is important because it helps to understand how nutrients are transported and distributed within different parts of the plant.

1. **Highly mobile nutrients:** These nutrients are easily translocated within the plant and can move from older to younger tissues. Examples of highly mobile nutrients include nitrogen (N), phosphorus (P), and potassium (K). Deficiencies of these nutrients typically show up first in older leaves.
2. **Moderately mobile nutrients:** These nutrients can be translocated within the plant, but the rate of movement is slower than highly mobile nutrients. Zinc (Zn) is an example of a moderately mobile nutrient. Deficiencies of these nutrients usually show up first in the middle leaves.
3. **Less mobile nutrients:** These nutrients are not easily translocated within the plant and do not move from older to younger tissues. Examples of less mobile nutrients include sulfur (S), iron (Fe), manganese (Mn), chlorine (Cl), molybdenum (Mo), and copper (Cu). Deficiencies of these nutrients typically show up first in the younger leaves.
4. **Immobile nutrients:** These nutrients remain fixed in one location and cannot be translocated within the plant. Calcium (Ca) and boron (B) are examples of immobile nutrients. Deficiencies of these nutrients show up first in the growing points of the plant.

Understanding the mobility of nutrients within the plant is important for identifying and addressing nutrient deficiencies. Foliar application of nutrients is often used for less mobile nutrients since they cannot be easily translocated within the plant. In contrast, highly mobile nutrients can be addressed by applying fertilizers to the soil.

Nutrient Deficiency Symptoms in Plants

Nutrient deficiency symptoms in plants can be observed in different parts of the plant. Here are the common deficiency symptoms and the parts of the plant where they can be observed:

Old Leaves:

- **Nitrogen (N) deficiency:** Yellowing of lower leaves, starting from tips and spreading to the base of the leaves.
- **Phosphorus (P) deficiency:** Purple or reddish color on the underside of leaves, reduced growth and smaller leaves.
- **Potassium (K) deficiency:** Yellowing of the edges and between veins of leaves, curling of leaves and necrosis.
- **Magnesium (Mg) deficiency:** Yellowing of older leaves starting from the edges and spreading towards the base of the leaves, have a reddish-brown color on the edges.

New Leaves:

- **Iron (Fe) deficiency:** Yellowing between veins of new leaves, leaves turn pale and the veins remain green.
- **Copper (Cu) deficiency:** Leaves become twisted and wilted, reddish-brown spots appear on leaves.
- **Chlorine (Cl) deficiency:** Yellowing of leaves, chlorosis in veins, necrosis of leaves.
- **Sulfur (S) deficiency:** Leaves turn yellow and small, reduced growth.

Old and New Leaves:

- **Zinc (Zn) deficiency:** Chlorosis between veins of new leaves, reduced growth and smaller leaves, leaves may have brown spots.

Apical Bud:

- **Calcium (Ca) deficiency:** Young leaves and growing points become twisted and distorted, dead tips and buds.
- **Boron (B) deficiency:** Bud dieback, stem and root tips die, growth slows down.

Essential plant nutrients

There are many essential plant nutrients that are required for optimal growth and development of plants. These nutrients can be grouped into two categories based on their availability to plants - macronutrients and micronutrients.

Macronutrients

- **Nitrogen (N):** Nitrogen is an essential component of amino acids, nucleic acids, and chlorophyll. It is required for the development of plant leaves, stems, and roots. Nitrogen is also involved in many important plant processes, including photosynthesis, respiration, and the uptake of other nutrients.
- **Phosphorus (P):** Phosphorus is essential for energy transfer within the plant, as well as for the formation of DNA and cell membranes. It is particularly important for root growth and flower and seed formation. Phosphorus also plays a role in the regulation of many plant processes, including photosynthesis, respiration, and the uptake of other nutrients.
- **Potassium (K):** Potassium is involved in the regulation of water movement in plant cells and is essential for the proper functioning of enzymes. It is also important for overall plant growth and development, as well as for the regulation of many plant processes such as photosynthesis, respiration, and the uptake of other nutrients.
- **Calcium (Ca):** Calcium is essential for the formation of cell walls and for the regulation of cell division and growth. It is also involved in the movement of other nutrients within the plant, and plays a role in the regulation of plant processes such as photosynthesis, respiration, and the uptake of other nutrients.
- **Magnesium (Mg):** Magnesium is a central component of chlorophyll and is therefore essential for photosynthesis. It is also involved in the activation of many enzymes and plays a role in the regulation of plant processes such as photosynthesis, respiration, and the uptake of other nutrients.
- **Sulfur (S):** Sulfur is a component of many important plant compounds, including amino acids, proteins, and vitamins. It is also involved in the production of chlorophyll and plays a role in the regulation of plant processes such as photosynthesis, respiration, and the uptake of other nutrients.

Micronutrients

- **Boron (B):** Boron is involved in the formation of cell walls and in the regulation of many important plant processes, including the uptake of other nutrients. It also plays a role in the production of nucleic acids and in the regulation of hormone levels in plants.
- **Copper (Cu):** Copper is involved in the formation of lignin, which is a component of cell walls. It is also important for the production of enzymes that are involved in photosynthesis and respiration. Copper also plays a role in the regulation of plant processes such as the uptake of other nutrients.
- **Iron (Fe):** Iron is essential for the formation of chlorophyll and is involved in many other plant processes, including respiration and photosynthesis. It is also important for the regulation of plant processes such as the uptake of other nutrients.
- **Manganese (Mn):** Manganese is involved in the formation of chloroplasts and in the production of enzymes that are important for photosynthesis. It also plays a role in the regulation of plant processes such as the uptake of other nutrients.
- **Zinc (Zn):** Zinc is involved in the production of auxins, which are plant hormones that regulate growth and development. It is also involved in the formation of chlorophyll and in the regulation of carbohydrate metabolism. Zinc also plays a role in the regulation of plant processes such as the uptake of other nutrients.
- **Molybdenum (Mo):** Molybdenum is involved in the production of enzymes that are important for nitrogen fixation and for the conversion of inorganic phosphorus to organic forms.
- **Chlorine (Cl):** Chlorine is involved in the regulation of water movement within plant cells and plays a role in photosynthesis by helping to maintain the balance of positive and negative charges within the plant. Chlorine deficiency can lead to wilting, stunted growth, and leaf damage.
- **Cobalt (Co):** Cobalt is involved in the production of vitamin B12, which is important for many plant processes, including the formation of nucleic acids.
- **Nickel (Ni):** Nickel is involved in the production of enzymes that are important for nitrogen metabolism.
- **Vanadium (V):** Vanadium is involved in the regulation of many plant processes, including the uptake and transport of other nutrients.
- **Sodium (Na):** Sodium is involved in the regulation of water movement within plant cells and plays a role in the maintenance of cell turgor.
- **Silicon (Si):** Silicon is involved in the formation of cell walls, and it can also help to increase plant resistance to pests and diseases.

All of these essential plant nutrients play crucial roles in the growth, development, and survival of plants. Deficiencies in any one of these nutrients can lead to a range of problems, including stunted growth, poor flowering or fruiting, and susceptibility to pests and diseases. It is important for farmers and gardeners to ensure that their plants are receiving the right balance of essential nutrients to support their growth and development.

SOIL TYPES OF INDIA AND THEIR CHARACTERISTICS

Classification of Soils

India has varied relief features, landforms, climatic realms and vegetation types. These have contributed in the development of various types of soils in India. In ancient times, soils used to be classified into two main groups – Urvara and Usara, which were fertile and sterile, respectively. In the 16th centrury A.D., soils were classified on the basis of their inherent characteristics and external features such as texture, colour, slope of land and moisture content in the soil. Based on texture, main soil types were identified as sandy, clayey, silty and loam, etc. On the basis of colour, they were red, yellow, black, etc. Since Independence, scientific surveys of soils have been conducted by various agencies. Soil Survey of India, established in 1956, made comprehensive studies of soils in selected areas like in the Damodar Valley.

The National Bureau of Soil Survey and the Land Use Planning an Institute under the control of the Indian Council of Agricultural Research (ICAR) did a lot of studies on Indian soils. In their effort to study soil and to make it comparable at the international level, the ICAR has classified the Indian soils on the basis of their nature and character as per the United States Department of Agriculture (USDA) Soil Taxonomy.

On the basis of genesis, colour, composition and location, the soils of India have been classified into:

(*i*) Alluvial soils
(*ii*) Black soils
(*iii*) Red and Yellow soils
(*iv*) Laterite soils
(*v*) Arid soils
(*vi*) Saline soils
(*vii*) Peaty soils
(*viii*) Forest soils

Alluvial Soils

Alluvial soils are widespread in the northern plains and the river valleys. These soils cover about 40 per cent of the total area of the country. They are depositional soils, transported and deposited by rivers and streams. Through a narrow corridor in Rajasthan, they extend into the plains of Gujarat. In the Peninsular region, they are found in deltas of the east coast and in the river valleys. The alluvial soils vary in nature from sandy loam to clay. They are generally rich in potash but poor in phosphorous. In the Upper and Middle Ganga plain, two different types of alluvial soils have developed, viz. Khadar and Bhangar.

Khadar is the new alluvium and is deposited by floods annually, which enriches the soil by depositing fine silts. Bhangar represents a system of older alluvium, deposited away from the flood plains. Both the Khadar and Bhangar soils contain calcareous concretions (Kankars). These soils are more loamy and clayey in the lower and middle Ganga plain and the Brahamaputra valley. The sand content decreases from the west to east. The colour of the alluvial soils varies from the light grey to ash grey. Its shades depend on the depth of the deposition, the texture of the materials, and the time taken for attaining maturity. Alluvial soils are intensively cultivated.

Black Soil

Black soil covers most of the Deccan Plateau which includes parts of Maharashtra, Madhya Pradesh, Gujarat, Andhra Pradesh and some parts of Tamil Nadu. In the upper reaches of the Godavari and the Krishna, and the northwestern part of the Deccan Plateau, the black soil is very deep. These soils are also known as the 'Regur Soil' or the 'Black Cotton Soil'.

The black soils are generally clayey, deep and impermeable. They swell and become sticky when wet and shrink when dried. So, during the dry season, these soil develop wide cracks. Thus, there occurs a kind of 'self ploughing'. Because of this character of slow absorption and loss of moisture, the black soil retains the moisture for a very long time, which helps the crops, especially, the rain fed ones, to sustain even during the dry season. Chemically, the black soils are rich in lime, iron, magnesia and alumina. They also contain potash. But they lack in phosphorous, nitrogen and organic matter. The colour of the soil ranges from deep black to grey.

Red and Yellow Soil

Red soil develops on crystalline igneous rocks in areas of low rainfall in the eastern and southern part of the Deccan Plateau. Along the piedmont zone of the Western Ghat, long stretch of area is occupied by red loamy soil. Yellow and red soils are also found in parts of Odisha and Chattisgarh and in the southern parts of the middle Ganga plain. The soil develops a reddish colour due to a wide diffusion of iron in crystalline and metamorphic rocks. It looks yellow when it occurs in a hydrated form. The fine-grained red and yellow soils are normally fertile, whereas coarse-grained soils found in dry upland areas are poor in fertility. They are generally poor in nitrogen, phosphorous and humus.

Laterite Soil

Laterite has been derived from the Latin word 'Later' which means brick. The laterite soils develop in areas with high temperature and high rainfall. These are the result of intense leaching due to tropical rains. With rain, lime and silica are leached away, and soils rich in iron oxide and aluminium compound are left behind.

Humus content of the soil is removed fast by bacteria that thrives well in high temperature. These soils are poor in organic matter, nitrogen, phosphate and calcium, while iron oxide and potash are in excess. Hence, laterites are not suitable for cultivation; however, application of manures and fertilisers are required for making the soils fertile for cultivation. Red laterite soils in Tamil Nadu, Andhra Pradesh and Kerala are more suitable for tree crops like cashewnut. Laterite soils are widely cut as bricks for use in house construction. These soils have mainly developed in the higher areas of the Peninsular plateau. The laterite soils are commonly found in Karnataka, Kerala, Tamil Nadu, Madhya Pradesh and the hilly areas of Odisha and Assam.

Arid Soils

Arid soils range from red to brown in colour. They are generally sandy in structure and saline in nature. In some areas, the salt content is so high that common salt is obtained by evaporating the saline water. Due to the dry climate, high temperature and accelerated evaporation, they lack moisture and humus. Nitrogen is insufficient and the phosphate content is normal. Lower horizons of the soil are occupied by 'kankar' layers because of the increasing calcium content downwards.

The 'Kankar' layer formation in the bottom horizons restricts the infiltration of water, and as such when irrigation is made available, the soil moisture is readily available for a sustainable plant growth. Arid soils are characteristically developed in western Rajasthan, which exhibit characteristic arid topography. These soils are poor and contain little humus and organic matter.

Saline Soils

They are also known as Usara soils. Saline soils contain a larger proportion of sodium, potassium and magnesium, and thus, they are infertile, and do not support any vegetative growth. They have more salts, largely because of dry climate and poor drainage. They occur in arid and semi-arid regions, and in waterlogged and swampy areas. Their structure ranges from sandy to loamy.

They lack in nitrogen and calcium. Saline soils are more widespread in western Gujarat, deltas of the eastern coast and in Sunderban areas of West Bengal. In the Rann of Kuchchh, the Southwest Monsoon brings salt particles and deposits there as a crust. Seawater intrusions in the deltas promote the occurrence of saline soils. In the areas of intensive cultivation with excessive use of irrigation, especially in areas of green revolution, the fertile alluvial soils are becoming saline.

Excessive irrigation with dry climatic conditions promotes capillary action, which results in the deposition of salt on the top layer of the soil. In such areas, especially in Punjab and Haryana, farmers are advised to add gypsum to solve the problem of salinity in the soil.

Peaty Soils

They are found in the areas of heavy rainfall and high humidity, where there is a good growth of vegetation. Thus, large quantity of dead organic matter accumulates in these areas, and this gives a rich humus and organic content to the soil. Organic matter in these soils may go even up to 40-50 per cent. These soils are normally heavy and black in colour. At many places, they are alkaline also. It occurs widely in the northern part of Bihar, southern part of Uttaranchal and the coastal areas of West Bengal, Odisha and Tamil Nadu.

Forest Soils

As the name suggests, forest soils are formed in the forest areas where sufficient rainfall is available. The soils vary in structure and texture depending on the mountain environment where they are formed. They are loamy and silty on valley sides and coarse-grained in the upper slopes. In the snow-bound areas of the Himalayas, they experience denudation, and are acidic with low humus content. The soils found in the lower valleys are fertile. It is evident from the foregoing discussions that soils, their texture, quality and nature are vital for the germination and growth of plant and vegetation including crops. Soils are living systems. Like any other organism, they too develop and decay, get degraded, respond to proper treatment if administered in time. These have serious repercussions on other components of the system of which they themselves are important parts.

Types of Cropping Systems

Different types of cropping systems are adopted on farms depending on the climate, soil, and available resources.

Monoculture: Monoculture is a cropping system in which a single crop is cultivated on a particular piece of land over an extended period. In this system, the same crop is grown repeatedly on the same land, often for several years in a row.

1. **Advantages of Monoculture:** One of the main advantages of monoculture is that it allows for the efficient use of resources such as water, fertilizers, and pesticides. Farmers can optimize their production by using the same techniques for each crop and minimizing input costs. Monoculture can also simplify the management of crops and improve harvest efficiency.
2. **Disadvantages of Monoculture:** One of the main disadvantages of monoculture is that it can lead to soil degradation and reduced soil fertility. Repeated planting of the same crop can deplete the soil of

specific nutrients and encourage pest infestations, leading to lower crop yields over time. Monoculture can also reduce biodiversity and create favorable conditions for pests and diseases to spread, which can increase the risk of crop failure.

3. **Strategies to mitigate the disadvantages of monoculture:** Farmers can adopt several strategies to mitigate the disadvantages of monoculture. Crop rotation involves alternating the crops grown on a particular piece of land to reduce soil depletion and pest infestations. Inter-cropping involves growing multiple crops simultaneously on the same land to reduce pest infestations and improve nutrient cycling. Cover crops can also be used to protect the soil from erosion and maintain soil fertility.
4. **Examples of monoculture:** Monoculture is commonly used in agriculture to grow crops such as wheat, rice, and corn. Large-scale agricultural operations often rely on monoculture to maximize production and reduce costs. However, small-scale farmers may also use monoculture to produce cash crops that have a high demand in the market.

Monoculture is a common cropping system used in agriculture that has both advantages and disadvantages. While it allows for efficient use of resources, it can also lead to soil degradation and reduced crop yields over time. Farmers can adopt strategies such as crop rotation, inter-cropping, and cover cropping to mitigate the disadvantages of monoculture and maintain soil fertility.

Multiple cropping: Multiple cropping is a cropping system in which two or more crops are grown on the same piece of land in a single growing season. This system allows farmers to maximize the use of available resources and increase crop yields.

1. **Advantages of Multiple cropping:** Multiple cropping allows farmers to make efficient use of available resources such as water, sunlight, and nutrients. It can increase crop yields by optimizing the use of resources and reducing the risk of crop failure due to adverse weather conditions. Multiple cropping can also improve soil fertility by reducing nutrient depletion and increasing nutrient cycling.
2. **Types of Multiple cropping:** There are several types of multiple cropping, including mixed cropping, intercropping, and sequential cropping. In mixed cropping, two or more crops are grown simultaneously on the same piece of land. In intercropping, two or more crops are grown in alternate rows or in the same row. Sequential cropping involves growing two or more crops in sequence on the same piece of land.
3. **Factors that influence Multiple cropping:** The success of multiple cropping depends on several factors, including the availability of resources such as water, sunlight, and nutrients. Soil fertility is also an essential factor, as multiple cropping can deplete the soil of specific nutrients. Climate and weather conditions can also influence the success of multiple cropping.
4. **Challenges of Multiple cropping:** Multiple cropping can present some challenges for farmers. Managing multiple crops can be labor-intensive, and coordinating the timing of planting, harvesting, and other activities can be difficult. Pest and disease management can also be challenging, as some crops may be more susceptible to specific pests or diseases.
5. **Examples of Multiple cropping:** Multiple cropping is common in many parts of the world, particularly in areas with limited resources. Examples of multiple cropping include growing wheat and legumes together, or growing maize and beans in alternate rows.

Multiple cropping is a cropping system that can help farmers maximize the use of available resources and increase crop yields. There are several types of multiple cropping, including mixed cropping, intercropping, and sequential cropping. While multiple cropping can present some challenges, it is a valuable tool for farmers looking to optimize their production and maintain soil fertility.

Intercropping is a cropping system in which two or more crops are grown simultaneously on the same piece of land. In this system, crops are planted in alternate rows or in the same row, and each crop benefits from the presence of the other

1. **Advantages of Intercropping:** Intercropping has several advantages, including better use of resources such as water, sunlight, and nutrients. By growing different crops together, intercropping can improve soil fertility, reduce pest and disease pressure, and increase crop yields. Intercropping can also help farmers diversify their production and reduce their dependence on a single crop.
2. **Types of Intercropping:** There are several types of intercropping, including mixed intercropping, row intercropping, and relay intercropping. In mixed intercropping, different crops are grown together in the same field. In row intercropping, different crops are grown in alternate rows. Relay intercropping involves planting a second crop after the first crop has reached maturity.
3. **Factors that influence Intercropping:** The success of intercropping depends on several factors, including the crop combination, the spacing between plants, and the management practices used. Crop combinations must be carefully chosen to ensure that the crops benefit from each other and do not compete

for resources. Spacing between plants must also be carefully managed to avoid overcrowding and ensure adequate light and nutrients for each crop.

4. **Challenges of Intercropping:** Intercropping can present some challenges for farmers. Managing multiple crops can be labor-intensive, and coordinating the timing of planting, harvesting, and other activities can be difficult. Pest and disease management can also be challenging, as some crops may be more susceptible to specific pests or diseases.
5. **Examples of Intercropping:** Intercropping is common in many parts of the world, particularly in areas with limited resources. Examples of intercropping include growing beans and maize together, or growing legumes with cereals.

Intercropping is a valuable cropping system that can help farmers maximize the use of available resources, increase crop yields, and maintain soil fertility. There are several types of intercropping, and each type presents its own unique advantages and challenges. By carefully managing crop combinations, spacing, and management practices, farmers can successfully implement intercropping and improve their production.

Mixed cropping: Mixed cropping is a type of multiple cropping system where two or more crops are grown simultaneously on the same piece of land in the same row, without any distinct pattern or arrangement. The crops are selected based on their complementary growth habits and requirements, and they help to maximize the use of resources such as sunlight, water, and nutrients.

1. **Advantages of Mixed cropping:** Mixed cropping has several advantages, including better utilization of available resources and a reduced risk of crop failure. By growing different crops together, mixed cropping can improve soil fertility, reduce pest and disease pressure, and increase crop yields. It can also help farmers diversify their production and reduce their dependence on a single crop.
2. **Types of Mixed cropping:** There are several types of mixed cropping, including pure or simple mixed cropping, mixed intercropping, and crop rotation. In pure mixed cropping, two or more crops are grown together without any distinct pattern or arrangement. In mixed intercropping, different crops are grown together in the same field, but in alternate rows or specific patterns. In crop rotation, different crops are grown in the same field in a specific sequence to maintain soil fertility.
3. **Factors that influence Mixed cropping:** The success of mixed cropping depends on several factors, including the crop combination, the spacing between plants, and the management practices used. Crop combinations must be carefully chosen to ensure that the crops benefit from each other and do not compete for resources. Spacing between plants must also be carefully managed to avoid overcrowding and ensure adequate light and nutrients for each crop.
4. **Challenges of Mixed cropping:** Mixed cropping can present some challenges for farmers. Managing multiple crops can be labor-intensive, and coordinating the timing of planting, harvesting, and other activities can be difficult. Pest and disease management can also be challenging, as some crops may be more susceptible to specific pests or diseases.
5. **Examples of Mixed cropping:** Mixed cropping is common in many parts of the world, particularly in areas with limited resources. Examples of mixed cropping include growing beans and maize together, or growing legumes with cereals.

Mixed cropping is a valuable cropping system that can help farmers maximize the use of available resources, increase crop yields, and maintain soil fertility. By carefully managing crop combinations, spacing, and management practices, farmers can successfully implement mixed cropping and improve their production.

Strip cropping: Strip cropping is a type of cropping system in which two or more crops are grown in alternating strips across a field. The strips are arranged in a way that maximizes the use of resources such as water, sunlight, and nutrients, and can help to reduce soil erosion and improve soil fertility.

1. **Advantages of Strip cropping:** Strip cropping has several advantages, including reduced soil erosion, increased soil fertility, and improved water management. By planting crops in alternating strips, the soil is better able to absorb water, reducing runoff and erosion. Strip cropping can also help to maintain soil fertility by reducing nutrient depletion, and can provide habitats for beneficial insects and wildlife.
2. **Types of Strip cropping:** There are several types of strip cropping, including contour strip cropping, crop rotation strip cropping, and alley cropping. Contour strip cropping involves planting crops in strips that follow the contour of the land, while crop rotation strip cropping involves alternating strips of different crops in a specific rotation. Alley cropping involves planting crops in strips between rows of trees or shrubs.
3. **Factors that influence Strip cropping:** The success of strip cropping depends on several factors, including the slope of the land, the types of crops used, and the management practices employed. Sloping land is particularly suited to contour strip cropping, as it can help to reduce erosion and runoff. The types of crops used must be carefully selected to ensure that they complement each other and do not compete for resources.

4. **Challenges of Strip cropping:** Strip cropping can present some challenges for farmers. Managing multiple crops can be labor-intensive, and coordinating the timing of planting, harvesting, and other activities can be difficult. Pest and disease management can also be challenging, as some crops may be more susceptible to specific pests or diseases.
5. **Examples of Strip cropping:** Strip cropping is used in many parts of the world, particularly in areas with steep slopes or other conditions that make traditional row cropping difficult. Examples of strip cropping include planting alternating strips of corn and soybeans, or alternating strips of wheat and clover.

Strip cropping is a valuable cropping system that can help farmers maximize the use of available resources, reduce soil erosion, and improve soil fertility. By carefully managing crop combinations, spacing, and management practices, farmers can successfully implement strip cropping and improve their production.

Sequence cropping: Sequence cropping is a farming practice where a sequence of different crops is grown in the same field over time. Each crop is planted and harvested in a specific order, with the goal of maximizing yields and reducing the risk of crop failure.

1. **Advantages of Sequence cropping:** Sequence cropping has several advantages, including reduced risk of crop failure, increased soil fertility, and improved weed and pest control. By rotating crops, the soil is less likely to become depleted of nutrients and less likely to develop pest and disease problems. This can result in higher yields and better crop quality over time.
2. **Types of Sequence cropping:** There are several types of sequence cropping, including simple crop rotation, double cropping, and triple cropping. Simple crop rotation involves planting two or more different crops in a specific sequence over time. Double cropping involves planting two different crops in the same field during the same growing season, while triple cropping involves planting three different crops in the same field in a single year.
3. **Factors that influence Sequence cropping:** The success of sequence cropping depends on several factors, including soil type, climate, crop types, and available resources. Some crops are better suited to specific soil types or climates, and the timing of planting and harvesting must be carefully managed to ensure that each crop has the optimal growing conditions.
4. **Challenges of Sequence cropping:** Sequence cropping can present some challenges for farmers, including managing multiple crops, coordinating planting and harvesting schedules, and controlling pests and diseases. Additionally, different crops may have different soil and nutrient requirements, which must be carefully managed to ensure that each crop receives the appropriate level of resources.
5. **Examples of Sequence cropping:** Sequence cropping is commonly used in many parts of the world, particularly in areas where small farms are common. Examples of sequence cropping include rotating corn and soybeans, rotating wheat and legumes, and planting different crops in the same field over time.

Sequence cropping is a valuable farming practice that can help to maximize yields, reduce the risk of crop failure, and improve soil fertility. By carefully managing crop types, planting and harvesting schedules, and soil and nutrient requirements, farmers can successfully implement sequence cropping and improve their production.

Relay cropping: Relay cropping is a farming practice in which a second crop is planted before the first crop is harvested. This practice can help to increase yields, reduce the risk of crop failure, and improve soil health.

1. **Advantages of Relay cropping:** Relay cropping can offer several advantages, including improved soil health, increased yields, and reduced risk of crop failure. By planting a second crop before the first is harvested, farmers can help to reduce soil erosion, improve soil fertility, and maintain a healthy soil ecosystem.
2. **Types of Relay cropping:** There are several types of relay cropping, including intercropping, double cropping, and multi-cropping. Intercropping involves planting two or more crops in the same field at the same time, while double cropping involves planting two crops in the same field during the same growing season. Multi-cropping involves planting three or more crops in the same field during a single growing season.
3. **Factors that influence Relay cropping:** The success of relay cropping depends on several factors, including soil type, climate, crop types, and available resources. Some crops are better suited to specific soil types or climates, and the timing of planting and harvesting must be carefully managed to ensure that each crop has the optimal growing conditions.
4. **Challenges of Relay cropping:** Relay cropping can present some challenges for farmers, including coordinating planting and harvesting schedules, controlling pests and diseases, and managing soil and nutrient requirements. Additionally, different crops may have different soil and nutrient requirements, which must be carefully managed to ensure that each crop receives the appropriate level of resources.-

5. **Examples of Relay cropping:** Relay cropping is commonly used in many parts of the world, particularly in areas where small farms are common. Examples of relay cropping include planting wheat before soybeans are harvested, planting beans before corn is harvested, and planting a cover crop before the main crop is harvested.

Relay cropping is a valuable farming practice that can help to improve soil health, increase yields, and reduce the risk of crop failure. By carefully managing crop types, planting and harvesting schedules, and soil and nutrient requirements, farmers can successfully implement relay cropping and improve their production.

Multistoried cropping: Multistoried cropping is a farming practice in which crops of different heights are grown in the same field, often on different levels or stories. This practice can help to increase yields, maximize land use, and improve soil health.

1. **Advantages of Multistoried cropping:** Multistoried cropping can offer several advantages, including increased yields, improved soil health, and reduced water use. By planting crops at different levels, farmers can maximize land use and improve the efficiency of water and nutrient use. Additionally, the diverse crop types can help to maintain a healthy soil ecosystem and reduce the risk of pests and diseases.
2. **Types of Multistoried cropping:** There are several types of multistoried cropping, including agroforestry, alley cropping, and vertical farming. Agroforestry involves planting trees and crops together in the same field, while alley cropping involves planting crops in the spaces between rows of trees. Vertical farming involves growing crops on multiple levels, often in a controlled environment.
3. **Factors that influence Multistoried cropping:** The success of multistoried cropping depends on several factors, including climate, soil type, crop types, and available resources. Some crops are better suited to specific soil types or climates, and the timing of planting and harvesting must be carefully managed to ensure that each crop has the optimal growing conditions.
4. **Challenges of Multistoried cropping:** Multistoried cropping can present some challenges for farmers, including managing the different crop heights and spacing, coordinating planting and harvesting schedules, and managing soil and nutrient requirements. Additionally, different crops may have different water and nutrient requirements, which must be carefully managed to ensure that each crop receives the appropriate level of resources.
5. **Examples of Multistoried cropping:** Multistoried cropping is becoming increasingly popular in many parts of the world, particularly in urban areas where space is limited. Examples of multistoried cropping include planting tomatoes on trellises, growing mushrooms in stacked trays, and growing herbs and lettuce in a vertical garden.

Multistoried cropping is a valuable farming practice that can help to maximize land use, improve yields, and promote a healthy soil ecosystem. By carefully managing crop types, planting and harvesting schedules, and soil and nutrient requirements, farmers can successfully implement multistoried cropping and improve their production.

Catch cropping: Catch cropping, also known as intercropping or relay cropping, is a farming practice in which a quick-growing crop is grown in the same field after the main crop has been harvested.

1. **Advantages of Catch cropping:** Catch cropping can offer several advantages, including improved soil health, reduced erosion, and increased yields. By planting a quick-growing crop after the main crop has been harvested, farmers can help to maintain soil structure and nutrient levels, prevent soil erosion, and improve the efficiency of water and nutrient use. Additionally, catch crops can provide additional yields and income for farmers.
2. **Types of Catch cropping:** There are several types of catch cropping, including cover crops, green manure crops, and forage crops. Cover crops are planted primarily to protect the soil, while green manure crops are grown primarily to add organic matter to the soil. Forage crops are grown to provide feed for livestock.
3. **Factors that influence Catch cropping:** The success of catch cropping depends on several factors, including climate, soil type, crop types, and available resources. Some crops are better suited to specific soil types or climates, and the timing of planting and harvesting must be carefully managed to ensure that each crop has the optimal growing conditions.
4. **Challenges of Catch cropping:** Catch cropping can present some challenges for farmers, including managing the different crop types and spacing, coordinating planting and harvesting schedules, and managing soil and nutrient requirements. Additionally, different crops may have different water and nutrient requirements, which must be carefully managed to ensure that each crop receives the appropriate level of resources.
5. **Examples of Catch cropping:** Catch cropping is a popular farming practice in many parts of the world, particularly in areas where the growing season is short

or the soil is prone to erosion. Examples of catch cropping include planting a cover crop of clover or rye after harvesting wheat or corn, or planting a forage crop of oats or barley after harvesting soybeans.

Farmers adopt different types of cropping systems based on their resources, climate, and soil conditions. Each system has its own advantages and disadvantages, and farmers must choose the right system to maximize their crop yield and maintain soil fertility.

ORGANIC MANURE

Organic manure refers to the natural substances that are added to the soil to improve its fertility and texture. These are usually derived from plants and animal waste, and are an important aspect of sustainable agriculture. Here are some important details about organic manure:

- **Types of organic manure:** Organic manure can be broadly classified into two types - plant-based and animal-based. Plant-based manure includes green manure, compost, and crop residues. Animal-based manure includes dung, urine, and other animal waste.
- **Benefits of organic manure:** Organic manure has several benefits for the soil and crops. It improves soil structure and texture, enhances water retention, and increases soil organic matter content. It also improves nutrient availability, promotes healthy microbial activity, and reduces soil erosion. Organic manure can also improve crop yield, quality, and disease resistance.
- **Methods of application:** Organic manure can be applied to the soil in various ways, such as broadcast application, furrow application, and band application. The method of application depends on the type of crop, soil texture, and nutrient requirements.
- **Precautions while using organic manure:** While organic manure is beneficial for the soil and crops, it is important to use it judiciously. Over-application of manure can lead to nutrient imbalances and soil pollution. Also, manure from diseased animals or plants should not be used as it can spread the disease to healthy plants.
- **Sources of organic manure:** Organic manure can be obtained from various sources, such as farmyard manure, compost pits, vermicomposting, and green manure crops. It is important to choose the right source of manure based on the nutrient requirements of the crops and the availability of resources.

Organic manure is an important aspect of sustainable agriculture and plays a crucial role in maintaining soil fertility and improving crop yield and quality.

COMMON FERTILIZERS INCLUDING STRAIGHT, COMPLEX, FERTILIZER MIXTURES AND BIOFERTILIZERS

Fertilizers are an essential component of modern agricultural practices as they provide the necessary nutrients for plant growth and development. There are several types of fertilizers available in the market, including straight fertilizers, complex fertilizers, fertilizer mixtures, and biofertilizers.

1. **Straight Fertilizers:** These are fertilizers that contain only one primary nutrient. For example, urea is a straight fertilizer that provides only nitrogen to plants.
2. **Complex Fertilizers:** These are fertilizers that contain two or more primary nutrients. For example, NPK (Nitrogen, Phosphorus, and Potassium) fertilizers are complex fertilizers that provide a balanced ratio of these essential nutrients to plants.
3. **Fertilizer Mixtures:** These are combinations of straight and complex fertilizers. They provide a balanced combination of essential nutrients to plants.
4. **Biofertilizers:** These are natural fertilizers that contain living organisms, such as bacteria, fungi, and algae, which help in nutrient fixation and improve soil health.

In addition to these fertilizers, micronutrient fertilizers are also used to provide essential trace elements such as iron, zinc, copper, and manganese, which are required in small quantities for plant growth and development.

It is essential to use fertilizers in the right amounts and at the right time to avoid overuse, which can lead to soil and water pollution. Proper soil testing and analysis can help determine the right type and amount of fertilizer required for a specific crop and soil type.

The use of fertilizers is crucial for ensuring sustainable and efficient agricultural practices that can help meet the growing demand for food in a world with a rapidly growing population.

INTEGRATED NUTRIENT MANAGEMENT SYSTEM

Integrated Nutrient Management (INM) is a comprehensive approach that aims to optimize nutrient use efficiency and promote sustainable agriculture. It involves the integration of various sources of plant nutrients, including chemical fertilizers, organic manures, biofertilizers, and other soil amendments, in a balanced and optimal manner to meet the crop's nutrient requirements.

INM includes the following components:

1. **Soil Testing:** Soil testing is the first step in INM, which involves determining the soil's nutrient status and pH. Based on the results of the soil test, nutrient

deficiencies can be identified, and a suitable fertilizer and manure application plan can be developed.

2. **Balanced Fertilizer Application:** INM aims to apply the right amount of fertilizers based on the crop's needs. It involves the use of both chemical and organic fertilizers, which are applied in a balanced manner to provide optimal nutrition to the plants.
3. **Organic Manure Application:** Organic manure is a vital component of INM, and its use is encouraged to improve soil fertility and promote sustainable agriculture. It includes the use of farmyard manure, compost, green manure, and other organic materials.
4. **Biofertilizer Application:** INM also promotes the use of biofertilizers, which are microbial inoculants that help fix atmospheric nitrogen and solubilize soil nutrients, making them more available to the plants.
5. **Crop Rotation:** Crop rotation is an essential component of INM, which involves growing different crops in a sequence. It helps in maintaining soil health and fertility, reducing pest and disease incidence, and improving the overall productivity of the farm.
6. **Conservation Agriculture:** Conservation agriculture practices, such as minimum tillage, residue retention, and crop diversification, are promoted under INM. These practices help in conserving soil moisture, improving soil health, and reducing the use of synthetic fertilizers and pesticides.

Benefits of INM:

1. **Improved Soil Fertility:** INM helps in maintaining and improving soil fertility by providing a balanced supply of plant nutrients.
2. **Increased Crop Productivity:** INM promotes the efficient use of nutrients, resulting in increased crop productivity.
3. **Reduced Environmental Pollution:** INM reduces the environmental pollution caused by excess use of synthetic fertilizers and pesticides.
4. **Sustainable Agriculture:** INM promotes sustainable agriculture practices by reducing the dependence on chemical fertilizers and promoting the use of organic and biofertilizers.

INM is an effective approach to optimize nutrient use efficiency and promote sustainable agriculture.

IRRIGATION AND DRAINAGE

SOURCES OF IRRIGATION

Sources of irrigation refer to the different methods or means of supplying water to crops in agricultural fields. Here are some important details about the various sources of irrigation:

1. **Rain:** Rainfall is a natural source of irrigation that is dependent on the season and location of the agricultural field. It is the most common source of irrigation in regions that receive adequate rainfall throughout the year.
2. **Canals:** Canals are man-made channels that carry water from rivers or other sources to agricultural fields. They are used for irrigation in areas that do not receive enough rainfall and require additional water to support crop growth.
3. **Tanks:** Tanks or reservoirs are artificial water storage structures that are used to store rainwater and surface water. They are often used in areas that experience frequent droughts or do not have access to other sources of irrigation.
4. **Rivers:** Rivers are a natural source of water that can be used for irrigation. They are often used in areas that are situated near a river and have the infrastructure to channel water from the river to agricultural fields.
5. **Wells:** Wells are man-made structures that are dug into the ground to extract groundwater. They are often used in areas that do not have access to other sources of irrigation.
6. **Tubewells:** Tubewells are a type of well that uses a motorized pump to extract groundwater. They are often used in areas that have high water tables and are situated near aquifers.

The choice of irrigation source depends on the location and the availability of water resources. Each source of irrigation has its advantages and disadvantages, and the selection of the appropriate source of irrigation is essential for sustainable crop production.

SCHEDULING OF IRRIGATION

Scheduling of irrigation is an important aspect of agriculture, as it helps to optimize water usage and increase crop productivity. Here are some important details about the scheduling of irrigation:

1. **Critical stages of growth:** Different crops have different critical stages of growth, during which they require more water. For example, during the vegetative stage, plants require more water to support their growth, while during the reproductive stage, they require more water for flowering and fruit development.
2. **Time interval:** The time interval between two irrigations depends on various factors, such as the crop type, soil type, weather conditions, and water availability. For example, some crops may require irrigation every 3-4 days, while others may require irrigation once a week.

3. **Soil moisture content:** Soil moisture content is an important parameter for scheduling irrigation. The moisture content of the soil should be maintained at an optimal level to ensure proper plant growth and development. Soil moisture can be measured using various techniques, such as tensiometers, gypsum blocks, and neutron probes.
4. **Weather parameters:** Weather conditions such as temperature, humidity, and wind speed can affect the water requirement of crops. For example, on hot and dry days, crops may require more water than on cool and humid days.
5. **Irrigation methods:** The scheduling of irrigation also depends on the irrigation method used. For example, in drip irrigation, water is supplied directly to the roots of the plants, which reduces water loss due to evaporation and increases water use efficiency.

Overall, scheduling of irrigation based on critical stages of growth, time interval, soil moisture content, and weather parameters can help to ensure optimal water usage and increase crop productivity.

WATERSHED MANAGEMENT

Watershed management is an important aspect of agricultural and environmental management. It involves the planning, development, and management of land and water resources within a specific watershed to ensure sustainable use and conservation of natural resources. Here are some important details about watershed management:

1. **Definition:** Watershed management refers to the process of managing land and water resources within a specific watershed to optimize the use of resources and minimize the impact of human activities on the environment.
2. **Importance:** Watershed management is important for several reasons, including the conservation of water resources, prevention of soil erosion, enhancement of agricultural productivity, protection of natural habitats, and mitigation of the impacts of climate change.
3. **Components:** The key components of watershed management include land-use planning, soil conservation, water conservation, water quality management, and biodiversity conservation.
4. **Techniques:** Several techniques are used in watershed management, including the construction of check dams, contour bunds, and contour trenches to prevent soil erosion and retain moisture; the use of crop rotation, mulching, and intercropping to enhance soil fertility and productivity; and the establishment of water harvesting systems, such as ponds, lakes, and wells, to conserve water resources.
5. **Challenges:** Some of the major challenges in watershed management include inadequate funding, lack of awareness and participation of local communities, inappropriate land-use practices, and conflicting interests of stakeholders.
6. **Benefits:** Effective watershed management can lead to several benefits, including increased agricultural productivity, improved water quality, enhanced biodiversity, and better management of natural resources.

Objectives of Watershed Management

- To control damaging run off and degradation and thereby conservation of soil and water.
- To promote sustainable farming and stabilize crop yield by adopting suitable cropping and crop management system.
- To check soil erosion and increase water infiltration rate.
- To cover non-arable area effectively through afforestation and pasture land.
- To restore ecological balance.
- To enhance the income of the individuals by adopting alternate enterprises.
- To minimize the risk of flood, drought and land slide.
- Supply and securing of clean and sufficient drinking water.

Watershed management is an important approach to sustainable agricultural and environmental management. It involves the planning and management of land and water resources within a specific watershed to optimize their use and minimize their impact on the environment.

WEED CONTROL

Weeds are unwanted plants that grow in crops and compete with them for nutrients, water, and light. They can also serve as hosts for pests and diseases. Therefore, weed control is an essential part of crop management. Here are some important details about the principles and methods of weed control:

PRINCIPLES OF WEED CONTROL

1. **Prevention:** One of the most effective ways to control weeds is to prevent their establishment. This can be done by using certified seeds, proper land preparation, and timely planting.
2. **Early detection:** Weeds should be detected early so that they can be removed before they become established.
3. **Integrated weed management:** This involves the use of a combination of control methods to manage weeds. This can include cultural, mechanical, chemical, and biological control methods.

4. **Selectivity:** Weed control methods should be selective, so they do not harm the crop.

METHODS OF WEED CONTROL

1. **Cultural control:** This involves the use of practices that prevent or suppress weed growth. These practices include crop rotation, intercropping, cover cropping, and timely planting.
2. **Mechanical control:** This involves the use of equipment to physically remove weeds. These methods include hand weeding, hoeing, and cultivation.
3. **Chemical control:** This involves the use of herbicides to kill or suppress weeds. Herbicides can be applied pre-emergence or post-emergence of weeds.
4. **Biological control:** This involves the use of natural enemies of weeds, such as insects or diseases, to suppress weed growth.
5. **Integrated weed management:** This involves the use of a combination of the above control methods to manage weeds. Integrated weed management is the most effective way to control weeds because it reduces the dependence on any single control method.

Weed control is an important aspect of crop management. Farmers should use a combination of control methods to manage weeds effectively. The choice of control method will depend on the type of weed, the crop, and the environment.

CROPS

SEED BED PREPARATION

Seed bed preparation is the process of creating a suitable environment for the germination and growth of seeds. Some important details about seed bed preparation in agriculture:

- **Purpose:** The main purpose of seed bed preparation is to create an optimal environment for seed germination and growth. This involves preparing the soil by breaking up clumps, removing weeds, and improving soil fertility.
- **Soil preparation:** Soil preparation is the first step in seed bed preparation. The soil should be plowed or tilled to a depth of 15-20 cm to break up any clumps or compacted soil. This also helps to incorporate organic matter into the soil, which improves soil fertility.
- **Levelling:** After plowing or tilling, the soil should be levelled to ensure uniform seed distribution and seedling emergence. This can be done using a harrow or a drag.
- **Weed control:** Weeds can compete with crops for nutrients, sunlight, and water, and can reduce crop yield. It is important to remove weeds before planting. This can be done mechanically, chemically, or by hand.
- **Fertilization:** Fertilizers are added to the soil to improve soil fertility and provide essential nutrients for plant growth. The type and amount of fertilizer used depends on the type of crop and soil conditions.
- **Irrigation:** Adequate moisture is essential for seed germination and plant growth. Irrigation should be done after seed bed preparation to ensure that the soil is moist but not waterlogged.
- **Timing:** Seed bed preparation should be done at the right time to ensure that the soil is at the right temperature and moisture level for seed germination. The timing varies depending on the crop and local weather conditions.

Seed bed preparation is an important step in agriculture that involves preparing the soil for seed germination and growth. This involves plowing or tilling the soil, levelling, weed control, fertilization, irrigation, and timing. Proper seed bed preparation can improve crop yields and ensure a successful harvest.

SEED TREATMENT

Seed treatment is a process of treating seeds with various chemicals or biological agents to protect them from pests, diseases, and other environmental stresses. Here are some important details about seed treatment:

1. **Purpose:** The primary purpose of seed treatment is to improve seed quality, germination rate, and crop yield by protecting the seeds from pests, diseases, and other environmental stresses.
2. **Chemicals used:** The chemicals used for seed treatment include fungicides, insecticides, nematicides, and herbicides. These chemicals can be applied to seeds using various methods such as seed coating, seed soaking, and seed dressing.
3. **Biological agents:** In addition to chemicals, biological agents such as biofungicides, bioinsecticides, and biofertilizers can also be used for seed treatment. These agents are derived from natural sources such as bacteria, fungi, and algae and are considered eco-friendly and safe for the environment.
4. **Methods of application:** Seed treatment can be done using various methods such as dusting, soaking, and coating. In the dusting method, the seeds are coated with a powder containing the required chemical or biological agent. In the soaking method, the seeds are soaked in a solution containing the required agent. In the coating method, the seeds are coated with a layer of material containing the required agent.

5. **Benefits:** Seed treatment has several benefits such as improving seed quality, enhancing germination rate, protecting the seeds from pests and diseases, and reducing environmental pollution by reducing the amount of chemicals required for crop protection.
6. **Precautions:** Seed treatment should be done with caution as some chemicals used for seed treatment can be toxic to humans and animals. It is important to follow the instructions on the product label and use appropriate protective gear when handling chemicals.

Seed treatment is an important practice in modern agriculture that helps improve seed quality, protect crops from pests and diseases, and increase crop yield.

TIME AND METHOD OF SOWING/ PLANTING

Time and method of sowing/planting are critical factors in crop production as they determine the crop's yield potential and performance. Some important details about time and method of sowing/planting:

1. **Time of sowing/planting:** The time of sowing/ planting varies depending on the crop and the region where it is grown. Generally, crops are sown/planted during the optimal season for growth and development. For example, wheat is sown in the winter season, while rice is sown in the rainy season.
2. **Method of sowing/planting:** The method of sowing/ planting also varies depending on the crop and the farming system. Some of the commonly used methods are:
    - **Broadcasting:** This involves spreading the seeds uniformly over the entire field without any specific arrangement. This method is commonly used for crops like wheat, barley, and mustard.
    - **Dibbling:** This involves making holes in the soil with a pointed stick or dibber and placing the seed in the hole. This method is commonly used for crops like maize and sorghum.
    - **Transplanting:** This involves raising seedlings in a nursery and then transplanting them in the field. This method is commonly used for crops like rice and vegetables.
    - **Drilling:** This involves sowing the seeds in rows at a predetermined depth using a drill machine. This method is commonly used for crops like wheat, maize, and soybean.
3. **Planting density:** The planting density refers to the number of plants per unit area of land. The optimal planting density varies depending on the crop and the farming system. In general, a higher planting density results in a higher yield but may also increase the risk of pest and disease outbreaks.
4. **Seed rate:** The seed rate refers to the amount of seed required to sow a unit area of land. The optimal seed rate varies depending on the crop and the farming system. In general, a higher seed rate results in a higher yield but also increases the cost of production.
5. **Seed treatment:** Seed treatment is the process of treating seeds with fungicides, insecticides, or other chemicals to protect them from pests and diseases. This is often done before sowing/planting to ensure better germination and establishment of the crop.

The time and method of sowing/planting, planting density, seed rate, and seed treatment are important factors that farmers need to consider when planning crop production.

SEED RATE

Seed rate refers to the amount of seed that is sown per unit area of land. The appropriate seed rate varies depending on the crop, variety, soil type, and other environmental factors. The goal of selecting the right seed rate is to achieve an optimum plant population that can provide the highest possible yield.

The seed rate is usually expressed as weight or number of seeds per unit area. For example, in wheat, the recommended seed rate is usually around 100-120 kg per hectare (ha), while for maize, it can be between 18-25 kg/ha. For vegetable crops, the seed rate is often given as the number of seeds per meter or row.

Factors that influence seed rate include seed size, seed viability, seed dormancy, germination percentage, and plant stand desired. Seed rate can be adjusted based on the fertility of the soil, expected yield, and management practices.

Planting too much seed can result in overcrowding, which can lead to competition for nutrients, water, and light, resulting in reduced yields, increased pest and disease pressure, and lodging. On the other hand, planting too few seeds can result in low plant populations, reduced yields, and wastage of land and other resources.

Therefore, it is important for farmers to follow recommended seed rates, which are usually based on research and experience, to ensure optimal plant populations and maximum yields.

DOSE, METHOD, AND TIME OF FERTILIZER APPLICATION

Dose, method, and time of fertilizer application are important considerations for optimizing crop productivity and minimizing nutrient loss. Here are some details:

1. **Dose:** The dose of fertilizer needed varies depending on the crop, soil fertility, and cropping system. It is important to determine the appropriate dose for a specific crop in a given field to avoid under or over

application. Soil testing can provide information on the nutrient status of the soil and guide the appropriate dose of fertilizer.

2. **Method:** There are different methods of fertilizer application including broadcasting, band placement, and fertigation. Broadcasting involves spreading fertilizer uniformly over the entire field. Band placement involves placing fertilizer in a narrow band near the seed or plant. Fertigation involves applying fertilizer through the irrigation system.
3. **Time:** The timing of fertilizer application is critical for maximizing nutrient use efficiency and crop productivity. Generally, fertilizers can be applied in pre-planting, at planting, and during the crop growing period. Pre-planting application can be done several weeks before planting to allow sufficient time for the fertilizer to mix with the soil. At planting application involves placing the fertilizer in the soil near the seed. During crop growing period, the fertilizer can be applied as a top dressing.

In addition to these considerations, it is important to follow recommended application rates and timing, avoid nutrient imbalances, and use fertilizers that are appropriate for the soil and crop needs.

IRRIGATION

Irrigation is the process of artificially applying water to crops for their growth and development. It is essential in areas where rainfall is insufficient or unreliable, or during certain stages of crop growth. Here are some details on irrigation:

1. **Types of Irrigation:** There are different types of irrigation systems, including surface irrigation, sprinkler irrigation, and drip irrigation. The type of system used depends on factors such as soil type, crop type, topography, and water availability.
2. **Water Requirements:** The amount of water required for irrigation varies depending on the crop, soil type, and climate. The water requirement is usually expressed in terms of the crop water requirement (CWR), which is the amount of water required to meet the evapotranspiration (ET) needs of the crop.
3. **Irrigation Scheduling:** The timing of irrigation is crucial for efficient water use and crop growth. Over-irrigation can lead to waterlogging, leaching of nutrients, and soil erosion, while under-irrigation can result in reduced crop yields. Irrigation scheduling involves determining the frequency and amount of water required for irrigation based on the crop growth stage, soil type, weather conditions, and other factors.
4. **Water Quality:** The quality of water used for irrigation is also important. Poor quality water can contain high levels of salts, which can accumulate in the soil and damage the crop. Water with high salinity or sodium content should be avoided or treated before use.
5. **Irrigation Management:** Effective irrigation management involves ensuring that the irrigation system is functioning properly and efficiently, and that water is being applied evenly across the field. Monitoring soil moisture levels and adjusting irrigation schedules accordingly can help to improve water use efficiency and crop yields.

Overall, irrigation is a critical component of crop production, and proper irrigation management can help to improve crop yields and reduce water use.

INTERCULTURE

Interculture is the process of managing the growth of crops between rows and within the crop itself. The objective of interculture is to control weeds, loosen the soil, and provide appropriate soil aeration and water-holding capacity. This practice is also known as cultivation or tillage.

Interculture activities vary depending on the type of crop, the stage of crop growth, and the specific needs of the soil. Some common interculture practices include:

1. **Weed control:** Weeds compete with crops for nutrients, water, and sunlight. Regular weeding helps to keep the weed population under control, reducing the competition with the crop.
2. **Soil aeration:** Regular interculture helps to loosen the soil, increasing its porosity, and allowing air and water to penetrate more easily. This can improve root development and increase water holding capacity.
3. **Fertilizer application:** Fertilizer can be applied during interculture by broadcasting, top-dressing, or banding. The timing and method of application depend on the type of fertilizer and the crop.
4. **Pest control:** Interculture can also help to control pests that may be damaging the crop. By breaking up soil clods and removing debris, interculture can disrupt the habitat of pests, reducing their population.
5. **Mulching:** Mulching involves covering the soil around the plants with organic material such as straw or leaves. This helps to suppress weed growth, retain moisture, and improve soil structure.

Interculture practices should be carefully timed to avoid damage to the crop. For example, interculture should not be performed during sensitive stages of crop growth, such as when the crop is flowering or fruiting.

WEED CONTROL

Weed control is an important aspect of crop management as weeds compete with crops for nutrients, sunlight, and water. Effective weed control can increase crop yield and quality. There are several methods of weed control including:

1. **Mechanical methods:** This involves the physical removal of weeds through hand weeding, hoeing, or plowing. These methods are effective but can be time-consuming and labor-intensive.
2. **Chemical methods:** The use of herbicides is a common method of weed control. Herbicides can be selective or non-selective, with selective herbicides targeting specific weed species and non-selective herbicides killing all vegetation. Herbicides should be applied according to the label instructions to ensure safety and effectiveness.
3. **Cultural methods:** Crop rotation, intercropping, and proper irrigation and fertilization can reduce weed growth and competition with crops.
4. **Biological methods:** The use of natural enemies such as insects, mites, or pathogens to control weeds can be effective, but requires careful management to prevent negative impacts on non-target organisms.

The timing of weed control is also important. Weeds should be controlled as early as possible before they compete with crops for resources. Herbicides should be applied when weeds are actively growing and at the correct stage of growth for maximum effectiveness. Regular monitoring and early detection of weeds is crucial for effective weed control.

COMMON PESTS, DISEASES AND THEIR CONTROL

Common pests and diseases in agriculture can cause significant damage to crops and result in yield loss if not properly controlled. Here are some important details about common pests and diseases and their control:

1. **Bacterial diseases:** Bacterial diseases in crops are caused by various bacteria that infect plants through wounds or natural openings. Some common bacterial diseases include bacterial blight, bacterial wilt, and bacterial spot. Control measures include the use of resistant varieties, crop rotation, sanitation, and copper-based bactericides.
2. **Fungal diseases:** Fungal diseases are caused by various types of fungi that infect plants and cause symptoms such as leaf spots, blights, and rots. Some common fungal diseases include powdery mildew, downy mildew, and rusts. Control measures include the use of resistant varieties, crop rotation, fungicides, and cultural practices such as pruning and removal of infected plant parts.
3. **Viral diseases:** Viral diseases in plants are caused by various viruses that are transmitted by insects or other vectors. Symptoms of viral diseases include stunting, yellowing, and mottling of leaves. Control measures include the use of virus-free seed or planting material, insecticides to control vectors, and removal of infected plants.
4. **Nematode diseases:** Nematodes are microscopic roundworms that live in soil and feed on plant roots. Symptoms of nematode damage include stunting, yellowing, and wilting of plants. Control measures include the use of resistant varieties, crop rotation, and soil fumigation with nematocides.

Integrated pest management (IPM) is an approach that combines different control measures to manage pests and diseases in a sustainable manner. It includes cultural practices such as crop rotation, sanitation, and use of resistant varieties, as well as biological control methods such as the use of natural enemies and biopesticides. Chemical control measures such as the use of pesticides are also used in IPM, but only as a last resort and with proper application techniques to minimize environmental impact.

STORAGE, PROCESSING AND MARKETING OF MAJOR FIELD CROPS

Storage, processing, and marketing of major field crops are essential components of agriculture. Proper storage and processing ensure the quality of the crops, while effective marketing helps in earning a better price for the farmers. Here are the important details regarding storage, processing, and marketing of some major field crops in India:

1. RICE

Rice (Oryza sativa) is a crucial staple food for over 3 billion people globally. It is cultivated in more than 100 countries across 154 million hectares, producing approximately 600 million tonnes with an average productivity of 3.9 tonnes per hectare. Among the rice-growing nations, India holds the largest area under cultivation. However, in terms of production, India ranks second with 131.2 million tonnes of coarse rice.

In India, rice is grown on an area of 44.6 million hectares, producing 132 tonnes with an average productivity of 2.97 tonnes per hectare. Rice is cultivated in almost all states in India, with Uttar Pradesh, West Bengal, and Punjab being the leading states in terms of area, production, and productivity, respectively. Punjab has the highest rice productivity among all states.

Around 90% of the world's rice is grown in Asia, and it provides approximately 29.4% of the total calories per capita per day in Asian countries. Milled rice generally contains 6-7% protein, with low fat content (2.0-2.5%), and most of the fat is lost during the milling process.

Climatic and Soil Requirements

Rice cultivation extends from sea level to as high as 3000 m above mean sea level (amsl) in India. High temperature, high humidity and high rainfall have considerable effect on growth and development of rice plant. Rice crop is grown during Kharif season in north-western plains zone, but in south and north-eastern parts of the country, it is grown in all the three seasons, as these areas do not have very cold weather during winter. Rice crop needs a hot and humid climate. It is essentially a C3 plant.

The wide range of agro-climatic conditions suggests an equally wide variety of soils. As regards texture, rice is grown on loamy sands in Punjab to heavy clay loams or clays in Andhra Pradesh and some other states. Soils having good water holding capacity with good amount of clay and organic matter are ideal for puddled rice.

Rice Eco-systems in India

Rice farming is practiced in several agro-ecological zones in India. No other country in the world has such diversity in rice ecosystems than India. Rice cultivation in India is done in four distinct types of ecosystems:

- Irrigated rice eco-system
- Rainfed upland rice eco-system
- Rainfed lowland rice eco-system
- Flood prone rice eco-system

Rice cropping pattern in India vary widely from region to region and to a lesser extent from one year to another year depending on a wide range of soil and climatic conditions. Some of the rice based cropping patterns being followed in the country are: Rice-wheat, rice-wheat-mungbean, rice-toria-wheat, rice-toria/chickpea, rice-wheat/barley/potato, rice-potato-blackgram, rice -pea-greengram and rice-rice-rice

Recommended Varieties

A good number of rice varieties/hybrids having resistance to various biotic and abiotic stresses and grain quality have been developed in India.

Some of the improved cultivars of rice are described as under:

Important Rice Cultivars Recommended for Different States

Cultivar type	Rice cultivars
Hybrids	APHR 1, DRRH-3, PA 6201, Pusa RH 10, HRI 120, Sahyadri-2, UPRH 27, Rajalaxmi, Pant Sankar Dhan 1, Pant Sugandh Dhan-17, PHB 71
Basmati/ scented varieties	Basmati 370, Pusa Basmati 1, Taraori Basmati (Karnal local), Pusa Sugandh 3, Pusa Sugandh 4, Pusa Sugandh 6, PRH 10, Pant Dhan 15, Punjab Basmati-1, Pusa Basmati 1121, Pusa Basmati 6, Pusa Basmati 1509
Other improved varieties	Mahamaya, GK 5003, Pusa 33, Pusa 169, Mehsuri, JKRH-401, Gurjari, GR-6, Dandi, HKR-127, Bhrigu Dhan, Himalaya 2216, SKAU 23, SKAU 27, GK 5003, Gauri, Sweta, Ratnagiri 24, Rajeshwari, PR 108, PR 109, PMK 2, Pant Dhan 10, Pant Dhan 11, VL Dhan 221, IR 20, Jayanthi

Methods of Cultivation

Rice is generally grown under dry or wet cultivation methods, which are briefly described below:

(a) Dry Cultivation

1. **Direct seeded rice:** Rice is sown directly in dry soil (dry seeding) or wet soil (wet seeding), and irrigation is given to keep the soil sufficiently moist for good plant growth, but the soil is never flooded. Dry system of rice cultivation is followed in uplands. Sowing of rice is usually done in May-June in the case of the crop dependent on south-west monsoon and in September for the crop dependent on north-east monsoon.

   Three methods are commonly followed in sowing dry and semi-dry crop. These are broadcasting, drilling or sowing in furrows behind country plough, and dibbling in general, a seed rate of 30-50 kg ha^{-1} is required for drilling, while 60-100 kg ha^{-1} is required for broadcasting. A row spacing of 15-20 cm is optimum for upland rice. There are mainly two methods of direct seeding.

   - **Dry seeding:** In dry seeding, seed is directly sown in dry soil either by seed drill or broadcasting of un-sprouted seed in well prepared and leveled dry soil.
   - **Wet seeding:** In wet seeding, seed is directly sown in puddled soil either by drum seeder or broadcasting of sprouted seed in wet soil.

2. **Aerobic rice:** It is a high-yielding rice, grown in non-puddled, aerobic soils under irrigation and high external inputs. Irrigation is applied when the soil becomes dry, and the quantity of applied water is sufficient to bring the soil to field capacity. The realization of water savings combined with high yields depends on good water management. Dry seeding of rice can be done by drilling the seed into a fine seedbed at a depth of 2–3 cm. Weed management is a critical factor in aerobic rice. Timely application of herbicides and two or three hand-weeding may provide effective control. Seeding under dry situations is done in three different ways viz. drilling, dibbling, and broadcasting.

(b) Wet Cultivation

Conventional rice cultivation: The conventional rice cultivation is a wet system of cultivation and rice is grown under wet season right from the start. In this system, the field is brought to a soil puddle by repeated ploughing with 5-7 cm standing water. After getting the requisite puddle, rice seedlings are transplanted or sprouted seeds are direct seeded. The seedlings of rice are grown in nursery before transplanting.

Transplanting Operation

Time of planting is the most important factor influencing the yield of the crop. In general, timely transplanting of 20-25 days old seedlings in wet season is ideal. In general, 20 cm × 10 cm, 20 cm × 15 cm or 15 cm × 15 cm spacing is ideal in transplanted rice. For realizing the yield potential of high yielding varieties of rice, 2-3 seedlings per hill is generally recommended. In rice hybrids where the tillering is more profuse, 1-2 seedlings per hill is sufficient. Depth of transplanting rice seedlings is 2-4 cm.

System of Rice Intensification (SRI)

SRI is an unusual innovation that can raise productivity of land, labour, water, and capital invested in irrigated and rainfed rice production. SRI has evoked considerable interest among Agronomists over last decade and posed interesting research issues.

SRI may prove as a boon to enhance productivity while using less seed and irrigation water than conventional rice farming. The SRI essentially comprises the following methodological components:

- Shallow (1–2 cm) transplanting of young seedlings at the two-leaf stage into a moist seedbed.
- Transplanting of single rice seedling at 25 cm × 25 cm spacing.
- A minimum of three hand weedings at 10–12, 22–25 and 40–42 days after transplanting.
- Farmers may use mechanical weeding tool called weeder to remove weeds and aerate soil surface.
- Alternation of wetting and drying of the field for soil aeration during vegetative growth.
- Addition of organic manures to supply adequate nutrients and to improve soil structure. If necessary, chemical fertilizers may be used as a supplement.

Nutrient Management

Adequate supply of all the essential plant nutrients is a must for getting good yield of rice. A dose 100-150 kg N/ha is generally recommended for high yielding varieties of rice. A dose of 45-60 kg P_2O_5/ha and 40 kg K_2O/ ha is generally recommended for rice. Zn deficiency in rice-growing areas of India is widespread. Zinc sulphate @ 20-25 kg / ha is generally recommended in zinc-deficient soils.

Water Management

Rice is the largest consumer of water; about 3000-5000 litres water is required to produce 1 kg rice. The principal water loss processes from paddy fields are via run- off, percolation, seepage and evapotranspiration or consumptive water use. The submergence (2-5 cm) throughout the crop growth period is conducive to higher yields. Under water scarcity, the practice of intermittent submergence during the critical stages (tillering, flowering) and maintenance of saturation or field capacity in rest of the growth stages is recommended.

Weed Management

Hand weeding is most widely used method for controlling weeds in rice. Normally two weedings are done. Time of weeding slightly varies in different regions but weedings are generally done within 15 to 45 days after sowing. Weeding with some implements such as hand hoes, weeders and bullock drawn desi plough can be done to control weeds in rice. Use of herbicides is gradually increasing in rice culture. Herbicides are expensive to small farmers but not to the large farmers who face the problem of labour shortage.

Chemical Weed Management in Rice

Rice	Herbicides	Dose (kg a.i./ha)	Application time and remarks
Rice nursery	Butachlor	1.0-1.5	Pre-emergence at 5-6 days after sowing (DAS); If moisture is less in soil, irrigation should be done immediately.
	Pendimethalin	1.0-1.5	Pre-emergence at 5-6 DAS; If moisture is less in soil, irrigation should be done immediately.
	Pretilachlor (S)	0.3-0.4	Pre-emergence at 3-5 DAS.
Direct-seeded upland rice	Butachlor	1.0-1.5	To be applied before emergence of crop; One hand weeding at 30-35 DAS will supplement herbicide treatment.
	Pendimethalin	1.0-1.5	To be applied before emergence of crop; One hand weeding at 30-35 DAS will supplement herbicide treatment.

	Pretilachlor (S)	0.3-0.4	Pre-emergence at 3-5 DAS.
	Metsulfuron-methyl	0.010-0.015	Post-emergence at 30-35 DAS; basically a broad-leaved weed killer and recommended as a substitute of 2,4-D.
Direct-seeded puddled and transplanted rice	Butachlor	1.0-1.5	Pre-emergence at 3-5 days after transplanting (DAT) on saturated soil; No irrigation or standing water impounded for at least 3 days after treatment.
	Pendimethalin	1.0-1.5	Pre-emergence at 3-5 DAT on saturated soil; No irrigation or standing water impounded for at least 3 days after treatment.
	Pretilachlor (S)	0.3-0.4	Pre-emergence at 3-5 DAT.
	Metsulfuron-methyl	0.010-0.015	Post-emergence at 30-35 DAS; basically a broad-leaved weed killer and recommended as a substitute of 2,4-D.

Disease Management

To overcome the diseases, the seed should be disease free. For fungal and bacterial diseases, seed should be treated with bavistin @ 2g kg^{-1} seed. Fungicides can be sprayed to control a diseases

Symptoms and Management of Important Diseases of Rice in India

Disease and its causal organism	Symptoms	Management
Leaf and neck blast	Initial symptoms on the leaves are white to grayish green circular lesions/spots with dark green borders, which may enlarge and coalesce to kill the entire leaves. Lesions on the neck cause the girdling of the neck and the panicle to fall over.	• Early sowing of seeds and balanced use of fertilizers. • Planting resistant varieties against the rice blast is the most practical and economical way. • Systemic fungicides are effective against the disease.
Bacterial leaf blight	Water-soaked to yellowish stripes on leaf blades or starting at leaf tips. Severely infected leaves tend to dry quickly.	• Field sanitation such as removing weed hosts, rice straws, ratoons, and volunteer seedlings. • Use of resistant varieties. • Seed treatment with bleaching powder (100 μg/ml) and zinc sulfate (2%) reduce bacterial blight.

Pest Management

Most of the rice pests are distributed throughout India, however, only a few pests are economically important in different regions. Agronomic practices and use of resistant cultivars should be given preference for pest management. The use of selective pesticides should also be stressed for efficient pest management.

Important Insect Pest, Nature of Damage and Pest Management in Rice

Insect-pest	Nature of damage	Management
Stem borer (yellow)	Symptoms of stem borer damage are deadhearts and whiteheads. Whiteheads are discolored panicles with empty or partially filled grains. Larvae feed on the tissues around the node.	• Adopt seedling root dip treatment in 0.05% chlorpyriphos emulsion forone minute before transplanting in endemic areas. • Apply carbofuran 3G @ 20 kg ha^{-1} or phorate 10 G @ 12.5 kg ha^{-1} or fenitrothion 50EC @ 0.1%.

Harvesting, Threshing and Yield

The plant should be cut close to the ground at ripening and left for drying. Threshing can be accomplished by manual methods, pedal threshers or power driven stationary threshers. Combine machines can be employed for combined harvesting and threshing. The produce should be properly sun-dried. The optimum moisture content for storage of rice grains is 12%. A well managed crop of mid-late duration (135-150 days) varieties and hybrids yield about 6–7 t/ha, whereas short duration cultivars yield about 4.5–5.5 t/ha.

2. WHEAT

Wheat (Triticum aestivum) is one of the most important cereal crops in the world, cultivated on a large scale for its edible seeds, which are used to make flour and a wide range of food products. It is a member of the grass family and belongs to the genus Triticum, which also includes other cereal crops such as barley and rye.

Wheat is widely grown in temperate regions, and it is the second most produced cereal crop after corn. It is a staple food for a large portion of the world's population, particularly in Europe, North America, and Asia. Wheat is a rich source of carbohydrates, protein, and essential nutrients, making it an important component of a healthy and balanced diet.

Climatic and Soil Requirements

Wheat is grown over a wide range of latitudes ranging between 60°N and 60°S and altitudes ranging from sea level to 3500 m amsl in the tropics and subtropics. Normally, the most ideal conditions for wheat cultivation are cool and moist weather during the vegetative growth period and warm and dry weather during grain formation. The optimum temperature for the germination of wheat is between 20-22°C, though wheat grain can also germinate at 4°C. The optimum temperature for vegetative growth ranges from 16 to 22°C. During the grain development, wheat requires a mean maximum temperature of about 25°C for at least four to five weeks. Wheat grows well in those areas where annual rainfall ranges between 250 and 1800 mm. Wheat crop also cannot withstand extended periods of soil moisture stress. Rainfed wheat requires a minimum evenly distributed winter rainfall of 15 to 20 cm. Wheat is grown on a wide variety of soils.

Major Cultivated Species of Wheat

- **Common wheat or bread wheat (T. aestivum):** A hexaploid species that is the most widely cultivated in the world.

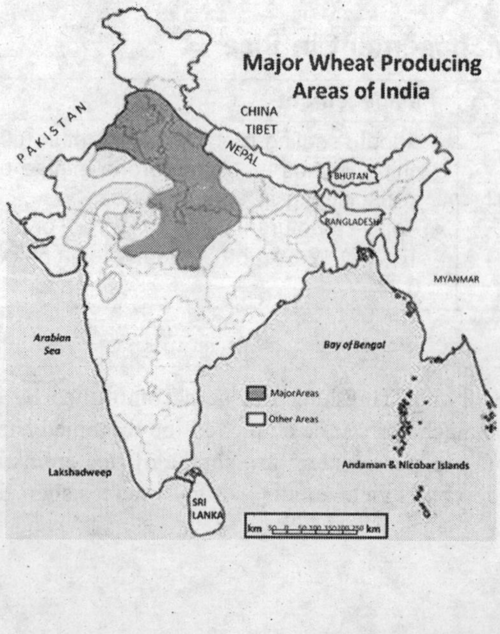

- **Durum wheat (T. durum):** The tetraploid form of wheat and the second most widely cultivated wheat today.

Seed and Sowing

Under irrigated timely sown condition, wheat sowing may be done in the first fortnight of November in north India and the middle of November in north-east and central India. Under late sown conditions, the wheat is sown in first fortnight of December. Rainfed wheat is generally sown from second fortnight of October to early-November to get maximum benefit from residual soil moisture. Seeds can be sown through broadcasting or in lines in rows 20 cm apart. Under normal conditions, a seed rate of 100 kg/ha is sufficient. Under late sown conditions, seed rate should be increased by 25 per cent. Irrigated wheat is spaced 22.5 cm between rows and 8-10 cm between plants. Rainfed wheat is spaced 25-30 cm between rows and 5-6 cm between plants. Seed depth should be around 5 cm.

Nutrient Management

The general N + P_2O_5 + K_2O recommendations for irrigated and rainfed wheat are 120 + 60 + 30 kg/ha and 80 + 40 + 20 kg/ha, respectively. Full dose of phosphorus and potassium and half of nitrogen should be applied at the time of sowing, while remaining half dose should be top dressed in two equal splits one at first irrigation and other at flowering stage. Farmyard manure (FYM) or organic manures @ 10 t/ha at the time of sowing is beneficial for long-term fertility maintenance.

Water Management

Wheat requires about 300-400 cm of irrigation water (4-6 irrigations), depending upon climatic factors, soil characteristics and the duration of the variety. If irrigation water is a constraint, then apply irrigation at critical stages.

Number of irrigations based on the availability of water

No of irrigations	Critical stages for irrigation
1	CRI
2	CRI + LJ
3	CRI + B + M
4	CRI + LT + F + M
5	CRI + LT + LJ + F + M
6	CRI + LT + LJ + F + M + D

CRI – Crown root initiation (21 DAS), LT – Late tillering (42 DAS), LJ – Late jointing (60 DAS), F – Flowering (80 DAS), M – Milk (95 DAS), D – Dough (115 DAS).

Weed Management

The critical period of weed competition in wheat is 30-45 days after sowing (DAS). Hand weeding with a khurpi or hand hoe after 20-25 DAS is used as conventional practice. A pre-emergence application of pendimethalin (Stomp 30 EC) @ 1 kg a.i./ha in 500- 750 L/ha of water within 3 DAS provides a broad spectrum control of weeds in wheat. However, post-emergence application (25-30 DAS) of herbicides like sulfosulfuron @ 25 g/ha or fenaxaprop-p ethyl @ 100-120 g/ha is necessary for effective weed control.

Disease Management

Rusts: Wheat is infected by brown, yellow and black rusts. Brown or leaf rust is caused by a fungus known as Puccinia recondite tritici. Yellow or stripe rust is caused by the fungus, Puccinia striiformis. Black or stem rust of wheat is caused by the fungus Puccinia graminis tritici. For controlling rusts, treat the seed with Trichoderma viride @ 4 g/kg seed. Late sown crop is more susceptible to rust. Hence avoid late sowing of wheat. High nitrogen dose favours rust infection, whereas high potash dose reduces rust infection. Hence there is need for balanced fertilization. Spray the crop with propiconazole (Tilt 25 EC) @ 0.1% at yellow rust initiation. This spray will also help in the control of powdery mildew and Karnal bunt diseases. Second and third spray may be repeated with an interval of 10-15 days.

Loose smut: Loose smut is caused by fungus Ustilago nuda tritici. Terminal symptom of loose smut is the production of black powder in place of wheat grains in the ears. As the ear formation starts, fungus accumulates in the floral parts, which are completely destroyed due to formation of the black powder. Loose smut can be controlled by growing loose smut resistant varieties. Seed treatment should be done with carboxin (Vitavax 75 WP) @ 1.25 g/kg seed. Uproot the infected plants, bury them underground or burn to avoid further field infection.

Karnal bunt: Karnal bunt or partial bunt is caused by fungus Neovossia indica. A portion of infected grain along its groove is converted into a black powdery mass. The black powder gives a foul smell due to presence of trimethylamine. Do not grow highly susceptible wheat varieties. One spray of propiconazole (25 EC) @ 0.1% at ear head emergence stage can be given to attain near complete control.

Pest Management

Termites: The damaged plants dry up completely and can be easily pulled out. Infestation is heavy under unirrigated conditions and in the fields where undecomposed FYM is applied before sowing. Termites can be controlled by seed treatment with fipronil (Regent 5FS @ 0.3 g a.i./kg seed).

Harvesting, Threshing and Yield

The most suitable stage for harvesting wheat is when plants are completly dry and the grains becomes hard and contain 20-25% moisture. Wheat crop harvested manually or by reapers, is dried for 3-4 days on the threshing floor and then threshing is done by threshers. A well managed crop may yield about 3.5 to 4.5 t grains/ha.

3. MAIZE

Maize (Zea mays L.) is a highly versatile crop that can adapt to various agro-climatic conditions. It is the only grain crop with multiple types and is grown for diverse purposes such as normal yellow/white grain, sweet corn, baby corn, popcorn, quality protein maize (QPM), waxy corn, high amylase corn, high oil corn, fodder maize, etc. Globally, maize is known as the "queen of cereals" due to its high genetic yield potential among cereals.

In India, maize is the third most important food crop after rice and wheat.

It is cultivated in 8.78 m ha mainly during Kharif season which covers 80% area. Predominant maize growing states collectively contributing to more than 80% of total national maize production are Andhra Pradesh (20.9%), Karnataka (16.5%), Rajasthan (9.9%), Maharashtra (9.1%), Bihar (8.9%), Uttar Pradesh (6.1%), Madhya Pradesh (5.7%) and Himachal Pradesh (4.4%).

Climatic and Soil Requirement

Maize is grown globally from 50°N to 40°S, and from sea level up to 4000 m altitude. Maize crop requires good amount of moisture and can be grown in areas receiving well distributed rainfall of 500 to 1000 mm. It uses water more efficiently and relatively drought resistant from establishment to tasseling stage of the crop where it can stands with less moisture. Maize is relatively well adapted to a wide range of soils with pH 5.0 to 8.0. Maize can be grown successfully in a variety of soils, ranging from loamy-sand to clay-loam. Being a sensitive crop to excess soil moisture; it is desirable to have provision of proper drainage in maize.

Maize Based Cropping Systems in India

Maize-wheat is the 3rd most important cropping systems after rice-wheat and rice-rice that contributes about 3% in the national food basket. The other major maize systems in India are maize-mustard, maize-chickpea, maize-maize, cotton-maize etc.

Time of Sowing

Maize can be grown in all seasons viz; Kharif (monsoon), post monsoon, Rabi (winter) and spring. The optimum time of sowing are given below:

Season	Optimum time of sowing
Kharif	Last week of June to first fortnight July
Rabi	Last week of October for inter cropping and up to 15th of November for sole crop
Spring	First week of February

Seed Rate and Plant Geometry

The seed rate depends on purpose, seed size, plant type, season, sowing methods etc. The following crop geometry and seed rate should be adopted.

S.No.	Purpose	Seed rate (kg/ha)	Plant geometry (plant × row in cm)
1	Normal grain maize	20	60 × 20
2	Quality protein maize (QPM)	20	60 × 20
3	Sweet corn	8	75 × 25
4	Pop corn	12	60 × 20
5	Green cob (normal maize)	20	60 × 20
6	Fodder maize	50	30 × 10

Tillage and Crop Establishment

Generally, the raised bed planting is considered as best planting method for maize during monsoon and winter seasons both under excess moisture as well as limited water availability/rainfed conditions. Maize can also be successfully grown without any primary tillage under no-till situation with less cost of cultivation, higher farm profitability and better resource use efficiency.

Nutrient Management

Application of 10-15 t FYM/ha alongwith NPK fertilizers @ 120-150 kg N, 60-80 kg P_2O_5, 60-70 kg K_2O and 25 kg $ZnSO_4$ /ha is recommended in general for getting higher yield of HYV/hybrid maize. Full dose of P & K and half of N should be applied at the time of sowing, while remaining half N dose should be top dressed in two equal splits one dose at around knee high stage and other dose at tasseling stage of the crop keeping in view moisture availability in the field.

Water Management

The irrigation water management depends on season as about 80% of maize is cultivated during monsoon season particularly under rainfed conditions. In general, the irrigation should be applied in furrows up to 2/3rd height of the ridges/beds. Young seedling, knee high stage, flowering and grain filling are the most sensitive stages for water stress and hence irrigation should ensured at these stages.

Weed Management

Weeds are serious problem in maize particularly during Kharif season and they cause upto 35% yield losses. Thus, timely weed management is must to achieve higher yields. Pre-emergence application of atrazine (Atratraf 50 WP) @ 1.0-1.5 kg a.i./ha in 600 L water or pendimethalin (Stomp 30 EC) @ 1-1.5 kg a.i./ in 500-750 L is effective way for weed control. One-to-two hoeing are recommended for aeration and uprooting of the remaining weeds, if any.

Disease Management

The major diseases of maize and their management practices are described below:

Turcicum leaf blight: The disease is prevalent in cooler conditions or with high humidity. Long, elliptical, grayish-green or tan lesions (2.5-15 cm) appear on lower leaves progressing upward. Resistant varieties alongwith need-based sprays of mancozeb @ 2.5 g/L (with adjuant @ 0.05%) at 8-10 days interval decreases its incidence.

Maydis leaf blight: It is a major disease in the areas having warm humid temperate to tropical climate. Lesions on the leaves elongated between the veins, tan with buff to brown or dark reddish brown borders. Growing of resistant varieties with need based sprays of mancozeb or zineb @ 2.5g/L of water are recommended to control this disease.

Pest Management

Stem Borer: Major pest of maize in India is stalk borer. Its attack occurs during monsoon season. It lays eggs 10-25 days after germination on lower side of the leaves. The larva of the Chilo enters in the whorl and cause damage in the leaves.

Termites: Termite is also an important pest in many areas especially zero-tilled maize. For control of termite, fipronil granules @ 20 kg/ha on termite appearance followed by light irrigation is the recommended practice. If the termite incidence is in patches, the spot application of fipronil @ 2-3 granules/plant should be done.

Harvesting, Threshing and Yield

The crop acquires physiological maturity when black layer starts forming on the tip of the grains. The crop must be harvested at less than 22 to 25% moisture in grains with husk colour turning pale brown. The harvesting of the cob is done manually. After de-cobbing and threshing, the maize grains must be dried upto 12% moisture level for safe storage. A well managed maize HYV's and hybrid maize may yield about 4-5 and 5-7 t grains/ha, respectively.

4. SORGHUM

Sorghum is a versatile cereal crop that has been cultivated for thousands of years around the world, especially in Africa, Asia, and the Americas. It is a major staple food for millions of people, particularly in the arid and semi-arid regions where other crops are difficult to grow due to water scarcity and high temperatures. Sorghum is also used for animal feed, fuel, and industrial purposes, such as making paper, syrup, and biofuels. In recent years, there has been renewed interest in sorghum as a sustainable crop that can help address food and energy security, climate change, and rural development challenges. Sorghum is known for its ability to tolerate drought and extreme temperatures, adapt to different soil types, and resist pests and diseases, making it a resilient and valuable crop for farmers and communities.

Climatic and Soil Requirements

- Sorghum is a versatile crop that can grow in a wide range of climates, from tropical to subtropical and temperate regions.
- The crop requires a temperature range of 20-35°C for optimum growth and yield.
- Sorghum is relatively drought-tolerant and can grow on soils with low fertility, but performs best on well-drained soils with a pH range of 6-7.

Seed Rate and Sowing Method

- The recommended seed rate for sorghum is 15-20 kg/ha.
- The crop can be sown either by broadcasting or drilling method.
- The optimal time of sowing is between May to June in India, depending on the rainfall pattern.

Cultivars

- There are many cultivars of sorghum available, each adapted to specific agro-climatic regions and intended use.
- Some of the popular cultivars in India are CSH 9, CSV 15, Maldandi, and SPV 462.

Nutrient Management

- Sorghum requires a moderate amount of nutrients for optimum growth and yield.
- The recommended dose of NPK (nitrogen, phosphorus, and potassium) for sorghum is 60-80:40:40 kg/ha.
- Organic manures like farmyard manure (FYM) and green manure can also be used to enhance soil fertility.

Water Management

- Sorghum is relatively drought-tolerant, but requires timely irrigation during the critical growth stages.
- The crop needs about 450-500 mm of water during the growing season.
- Irrigation should be applied at an interval of 10-15 days during the vegetative stage and 20-25 days during the reproductive stage.

Weed Management

- Sorghum is vulnerable to weed competition, especially during the early growth stages.
- Hand weeding and hoeing are the common methods of weed control in sorghum.
- Pre-emergence herbicides like atrazine, metribuzin, and pendimethalin can also be used to control weeds.

Harvesting and Yield

- Sorghum takes about 100-120 days to mature, depending on the variety and environmental conditions.
- The crop is harvested when the grain moisture content reaches 18-22%.
- The yield of sorghum ranges from 1-2 t/ha under rainfed conditions and can go up to 3-4 t/ha with proper nutrient and water management.

Sorghum is a versatile crop that can grow in a wide range of climates and soil types. The crop has a good potential to provide food, feed, and fuel in areas with limited water resources. With proper management practices, sorghum can be a profitable crop for farmers.

5. PEARL MILLET

Pearl Millet, also known as Bajra, is a warm-season crop that is grown primarily for its nutritious grain. It is one of the oldest cultivated grains in the world, with a history of domestication dating back more than 4000 years in Africa and Asia. Pearl Millet is a major staple food in many parts of India, Africa, and Asia, particularly in regions with low rainfall and poor soil fertility. It is a hardy crop that can tolerate drought, heat, and pests, making it an important food and income source for millions of smallholder farmers.

Besides its nutritional value, Pearl Millet has many other uses, including fodder for livestock, fuel, and thatching material. In recent years, there has been a growing interest in Pearl Millet as a climate-resilient and sustainable crop that can contribute to food security, poverty reduction, and rural development. With its high tolerance to environmental stresses and adaptability to different agro-climatic conditions, Pearl Millet has the potential to play a crucial role in meeting the growing demand for food and feed in a changing world.

Climatic and Soil Requirements

- Pearl millet is best adapted to warm and dry climates with average temperatures between 25-30°C.
- The crop can tolerate temperatures up to 42°C and can survive in areas with annual rainfall as low as 200 mm.
- Pearl millet can grow on a wide range of soils, from sandy to clay soils, but performs best on well-drained soils with a pH range of 6.5-7.5.

Seed Rate and Sowing Method

- The recommended seed rate for pearl millet is 5-7 kg/ha.
- The crop can be sown either by broadcasting or drilling method.
- The optimal time of sowing is between mid-May to mid-July in India, depending on the rainfall pattern.

Cultivars

- There are many cultivars of pearl millet available, each adapted to specific agro-climatic regions and intended use.
- Some of the popular cultivars in India are HHB 67, J 104, Pusa 704, Pusa 345, and ICTP 8203.

Nutrient Management

- Pearl millet requires a moderate amount of nutrients for optimum growth and yield.
- The recommended dose of NPK (nitrogen, phosphorus, and potassium) for pearl millet is 30-40:20:20 kg/ha.
- Organic manures like farmyard manure (FYM) and green manure can also be used to enhance soil fertility.

Water Management

- Pearl millet is a drought-tolerant crop, but requires timely irrigation during the critical growth stages.
- The crop needs about 350-450 mm of water during the growing season.
- Irrigation should be applied at an interval of 10-15 days during the vegetative stage and 20-25 days during the reproductive stage.

Weed Management

- Pearl millet is vulnerable to weed competition, especially during the early growth stages.
- Hand weeding and hoeing are the common methods of weed control in pearl millet.
- Pre-emergence herbicides like atrazine, metribuzin, and pendimethalin can also be used to control weeds.

Harvesting and Yield

- Pearl millet takes about 70-100 days to mature, depending on the variety and environmental conditions.
- The crop is harvested when the grain moisture content reaches 20-25%.
- The yield of pearl millet ranges from 1-2 t/ha under rainfed conditions and can go up to 3-4 t/ha with proper nutrient and water management.

Pearl millet is a hardy crop that can thrive in arid and semi-arid regions with proper management practices. The crop has a good potential to provide food and feed in areas with limited water resources.

6. GROUNDNUT

Groundnut, also known as peanut or mungfali (Arachis hypogaea L), is a legume that contains about 45% oil and 26% protein in its seed. It is a rich source of essential nutrients such as niacin, folate, fiber, magnesium, vitamin E, manganese, and phosphorus. Globally, India has the largest acreage and is the second largest producer of groundnuts. In India, groundnuts are grown on an area of 5.86 million hectares, with a production of 8.26 million tonnes and an average productivity of 1411 kg/ha. The major groundnut-growing states in India are Gujarat, Tamil Nadu, Andhra Pradesh, Maharashtra, Karnataka, and Rajasthan. Morphologically, groundnuts are classified into two groups: (i) erect or bunch type (Arachis hypogaea subspecies fastigiata), and (ii) trailing or spreading type (Arachis hypogaea subspecies procumbens).

Climatic and Soil Requirements

Groundnut is grown in the tropical and subtropical countries and up to an altitude of 1000 m. The crop can be grown successfully in places receiving a minimum rainfall of 500 mm and a maximum of 1250 mm. The rainfall should be well distributed during flowering and pegging stages. The groundnut cannot withstand long and severe drought or water stagnation. During ripening period, it requires about a month of warm and dry weather.

Most suitable soils for groundnut production are well-drained, light-textured, loose sandy-loam or sandy clay loam with good drainage. Soils should have reasonable high calcium, pH 5.5 to 7.0 and a moderate organic matter.

Cropping Systems

Groundnut is grown in rotation with wheat, lentil, chickpea, pea, barley, etc. It is grown as a mixed crop with pearl millet, maize, sorghum, castor and cotton. The most common cropping systems are: groundnut-wheat/barley/chickpea/field pea/lentil.

Varieties

Some promising varieties recommended for different states are ICGS 76, Tirupati 2, Girnar 1, ICGS 37, ALR 3, ICGS 11, HNG 10, Punjab Mungphali 1, Mukta, Chitra, Jyoti, RS-1, M-335, MH-4, BG-2, TG-1, and TMV-6.

Seed Rate and Sowing Method

A seed rate of 80-100 kg/ha is enough for bunch type and 60-80 kg/ha for spreading type groundnut cultivars. In bunch types, the row to row distance is kept 30-40 cm and in spreading types 45-60 cm. Plant to plant distance would be 15 and 20-22.5 cm for bunch and spreading types, respectively. Sowing can be done through tractor-mounted groundnut planter. The depth of sowing should be 5 cm. One ploughing with soil turning plough followed by two harrowings would be sufficient to achieve a good surface tilth up to 12-18 cm depth.

In India, groundnut is grown over four seasons. Sow the rainfed crop with the onset of monsoon in the last week of June to first week of July. In irrigated conditions, sow in last week of June. In rabi, groundnut is sown during November-December. Summer groundnut is sown during mid-February. For seed purposes, pods should be shelled by hand one week before sowing. Hand shelling ensures little damage to seeds. Treat the selected kernels with thiram or captan or ceresan @ 5 g/kg kernels to check seed and soil borne diseases.

Nutrient Requirement

Groundnut, being legume, needs more phosphorous, and being an oilseed requires more sulphur. Seed should be inoculated with efficient strains of Rhizobium culture. Well decomposed FYM or compost @ 5-10 t/ha should be applied about 15-20 days before sowing. Apply 15 kg N, 50 kg P_2O_5 and 25 kg K_2O /ha at the time of sowing. Use of gypsum @ 100-150 kg/ha during field preparation can add to the yield. Calcium too has pronounced effect on proper development of pods and kernels.

Water Management

Being a rainy season crop, groundnut does not require irrigation. The field should be well drained. Flowering and pegging are the most critical stages for irrigation.

Weed Management

Two weedings 20 and 45 DAS are recommended. Pre-emergence application of pendimethalin @ 1 kg a.i./ha in 800-1000 L water/ha along with 2 intercultures at 30 and 45 DAS have been recommended in irrigated conditions.

Disease Management

Tikka disease or leaf spot (ansal organisation): The spots on leaves are circular to irregular and are surrounded by a yellow halo. The spots on the upper surface look like reddish brown to black, whereas on lower surface these spots are smooth and light brown in colour. Spray the crop two to three times with dithane M- 45 or blitox-50 @ 1.5-2.0 kg/ha at 10-15 days interval starting from the first appearance of spot.

Pest Management

White grub: The young grubs are white and translucent. Fully grown larvae are larger than a thumb. The larvae feed on soil organic matter for a few weeks and then they eat roots. They also damage pods. The grubs cut and eat the plant roots, and consequently the plants wilts and dies. White-grub is a menace in the light soils, which can be controlled effectively by treating seed with chlorpyriphos 20 EC @ 15 ml/kg seed.

Harvesting, Threshing and Yield

Harvesting of groundnut should be done at blackening of inner shell and development of testa colour. Harvest the crop at 80% pod maturity. After harvesting, the pods are dried in sun to reduce moisture content to 20-25% for threshing. After threshing, kernels are dried to reduce the moisture content to 8-10%. Under normal conditions, groundnut yields about 15-25 q pods/ha with shelling percentage of 68-69.

7. MUSTARD

Mustard is a versatile and popular plant that has been cultivated for centuries for its edible leaves, seeds, and oil. It belongs to the Brassicaceae family and is closely related to other well-known crops such as broccoli, cauliflower, and cabbage. Mustard is grown in many parts of the world, including India, Canada, and Europe, and is used in various culinary traditions, including Indian, French, and American. Mustard plants require specific soil and climatic conditions, and the crop requires proper care and attention to ensure a good yield. In this context, it is important to have a good understanding of the plant's growth habits, propagation, planting distance and time, pruning, manures and fertilizers, irrigation, plant protection, diseases, physiological disorders, maturity, and harvesting.

Soil and Climatic Requirements

Mustard grows well in well-drained loamy soils with a pH range of 6.0 to 7.5. It requires a cool and moist climate with a temperature range of 10 to 25°C during the growing season. The crop can tolerate light frost but not heavy frost. Mustard can be grown in both tropical and temperate climates.

Varieties

There are many varieties of mustard, including black, brown, and white mustard. Some popular varieties include Pusa Bold, Pusa Agrani, Pusa Mahak, and Pusa Jaikisan.

Propagation

Mustard is propagated by seeds. Seeds are sown directly in the field or in a nursery for transplanting.

Planting Distance and Time

Mustard is usually sown in rows with a spacing of 30 to 45 cm between rows and a spacing of 10 to 20 cm between plants. The best time to plant mustard is in the autumn season (September to November) in temperate regions and in the winter season (November to February) in tropical regions.

Pruning

Mustard does not require pruning, but if the plant becomes too tall and leggy, it can be pruned to promote bushy growth.

Manures and Fertilizers

Mustard requires a moderate amount of nitrogen, phosphorus, and potassium. A dose of 50-60 kg/ha of nitrogen and 40-50 kg/ha of phosphorus should be applied before sowing. A top dressing of nitrogen can be applied 4 to 6 weeks after sowing.

Irrigation

Mustard requires regular irrigation during the growing season, especially during the flowering and pod formation stages. The frequency and amount of irrigation depend on the soil moisture level and climatic conditions.

Plant Protection

Mustard can be attacked by pests such as aphids, flea beetles, cutworms, and cabbage loopers. It can also be affected by diseases such as blackleg, white rust, and downy mildew. The use of pesticides and fungicides can help control these pests and diseases.

Diseases

Mustard can be affected by various diseases such as blackleg, white rust, and downy mildew. These diseases can be controlled by the use of resistant varieties and proper plant protection measures.

Physiological Disorders

Mustard can also be affected by physiological disorders such as lodging and bolting. Lodging occurs when the plant falls over due to its own weight or strong winds. Bolting is the premature formation of a flowering stem before the plant has produced enough leaves.

Maturity and Harvesting

Mustard is ready for harvest in about 90 to 120 days after sowing. The crop is harvested when the pods turn yellow and the seeds are mature. The crop is harvested by cutting the plants close to the ground and threshing the seeds. The seeds can be dried and stored for later use or sold in the market.

8. PIGEON PEA

Pigeon pea *(Cajanus cajan L.)* or Redgram is a popular pulse crop in India, occupying approximately 90% of global area and 85% of world production. Known as arhar or Tur in Hindi, it is the second most important pulse crop in India, following chickpea, in terms of area and production. Pigeon pea seeds, used as dal, are an excellent source of protein (21%), iron, and iodine. They are also rich in essential amino acids such as lycine, tyrocene, cystine, and arginine. Being a legume, pigeon pea possesses valuable properties as a restorer of nitrogen in soil. It is mainly a kharif crop, but the cultivation of pigeon pea in summer season is also gaining attention, especially in intercropping systems in north and northeast states, with the development of short duration varieties. India has the largest area (3.38 million ha) under pigeon pea. Pigeon pea's maturity duration varies from about 90 days for extra-early varieties to over 260 days for late maturing varieties that fit well in various niches and cropping systems.

Climate and Soil Requirements

Pigeon pea is a crop of arid and semi-arid climates grown between 30°N and 35°S latitudes and thrives well in areas with 500-1000 mm of rainfall. Its drought hardy nature due to deep tap root system makes it a crop of low rainfall situations. It is grown in the temperature ranges of 20-40°C and can withstand a minimum temperature of 10°C and maximum temperature of 40°C.

Sandy-loam to loam soil with sufficient organic matter content is ideal for cultivation of pigeon pea. The soil should be deep, well-drained and free from soluble salts. It can be grown on soils with a pH range of 5.5-8.0 successfully, but most favourable pH for its growth and development is 6.0-6.5.

Varieties

Based on time required for maturity, all the varieties have been classified into 3 groups viz.

(*i*) Short duration (120-150 days)

(*ii*) Medium duration (150-180 days)

(*iii*) Long duration (180-300 days)

Selection of varieties should be done carefully keeping in mind the climate, water retention capacity of the soil, water availability and irrigation conditions. In case of rain-fed conditions with low to no moisture availability beyond October and poor soils, early maturing varieties (120-150 days) should be preferred over medium and long duration. Some of improved pigeon pea cultivars are: Pusa 855, Pusa 991, Pusa 992, Pusa 2001, Pusa 2002, UPAS 120, Manak, AL-15, and AL 201. For arhar-wheat rotation, Pusa 991, Pusa 992, Pusa 2001 and Pusa 2002 are suitable cultivars.

Sowing Time

Redgram is grown during June to July. Ideal time for sowing is second week of June to second week of July. Under delayed monsoon conditions, it can be sown up to end of August. Treat the seeds with Trichoderma viride (8 g/kg of seed). Dry the seeds in shade. Then again treat the seeds with redgram Rhizobium and PSB biofertilizer (5 g/ kg seed) and dry the treated seeds in shade. Such treated seeds should be sown within 4-6 hour of treatment.

Seed Rate and Sowing

In general, a seed rate of 8-10 kg for long duration, 10-12 kg for medium and 12-15 kg/ ha for short duration varieties is sufficient in pigeon pea. Seeds are sown 4-6 cm deep, when the soil is wet. In short duration varieties, a row spacing of 40-60 cm and intra- row spacing of 10-15 cm is optimum. While long duration varieties require 60-120 cm inter-row and 10-20 cm intra-row spacing. Quantity of seed and spacing depending upon the variety and its crop duration are as follows:

Very early maturing:	Monocrop: 20 kg/ha, spacing 120 × 30 cm
Early maturing:	Monocrop: 20 kg/ha, spacing 120 × 30 cm
Medium duration:	Monocrop: 15 kg/ha, spacing 60 × 20 cm
	Intercrop: 5 kg/ha, spacing 30 × 20 cm
Long duration:	Monocrop: 12 – 15 kg/ha, spacing 60 × 20 cm
	Intercrop: 5 kg/ha, spacing 90 × 20 cm

Cultural Operations

Between 50 and 60 days of germination, the main shoot tip and the secondary branch tips are pruned. This promotes development of large number of tertiary shoots, which bear more number of pods, thus increasing the yield by 30-50%.

Nutrient Management

As redgram is a deep-rooted crop, it requires at least one deep tilling up 1 to 1.5 feet and one shallow tilling. Application of 5-10 t FYM mixed with 5 kg PSB during last tilling, when soil is wet is highly beneficial. Apply 20 kg nitrogen, 50 kg P_2O_5, 20-30 kg K_2O + 20 kg sulphur per ha as a basal dressing. Fertilizer should be broadcasted evenly and mixed thoroughly in the soil at the time of final preparation of land before sowing.

Water Management

Redgram requires 35-40 cm water during its entire growth period. Optimum moisture is necessary during budding, flowering and pod formation stages. Redgram grown in assured rainfall areas, usually it does not require any irrigation. If there is water stress, protective irrigation may be given in alternate rows at these three stages. Use harvested intercrops' biomass as mulch to preserve soil moisture and to maintain microbial activity.

Weed Management

Weed management is required only up to 60 days of crop growth, as this is the time when weeds compete with the crop for nutrients. First weeding is done at 20-25 DAS, while second hoeing is done at 50-60 DAS. Pre-emergence application of pendimethelin @ 1.0 kg a.i./ha is quite effective in controlling weeds.

Disease Management

During the growing phase, incidence of yellow mosaic can be seen. The affected plants show yellow mottled symptoms. These plants can be rouged out as and when they appear. White fly is known to spread this disease; hence after removal of the affected plants, an insecticide spray is important. Apart from this, redgram is also affected by root rot and wilt, where the affected areas are sprayed with 0.1% bavistin solution.

Pest Management

Pod borer: Pod borer survives on many host plants across different seasons, including cotton and legumes. Redgram is its preferred choice. Monocrotophos (0.04%) spray at pre and post-flowering stage is effective in controlling this pest.

Harvesting, Threshing and Yield

When most of the leaves are shed and 80% pods turn brown, is the best time for harvest. A grain yield of 15-20 q/ha as rainfed intercrop and 25-30 q/ha as irrigated monocrop can be obtained. Very early and early varieties yield 20-30% less. Dry clean seeds in sun to ensure moisture below 8%. Beetles affect redgram in storage. Mix crushed neem leaves with grain and store in gunny bags. Gunny bags can also be treated with 5% neem oil.

9. GRAM

Gram, also known as chickpea, is a popular pulse crop that is widely grown in many parts of the world, including India, Pakistan, and Australia. The crop is an excellent source of protein and other essential nutrients, making it an important part of many diets. Gram belongs to the Fabaceae family and is closely related to other leguminous crops such as lentils, beans, and peas. Gram requires specific soil and climatic conditions, and the crop requires proper care and attention to ensure a good yield. In this context, it is important to have a good understanding of the plant's growth habits, propagation, planting distance and time, pruning, manures and fertilizers, irrigation, plant protection, diseases, physiological disorders, maturity, and harvesting.

Soil and Climatic Requirements

Gram prefers well-drained loamy soils with a pH range of 6.0 to 7.5. It requires a warm and dry climate with a temperature range of 20 to 30°C during the growing season. The crop can tolerate moderate drought conditions but not waterlogged soils. Gram can be grown in both tropical and temperate climates.

Varieties

There are many varieties of gram, including desi and kabuli. Some popular desi varieties include KAK-2, H-208, and JAKI-9218, while popular kabuli varieties include Pusa 391 and BG 256.

Propagation

Gram is propagated by seeds. Seeds are sown directly in the field or in a nursery for transplanting.

Planting Distance and Time

Gram is usually sown in rows with a spacing of 30 to 45 cm between rows and a spacing of 10 to 20 cm between plants. The best time to plant gram is in the winter season (October to December) in tropical regions and in the spring season (February to March) in temperate regions.

Pruning

Gram does not require pruning, but if the plant becomes too tall and leggy, it can be pruned to promote bushy growth.

Manures and Fertilizers

Gram requires a moderate amount of nitrogen, phosphorus, and potassium. A dose of 20-25 kg/ha of nitrogen and 40-50 kg/ha of phosphorus should be applied before sowing. A top dressing of nitrogen can be applied 4 to 6 weeks after sowing.

IRRIGATION

Gram requires regular irrigation during the growing season, especially during the flowering and pod formation stages. The frequency and amount of irrigation depend on the soil moisture level and climatic conditions.

Plant Protection

Gram can be attacked by pests such as pod borers, aphids, and cutworms. It can also be affected by diseases such as wilt, blight, and rust. The use of pesticides and fungicides can help control these pests and diseases.

Diseases

Gram can be affected by various diseases such as wilt, blight, and rust. These diseases can be controlled by the use of resistant varieties and proper plant protection measures.

Physiological Disorders

Gram can also be affected by physiological disorders such as lodging and pod shattering. Lodging occurs when the plant falls over due to its own weight or strong winds. Pod shattering is the premature opening of pods before the crop is harvested.

Maturity and Harvesting

Gram is ready for harvest in about 90 to 120 days after sowing. The crop is harvested when the pods turn yellow and the seeds are mature. The crop is harvested by cutting the plants close to the ground and threshing the seeds. The seeds can be dried and stored for later use or sold in the market.

10. SUGARCANE

Sugarcane is a perennial plant belonging to the genus Saccharum, which encompasses five important species: *Saccharum officinarum, S. sinense, S. barberi, S. robustum,* and *S. spontaneum*. Of these, the first three are cultivated species, while the last two are wild. Among the cultivated species, *S. officinarum* is highly prized due to its high sucrose content. Sugarcane is a tall plant that can grow up to 5-6 meters, producing multiple stems. It is a C4 plant that efficiently stores solar energy and is the most effective converter of solar energy to sucrose. Brazil is the largest producer of sugarcane, followed by India.

Climatic and Soil Requirement

In the tropical region, sugarcane gets more or less ideal climatic conditions for its growth. The different critical stages are germination, tillering, early growth, active growth and elongation. Optimum temperature for sprouting (germination) of stem cuttings is 32° to 38°C. For ripening, however, relatively low temperatures in the range of 12° to 14°C are desirable. Sugar recovery is highest when the weather is dry with low humidity; bright sunshine hours, cooler nights with wide diurnal variations and very little rainfall during ripening period.

A well drained, deep, loamy soil with ample available water holding capacity is considered ideal for sugarcane cultivation. The optimum soil pH is about 6.5 but sugarcane can tolerate considerable degree of soil acidity and alkalinity. Hence, it is found growing in soils with pH in the range of 5 to 8.5.

Seed Rate and Sowing Method

Seed rate in sugarcane varies from region-to-region. In north India, seed rate generally varies from 35,000 three budded sets/ha while in south it ranges between 25,000 to 40,000 three budded sets/ha. The row spacing in subtropical part ranges from 60 to 120 cm whereas, it is 90-150 cm in tropical regions.

Sugarcane take generally one year to mature in subtropical states called "Eksali" however in some tropical states, it matures in 18 months called "Adsali". In India planting seasons of sugarcane in subtropical regions are September to October (Autumn) and February to March (spring). Whereas in tropical regions, it is June to August (Adsali) and January-to-February and October-to-November (Eksali). Sugarcane can be planted by improved method of planting like, deep furrow, trench methods, ring pit method and paired row method instead of furrow system.

Cultivars

Some of the promising sugarcane cultivars are: COS 687, COS 8436, COS 767, BO 106, BO 108, BO 90, CO 7508, CO 7704, CO 1108, COJ 83, CO 89003, CO 29, CO 997, CO 527, CO 775, CO 419, CO 775, CO 8021, CO 8011, CO 671, CO 8208, COG 93076.

Nutrient Management

The NPK recommendation for sugarcane crop varies from region-to-region. The recommendation of N is from 70-400 kg/ha, P_2O_5 is 27-74 kg/ha and K_2O is 25-141 kg/ha. Apply FYM or compost @ 10-15 t/ha. Recommended dose of bio-fertilizers for sugarcane crop is 10-12 kg/ha. Acetobacter, Azotobacter, Azospirillum and PSB are the major biofertilizers, which are being used in sugarcane crop.

Water Management

In tropical area, irrigations are to be given once in 7 days during germination phase, once in 10 days during tillering phase, again in 7 days during grand growth phase and once in 15 days during maturity phase, adjusting it to the rain fall pattern of the area. About 30 to 40 irrigations are needed. Whereas in subtropics, about 7-10 irrigations are being given to the sugarcane crop. Sugarcane is a high water requirement crop. About 250 tonnes of water is needed to produce one tonne of sugarcane. Methods like alternate furrow irrigation, drip irrigation and trash mulching could be of use to economize irrigation water during water scarcity periods.

Weed Management

In pure crop of sugarcane spray atrazine 2 kg or oxyflurofen 750 ml/ha mixed in 500 L water as pre-emergence herbicide on 3rd day of planting. Pre-mergence application of thiobencarb @ 1.25 kg a.i./ha under intercropping system in sugarcane with soybean, blackgram or groundnut gives effective weed control.

Plant Protection

Sugarcane is liable to be attacked by a number of insect-pests and diseases. Due to diversity in agro-ecological conditions, the importance of insect-pests and diseases varies and therefore, management strategy should be adopted accordingly. Top borer and stalk borer are found pre-dominantly in sub-tropical areas whereas early shoot borer and among diseases rust & eye spot are prevalent in tropical region.

Harvesting and Yield

Harvesting and collection of cane should either be mechanical or manual. In subtropical India, it has been shown that spring harvested crop would result in a better ratoon than that obtained by harvesting in the autumn. Sugarcane crop is harvested after attending maturity, generally it starts from the month of October and continue till the month of May in sub-tropical states whereas in Tropical states, it starts from the month of December and continues till the month of May. Cane tonnage at harvest with best management practices can vary between 120 and 150 t/ha, which depends on the length of the total growing period and whether it is a main or ratoon crop. The sugar recovery in sugarcane varies from state-to-state. Average sugar recovery in the country is 10.25%.

11. COTTON

Cotton, also known as "white gold", is a significant commercial crop in India. It is primarily grown for its fibers, but its seeds are also a source of oil, known as cottonseed oil. The Gossypium species, which belong to the Malvaceae family, include 52 species, of which four are commercially cultivated worldwide, namely *Gossypium arboreum, Gossypium herbaceum, Gossypium hirsutum,* and *Gossypium barbadense*. In India, *G. hirsutum* and *G. arboreum* are grown in all major cotton-growing states. India has the largest acreage of cotton in the world, with 11.99 million hectares, producing 6 million tons and an average yield of 512 kg/ha.

Climatic and Soil Requirements

Cotton is a warm season loving shrub, adapted to a wide range of climate. A frostless season of 180-240 days is required for successful cotton production. The cotton-picking period from mid-September to November must have bright sunny days to ensure a good quality of the produce. Abundant sunshine during the period of boll maturity and harvesting is essential to obtain a good quality produce.

It is raised mainly as a rainfed crop in the black cotton and medium soils and as an irrigated crop in the alluvial soils. Proper drainage of excess water during rains is essential. Soils with a pH >9.0 and <6.5 and $CaCO_3$ content >10% are not suitable for cotton cultivation.

Cropping Systems

Cotton–fallow, cotton–wheat/barley, cotton–sunflower, cotton–senji/barseem/oats, cotton–sunflower-paddy-wheat, cotton–raya.

Varieties

Zone	G. arboreum	G. herbaceum	G. hirsutum	G. barbadense
North Zone	Lohit, Shyamali, RG 1, LD 230, HD 11	Digvijay	Ganganagar Ageti, Pusa 31, Pusa 8-3, H 1117	—
Central Zone	Sanjay, G 22, AKH 4, AKA 1	F 46, V 797, Digvijay, CNH 36	Laxmi, Badnawar 1, Nimbakar 1, Deviraj	Suvin
South Zone	Nardium, Srisailam, Mahanandi	Jayadhar, Raichur 51, Ajanta	Laxmi, Mysore Vijay, Hampi, Krishna, Supriya	Suvin, Sujata, TNB 1

Hybrids

The currently cultivated hybrids include H6, H8, H10 in Gujarat; DCH 32, DHB 105 and DHH 11 in Karnataka; Savita, TCHB 213, Surya and Sruthi in Tamil Nadu, LAHH 4 and JKHy-1 and JKHy-2 in Madhya Pradesh.

Seed Rate and Sowing Method

The seed rate varies with species, growing zone and irrigation availability. The general seed rate for different species/cultivars is as under:

Varieties/hybrids	Seed-rate (kg/acre)
American Cotton Bt Hybrids	0.750
Non Bt Hybrid: LHH 144	1.5
Varieties: LH 2108, LH 2076 and F 1861	3.5
Desi Cotton Hybrid	1.25
Varieties	3.0

Time of sowing is first April to 15th May. Sowing during this period ensures better yield and escapes the attack of insect pests and diseases. Sowing should be done in morning and evening hours. Sow in lines 67.5 cm apart with a cotton sowing drill. The plants within rows be kept 45-60 cm apart by thinning. However for hybrids (both Bt and non-Bt), the plant to plant distance should be kept at 75 cm. It may be done after first irrigation or heavy shower. For desi cotton hybrid, the plant to plant spacing should be kept at 60 cm. A fine seed-bed is essential for securing a good plant stand.

Weed Management

A deep summer ploughing is desirable once in 3 years to kill perennial weeds, pests and disease propagules hibernating in the soil. For this, hoeing should be done two or three times. The first hoeing should be done before first irrigation. For chemical weed control, apply pendimethalin @ 1.0 kg a.i./ha as pre-emergence spray.

Nutrient Management

Apply 75 kg N/ha, 30 kg P_2O_5/ha in HYVs and 150 kg N/ha, 60 kg P_2O_5/ha in Bt and non-Bt hybrids. Apply whole P & K as basal dose while half N is applied at thinning and the remaining half N at flowering. Apply 20 kg muriate of potash in soils medium in available potassium and 25 kg zinc sulphate heptahydrate (21%) per ha to cotton on light soils.

Water Management

Cotton requires four to six irrigations, depending upon the seasonal rainfall. The first irrigation should be given 4 to 6 weeks after sowing and the subsequent ones at interval of two or three weeks. Sowing of cotton on ridges and irrigation in furrows save considerable amount of water. In cotton, four critical stages of irrigation have been identified viz. commencement of sympodial branching (60-70 DAS), flowering (90-100 DAS), boll formation (125 DAS) and boll bursting (140 DAS). Drain out the stagnant water, if such a situation arises.

Disease Management

Root rot: The loss in yield occurs due to reduction in sudden death of plants. Due to this disease, healthy plants may wilt within 24 hr with leaves drooping without showing any discoloration. Soil should be drenched with 0.2% carbendazim.

Fusarium wilt: In young as well as old plants the initial symptoms are stunning followed by yellowing, wilting and dropping of most of the leaves. Soak 4 kg seed in 8 L water containing 8 g of bavistin for 6-8 hr and 2-3 hr in case of delinted cotton.

Pest Management

Pink boll worm: It is a notorious pest of cotton in all cotton growing areas. Bt cotton provides effective protection against all cotton bollworms.

Harvesting Threshing and Yield

Cotton is harvested in 3-4 pickings by hand as the bolls mature. By adopting improved technology, it is possible to harvest about 1.5-2 t/ha of seed cotton (kapas). However, much higher yields may be obtained from hybrid cottons. Cotton lint production is 33% of kapas production, while cotton to seed production is 66% of kapas production. Oil to seeds crushed is 14-18% and cake to seeds crushed is 82-86%.

12. BERSEEM

Berseem, scientifically known as *Trifolium alexandrinum L.*, is a highly valued forage legume in India, primarily cultivated as a winter annual in tropical and subtropical regions. It serves as an excellent source of nutritious, succulent, and palatable forage for milch animals. Berseem forage is rich in crude protein, containing about 20% protein, and has high digestibility, up to 65%, making it a preferred choice among livestock farmers.

Climatic and Soil Requirements

Berseem is adapted to cool and moderately cold climate. Such conditions prevail during winter and spring seasons in north India, which is considered as favourable and productive zone for this crop. It can be grown successfully in areas which receive annual rainfall of 150-250 cm or even lower but the irrigation must be assured.

Berseem can be grown on all types of soils except very light sandy soils. Well-drained clay to clay-loam soils rich in humus, calcium and phosphorus are suitable for berseem.

Varieties

Some of the promising cultivars of fodder berseem are Pusa Giant, Mescavi, Berseem Ludhiana-1, Jawahar Berseem-1, Wardan, BL-10, BL-22, UPB-10, Bundel Berseem-2, Bundel Berseem-3, BL-180, Hisar Berseem-1 and JB-5.

Seed Rate and Sowing Method

The optimum seed rate is 25 kg/ha, which may be increased up to 35 kg in early or late sown conditions. For yield compensation in first cutting, 1.5 kg mustard should be sown alongwith berseem. Being a legume, berseem enriches the soil with biological nitrogen fixation. Therefore, berseem seed should be inoculated with Rhizobium trifollii. The seeds being very small, berseem requires a fine seedbed. After the arrest of rains, sowing of berseem can be done from last week of September to first week of December in north-west to eastern and central India.

Nutrient Management

Top dressing of 10 kg N/ha is done after each cut in addition to 30 kg N/ha basal dose to encourage good regeneration, quick growth and high yield. In general, the crop responds significantly upto 80-90 kg P_2O_5/ha. The potassium requirement of berseem has been found to be 30 to 40 kg K_2O/ha in low potassium soils.

Water Management

Berseem requires huge quantities of water for producing high succulent biomass. Normally, the crop should be irrigated after each cutting. About 12-15 irrigations will be needed during the entire crop season.

Weed Management

The major associated weed of berseem is chicory *(Chicorium intybus)*. Chicory infestation can be minimized by seed cleaning in 10% solution of common salt, besides deep summer ploughing.

Cutting Management and Forage Yield

The first cutting should be taken at 50-55 days after sowing of crop. The subsequent cuttings should be taken at 25-30 days interval. The number of cuts depends upon rate of growth and temperature during the life cycle of the crop. The crop is capable of producing 100 to 120 t/ha of green forage and 15-20 tonnes/ha dry fodder under improved agronomic management practices and favorable weather conditions.

MULTIPLE CHOICE QUESTIONS

1. Match the following:

List-I (Herbicide)	List-II (Example)
(a) Selective herbicide	I. Diquat
(b) Foliage active herbicide	II. Glycophosate
(c) Contact herbicide	III. 4-D
(d) Translocated herbicide	IV. Isoproturon

Choose the correct answer from the options given below:

	(a)	(b)	(c)	(d)
A.	I	III	II	IV
B.	III	IV	I	II
C.	II	I	IV	III
D.	IV	II	III	I

2. Match List-I with List-II.

List-I (Weed)	List-II (Bio control agent)
(a) Prickly pear	I. Sameodes albiguttalis
(b) Water hyacinth	II. Chrosidosima lantana
(c) Lantana camara	III. Conchineal insect
(d) Carrot grass	IV. Zygograma bicholoreta

Choose the correct answer from the options given below:

	(a)	(b)	(c)	(d)
A.	I	II	III	IV
B.	III	I	II	IV
C.	II	III	IV	I
D.	IV	I	II	III

3. Atrazine is an example of:
A. herbicide B. insecticide
C. fungicide D. miticide

4. The chemical which is used to kill or control weed is called as:
A. Fungicide B. Insecticide
C. Herbicide D. Acaricide

5. _______ was the first person to use the word weed.
A. Jenny B. Jethro Tull
C. Marshal D. Philip Kotler

6. Which of the following is NOT a method of asexual reproduction in plants?
A. Fragmentation B. Budding
C. Grafting D. Apomixis

7. Which of the following can NOT be further hydrolyzed to simple sugars?
A. Disaccharides B. Trisaccharides
C. Monosaccharides D. Polysaccharides

8. _______ is called as anti-hemorrhagic vitamin.
A. Vitamin K B. Vitamin E
C. Vitamin D D. Vitamin A

9. Vitamin C is also known as _______.
A. Carotene B. Ascorbic acid
C. Folic acid D. Thiamine

10. Scurvy disease is caused by deficiency of:
A. Vitamin A B. Vitamin B
C. Vitamin C D. Vitamin D

11. ______ is caused due to the deficiency of vitamin A.
A. Skin disease B. Scurvy
C. Night blindness D. Rough skin

12. Koshland's theory of enzyme action is known as ____.
A. Lock and Key theory
B. Reduced fit theory
C. Induced fit theory
D. Enzyme co-enzyme theory

13. Enzyme that catalyzes the transfer of a group, other than hydrogen, belongs to the class:
A. Oxidoreductase B. Transferase
C. Hydrolase D. Ligase

14. All the carbon compounds that we get from living tissues can be called as ____.
A. Bioresource B. Bio-informatics
C. Biovar D. Biomolecules

15. A non-proteinaceous enzyme is:
A. Ribozyme B. Ligase
C. Deoxyribonuclease D. Lysozyme

16. Deficiency of ______ affects the clotting of blood in human beings.
A. Vitamin B12 B. Vitamin B2
C. Vitamin E D. Vitamin K

17. Gas which is produced during the processes of fermentation of dough, cheese making, and beverage production?
A. CO_2 B. H_2S
C. H_2O D. O_2

18. Which crop is commonly affected by tikka disease in India?
A. Paddy B. Groundnut
C. Gram D. Wheat

19. Which biological agent is commonly used as seed inoculant for symbiotic nitrogen fixation in groundnut crop?
A. Azotobacter B. Azolla
C. Rhizobium D. Acetobacter

20. Potato spindle tuber diseases is caused by which type of pathogen?
A. Virus B. Viroids
C. Prions D. Bacteria

21. Match List-I with List-II:

List-I (Crop name)	**List-II (Botanical name)**
(*a*) Soyabean	I. *Zea mays*
(*b*) Blackgram	II. *Cicer arietinum*
(*c*) Maize	III. *Glycine max*
(*d*) Chickpea	IV. *Vigna mungo*

Choose the correct answer from the options given below:

	(*a*)	(*b*)	(*c*)	(*d*)
A.	II	I	III	IV
B.	IV	II	I	III
C.	IV	III	II	I
D.	III	IV	I	II

22. Which of the following is an appropriate use of mulching?
A. Plant propagation
B. Watershed management
C. Livestock management
D. Soil management

23. Organic matter of soil plays a vital role in the plant productivity because of:
A. Presence of appropriate combination of plants protecting chemicals
B. Saving time and labour in its application
C. Contains two or three primary plant nutrients
D. Acts as a source of food for soil bacteria and fungi

24. Soil sampling and testing is essential to:
(*a*) identify fertility status
(*b*) identify seed viability
(*c*) identify fertilizer requirement
(*d*) identify physical properties
(*e*) control pest population

Choose the correct answer from the options given below:

A. (*a*), (*b*) and (*d*) only
B. (*a*), (*c*) and (*d*) only
C. (*a*), (*b*) and (*e*) only
D. (*a*), (*b*) and (*c*) only

25. ______ means the physical condition of soil resulting from tillage operations.

A. Threshing B. Soil tilth
C. Mulching D. Harvesting

26. Jowar seedlings of upto 8 weeks age contain ______.

A. Hydrocyanic acid
B. Carbonic acid
C. Oxalic acid
D. Malic acid

27. Botanical name of paddy is:

A. *Oryza sativa* B. *Cicer arientinum*
C. *Tritim nestivum* D. *Aracitis irypogea*

28. Which of the following is/are the diseases of groundnut:

(*a*) Tikka
(*b*) Root rot
(*c*) Stem borer
(*d*) Downey mildew
(*e*) Rust

Choose the correct answer from the options given below:

A. (*c*) & (*d*) only B. (*c*), (*d*), (*e*) only
C. (*a*) only D. (*a*) & (*b*) only

29. Which of the following is an important oilseed as well as pulse crop:

A. Soyabean B. Groundnut
C. Gram D. Redgram

30. The diseases of sugarcane are:

(*a*) Red rot
(*b*) Whip smut
(*c*) Black arm
(*d*) Grey mildew
(*e*) Grassy shoot disease

Choose the correct answer from the options given below:

A. (*c*) only B. (*d*) only
C. (*c*) & (*d*) only D. (*a*), (*b*), & (*e*) only

31. Match List-I with List-II:

List-I	List-II
(*a*) Paddy	I. *Oryza Sativa*
(*b*) Wheat	II. *Triticum*
(*c*) Gram	III. *Cicer argenteum*
(*d*) Groundnut	IV. *Arachis hypogea*

Choose the correct answer from the options given below:

	(*a*)	(*b*)	(*c*)	(*d*)
A.	IV	III	II	I
B.	III	IV	II	I
C.	I	II	III	IV
D.	II	III	IV	I

32. *Glycine max* is the botanical name of:

A. Soyabean B. Gram
C. Red gram D. Black gram

33. Emitters are the main components of which of the following irrigation system?

A. Sprinkler B. Surface
C. Subsurface D. Drip

34. Match List-I with List-II:

List-I (Crop)	List-II (Water requirement)
(*a*) Rice	I. 450 – 700 mm
(*b*) Cotton	II. 500 – 700 mm
(*c*) Soyabean	III. 700 – 1300 mm
(*d*) Potato	IV. 900 – 2500 mm

Choose the correct answer from the options given below:

	(*a*)	(*b*)	(*c*)	(*d*)
A.	I	II	III	IV
B.	IV	III	I	II
C.	IV	II	I	III
D.	IV	III	II	I

35. Milli watershed is which type of watershed?

A. Long watershed B. Short watershed
C. Broad watershed D. Milli watershed

36. _____ is the total depth of water required by a crop during the period of the crop.

A. Gamma B. Delta
C. Alpha D. Beta

37. Water harvesting is defined as the collection of runoff for its productive use.

A. Scheduling of Irrigation
B. Water storage
C. Flood irrigation
D. Water harvesting

38. Which irrigation system uses emitters as the main components?

A. Sprinkler B. Ring & basin
C. Drip D. Border strip

39. Soils with a pH above 7.5 is said to be:

A. Acidic B. Basic
C. Alkaline D. Organic

40. Which of the following is NOT an example of straight nitrogenous fertilizer?

A. Diammonium phosphate (DAP)
B. Ammonium sulphate
C. Ammonium chloride
D. Urea

41. The capacity of soil to provide essential nutrients in proper quantity and proportion for plant growth is called:
A. Soil profile B. Soil fertility
C. Soil age D. Soil erosion

42. Soil texture is a property of soil in terms of its:
A. Biochemical composition
B. Physical structure
C. Chemical composition
D. Biological activity

43. Muriate of potash is an example of which type of fertilizer?
A. Soil amendment B. Straight
C. Mixed D. Complex

44. Primary essential nutrients for plants are:
(*a*) Manganese
(*b*) Calcium
(*c*) Nitrogen
(*d*) Phosphorus
(*e*) Potassium

Choose the correct answer from the options given below:
A. (*a*) and (*c*) only
B. (*b*) and (*d*) only
C. (*a*), (*b*), and (*c*) only
D. (*c*), (*d*), and (*e*) only

45. _______ is a straight fertilizer.
A. Single super phosphate
B. 20 ÷ 20:00
C. Diammonium phosphate (DAP)
D. Mono ammonium phosphate

46. _______ refers to the size of soil particles.
A. Soil structure B. Soil pH
C. Soil plasticity D. Soil texture

47. Nitrogen, Phosphorus, and Potassium are the plant nutrients:
A. Primary B. Secondary
C. Trace D. Minor

48. Which one of the following solutions is a buffer solution:
(*a*) HNO_2
(*b*) HCl
(*c*) HNO_3
(*d*) NaOH
(*e*) H_2SO_4

Choose the correct answer from the options given below:
A. (*a*) only B. (*b*) & (*c*) only
C. (*d*) & (*e*) only D. (*e*) only

49. Gypsum is a:
A. Soil amendment
B. Straight fertilizer
C. Complex fertilizer
D. Micronutrient

50. An example of a secondary nutrient is:
A. Nitrogen B. Phosphorus
C. Calcium D. Potash

51. Which of the following is a leguminous crop?
A. Wheat B. Maize
C. Paddy D. Gram

52. Which of the following is a root crop?
A. Sugarcane B. Cotton
C. Potato D. Tobacco

53. Which of the following crops is used for making paper?
A. Jute B. Sugarcane
C. Wheat D. Bamboo

54. Which crop is known as the 'King of cereals'?
A. Rice B. Wheat
C. Maize D. Barley

55. Which of the following is not a major oilseed crop in India?
A. Groundnut B. Mustard
C. Sunflower D. Wheat

56. What is the main cause of bacterial diseases in crops?
A. Fungal infection B. Viral infection
C. Bacterial infection D. Nematode infection

57. Which of the following is a fungal disease of wheat?
A. Bacterial blight B. Rust
C. Root knot D. Leaf curl

58. What is the most common method of controlling nematode infestation in crops?
A. Use of chemical pesticides
B. Use of biopesticides
C. Crop rotation
D. None of the above

59. What is the most common viral disease of tomato plants?
A. Bacterial wilt B. Mosaic virus
C. Anthracnose D. Fusarium wilt

60. Which of the following is a biopesticide used to control insect pests?
A. Malathion
B. Carbaryl
C. Bacillus thuringiensis
D. Glyphosate

61. What is the main goal of integrated pest management (IPM) in agriculture?
A. To completely eliminate all pests from the crops
B. To minimize the use of pesticides while maintaining pest control
C. To use only organic methods for pest control

D. To increase crop yield without considering pest control

62. Which of the following is NOT a step in the IPM process?
A. Monitoring and identifying pests
B. Applying pesticides at regular intervals
C. Setting economic thresholds for pest control
D. Implementing appropriate control measures

63. What is the purpose of threshing in agriculture?
A. To remove weeds from the crop
B. To separate the grain from the chaff
C. To apply fertilizer to the crop
D. To irrigate the crop

64. Which of the following post-harvest technologies is used to slow down the ripening of fruits and vegetables?
A. Drying B. Canning
C. Refrigeration D. Freezing

65. What is the main objective of crop harvesting in agriculture?
A. To prepare the field for the next crop
B. To collect the crops for storage and processing
C. To remove pests and diseases from the field
D. To apply fertilizer to the field

66. Which of the following is not a method of irrigation?
A. Sprinkler irrigation
B. Drip irrigation
C. Solar irrigation
D. Flood irrigation

67. Which of the following is a disadvantage of flood irrigation?
A. High water use efficiency
B. Uniform water distribution
C. Low labor requirements
D. Waterlogging and soil erosion

68. Which method of irrigation is most suitable for fruit crops?
A. Sprinkler irrigation
B. Drip irrigation
C. Flood irrigation
D. Furrow irrigation

69. Which of the following is not a method of drainage?
A. Surface drainage
B. Subsurface drainage
C. Ditch drainage
D. Furrow drainage

70. Which of the following is not a component of watershed management?
A. Soil conservation
B. Water conservation
C. Forest conservation
D. Monoculture crop production

ANSWERS

1	2	3	4	5	6	7	8	9	10
B	B	A	C	B	C	C	A	B	C
11	**12**	**13**	**14**	**15**	**16**	**17**	**18**	**19**	**20**
C	C	B	D	A	D	A	B	C	B
21	**22**	**23**	**24**	**25**	**26**	**27**	**28**	**29**	**30**
D	D	D	B	B	A	A	D	A	D
31	**32**	**33**	**34**	**35**	**36**	**37**	**38**	**39**	**40**
C	A	D	B	D	B	D	C	C	A
41	**42**	**43**	**44**	**45**	**46**	**47**	**48**	**49**	**50**
B	B	B	D	A	D	A	A	A	C
51	**52**	**53**	**54**	**55**	**56**	**57**	**58**	**59**	**60**
D	C	D	B	D	C	B	C	B	C
61	**62**	**63**	**64**	**65**	**66**	**67**	**68**	**69**	**70**
B	B	B	C	B	C	D	B	D	D

•••

UNIT 4

Horticulture

IMPORTANCE OF FRUITS AND VEGETABLES IN HUMAN DIET

Fruits and vegetables are an essential part of a balanced and healthy diet for human beings. Here are some important details about their importance:

1. **Nutritional value:** Fruits and vegetables are a rich source of vitamins, minerals, and dietary fiber. They are low in fat and calories, making them an excellent food choice for maintaining a healthy weight.
2. **Disease prevention:** Eating a diet rich in fruits and vegetables can help reduce the risk of chronic diseases such as heart disease, stroke, and certain types of cancer. This is because they contain various antioxidants and other nutrients that help protect the body from damage caused by free radicals.
3. **Digestive health:** The fiber content in fruits and vegetables helps promote healthy digestion and prevents constipation. They also contain enzymes that aid in digestion and absorption of nutrients.
4. **Hydration:** Many fruits and vegetables have a high water content, which helps to keep the body hydrated and maintain healthy skin.
5. **Versatility:** Fruits and vegetables can be eaten raw, cooked, or used in a variety of recipes. This makes them a versatile and delicious addition to any meal or snack.

Consuming a diet rich in fruits and vegetables is essential for maintaining optimal health and preventing chronic diseases.

CROP DIVERSIFICATION & PROCESSING INDUSTRY

Crop diversification is a process of shifting the cropping pattern from mono-cropping to multiple cropping. It is essential for sustaining agriculture and the environment, improving food security and income generation, and reducing risks associated with single-crop cultivation. Here are some important details about crop diversification:

- **Benefits of crop diversification:** Crop diversification has several benefits such as reducing soil degradation and erosion, improving soil health and fertility, reducing pest and disease incidence, increasing biodiversity, providing alternative sources of income, and ensuring food security.
- **Types of crop diversification:** There are two types of crop diversification - intercropping and mixed cropping. Intercropping involves growing two or more crops simultaneously on the same land, while mixed cropping involves growing two or more crops in the same field at different times.
- **Processing industry:** Crop processing industry refers to the conversion of raw agricultural products into processed products that are more valuable and have a longer shelf life. The processed products include fruits and vegetables, grains, oilseeds, dairy, meat, and poultry products. The processing industry provides employment opportunities, enhances the value of agricultural produce, and helps in reducing post-harvest losses.
- **Importance of processing industry:** The processing industry is important for reducing the post-harvest losses, enhancing the shelf life of the products, reducing transportation costs, and ensuring availability of food products throughout the year. It also provides employment opportunities and helps in value addition to the agricultural produce.
- **Challenges in crop diversification and processing industry:** The challenges in crop diversification include lack of knowledge and skills, inadequate infrastructure, insufficient credit facilities, and market linkages. Similarly, the challenges in the processing industry include high capital investment, lack of proper technology and infrastructure, lack of skilled manpower, and low market demand.

Crop diversification and processing industry are important for sustaining agriculture, enhancing food security, and ensuring economic development. The government should take necessary steps to promote these activities by providing necessary infrastructure, credit facilities, and market linkages to farmers and entrepreneurs.

ORCHARD-LOCATION AND LAYOUT

An orchard is a cultivated area of land where various fruit trees are grown for commercial purposes. Here are some important details about the location and layout of an orchard:

1. **Location:** The location of the orchard should be selected based on factors such as soil type, climate, rainfall, and availability of water. It is important to choose a location that has good drainage and is free from waterlogging. The orchard should also be protected from strong winds and frost.
2. **Layout:** The layout of an orchard is an important aspect of its management. It involves the arrangement of trees in a manner that facilitates easy access for planting, pruning, harvesting, and other operations. The following are some important points to consider when designing an orchard layout:
    - **Row spacing:** The distance between rows should be wide enough to allow for machinery and equipment to move through, but narrow enough to ensure efficient use of land.
    - **Tree spacing:** The distance between trees should be based on the type of tree, rootstock, and the desired yield. It is important to ensure that trees are not overcrowded, as this can lead to poor growth and yield.
    - **Orientation:** The orientation of the orchard rows should be based on the prevailing winds and sun exposure. This can help to minimize the risk of damage from wind and frost, and ensure optimal photosynthesis for the trees.
    - **Water management:** The orchard layout should be designed in a manner that facilitates efficient irrigation and drainage. The irrigation system should be designed to ensure that water reaches the root zone of the trees and is not wasted through run-off or evaporation.
    - **Access roads:** The orchard layout should also include access roads for machinery and equipment. These roads should be wide enough to allow for easy movement of equipment, and should be designed to minimize soil compaction and erosion.

The location and layout of an orchard play a critical role in its productivity and profitability. Proper planning and design can help to ensure efficient use of resources and optimal growth and yield of fruit trees.

ORNAMENTAL GARDENING AND KITCHEN GARDEN

Ornamental gardening and kitchen gardening are two popular types of gardening that serve different purposes. Here are some important details about each type:

1. **Ornamental Gardening:** This type of gardening involves growing plants for their aesthetic beauty rather than for consumption. It is often used for landscaping, decoration of public spaces, and beautification of private gardens. Some common plants used for ornamental gardening include flowers, shrubs, and trees. Ornamental gardening requires careful planning, soil preparation, and regular maintenance to ensure the health and vitality of the plants.
2. **Kitchen Gardening:** This type of gardening involves growing vegetables, fruits, and herbs for personal consumption. It is often done in small spaces such as balconies, terraces, and backyard gardens. Kitchen gardening promotes healthy eating habits and can be a fun and rewarding hobby. Some common plants used for kitchen gardening include tomatoes, peppers, lettuce, basil, and mint. Kitchen gardening requires good soil, adequate sunlight, and regular watering and fertilization to produce healthy and nutritious plants.

Both ornamental gardening and kitchen gardening have their unique benefits and are important aspects of horticulture. Ornamental gardening enhances the aesthetic appeal of public and private spaces, while kitchen gardening promotes healthy eating habits and provides fresh produce for personal consumption.

PLANTING SYSTEM AND PROTECTION FROM FROST AND SUNBURN

Planting system: The planting system refers to the arrangement of plants in an orchard or garden. The two main planting systems are square and hexagonal. In square planting, trees are planted in rows with equal distances between trees in the same row and between rows. In hexagonal planting, the trees are planted in a pattern that forms equilateral triangles.

Training: Training is a technique of directing the growth of plants to achieve a desired shape and structure. Proper training is important for the development of healthy and productive trees. There are several methods of training, including central leader, open center, and modified central leader.

Pruning: Pruning is the removal of unwanted parts of the plant to improve its health, shape, and productivity. Pruning is done to remove diseased or damaged branches, promote new growth, and shape the tree. Pruning should be done in the dormant season for most fruit trees.

Intercropping: Intercropping is a technique of growing two or more crops in the same field at the same time. It is done to maximize the use of available resources, such as sunlight, water, and nutrients, and to minimize the risk of pests and diseases. For example, legumes can be grown between rows of fruit trees to fix nitrogen in the soil.

Protection from frost and sunburn: Frost and sunburn can damage fruit trees, especially young trees. Frost damage occurs when the temperature drops below freezing, and sunburn occurs when the tree bark is exposed to high-intensity sunlight. Protection measures include covering the trees with blankets or burlap during frosty nights, painting the trunk with white latex paint to reflect sunlight, and providing shade using screens or cloth covers.

TREES, SHRUBS, CLIMBERS, ANNUALS AND PERENNIALS

In agriculture, there are various types of plants that can be classified based on their life cycle, growth habit, and other characteristics. Some of the most common categories include trees, shrubs, climbers, annuals, and perennials.

1. **Trees:** Trees are perennial plants that have a single main stem or trunk and typically grow to a significant height. They can be either deciduous (shed their leaves seasonally) or evergreen (retain their leaves year-round). Some examples of trees include mango, coconut, neem, teak, and banyan.
2. **Shrubs:** Shrubs are woody plants that are smaller than trees and have multiple stems. They can be deciduous or evergreen and usually grow up to a maximum height of around 6 meters. Some examples of shrubs include rose, hibiscus, bougainvillea, and jasmine.
3. **Climbers:** Climbers are plants that require support to grow vertically and can be used to cover walls, fences, and other structures. They can be annual or perennial, and some examples include grapevine, passion fruit, ivy, and morning glory.
4. **Annuals:** Annuals are plants that complete their life cycle within a year. They grow from seed, produce flowers and fruits, and then die. Some common examples of annuals include tomato, chili, marigold, petunia, and sunflower.
5. **Perennials:** Perennials are plants that live for more than two years and can produce flowers and fruits repeatedly. They can be either herbaceous (non-woody) or woody, and examples include apple, banana, mango, papaya, and rosemary.

Understanding these different categories of plants is important in agriculture as it can help in selecting the appropriate planting techniques, fertilizers, pest management strategies, and other cultivation practices based on the specific needs of each type of plant.

PROPAGATION

Propagation is the process of producing new plants from a variety of sources. There are several methods of plant propagation including seed, cutting, budding, layering, and grafting. Each method has its advantages and disadvantages and is used for different types of plants.

1. **Seed Propagation:** This is the most common method of propagation and involves planting seeds in the soil or other growing medium. This method is relatively simple and requires minimal equipment, making it an affordable option for farmers. However, it can take longer to produce mature plants, and there is less control over the characteristics of the resulting plant.
2. **Cutting Propagation:** This involves taking a cutting from a parent plant and placing it in soil or another growing medium to grow roots and become a new plant. This method is useful for propagating plants that do not produce viable seeds, such as many ornamental plants. It is also useful for maintaining the genetic characteristics of a particular plant.
3. **Budding Propagation:** Budding is a form of grafting that involves taking a bud from a parent plant and grafting it onto a rootstock of another plant. This method is commonly used in fruit tree production to produce trees with desired characteristics.
4. **Layering Propagation:** This involves bending a low branch or stem of a plant to the ground and covering it with soil. Over time, roots will grow from the covered portion of the stem, and a new plant will develop. This method is commonly used for shrubs, climbers, and other plants with flexible branches.
5. **Grafting Propagation:** Grafting involves joining two different plants together so that they grow as a single plant. The scion is the top part of the plant that contains the desired characteristics, and the rootstock is the bottom part that provides the root system. Grafting is commonly used in fruit tree production to produce trees with desired characteristics.

Plant propagation is an important aspect of agriculture, and different methods of propagation are used for different types of plants. It is important for farmers to understand the advantages and disadvantages of each method to choose the appropriate method for the specific plant they are propagating.

CULTIVATION PRACTICES, PROCESSING AND MARKETING

MANGO

Mango *(Mangifera indica L.)* is a member of the Anacardiaceae family and the Mangifera genus with a basic chromosome number of X = 20. In India, it is considered the choicest fruit and is known as the “king of fruits”. It is an excellent source of vitamin A and a good source of vitamin C, as well as various minerals and vitamins.

Soil and Climatic Requirements: Mango can be grown in a variety of soils but clay-loam, well-drained soils with a pH range of 5.7 to 7.5 are considered to be the best for its cultivation. A temperature range of 24-27°C throughout the growing season is the best for its cultivation.

Commercial Varieties: In India, there are several varieties of mango but only 10-12 are grown commercially. For example, Dashehari, Langra, Chausa and Bombay Green are grown commercially in north, Banganpalli/Baneshan, Neelum, Totapuri in south, Alphonso and Kesar in west and Langra, Himsagar etc. in the east. On the basis of embryos, mango varieties have been classified as monoembryonic (Most of the varieties) and polyembryonic (Bapakai, Vellary, Chandrakaran, Kurrukan, Goa, Olour, Carabao, Paho, Peach, Apricot, Strawberry etc.)

Propagation: Mango can be propagated both by sexual and asexual means but it is mainly propagated by veneer grafting, stone grafting and soft-wood grafting in different parts of India.

Planting Distance and Time: Planting distance varies from variety-to-variety and locality-to-locality. In general, a planting distance of 10-12m is recommended for commercial varieties like Dashehari, Langra, Chausa, Alphonso, Banganpalli etc. Pits of 1 × 1 × 1 m size are dug out and kept open during May, which are refilled by the end of the June with the mixture of top soil and Farm Yard Manure in the ratio of 1 : 1. The best time for planting mango is the monsoon season.

Manures and Fertilizers: In general, ammonium sulphate, super phosphate and sulphate of potash should be mixed in the ratio of 1 : 3 : 1 and applied @ ½ kg in the first year, which should be increased by kg every year up to 15th year, and then 6-10 kg afterwards. Farm yard manure (FYM) is generally applied in September-October every year.

Irrigation: Young plants should be irrigated at weekly intervals in summer and at fortnightly intervals in winter. However, the bearing plants should be irrigated at 10-15 days interval from fruit set stage to maturity. It is, however, advised to withheld irrigation during flowering as it may result in shedding of flowers.

Plant Protection

Insect-pest	Control measures
Mango leaf hopper	Mango hoppers can be controlled by two sprays of carbaryl (0.1%) or diazinon (0.2%) during January-February at fortnightly intervals.
Mango mealy bug	Kill nymphs and females by spraying metasystox (0.2%). Follow banding of tree trunks with 30 cm wide alkathene.
Stone weevil	Difficult to control, however, bagging of fruits, destruction of affected fallen fruits and disposal of debris, etc., can bring out reduction in the insect number.
Fruit fly	Collect and destroy the affected fruits. Use baits (malathion (0.05%) + jaggery + eugenol) at 4-5 places in open containers to attract the adult flies, and control them effectively. Raking of soil in May-June is equally useful as it helps in the killing of pupae.

Diseases

Powdery mildew	Two sprays of karathane (0.1%) at fortnightly interval completely control this disease. One preventive spray of karathane (0.1%) as soon as cloudy weather appears during flowering time.
Anthracnose	Spray zineb (0.2%). However, a preventive spray of Bordeaux mixture (4:4:50) is always useful in humid areas before panicle emergence.

Physiological Disorders

Malformation: It is most dreaded disorder of mango in northern parts of India, the causal agent of which is still unknown. Most of the commercial varieties in subtropical parts of India are affected by malformation and southern parts are virtually free from it. Plants both in nursery and field are affected by this malady. The symptoms of this malady are characterized by the transformation of inflorescence into compact mass with predominating male flowers.

This disorder is commonly related to the prevailing environmental temperature. Panicles emerging during late-December or early- January (when the environmental temperature is comparatively low) are worst affected by malformation.

The following control measures reduce the incidence of malformation:

1. Remove and burn all the affected malformed panicles and branches as and when they emerge. Mango malformation is the most dreaded malady of mango in north India; its causes are not yet known, however, temperature plays a vital role. De-blossoming of malformed panicles during December-January is most useful solution.
2. Follow up de-blossoming in January.
3. Application of methanol leaf extract of Ruelia tuberosa (12 g leaf per litre solution) reduces malformation in cv. Dashehari. However, the concentration is variety specific, which needs to be standardized.
4. Spray NAA (200 ppm) in October.

Spongy tissue: Spongy tissue disorder accounts for more than 30 per cent loss in Alphonso mango. In this disorder, a non-edible, sour, yellowish and sponge like patch develops in one part of the fruit during ripening. The fruit pulp remains unripe but the fruits look normal in external appearance. On cutting, the fruits emit bad odour and are unfit for human consumption. The precise cause of this malady is still unknown. However, recent studies indicate that fruits low in Ca content are worst affected by spongy tissue disorder and the convecteric heat of the soil adds more to this disorder. Use of sod culture, green vegetation, leguminous crop cover or mulching at pre-harvest stage are some measures to reduce this disorder to some extent.

Maturity and Harvesting

Depending on variety and growing environment, mango fruits take 90-120 days to reach harvest maturity. Various indices have been suggested to determine the harvest maturity of mango, e.g., change of peel colour, natural falling of some fruits from the tree (tapka) formation of abscission layer at pedicel joint, specific gravity of fruits (1.01-1.02), etc. Harvesting is done manually. The most useful tool for this purpose is a long bamboo pole fitted with a cutting shear and a collecting net below it at the distil end of the pole.

PAPAYA

Papaya, also known as Carica papaya, is a tropical fruit tree native to Central America and Mexico but now widely cultivated in many parts of the world. Papayas are grown for their sweet and juicy fruits, which are high in vitamin C, fiber, and other nutrients. In addition to their culinary uses, papaya fruits and other parts of the tree are also used for medicinal purposes. The papaya tree is fast-growing and relatively easy to cultivate, making it an important crop in many tropical and subtropical regions.

Soil and Climatic Requirements: Papaya grows well in a warm and humid climate with a temperature range of 25-30°C. It requires well-drained, deep and fertile soils rich in organic matter, with a pH range of 6-7.

Commercial Varieties: Some popular papaya varieties are Solo Sunrise, Red Lady, Maradol, and Tainung No. 1.

Propagation: Papaya can be propagated through seeds or vegetative means like cuttings, air layering or budding.

Planting Distance and Time: The distance between plants in a papaya orchard depends on the cultivar and the soil fertility. Generally, plants are spaced 2.5-3 meters apart in rows that are 3-4 meters apart. Papaya can be planted throughout the year in tropical climates, but the best time to plant is during the monsoon season.

Manures and Fertilizers: Papaya requires regular application of organic manure such as well-rotted farmyard manure, compost or green manure. For optimal growth and yield, papaya requires balanced fertilization with macro and micro-nutrients like nitrogen, phosphorus, potassium, calcium, magnesium, sulfur, and iron.

Irrigation: Papaya requires frequent and adequate irrigation during the growing season. Inadequate irrigation can result in stunted growth, while over-irrigation can lead to root rot.

Plant Protection: Papaya is susceptible to pests like fruit flies, mealybugs, mites, aphids, and scale insects, as well as diseases like powdery mildew, anthracnose, and damping-off. Proper sanitation practices, use of biocontrol agents, and timely application of pesticides can help manage these problems.

Diseases: Papaya plants are susceptible to several fungal, bacterial, and viral diseases, including anthracnose, powdery mildew, root rot, bacterial wilt, and papaya ring spot virus. Crop rotation, proper sanitation practices, and use of disease-resistant cultivars can help control these diseases.

Physiological Disorders: Papaya can also suffer from physiological disorders like fruit drop, fruit cracking, and fruit splitting, which can be managed by providing proper irrigation, nutrition, and care.

Maturity and Harvesting: Papaya fruits are harvested when they reach physiological maturity and begin to change color from green to yellow or orange. The ideal stage for harvesting papaya is when it has 1/3 of yellow color on the fruit. Papaya fruits continue to ripen even after they are harvested, and they should be stored at room temperature until they reach desired ripeness.

BANANA

Banana, a popular fruit, belongs to the family Musaceae and the genus Musa. It has a basic chromosome number of X=11. The edible varieties of banana have been developed from two species, *Musa acuminata* and *Musa balbisiana,* based on their genomic constitution. Bananas are a good source of carbohydrates and minerals such as potassium and sodium. They can be consumed fresh or used to make value-added products like chips and puree. India is the second-largest banana-growing country after Brazil, with Kerala, Maharashtra, and Tamil Nadu being major contributors to its production and acreage.

Soil and Climatic Requirements: Clay to sandy clay-loam soil is the most suitable for banana cultivation. However, the best soil is medium textured soil, having pH between 5.5-8.0. It enjoys an annual rainfall ranging from 100 to 325 cm. Banana is well adapted to areas with temperature between 21-32°C, and annual rainfall between 1,000-2,000 mm.

Commercial Varieties/Clones: The major varieties are Poovan, Basrai, Monthan, Harichal, Rasthali, Hill Banana, Nendran, Sevazhai and Kunnan.

Propagation: Bananas are propagated from offshoots (suckers) or rhizomes.

Planting System: Square, rectangle and triangle system are recommended systems for banana planting. For mono-cultured cropping system, the recommended planting distance is 3.0 × 1.5 m. For high-density planting, distance is reduced significantly.

Thinning of Suckers or Desuckering: Thinning of suckers involves removal of unwanted suckers; normally weak unhealthy, mainly water sucker using sharp knife at the ground level, leaving 1 bearer, one follower and one sucker per clump at any time.

Fertilizer Application: Banana requires high fertilization due to its rapid and vigorous growth and high fruit yield. It removes nearly 250-300 kg N, 25-40 kg P and 800-1200 kg K, 150-180 kg Ca, 40-60 kg Mg and 14-20 kg S per hectare. Usually, 300 Kg N, 40-50 Kg P and 250-300 K should be given per ha.

Water Management: Banana plant should be irrigated to encourage development and healthy growth especially in the early years of growth. Micro-sprinkler or drip irrigation system is recommended. Areas with frequent flash flood, construction of in-field drainage is recommended.

Plant Protection

Insect-pests	Control measures
Corm weevil	Use healthy materials and treat rhizomes with hot water for 5-10 minutes. Ensure good sanitation. Drench with dieldrin.
Stem borer weevil	Ensure good sanitation. Spray with dieldrin.
Nematode	Hot water treatment. Sanitation. Drench with fenamiphos. Wrapping of fruit with polyethylene bags.

Diseases	Control measures
Leaf spot	Used resistant cultivar. Spray with benomyl (0.03%).
Panama disease (Fusarium wilt)	Use resistant variety. Ensure good sanitation. Use disease free planting material.
Bunchy top	Adoption of strict quarantine measures, destroy infected plant material. Control aphid by spraying metasystox or dimecron (0.01%)

Maturity, Harvesting and Yield: Depending on the variety, banana starts to bear fruit in 6-8 months after planting. It is ready for harvesting in about 7-11 weeks later.

GUAVA

Guava *(Psidium guajava L.)* belongs to the family Myrtaceae and the genus Psidium with a basic chromosome number of 11. It is known as the "apple of tropics" and "poor man's fruit" in India. Guava is a rich source of vitamin C, pectin, and a good source of vitamins, minerals like calcium and phosphorus. Its high pectin content makes it an excellent fruit for making jelly. In India, it is mainly cultivated in Uttar Pradesh, Madhya Pradesh, Bihar, and Maharashtra. The Allahabad region in Uttar Pradesh is known for producing the best quality guavas in the world.

Soil and Climatic Requirements: Guava is a hardy fruit plant and can thrive on all types of soils, ranging from heavy clay to light soils. However, the clay loam, deep, friable and well-drained soils are best. It can be grown in soils having pH up to 9.0, though the optimum range is 4.5 to 7.5. Under highly waterlogged, saline and alkaline conditions, its cultivation is adversely affected.

However, both yield and fruit quality are better in areas with distinct winter.

Commercial Varieties: Important varieties of guava are Allahabad Safeda, Sardar (Lucknow-49), Behat Coconut, Seedless, Apple Colour, Banarasi Surkha, Chittidar, Arka Kiran, Swetha.

Propagation: Guava can be propagated both by seed and a sexual means. Most important methods of vegetative propagation are air layering/gootee, stooling, softwood grafting and budding. Now-a-days, stooling is preferred.

Planting: The pits of 1 × 1 × 1 m size should be dug out at appropriate distance in a square system before monsoon. The pits are refilled with 25-30 kg well decomposed farm yard manure, mixed with top soil and irrigated. The best planting time is onset of monsoon. Guava is usually planted at a distance of 7 to 8 m.

Irrigation: Guava is a hardy fruit plant and requires very less water. However, in the early stages of orchard establishment, plants require frequent irrigation. Later, more frequent irrigation (fortnightly interval) is required from April to June for good growth and fruit yield. Due to regular growth, flowering and fruiting in south India, guava requires irrigation throughout the year.

Manuring and Fertilization: Ten-year-old guava tree should be given about 80 kg of FYM, 1 kg of ammonium sulphate or 800 g of calcium ammonium nitrate, 3 kg of super-phosphate and 2 kg of potassium sulphate. The fertilizers should be applied in two split doses (June and October) when there is sufficient moisture in the soil.

Flowering and Crop Regulation: Guava flowers twice a year in north India. First flowering takes place in April-May, which gives fruits in rainy season. The second flowering takes place in August-September to give fruiting in winter season. The rainy season crop is generally avoided as most of the fruits are infested by fruitfly and the fruits are insipid and of very poor quality. The winter crop is virtually free from fruitfly and the fruits are of high quality. Winter crop is therefore, preferred as it gives very high returns to the farmers. In central-southern India, guava flowers thrice a year, with flowers appearing in October also. In West Bengal, guava flowers once in April-May and again in September-October.

In areas where guava flowers twice or thrice a year, we need to regulate crop in such a way that only quality crop is harvested. In this process, winter and rainy season crop is avoided. This can be done by forcing the plants to take rest in the undesired season by stopping irrigation, and then applying fertilizers and manures in the desired season. De-blossoming can be done by spraying NAA (100 ppm) or 2,4-D (30 ppm) in summer.

Plant Protection

Insect pests	Damage	Control measures
Fruit fly	Most serious pest of rainy season crop, renders whole crop unfit for consumption. Maggots on hatching, enter the fruits, and feed inside.	Soil raking, destruction of infected fruits, use of baits (sugar + malathion) and spraying plants with malathion (0.05%) or dimecron (0.03%) during oviposition period are some useful measures.
Mealy bug	Causes damage by sucking cell sap from tender leaves, shoots, flowers and fruits. The affected leaves dry up and the fruits drop off, resulting in poor yield.	The banding of the tree trunk with polyethylene film or Ostico-sticky bands is the best method to prevent them climbing up the tree. Further, treatment of soil with aldrin or malathion is also effective.

Diseases	Symptoms	Control measures
Wilt	This disease is characterized by yellowing of leaves, followed by drying of the leaves. The twigs start drying from tip downwards. The plant may collapse slowly in several or within 15-20 days.	Remove and burn the infected plants, maintain proper drainage, grow wilt resistant varieties (L-49, Banarasi), avoid planting in highly alkaline soils, disinfect soil with 2 per cent formaldehyde solution before planting, and drench soil with brassicol or spray bavistin (0.1%) at an interval of 15 days at early stages of disease infection.
Anthracnose	Die-back starts from top of the branch. Other plant parts, like shoots, leaves and fruits are readily affected. High humidity and frequent rains favour the spread and intensity of disease.	Spray dithane-Z-78 or phytolan (0.2%) at fortnightly interval.

Maturity and Harvesting: Seedling guava plants have 5-6 years juvenile phase whereas the grafted or layered plants start bearing after 2-3 years. Change in fruit colour is usually taken as harvesting index. As soon as colour starts turning from greenish-to-yellowish, the fruits should be harvested. Hand picking of fruits at regular intervals is preferred. Harvesting by shaking of tree may cause severe damage to fruits and the tree. Guava starts giving economic yields after 8-10 years of planting. In general, grafted plant of 8-10 years age can yield 400 to 800 fruits weighing 80 to 100 kg. Guavas are highly perishable and must be marketed immediately after harvest.

CITRUS

Citrus fruits are a group of fruits that includes mandarin *(Citrus reticulata)*, sweet orange *(Citrus sinensis)*, lemon *(Citrus limon)*, lime *(Citrus aurantifolia)*, pummelo *(Citrus grandis)*, and grapefruit *(C. paradisi)*, all of which belong to the family Rutaceae and have a basic chromosome number of X = 8. The edible portion of these fruits is the juice present in the vesicles, which contains 12-14% sugars, citric acid, and ascorbic acid (Vitamin C). India has several major citrus producing states, including Maharashtra, Andhra Pradesh, Punjab, the northeastern states, Karnataka, and Bihar.

Soil and Climatic Requirements: Commercial citrus cultivation in India is done on soils ranging from coarse sands to heavy clays, Ideal pH ranges from 5.5 to 6.0. The growth and development in citrus is optimum in temperature regimes ranging from 25 to 30°C to minimum of 13°C. Annual rainfall of 800-900 mm, well distributed throughout the year is optimum for citrus growth and production.

Commercial Cultivars

Sweet oranges	Mosambi, Sathgudi, Valencia, Pineapple, Jaffa, Hamlin, Shamouti, Malta, Malta Blood Red, Ruby etc.
Mandarins	Owara, Silver Hill, King, Willow Leaf, Nagpuri, Khasi, Coorg, Kinnow and Satsuma.
Lemon	Eureka, Lisbon, Assam lemon, Pani Jamir, Meyer lemon, Karna Khatta, and *galgal* (hill lemon).
Lime	West Indian lime, Kagzi, Tahiti lime (Persian), Pond, etc.
Grapefruit	Duncan, Foster, Marsh Seedless Thompson Seedless, Red Blush.
Pummelo	Nagpur (chakotra), Common pummelo.

Propagation and Rootstock: Citrus trees are propagated by both vegetative mean and sexually by seeds. Vegetative methods are preferred because they ensure uniformity in quality and bearing. Seeds of several citrus species are polyembryonic and nuclear seedlings, which produce true-to-type plants. Mandarins and acid limes are mostly propagated as seedlings. Lemons, citrons, sweet limes are easily propagated by stem cuttings. Air-layering is mostly practiced in pummelo, mandarin, acid lime and seedless lemons. Most of citrus cultivars are propagated by 'T' budding on a suitable rootstock.

Rootstock and Polyembryony: Rootstocks commonly employed for citrus propagation are rough lemon, sour orange *(C. aurantium L.)*, Karna Khatta *(C. karna)*, Rangpur lime *(C. reticulata)*, sweet orange (*C. sinensis L.* Osbeck), Citranges like Troyer, trifoliate orange (*Poncirus trifoliata* L. Raf.), and Cleopatra mandarin.

Planting: Commonly planted in a square or rectangular system. In square system, the planting density of 4 × 4 m, 5 × 5 m, 3 × 3 m can accommodate 625, 400, 1111 plants/ha, respectively. Pits of size 50 × 50 cm are dug in summer according to the layout plan and mixed with 15-20 kg well rotten FYM and 50 g chloropyrophos (to kill white ants) and filled tightly with top soil. The best planting time is beginning of rainy season.

Nutrient Management: For sustainable production of fruits and for proper maintenance of plant and soil health, efficient nutrient management programme must be adopted. Citrus is a nutrient exhaustive crop as plants in the population density of 400 plants/ha can remove about 200 kg N, 50 kg P_2O_5 and 200 kg K_2O /ha. Foliar spray of micronutrients has given beneficial effect on improving the yield and quality. One to 2% urea, alongwith $ZnSO_4$, $MnSO_4$, $MgSO_4$ (each 0.5%) and $CuSO_4$ (0.25%) is beneficial for all citrus cultivars.

Physiological Disorders

Granulation: This is the major disorder of sweet orange, mandarin wherein the juice sacs become tough, enlarged, colourless and tastelss. There is a marked increase in the pectic substances, gels etc. and marked decline in sugars, organic acids and carotenoids. These fruits are insipid and fetch poor price in the market. Some of the factors associated with it are: high soil humidity, high relative humidity and temperature during fruit growth. Hamlin and Mosambi orange are highly prone to granulation. This malady can be kept under control with the application of 16 ppm of 2,4-D on developing fruits.

Similar, effect was also noted with the spray of $ZnSO_4$ + $CuSO_4$ + KCl each at 0.25% at monthly interval from August to October.

Fruit cracking: This is a common disorder of sweet orange and acid lime. The splitting starts at stylar end and progresses towards the pedicelar end. Splitting is basically caused due to factors like deficit soil moisture, atmospheric temperature and relative humidity. Borax (0.2%) spray can check splitting and timely application of irrigation water must be ensured.

Plant Protection

Insect-pest	Damage	Control measures
Aphids (Several species)	Aphids suck sap from young leaves and twigs thereby causing severe curling of leaves, stunting of plant and facilitate sooty mould growth by excreting honeydew. These aphids act as vector for Tristeza virus.	Sprays of monocrotophos (0.025%), phosphomidon (0.03%) or parathion (0.03%) are useful for the control of aphids.
Citrus psylla	Suck sap from young leaves and act as a vector for transmitting greening disease	Spray systemic insecticides like phosphomidon (0.03%), monocrotophos (0 025%) or oxydemeton methyl (0.03%).
Leaf minor	Young ones cause damage by mining the leaves	Synthetic pyrethroids viz., fenvalerate (0.01%), permethrin (0.005%) or cypetnethrin (0.001%) are most effective.
Lemon butterfly	Caterpillars defoliate entire leaves.	Dusting and spraying with sevin (0.1%) has been found very effective.
Fruit sucking moth	Adult insects suck sap from mature fruits, thereby leading to fruit rot and drop.	Use light traps

Diseases	Symptoms	Control measures
Tristeza	Symptoms like stem pitting, seedling yellows, etc. infected plants show poor growth, die back, defoliations and ultimately death.	Use tolerant rootstock like Rangpur lime, Cleopatra mandarin, Trifoliate orange, use certified bud-wood, control aphids by insecticides.

Greening	The symptoms appear as chlorosis resembling Zn deficiency, short twigs with upright yellow leaves, leaf drop, dieback, formation of multiple buds and disfigured fruits.	Tree injection with tetracycline or employing cross protection is found to be effective. Control citrus psylla by suitable insecticides.
Phytophthora rot or gummosis	Symptoms are noted as root rot, gummosis, blight of seedlings and fruit rot.	Use resistant rootstocks like *Poncirus trifoliata* or sour orange. Soil drenching with foltaf (0.2%) or avoiding water stagnation around tree trunk is widely adopted practices.
Bacterial canker	Acid limes are most susceptible. Development of lesions with halo on leaves, twigs and fruits.	Spray 1% Bordeaux mixture or 500 ppm streptomycin sulphate and control of leaf miner (insect vector) by metasystox (0.1%). Prune infected portions.

Maturity, Harvesting and Yield

Time of harvest in citrus varies with the region (tropical and subtropical) and the species. Marketable maturity is generally judged with the change in rind colour. Commercially, TSS: acid ratio is the most reliable method and it ranges from 10:1 to 16:1, depending upon citrus species and flush. 'Khasi mandarin' in Northern-Eastern states is harvested during October-January, while 'Darjeeling' mandarin is harvested during November-December. Kinnow in Punjab is harvested during January-February; Citrus canker during April-July. Mosambi is harvested in April-June (1st crop) in Maharashtra. Hand picking is the most popular method to collect fruits while in some regions, harvesting by shaking of main trunk is also done. Maximum productivity in citrus ranges from 700 to 1,000 fruits per tree which depends on the age of plant, cultivar, rootstock and management practices. Kinnow plant can yield 300 to 800 fruits/ plant, mandarin give 500 fruits per plant.

GRAPES

Grape *(Vitis vinifera L.)* is a highly desirable, refreshing, and nutritious fruit belonging to the family Vitiaceae. Grapes are versatile and can be utilized in many ways. The majority of the grape harvest, around 80 percent, is used for wine production, while the remaining 20 percent is utilized for raisins, juice, and canning. France, Italy, and Spain are the leading producers of wine, while in India, grapes are mainly consumed as fresh fruit.

Soil and Climatic Requirements: Well drained sandy-loam soil and fairly fertile soil, having good amount of organic matter is best for cultivation of grapes. Heavy clay, sand or slit are unsuitable for grape. Grape is relatively tolerant to soil salinity and alkalinity.

Grape requires a long, dry and moderately hot season during cane maturity and ripening of berries followed by cool winter. Rains during growing season are useful, but continuous rains, make it difficult to control diseases. Rains at the time of berry ripening are harmful as even a single shower of rain during berry ripening can destroy the whole crop. Bright sunny days help in accumulation of sugar in berries.

Commercial Cultivars

Table grapes	Thompson Seedless, Pusa Seedless, Perlette, Beauty Seedless, Pusa Urvashi, Bhokri, Cardinal and Black Muskat.
Raisin grapes	Black Corinth, Thompson Seedless, Muscat of Alexandria, Sundekhani, Pusa Seedless and Kismish Beli.
Juice grapes	Early Muscat, Black Champa, Concord, Bangalore Blue, White Riesling, Arka Hans, and Pusa Navrang.
Wine grapes	White Riesling, Pinot Noir, Cabernet Sauvignon, Black Cheaper, Rubired, Madeleine Angevine, Cheema Sahebi and Pusa Navrang.
Canning grapes	Thompson Seedless, Pusa Seedless and Perlette.
Grape varieties can be seeded or seedless, as grouped hereunder:	
(a) Seeded cultivars	Anab-e-Shahi, Bangalore Blue, Bhokri (Panchdraksha), Cardinal, Cheema Sahebi, Gold, Gulabi, Pearl of Casaba, Pinot Noir, Arka Kanchan, Arka Shyam, Arka Hans, Pusa Navrang etc.
(b) Seedless cultivars	Beauty Seedless, Pusa Seedless, Perlette, Thompson Seedless, Delight, Himrod, Kishmish Charni, Arkavati, Pusa Urvashi etc.
(c) Selections	Some selections have been made by farmers. Tas-e-Ganesh, a selection from Thompson Seedless is popular in Maharashtra. Dilkush, Manik Chaman and Sonaka have been selected from Anab-e-Shahi.

Propagation and Rootstock: Grape is commercially propagated through hardwood cuttings. The length of cuttings should be 25-30 cm, having at least 4 buds and of pencil thickness. The best time for preparation of cutting in north India is at the time of annual pruning in mid-January. Under certain specific conditions to impart protection from soil borne diseases and advance soil conditions (e.g., salinity), commercial varieties are budded or grafted on desired rootstocks (e.g., Dog Ridge, Salt Creek). 'T' and 'Chip' budding are successful methods for grape propagation.

Planting: Normally, a spacing of 2 m × 2 m is recommended for head system, 3 × 3 m for trellis and bower system, for low and medium varieties. The poles should be fixed at a specific distance, depending on the training system. Usually, one-year-old rooted cuttings are planted. The planting is done during January-February in north India and during March- April and September-October in southern India.

Training: Training is done to give proper shape and desired growth for good quantity and quality of fruiting. The different training systems are bower, head, kniffin, trellis, telephone, etc. The most commonly followed training system is bower system, which is also called as Arbour or Pergola system of training. It is best suited for vigorous cultivars like Thompson Seedless, Anab-e-Shahi, Cheema Sahebi and Bhokri.

Pruning: Judicious removal of any plant part for increased productivity, facilitation of various cultural operation, regulation of crop and maintenance of vitality of vine is referred to as pruning. In north India, it is done during dormant season, from late-December to end-January, and in south, pruning for fruiting cycle is done during October-November and the foundation pruning for vegetative growth is done in April. After pruning, a single spray of blitox (0.2 per cent) should be done to avoid fungal attack on the cut portion of the vines. By staggered pruning, Bangalore Blue, Panch Drakshi and Anab-e-Shahi cultivars give two crops in a year.

Irrigation: In north India, the grape is irrigated at 7-10 days interval during growing season until beginning of sugar formation in berries.

Manuring and Fertilization:

(*a*) Vines under the age of 3-5 years, should be given 40-50 kg well rotten FYM, and fertilizer combination of 500 g N + 300 g P_2O_5 + 700 g K_2O.

(*b*) Vines above 5 years of age, should be given 50-70 kg well rotten FYM and fertilizer combination of 500 g N + 700 g P_2O_5 + 1000 g K_2O per year.

Crop regulation and quality improvement:

(*a*) Pruning and thinning: A sizeable number of canes should be retained during pruning. In general, 60-70 clusters are considered optimum on Bower system at 3 × 3 m spacing. Berry thinning helps in proper development of berries, good colour, ripening and quality.

(*b*) Girdling: It consists of removal of a complete ring (0.5 cm) of bark from the shoot, trunk or cane of a plant. The stage of girdling depends upon the cultivar and the grower's interest. For example, to improve berry set and yield, girdling is done one week before flowering, for increasing berry size, it is done at berry set or just after set and for advancing ripening, uniform colour and quality development, it is done at verasion within a month. This technique is very effective if integrated with pruning, thinning or growth regulators sprays.

(*c*) Growth regulators: GA3 has been found to be highly beneficial in loosening the bunches, increasing berry size and yield and in improving fruit quality in seedless varieties like Thompson Seedless, Beauty Seedless, Pusa Seedless etc.

Plant Protection

Insect-pest	Damage	Control measures
Chafer beetle	It feeds on buds, young and old leaves, eating away whole lamina, leaving only the skeleton of veins.	Dust chloropyriphos dust on plants.
Thrips	Thrips suck sap from the lower leaf surface, producing silvery blotches, affected parts turn brown, dry and brittle, which later drop off.	Spray malathion (0.5%) during March.

Causal Diseases	Symptoms	Control measures
Powdery mildew	Virulent in south India. Powdery growth of fungus develops on the leaves and berries, which may drop. Berries do not ripen properly, become hard and crack.	Sulphur dusting or spraying wettable sulphur (0.2%) or karathane (0.1%) protect the vine from powdery mildew.
Downy mildew	Initially, light-yellow translucent spots appear on the upper surface of leaf. Afterwards, white mould patches develop on the lower surface of the leaf. Severely affected leaves, flowers and young berries may dry and drop off.	Spraying Bordeaux mixture (1%) at a weekly interval or fytolan (0.25%) holds good for control of downy mildew.

Anthracnose	There is development of erupted brown to black spots on all green parts of the vine. The growth is completely checked, resulting in death of affected parts and splitting of bark.	Destroy affected plant parts. Spray 0.2 per cent copper oxychloride or blitox (0.3%) or fytolan (0.3%) or bavistin (0.2%) at fortnightly interval during rainy season.

Maturity, Harvesting and Yield: Grape is a non-climacteric fruit and does not ripen after harvest. Therefore, fully ripe fruits are harvested. Most commonly used maturity index is colour change, depending upon the cultivar. The bunches after harvesting should be kept in shade. Grading is done considering size, colour and variety. Packing is done in hard cardboard boxes with appropriate cushioning or packing material. Well-maintained vineyard of Perlette, Thompson Seedless may yield about 25-30 and 15-20 t/ha, respectively.

RADISH

Radish is an edible root vegetable belonging to the Brassicaceae family. It is widely cultivated and consumed throughout the world for its crisp texture and peppery flavor. Radishes come in a variety of shapes, sizes, and colors, ranging from small, round, red radishes to long, white daikon radishes. This vegetable is known for its ability to grow quickly, making it a popular choice for home gardeners and commercial farmers alike. In addition to being a tasty addition to salads and sandwiches, radishes are also packed with nutrients and are believed to have several health benefits.

Soil and Climatic Requirements: Radish is a cool-season crop that prefers well-drained, fertile soil with a pH range of 5.5 to 6.8. It grows well in cool weather and requires temperatures ranging from 10 to 25°C for optimal growth. It also requires a good amount of sunlight and prefers a slightly moist soil.

Commercial Varieties: There are many commercial varieties of radish available, including Cherry Belle, Early Scarlet Globe, French Breakfast, White Icicle, and Easter Egg.

Propagation: Radish is propagated by seeds. The seeds can be sown directly into the soil, usually at a depth of 1-2 cm.

Planting Distance and Time: The optimal time for planting radish is in early spring or late summer. The distance between the plants should be around 5-10 cm apart, and the rows should be spaced 20-30 cm apart.

Manures and Fertilizers: Radish requires a good amount of nutrients for optimal growth. Incorporating well-rotted organic manure or compost into the soil before planting can help improve soil fertility. Nitrogen-based fertilizers can also be added during the growth period to provide the necessary nutrients.

Irrigation: Radish requires regular watering, especially during dry spells. Irrigation should be done in the morning or evening to reduce water loss through evaporation.

Plant Protection: Radish plants are prone to attack by pests such as aphids, flea beetles, and cutworms. To prevent pest infestations, the plants can be covered with row covers or sprayed with insecticides. Weeds can also be a problem, and regular hoeing and weeding should be done to keep the area around the plants free of weeds.

Diseases: Radish plants are susceptible to diseases such as clubroot, damping-off, and white rust. To prevent the spread of diseases, infected plants should be removed from the garden and destroyed.

Physiological Disorders: Radish plants can also be affected by physiological disorders such as bolting, which is the premature flowering of the plant. This can be prevented by planting radish during the cooler months and by avoiding excessive nitrogen fertilization.

Maturity and Harvesting: Radish is a fast-growing crop that matures in around 3-4 weeks after planting. The crop is ready for harvesting when the radishes have reached their full size and the roots are firm. The radishes can be pulled out of the soil by hand, and the leaves and stems can be cut off before storage.

CARROT

Carrot (Daucus carota) is a root vegetable that is widely cultivated all over the world. It is a biennial plant that belongs to the Apiaceae family, which also includes other vegetables such as parsley, celery, and fennel. The edible part of the carrot is the taproot, which is typically long, cylindrical, and orange in color, although there are also other varieties with different colors such as white, purple, red, and yellow. Carrots are known for their high nutritional value, particularly their beta-carotene content, which is a precursor to vitamin A. They are commonly eaten raw, cooked, or juiced, and are used in various culinary dishes and recipes. Carrots are easy to grow, making them a popular crop for home gardeners and farmers alike.

Soil and Climatic Requirements: Carrots grow best in well-drained, loose soils that are rich in organic matter. The soil pH should be between 6.0 and 6.8. Carrots prefer cool weather and can tolerate temperatures between 15-20°C. They can be grown in a wide range of climatic conditions, but it's important to avoid extremes of temperature and moisture.

Commercial Varieties: There are many varieties of carrots available, ranging in color from white to deep purple.

Some popular varieties include Danvers, Nantes, Imperator, and Chantenay. Choose a variety that is well-suited to your growing conditions.

Propagation: Carrots are typically grown from seed. The seeds are small and should be sown shallowly, about 1/4 inch deep. They can be planted directly in the garden or started indoors and transplanted.

Planting Distance and Time: Carrots should be planted in rows spaced 12-18 inches apart, with the seeds planted about 2 inches apart within the row. The ideal time to plant depends on your climate, but in general, carrots should be planted in the spring or fall.

Manures and Fertilizers: Carrots don't require a lot of fertilizer, but they do benefit from a moderate amount of nitrogen. Too much nitrogen can cause the carrots to develop hairy roots. A well-balanced fertilizer can be applied before planting, or a side-dressing of nitrogen fertilizer can be applied when the carrots are about 3-4 inches tall.

Irrigation: Carrots require regular watering to grow properly, but it's important not to overwater them. The soil should be kept consistently moist but not waterlogged. Irrigate deeply and infrequently to encourage deep root growth.

Plant Protection: Carrots can be susceptible to pests such as carrot rust fly and carrot weevil. These pests can be controlled with insecticidal sprays or by using row covers. Carrots can also be affected by foliar diseases such as leaf blight and powdery mildew, which can be controlled with fungicidal sprays.

Diseases: Carrots are susceptible to several diseases, including damping off, leaf blight, and powdery mildew. It's important to practice good sanitation practices and rotate crops to avoid the buildup of disease pathogens in the soil.

Physiological Disorders: Carrots can be affected by several physiological disorders, including cracking, splitting, and forked roots. These disorders can be caused by uneven watering, soil nutrient imbalances, and other factors.

Maturity and Harvesting: Carrots are ready to harvest when the roots are mature and of a usable size. This usually takes around 70-80 days after planting. The tops of the carrots will start to push up out of the soil when they are ready to be harvested. The carrots can be pulled up by hand, taking care not to damage the roots. The tops should be cut off and the carrots should be stored in a cool, dry place.

POTATO

Potato (Solanum tuberosum L.) is a member of the Solanaceae family and is considered a staple food in many European countries. It is a valuable source of starch and an important dietary component. Potatoes are rich in carbohydrates, vitamins (B1, B2, B6, and C), minerals (calcium, phosphorus, and iron), and protein.

Soil and Climatic Requirements: It can grow in almost all types of soil. The well-drained clay-loam soil is considered as ideal for its cultivation.

It is a cool season crop and can tolerate moderate frost. It requires 20°C soil temperature for better germination. Young plant growth is good at 24°C but later growth is favoured by a temperature of 18°C. No tuberization takes place when the night temperature exceeds 23°C. Maximum tuberization occurs at 20°C. Tuber formation stops completely at about 29-30°C.

Varieties

Early varieties: These varieties are ready for harvest in 70-80 days such as Kufri Ashoka, Kufri Chandermukhi, Kufri Jawahar, and Kufri Lauvkar.

Main season varieties: They are ready for harvest in 90-95 days. Among the white coloured varieties, Kufri Jyoti, Kufri Sutlej, Kufri Pukhraj, Kufri Megha, Kufri Badshah, Kufri Anand, Kufri Bahar, Kufri Sadabahar, Kufri Deva, Kufri Sherpa are important.

Late varieties: Kufri Jeevan, Kufri Neelamani, Kufri Khasigaro, Kufri Naveen.

Processing varieties: Kufri Chipsona 1, Kufri Chipsona 2, Kufri Chipsona 3, and Kufri Himsona.

Soil Preparation and Planting: A well prepared soil provides sufficient room for the development of tubers and also helps to retain moisture. The fields are ploughed to a depth of 20-35 cm first with soil turning plough and afterwards by 4 to 5 ploughings with country plough/disc harrow. Clods must be broken to make the field well pulverized and levelled.

Planting Time

Region	Season	Planting time	Harvesting time
North western hills			
Very high hills	Summer	April-May	September-October
High hills	Summer	Mid-March-April	September-October
Mid hills	Spring	Jan-February	May-June
North western plains	Early	Mid-September	Mid November-December
	Autumn	Mid-October	February-March
	Spring	January	April
North Central Plains	Winter	Mid-October	February-March
North eastern plains	Winter	October end to 2nd week of November	January-February

Seed Rate and Propagation: 25-35 q tubers/ha. Potato is traditionally propagated through tubers. The eyes on the tuber surface contain axillary buds. The tubers have a dormancy of nearly 8-10 weeks after harvesting. The axillary buds on the tubers start germinating by producing sprouts only when this dormancy is over. The sprouted tubers put up fast and vigorous growth when planted in the soil.

Breaking of Dormancy: This dormancy can be broken by dipping cut tubers for 1-1½ hours in thiourea @ 1-2% solution or treating tubers with 5 ppm solution of GA3 for 10 seconds.

Seed Size and Spacing: Planting 40-50 g tuber with 40-50 mm diameter at a spacing of 45-60 cm between rows and 20-25 cm between the tubers within the rows. Tuber cutting is not recommended especially for the production of a seed crop as it transmits viruses and bacteria.

Manures and Fertilizers: Apply farmyard manure @100q/ha at the time of field preparation. However, fertilizers are applied @ 120:80:60 kg N: P_2O_5: K_2O/ha, respectively. Full dose of farmyard manure, phosphorus and potassium and half of N should be applied at the time of planting. Remaining part of N should be top dressed at the time of earthing up for effective utilization by the crop.

Irrigation: Water is applied effectively and economically at critical stages in crop development i.e. stolon formation, tuber initiation and tuber development stages of the crop. Irrigation is stopped about 10 days before harvesting of crop, to allow firming of tuber skin.

Plant Protection

Major diseases and their management		
Early blight	Concentric rings of brown to black colour are formed on the leaves. Heavily infected leaves fall off after drying. Spots also appear on stems.	Destroy crop debris. Spray ridomil MZ @ 2g/l or 0.3% blitox or 0.25% dithane - M - 45 / dithane - Z - 78 at fortnight intervals 3-4 times. Grow resistant varieties e.g. Kufri Naveen, Kufri Jeevan.
Late Blight	Lower leaves are infected having cottony growth. Water soaked lesions appear on the margins. Tubers decay under severe infection.	Use disease-free seed. Spray ridomil @ 2g per litre of water. Grow resistant varieties like Kufri Jawahar, Kufri Himsona, Kufri Jyoti, Kufri Swarnima, Kufri Kanchan.
Insect-pests and their management		
Cut worm	Adult moths cause extensive damage by cutting the plants.	Flood the infested fields, hand pick and destroy the larva, set up light trap @ 1/ha or pheramone traps @ 10/ ha to attract male moths and spray insecticides or chlorpyriphos 20EC @ 1 lit/ha or neem oil 3% @ 5.0ml/lit.
Potato tuber moth	It causes damage to tubers in the field and storage by tunneling the foliage, stem and tubers.	Avoid shallow planting of tubers, plant the tubers at depth of 10-15 cm, collect and destroy the infested tubers, and fumigate the stores with carbon disulphide.

Harvesting and Yield: The crop is harvested when it is fully matured, which can be characterized by yellowing of haulms and no pulling out of skin on rubbing of tubers. At the time of harvesting, field should not be too wet or too dry. Tractor operated potato diggers are available for digging the tubers from the fields. Early varieties may produce 200 q tubers/ha, and late varieties produce about 300 q tubers/ha.

ONION

Onion is a widely cultivated vegetable belonging to the Allium genus, which also includes garlic, chives, and leeks. It is grown for its edible bulbs, which can be eaten raw or cooked, and is used in a variety of dishes around the world. Onions are a popular crop due to their adaptability to different growing conditions and long storage life. They are also valued for their health benefits, as they are a good source of vitamins and minerals, including vitamin C, folate, and potassium. Onions can be grown in a variety of climates and soil types, making them a versatile crop for farmers and gardeners.

Soil and Climatic Requirements: Onions require well-drained soil with high organic matter content. They grow best in a soil pH range of 6.0 to 7.0. Onions grow well in cool climates, with a temperature range of 13°C to 30°C. They require plenty of sunlight and can tolerate light frost.

Commercial Varieties: Some of the popular varieties of onions are Red Creole, Texas Grano, White Bermuda, Yellow Granex, and Sweet Spanish.

Propagation: Onion seeds are sown in nurseries, and after 4-6 weeks, the seedlings are transplanted in the field. Onion can also be propagated through sets or small bulbs.

Planting Distance and Time: Onion seedlings are transplanted at a distance of 15cm x 15cm in rows 30cm apart. Planting is done during the cool season, between October and February.

Manures and Fertilizers: Onion plants require nitrogen, phosphorus, and potassium. Farmyard manure or compost is added to the soil before planting. Nitrogen fertilizer is applied in split doses at 20, 40, and 60 days after transplanting.

Irrigation: Onions require frequent and light irrigation, especially during the bulb formation period. The soil must be kept moist, but not waterlogged, to avoid rotting.

Plant Protection: Onion plants are prone to damage by thrips, aphids, and mites. Insecticides and pesticides can be used to control these pests.

Diseases: Onion plants are susceptible to diseases such as purple blotch, white rot, and downy mildew. Crop rotation, proper irrigation, and the use of disease-resistant varieties can help prevent these diseases.

Physiological Disorders: Onion plants can also suffer from physiological disorders such as bolting, splitting, and sunscald. Adequate irrigation, planting at the right time, and proper fertilization can help prevent these disorders.

Maturity and Harvesting: Onion bulbs are ready for harvest when the leaves turn yellow and start to fall over. The bulbs are lifted from the soil and allowed to dry in the field for a few days. The dried bulbs are then trimmed and stored in a cool and dry place.

CAULIFLOWER

Cauliflower (*Brassica oleracea* var. botrytis) is a cruciferous vegetable that belongs to the same family as cabbage, broccoli, and kale. It is an annual plant that is widely cultivated for its edible white, purple or green head or curd, which is composed of tightly clustered flower buds. Cauliflower is a highly nutritious vegetable and is a rich source of vitamins, minerals, and antioxidants. It is a versatile ingredient that can be roasted, boiled, mashed, or added to stir-fries, soups, and curries. Cauliflower is believed to have originated in ancient Asia and has been cultivated for over 2,000 years. Today, it is grown in many parts of the world and is a popular vegetable in many cuisines.

Soil and Climatic Requirements: Cauliflower can be grown in all types of soil with good fertility and good water holding capacity. It prefers a soil reaction ranging from pH 6 to 6.5.

Climatic factors play an important role during transformation from vegetative to curding and curd development stages. Temperature range of 10-21°C is good for germination and favourable temperature range is 17-20°C. On the basis of maturity, cauliflower varieties have been grouped as under:

Maturity group	Nursery sowing	Transplanting time	Opt. temp. range for curding	Varieties
Early I (A) Sept. maturity (mid Sept-mid Nov.)	Mid May	July beginning	20-25 °C	Early Kunwari, Pusa Early Synthetic, Pant Gobhi-3, Pusa Meghna, Pusa Kartik Sankar
Early I (B) Oct. maturity (Mid Oct-mid Nov)	May end to Mid June	Mid July	20-25°C	Pusa Katki, Pusa Deepali, Pant Gobhi-2
Mid Early (II) Nov. maturity (Mid Nov-mid Dec)	July end	Sept beginning	16-20°C	Improved Japanese, Pusa hybrid-2, Pusa Sharad, Pant Gobhi-4
Mid late (III) Dec maturity (mid Dec-mid Jan)	Aug end	Sept end	12-16 °C	Pusa Synthetic, Pusa Subhra, Palam Uphar, KT-25, Pant Subhra, Pusa HimJyoti, Pb Giant 35, Pusa Paushja, Pusa Shukti
Late (IV) Snowball (Jan-March)	Sept end to mid Oct	Oct end-mid Nov	10-16 °C	Snowball 16, Pusa Snowball-I, Pusa Snowball K-1, Dania, Ooty-1

Seed Rate and Spacing: The seed requirement for raising nursery for early varieties is 600-750g per hactare and for late varieties is 300g per hectare area. Early varieties 45cm × 30cm and mid and late season varieties 60cm × 45cm.

Soil Preparation and Transplanting: The soil should be well prepared by ploughing first with soil turning plough and afterwards with 4 to 5 ploughings with country plough. The manure should be applied at the time of field preparation. Drainage is a problem for early and some times for mid season crop when rains coincide with cropping period. Therefore, early crop should be transplanted on ridges or raised beds while the mid and late cultivars can be planted on flat beds. Transplanting should be done during late afternoon to avoid losses due to sun heat.

Manures and Fertilizers: Mix 200-250 q FYM/ha at the time of field preparation. Application of nitrogen, phosphorus and potash @ 120-180: 75-80: 60-75 kg per hectare, respectively is required to raise a healthy crop of cauliflower.

Irrigation: Cauliflower needs very careful irrigation that should be applied at right time and in sufficient quantity as both overwatering and insufficient irrigation are harmful to the standing crop. First light irrigation is given immediately after transplanting of the seedlings.

Maturity and Harvesting: The harvesting of curds is to be done as soon as the curds attain prime maturity and compactness. It is better to harvest little early than late if there is any doubt about the maturity. Delayed harvesting leads to the elongation of flowering stalk, loose, ricey, and fuzzy and over matured curds which deteriorates the quality of the curd. The curd should be cut-off with stalk along with sufficient number of jacket leaves to protect the curd. Severe trimming of leaves is to be done after unloading or before marketing.

Physiological Disorders

Buttoning: It means development of small curds or buttons. Planting of over-aged seedlings, which do not get sufficient time to initiate growth before transformation to curding or selection of wrong cultivars (planting early variety late) or root injury by insects or diseases result in buttoning.

Riceyness: A premature initiation of floral buds or elongation of peduncle stalk of inflorescence is characterized by riceyness. The curds are considered to be of poor quality for marketing. Temperature higher or lower than the optimum required for curding or application of high nitrogen results in riceyness.

Blindness: Blind plants are those, which are without terminal bud. They do not form curd. It is due to poor fertility of the soil or damage to the terminal portion during handling at the time of planting or by insects, diseases etc.

Whip tail: It is caused by the deficiency of molybdenum (Mo). Young plants become chlorotic and turn white particularly along the leaf margins. In older plants, the lamina of the newly formed leaves is irregular in shape and leaves have only a large bare midrib. This is because of this condition, the disorder is called as "Whip tail".

BRINJAL

Brinjal, also known as eggplant or aubergine *(Solanum melongena)*, is an important vegetable indigenous to India and belongs to the family Solanaceae. It is a rich source of nasunin, a potent antioxidant known to protect brain cells. Brinjal can be grown on a wide range of soils, from light sandy to heavy clay, with silt loam and clay loam being the preferred types. The ideal pH range for brinjal cultivation is 5.5-6.8. As a warm-season crop, it is vulnerable to severe frost and thrives in temperatures ranging from 21-29°C.

Important Varieties: Pusa Shymala, Pusa Purple Long, Pusa Purple Cluster, Pusa Kranti, Pusa Bhairav, Pusa Anmol, Arka Sheel, Arka Shirish, Arka Kusumkar, Arka Navneet Arka Keshav, Arka Neelkanth, Punjab Chamkila.

Nursery Sowing and Planting Time

Crop/ Region	Spring-summer crop	Rainy season crop	Autumn crop
Northern Indian (NI) plains	Nov (mid Jan-Feb)	Mar-May (April-June)	June-July (July-Aug)

Soil Preparation and Transplanting: Brinjal should be planted in well pulverized field by ploughing first with soil turning plough and afterwards with 4 to 5 ploughings with country plough.

Seed Rate and Spacing: 500-700g (OP), 350-400g (hybrids). Spacing for Dwarf varieties-60 × 45 cm and tall varieties- 90 × 60 cm.

Manures and Fertilizers: FYM @200-250 quintals per ha should be applied at the time of field preparation. In addition, apply 75-100 kg N, 50-60 kg phosphorus (P_2O_5) and 50-60 kg potassium (K_2O) per hectare.

Irrigation: Apply irrigation at an interval of one week in summer season and 10-15 days during winter.

Maturity Harvesting and Yield: Fruits should be harvested when they attain a good size, attractive colour and its surface should not loose its bright and glossy appearance. Timely harvesting of tender fruits increases the total growing period and number of pickings alongwith yield. The yield of open-pollinated varieties is 300-500 q/ha and of Hybrids, it is 600-800 q/ha.

Plant Protection

Diseases	Symptoms and management
Phomopsis blight	Portion of fruit is bleached and gives burning appearance. Seed treatment with thiram @3 gm per kg. Spray the crop in the nursery with dithane M-45. Grow resistant variety like Pusa Bhairav.
Bacterial wilt	Grow resistant varieties such as Arka Nidhi, Arka Keshav, Hisar Shyamal etc.
Little leaf	Caused by Mycoplasma and transmitted by leaf hoppers. The affected plants are shorter in structure. The leaves are malformed. Floral parts turn into leaf-like structures. No fruit bearing takes place.
Insect-pests and their Control	
Brinjal fruit and shoot borer	It is the most serious pest of brinjal crop. Plant shoots wilt and dry. Small holes appear below the calyx of fruits. Fruits are filled with frass. Grow resistant/tolerant varieties like Pusa Purple Cluster, Arka Kusumkar. Foliar application of carbaryl (0.1%)/ endosulfan (0.07%)/ fenvalerate (0.01%) is effective.

TOMATO

Tomato (Solanum lycopersicum) belongs to the Solanaceae family and is an essential ingredient in almost every Indian vegetable dish. The fruit of the tomato plant is used to make soup, juice, ketchup, puree, paste and powder. The red color of the tomato is due to the presence of lycopene pigment, which has anticarcinogenic properties. The orange color of the fruit is due to the presence of carotenoid pigment, which is a rich source of vitamin A.

Plant Growth Habit in Tomato: Tomato varieties are grouped into two broad categories based on their growth habit:

Determinate (Dwarf growth)	Indeterminate (Tall growth)
Inflorescence occurs more frequently on every internode until terminal ones are formed.	Inflorescence cluster occurs at every third internode.
Plant growth stops at terminal point with a flower cluster (self topping).	The main branch continues growing indefinitely with fruit formation until frost occurs.

Soil and Climatic Requirements: Well drained, fairly light fertile loam with a fair moisture holding capacity is the most ideal soil for tomato cultivation. Tomato is a warm season crop, which requires long season to produce a profitable crop and highly susceptible to frost. High temperature and high humidity favours development of foliar diseases. Night temperature is the critical factor in fruit setting; the optimum range is 15-20°C.

Varieties: Pusa Rohini, Pusa Early Dwarf, Pusa 120, Pusa Ruby, Pusa Sadabahar, Pusa Uphar, Pusa Sheetal, Pusa Gaurav, Arka Abha, Arka Vikas, Arka Saurabh, Arka Alok, Arka Abhijit, Arka Shreshtha, Arka Vardan, Arka Ananya, Kashi Amrit, Kashi Hemant, Kashi Sharad, Kashi Anupam, Kashi Vishesh are important varieties.

Hybrids: Kt-4, Pusa Hybrid 1, Pusa Hybrid 2, Pusa Hybrid 4, Arka Vardan, Arka Meghali, Arka Vishal, Arka Samrat, Kashi Hybrid 1, Kashi Hybrid 2 are some hybrids developed in our country.

Nursery Sowing & Transplanting Time in India

Crop/Region	Spring-summer	Autumn crop
North Indian plains	Late Nov (mid Jan)	July-Aug (Aug-Sept)
Eastern India	Nov (Late Dec)	Aug-Sept (Sept-Oct)

Nursery Raising: For better survival in the field, it is advisable to harden the seedlings. Plants are allowed to nearly wilt for 2-3 days before watering and this practice can be repeated two-three times. Such seedlings can withstand the extremes of temperature. Seedlings become ready for transplanting in 4-5 weeks time. Seedlings 5mm in diameter are better and about 15cm in length are the best for transplanting.

Soil Preparation and Transplanting: Tomato should be planted in well pulverized field by ploughing first with soil turning plough and afterwards with 4 to 5 ploughings with country plough. Ploughing should be followed by leveling. Tomato is normally planted in raised beds of 60-75 cm width. Transplanting should be done during late afternoon and the seedlings are placed on side of the beds. This provides ample moisture for the plants to survive.

Seed Rate and Spacing: For pen pollinated varieties 400-500g and for hybrids = 150-200g. Spacing of 60 cm × 45cm for determinate varieties & 90cm × 30cm for indeterminate varieties.

Manures and Fertilizers: Recommended dose of N, P and K fertilizers and their time of application is as under.

Recommended dose	Farmyard manure (q/ha)	Nitrogen (Kg/ha)	Phosphorus (Kg/ha)	Potassium (Kg/ha)
Open pollinated varieties	250	75-100	50-75	50-60
Hybrids	250	150-180	100-150	80-120

Irrigation: Careful irrigation is required for better growth of tomato crop which should be sapplied at right time. Both over-watering and insufficient irrigation is harmful. Irrigation of tomatoes can result in higher and more consistent yields, better quality, larger fruit, less blossom-end rot and less cracking. Recent research on processing tomatoes in Ontario has shown yield increases of up to 81% on a range of soil types with the use of properly scheduled irrigation. Tomato yields increased with irrigation in both wet and dry years and on sandy soils as well as on clay loams. On light soils, with their low water-holding capacity, the tomato crop can be very responsive to irrigation, but correct scheduling will provide maximum benefit. Proper scheduling is critical when irrigating tomatoes on heavier soils.

Maturity and Harvesting: Tomato fruits are harvested at different maturity stages depending upon the purpose for which these are used and distance over which they are to be transported. Fully developed mature green fruits are harvested for long distance transportation. Such fruits ripen after reaching the market and develop good colour under favourable conditions. Fruits at turning stage (1/4th of the fruit especially at blossom end shows pink colour), pink stage (3/4th of the surface shows pink colour) and hard ripe stage (nearly all red or pink with firm flesh) are harvested for local market. Over ripe fruits (Fully coloured and soft) are suitable for processing, which ensure desired quality and red colour in processed products.

Major diseases and their management		
Damping Off	The fungus attack usually starts on the germinating seed, and further spread to the hypocotyl, basal stem, and developing tap- root.	Drench the nursery bed with 5 litre formalin dissolved in 100 litres of water 15 days before sowing. Spray mancozeb or dithane- M-45 (25 gram in 10 litre of water), carbendazim or bavistin (10 gram in 10 litre of water) on nursery seedlings.
Bacterial wilt	Deadly disease of tomato, which results in wilting of plant, stunting plant growth, yellowing of entire plant, and brown vascular system	Follow crop rotation with Cruciferous vegetables, grow resistant varieties such as Arka Ananya, Arka Rakshak *etc.*, follow hot water seed treatment at 50°C for 25 minutes and spray with streptocycline @ 200ppm at 4-7 days interval.
Insect-pests and their management		
Tomato fruit borer	Initially, the larvae feed on tender foliage but later on, it moves to flower buds, flowers and developing fruits. The caterpillars make holes into fruits and render them unfit for market.	Follow late transplanting. Foliar application of endosulfan (0.07%)/ carbaryl (0.1%)/ deltamethrin (0.0028%) and acephate (0.05%) is effective.
Fruit fly	The maggots after hatching feed on pulp of the fruits and render them unfit for human consumption.	Remove and destroy affected fruits. Use pheromone traps for monitoring pest population. Spray of fenthion (0.05%)/ fenitrothion (0.05%), or bait spray adding 50 g gur + 10 ml malathion in 10 L water is effective.
Physiological disorders and their management		
Blossom end rot	A very common and destructive disorder. Rotting of fruits starts at blossom end of the fruit. Deficiency of Mg and Ca is the main cause.	It can be managed by spraying calcium chloride @ 0.5% at fruit development stage. Also apply balanced irrigation and ensure proper staking.
Cracking of fruits	Cracking of fruits at stem end is common in tomato and often results in large losses. Cracks appear to develop at maturity or ripening stage than mature green or turning stage. Deficiency of boron and long dry spell followed by heavy watering are the main reason of cracking.	Soil application of 20-30 kg of borax per hectare is beneficial. Application of proper irrigation at right stage is also very important.

SPINACH

Spinach (Spinacia oleracea) is a popular leafy green vegetable that is rich in vitamins, minerals and antioxidants. It is a cool-season crop that can be grown year-round in some regions. Here are some details about the climatic and soil requirements, varieties, soil preparation and planting, seed rate and propagation, plant protection, harvesting and yield of spinach.

Soil and Climatic Requirements: Spinach prefers to grow in a well-drained, fertile soil with a pH level between 6.0 to 7.5. It grows best in cool temperatures ranging from 15 to 20°C. High temperatures and long day lengths may cause bolting in the plants.

Varieties: There are several varieties of spinach available. Some popular varieties include Bloomsdale, Savoy, New Zealand, and Indian Summer.

Propagation: Spinach is typically propagated from seeds, which can be sown directly into the soil or started indoors and transplanted later. The seeds should be sown about 1 cm deep and 3-5 cm apart. Spinach seeds typically take about 5-14 days to germinate.

Planting Distance and Time: Spinach can be grown year-round in most climates, but it grows best in the cooler months. The ideal planting distance for spinach is 10-15 cm apart in rows that are spaced about 30-40 cm apart.

Pruning: Spinach doesn't require any pruning. However, you can remove any damaged or diseased leaves to prevent the spread of disease.

Manures and Fertilizers: Spinach requires a moderate amount of nitrogen, phosphorus, and potassium for healthy growth. Before planting, it is recommended to add well-rotted manure or compost to the soil. Once the plants are established, you can feed them with a balanced fertilizer every 2-3 weeks.

Irrigation: Spinach requires consistent moisture to grow well. It is important to water the plants regularly, especially during dry periods. Overhead irrigation should be avoided as it can increase the chances of disease.

Plant Protection: Spinach is susceptible to several pests and diseases, including aphids, leaf miners, and downy mildew. To protect the plants, it is important to keep the garden clean and remove any debris or dead leaves.

Diseases: Some common spinach diseases include downy mildew, powdery mildew, and white rust. These diseases can be prevented by practicing good sanitation practices, proper watering techniques, and using disease-resistant varieties.

Physiological Disorders: Spinach can suffer from physiological disorders such as bolting, tipburn, and yellowing. These disorders can be prevented by providing proper growing conditions such as cool temperatures, adequate water, and proper fertilization.

Maturity and Harvesting: Spinach typically reaches maturity in about 40-50 days after planting. The leaves can be harvested when they are young and tender, usually about 3-4 weeks after planting. Spinach can be harvested by cutting the leaves just above the soil level or by pulling the entire plant out of the ground.

CABBAGE

Cabbage (*Brassica oleracea* var. capitata) is a leafy vegetable belonging to the Brassicaceae family, and is widely cultivated throughout the world. It is an excellent source of vitamins, minerals, and dietary fiber. Cabbage is available in different colors, including green, red, and purple, and can be consumed cooked or raw, in salads, soups, stews, and a variety of other dishes. The cultivation of cabbage is a major agricultural activity in many countries, with China being the largest producer followed by India and Russia.

Varieties

Early Group: It takes 55-70 days for maturity. The commonly grown varieties are Golden Acre, Pride of India, Copenhagen Market, Pusa Ageti, Pusa Mukta, Pusa Sambandh (Synthetic variety).

Mid season Group: The cultivars fall between early and late maturity groups in September. Pusa Drum Head is the common variety from this group.

Late Group: It takes about 85-130 days for maturity e.g. Late Large Drum Head.

Soil and Climatic Requirements: The soil requirement for cabbage is almost same as that of cauliflower. On heavy soils, plant grows slowly and the keeping quality is improved because of compactness. Most cabbages are some what tolerant to salt. It can withstand extreme cold and frost better than cauliflower.

Planting Time: In the Northern Indian plains, transplanting of different varieties can be done from October-January.

Seed Rate and Spacing: Early season varieties need 600-800 g/ha & main season varieties need 200-500 g/ha. Late varieties 60 cm × 45 cm & for early varieties 45 cm × 30 cm.

Nutrient Management: Mix 200-250 q/ha farmyard manure thoroughly at the time of field preparation. Application of 120-180 kg nitrogen, 75-80 kg phosphorus and 60-75kg potassium per hectare is required to raise a healthy crop of cabbage.

Water Management: Cabbage is very sensitive to soil moisture. Irrigation may be applied at 10-15 days interval according to the season and soil but optimum soil moisture should be maintained regularly.

Maturity and Harvesting: In general, the heads are harvested when they are firm and solid. The heads are cut with a knife, frequently attached with some non-wrapper leaves. These non-wrapper leaves give protection to the heads from bruising injury.

Diseases and Insect-pests of Cole Crops

Major diseases and their management		
Black leg	It is a seed borne disease and hence infest crop plants at an early stage. Stem of the affected plant shows severe black discolouration. Whole root system decays from bottom upwards. Often, the affected plants collapse in the field.	Hot water treatment of seed before sowing. Spray the seed crop with copper oxychloride or with an organomercuric compound. Grow resistant varieties like Pusa Drum Head.
Downy mildew	It causes serious damage at all stages of plant growth. Discolouration occurs in the young seedlings and in severe cases, whole plant perishes.	Spray ridomil @ 0.5 g/litre of water at 10-15 days intervals or with dithane-M-45 @ 1.5-2.0 g/ litre of water.
Black rot	The tissue at the leaf margin becomes yellow; chlorosis progresses towards leaf center creating a V-shaped area at the mid rib.	Spray streptocycline @ 5g and blitox @ 100g per 10 litre of water after transplantation.
Bacterial soft rot	The affected plants show a soft, slimy, bad smelling rot that rapidly spreads throughout the plant under favourable conditions.	Control measures adopted for other diseases can check this disease as well. Spray 100- 200 ppm streptocycline or plantomycin combined with copper oxychloride (0.3%) at 15 days interval.

Insect- pests and their Management		
Diamond back moth	Spindle shaped pale yellowish green caterpillars feed on the lower side of leaves but later feed on the exposed leaves and enter the head/ curd affecting the produce as well as quality.	Grow Indian mustard as a trap crop. Spray of malathion (0.05%) or deltamethrin (0.028%), or cypermethrin (0.0075%) is very effective.
Aphids	Aphids cause serious damage by sap sucking. Seed setting stage is seriously affected.	Foliar application of malathion (0.05%) at 15 days interval is quite effective.
Cabbage butterfly	Damage is caused by caterpillars. The white winged butterflies deposit yellow coloured eggs in clusters on the undersurface of leaves.	Collect and destroy yellow egg masses and early stage larvae of cabbage butterfly. Spray of malathion (0.05%)/ deltamethrin (0.0028%)/ cypermethrin (0.0075%) and fenvalerate (0.01%) is quite effective.

GLADIOLUS

Gladiolus is a genus of flowering plants in the family Iridaceae. The plant is native to South Africa, but it is widely cultivated around the world for its attractive flowers. Gladiolus plants produce tall, graceful spikes of colorful blooms that are popular in cut flower arrangements and as garden plants. The flowers come in a wide range of colors, including pink, red, purple, yellow, orange, and white, and can be single or double blooms. The plant is easy to grow and care for, making it a popular choice for home gardeners and florists alike. In addition to its ornamental value, the Gladiolus has also been used in traditional medicine for its healing properties.

Soil and Climatic Requirements: Gladiolus plants thrive in well-drained soils that are rich in organic matter. The ideal pH range for soil is 6.0-7.0. Gladiolus plants require full sunlight exposure for proper growth and development. They can tolerate a wide range of temperatures, from 15-35°C, but grow best in warm and dry conditions.

Varieties: There are many gladiolus varieties available, which vary in size, color, and shape of the flowers. Some of the popular varieties are Atom, Black Star, Blue Bird, White Prosperity, Friendship, and Green Star.

Propagation: Gladiolus can be propagated through corms, which are underground stems that are similar to bulbs. Corms should be planted in well-draining soil, and the pointed end should be facing upwards. Corms can be planted directly in the ground, or in pots or containers.

Planting Distance and Time: Gladiolus should be planted in rows, with a spacing of 15-20 cm between plants and 60-90 cm between rows. The best time for planting is in early spring, after the danger of frost has passed. Planting can continue until early summer.

Pruning: Gladiolus plants require regular pruning to promote healthy growth and blooming. Dead or damaged flowers should be removed promptly to prevent the development of fungal diseases.

Manures and Fertilizers: Gladiolus plants require regular feeding with balanced fertilizers to promote healthy growth and blooming. A slow-release fertilizer can be applied at planting time, and a liquid fertilizer can be applied every 2-3 weeks during the growing season.

Irrigation: Gladiolus plants require regular watering, particularly during dry periods. They should be watered deeply once a week, or more often if the weather is hot and dry. However, care should be taken not to overwater, as gladiolus plants are susceptible to root rot.

Plant Protection: Gladiolus plants are susceptible to a number of pests and diseases, including thrips, spider mites, and fungal diseases such as botrytis and fusarium wilt. Regular monitoring and early intervention can help prevent serious damage.

Diseases: Gladiolus plants can be affected by a number of diseases, including botrytis, fusarium wilt, and rust. Good cultural practices such as regular pruning, proper spacing, and adequate irrigation can help prevent the development of these diseases.

Physiological Disorders: Gladiolus plants can also be affected by a number of physiological disorders, including stem rot, corm rot, and streaking. These disorders can be prevented by maintaining good soil drainage and avoiding overwatering.

Maturity and Harvesting: Gladiolus flowers are ready for harvesting when the first few flowers on the spike have opened. The spikes should be cut when about half of the flowers on the spike have opened. Flowers can be stored in a cool, dry place for several days before use.

CANNA

Canna is a genus of perennial flowering plants native to tropical and subtropical regions of the Americas, although some species are also found in Africa and Asia. These plants are widely grown for their colorful and attractive flowers, as well as their lush foliage, which can range from green to purple or bronze. Canna plants have been cultivated for centuries and have been hybridized extensively, resulting in a wide variety of cultivars with different flower colors, sizes, and shapes. They are often used in garden beds, borders, and containers, and can also be grown as houseplants. In addition to their ornamental value, some species of canna are also used for medicinal purposes, while others are cultivated for their edible rhizomes.

Soil and Climatic Requirements: Canna plants grow well in well-drained soil rich in organic matter with a pH range of 5.5 to 7.0. They require warm temperatures and plenty of sunlight to thrive. The ideal temperature range for canna cultivation is between 20 to 30°C (68 to 86°F). In areas with hot summers, it's best to plant them in partially shaded locations to protect them from the intense heat.

Varieties: There are many varieties of canna, with different colors and sizes. Some popular varieties include Canna indica, Canna 'Australia', Canna 'Durban', Canna 'Pink Sunburst', Canna 'Pretoria', and Canna 'Tropicanna'.

Propagation: Canna can be propagated through rhizomes or seeds. Rhizomes are the most common method of propagation. To propagate through rhizomes, separate the clumps of rhizomes during the dormant season, making sure each section has a bud. Plant the rhizomes 4 to 6 inches deep in well-prepared soil.

Planting Distance and Time: Canna plants should be planted 18 to 24 inches apart and 4 to 6 inches deep. They can be planted in the spring, after the last frost has passed, or in the fall. Planting in the fall allows for earlier blooming in the following year.

Pruning: Canna plants don't require much pruning, but deadheading spent flowers can promote additional blooms. Cut the flower stem down to the base of the plant after the flowers have faded.

Manures and Fertilizers: Canna plants benefit from regular feeding. A balanced fertilizer can be applied once a month during the growing season. Organic matter, such as compost or well-rotted manure, can also be added to the soil to provide nutrients.

Irrigation: Canna plants require regular watering, especially during hot and dry periods. They should be watered deeply, but not overwatered, as they don't tolerate waterlogged soil. Mulching around the plants can help to retain moisture in the soil.

Plant Protection: Canna plants can be susceptible to pests such as slugs, snails, and spider mites. Regular monitoring and removal of pests can help to prevent damage. Diseases such as fungal leaf spot and bacterial wilt can also affect canna plants. Avoid overhead watering and remove infected plant material to prevent the spread of disease.

Physiological Disorders: Canna plants can be prone to a condition known as canna rust. This is characterized by yellowing leaves with brown spots. It can be prevented by avoiding overhead watering and ensuring good air circulation around the plants.

Maturity and Harvesting: Canna plants will begin to flower in mid-summer and continue until the first frost. Flowers can be cut for use in floral arrangements when the lower blooms start to fade. The rhizomes can be dug up in the fall after the foliage has died back, dried, and stored for planting the following year.

CHRYSANTHEMUMS

Chrysanthemums are flowering plants that are native to Asia and northeastern Europe. They are widely cultivated as ornamental plants and are valued for their brightly colored, long-lasting blooms. Chrysanthemums are known for their variety of shapes and sizes, ranging from small, daisy-like flowers to large, showy blooms resembling pom-poms or spiders. They are commonly used in gardens, landscapes, and as cut flowers for floral arrangements.

Chrysanthemums have been cultivated for thousands of years and have a rich cultural history, particularly in East Asia where they have been used for medicinal and culinary purposes. Today, there are hundreds of cultivars of chrysanthemums available, each with its unique characteristics and growing requirements.

Soil and Climatic Requirements: Chrysanthemums prefer well-drained loamy soils with a pH of 6.0 to 7.5. They grow well in moderate temperatures ranging from 15 to 28°C. However, they can also tolerate low temperatures up to –5°C and high temperatures up to 35°C. These flowers need a lot of sunlight to grow, but they also require shade during the hottest part of the day. They can grow in both tropical and temperate regions.

Varieties: There are several types of chrysanthemums, including garden chrysanthemums, spray chrysanthemums, and exhibition chrysanthemums. The garden chrysanthemums are the most common type and are easy to grow. They come in different colors and flower shapes, including pompons, spider-like flowers, and daisy-like flowers.

Propagation: Chrysanthemums can be propagated from seeds, cuttings, and division of the roots. Seeds are sown in a nursery bed and transplanted when they are 6 to 8 weeks old. Cuttings are taken from mature plants and planted in a rooting medium. The roots division method involves dividing the roots of mature plants and replanting them.

Planting Distance and Time: The planting distance for chrysanthemums depends on the variety and the growing conditions. Generally, garden chrysanthemums should be planted 18 to 24 inches apart, while spray chrysanthemums should be planted 10 to 12 inches apart. They can be planted in spring or fall, depending on the climate.

Pruning: Pruning is essential for the growth and development of chrysanthemums. Pinching off the tips of the growing stems will encourage bushy growth and more flowers. Deadheading or removing faded flowers can also help promote more blooms.

Manures and Fertilizers: Chrysanthemums require a balanced fertilizer with a higher amount of phosphorus and potassium than nitrogen. A well-decomposed organic manure, such as compost or well-rotted manure, can be added to the soil to improve its fertility.

Irrigation: Chrysanthemums need regular watering, especially during the hot and dry season. Overwatering can lead to root rot and other diseases, so it's important to avoid waterlogging the soil. Drip irrigation is the best method for watering chrysanthemums.

Plant Protection: Chrysanthemums can be affected by pests such as aphids, spider mites, and thrips. They can also be susceptible to diseases such as powdery mildew, botrytis, and bacterial leaf spot. Proper sanitation practices, including removing plant debris and dead leaves, can help prevent the spread of diseases.

Physiological Disorders: Chrysanthemums can develop physiological disorders such as stem breakage, bud blast, and chlorosis. These can be caused by factors such as improper watering, nutrient deficiencies, and environmental stresses.

Maturity and Harvesting: Chrysanthemums bloom in the fall and can be harvested when the flowers are fully open but before they start to fade. The flowers should be cut in the morning and placed in a bucket of water immediately to keep them fresh. They can be stored in a cool place for up to two weeks.

ROSE

Rose (Rosa species) is a well-known and popular flower that has been cultivated for centuries around the world. In India, it is widely grown for commercial purposes, especially for cut flowers that are sold in traditional flower markets and florist shops. The loose petals of roses are also used for making garlands and for offering in temples, while cut roses with stems are primarily used for creating beautiful bouquets and floral arrangements. In addition to the commercial rose, the Damask rose (R. damascena) and Edouard rose (R. bourboniana) are grown for their attar and other products such as gulkand, gulabjal, and pankhurj.

Soil and Climatic Requirements: Roses are grown in cold climate of the hills as well as in the plains of northern and southern regions and well-drained, medium loam soil having a pH of 6.0–7.5 is ideal for rose growing.

Varieties: First Red, Grand gala, Gladiator, cocktail.

Propagation: Rose is commercially propagated through T-Budding.

Planting: The rose should be planted in pits of 60 cm diameter and 60–75 cm depth dug at appropriate distances in a bed and in northern plains, mid-October is good time for planting.

Pruning: The rose bushes are pruned once a year during second or third week of October in the northern plains. After about 6–7 weeks of pruning, the plants start flowering. The time of flowering can be adjusted according to the date of pruning. The pruning in northern plains, is done in October.

Manuring and Fertilization: Rose being a perennial crop, it requires regular nutrient feeding through manures and fertilizers at the time of pruning, plant growth and at the end of flowering, besides during land preparation and planting of new bushes.

Irrigation: The frequency of irrigation depends upon the soil texture and climate. Watering is more frequent in sandy soils and hot weather than in clay soils and humid/ rainy or cool season. During the rainy season in eastern/ southern or coastal areas, it may not be necessary to irrigate the plants. The frequency of watering during summer may be about twice a week, while in winter or cool season, it may be only once a week or 10 days.

Disbudding and Pinching: The young vegetative buds in the leaf axils of basal and lateral shoots are disbudded to encourage branching at the base and to obtain long terminal shoots. For obtaining long stemmed quality blooms, it is necessary to do disbudding and pinching or removal of side flower buds.

Harvesting and Postharvest Management: The rose flowers are cut while still in the bud stage after the sepals curl back and the colour is fully showing. In large-flowered roses, flowers along with the stem of prescribed length are cut when the first one or two petals start to unfold but do not open fully. The flowers in small-flowered clustered varieties are cut when these begin to open in the cluster. The flowers are harvested in early morning or late in the afternoon.

The cut roses are kept in plastic buckets/containers filled with clean water having disinfectant and preservative (silver thiosulphate) to enhance their shelf-life. These flowers are shifted to precooling chambers having a temperature of 10°C, and kept there for about 12hr. The grading is done on the grading tables. The graded flowers are bunched with 10 or 20 stems in each bunch and sleeved with thick paper or plastic film. These flowers are then packed in telescopic corrugated cardboard boxes.

Plant Protection

Pests	Diseases
Red spider mite	Powdry mildew
Scale	Dieback
Aphid	Black spot
Leaf eating caterpillar	Nematode

MARIGOLD

Marigold (*Tagetes* spp.) is an ornamental crop belonging to the family Asteraceae. It is cultivated for its loose flowers, which are popular in the market as garlands or as cut flowers. In addition to its ornamental value, Marigold is also a source of pigment for poultry feed. Its variable height and colourful flowers make it a popular choice for landscape designs and beautification purposes.

Botanical Description:

1. **Tagetes erecta (African marigold):** The African marigold plant is hardy, annual; about 90 cm tall erect and branched.
2. **Tagetes patula (French marigold):** The French marigold is a hardy annual, about 30 cm tall, forming a bushy plant.

Soil and Climatic Requirements: Marigold is adaptable to different types of soil conditions and thus can grow successfully in a wide variety of soils. However, a deep, fertile, friable soil having good water holding capacity, well drained and near to neutral in reaction (pH 7.0 – 7.5) is most desirable. Marigold requires mild climate for luxuriant growth and flowering.

Varieties:

1. **Tagetes erecta (African marigold):** Pusa Narangi Gainda, Pusa Basanti Gainda, Climax, Chrysanthemum, Charm etc.
2. **Tagetes patula (French marigold):** Pusa Arpita, Red Brocade, Rusty Red, Butter Scotch etc.

Plant Propagation: Marigold is mainly propagated by seeds. The seed rate is 42.5 kg/ha.

Transplanting: Mid-July, mid-October and February-March are suitable times for transplanting of marigold at spacing of 40 × 30 cm.

Nutrient Management: FYM is given @ 50 tones/ha at the time of field preparation. In African and French marigold, application of 400 kg N, 200 kg P and 60 kg K per hectare should be done.

Maturity and Harvesting: Marigold flowers are plucked when they have attained full size. Plucking of flowers should be done in cool hours of the day. The field should be irrigated before plucking so that flowers keep well for a longer period after harvest. Plucked flowers are collected in polythene bags or bamboo baskets for carrying to markets.

Plant Protection

Pests	Diseases
Red spider mite	Damping off
Hairy caterpillar	Collar rot
Alternaria dianthi	Flower bud rot

PRINCIPLES AND METHODS OF PRESERVATION OF FRUITS AND VEGETABLES

Preservation of fruits and vegetables is an important practice to increase their shelf life and maintain their nutritional value. The principles and methods of fruit and vegetable preservation vary depending on the type of produce and the desired preservation method. Here are some common principles and methods of fruit and vegetable preservation:

Temperature Control

Temperature control is one of the most important principles in fruit and vegetable preservation. The rate of respiration and ripening of fruits and vegetables is directly related to temperature. Therefore, controlling the temperature of fruits and vegetables is essential in maintaining their quality, shelf life, and preventing spoilage.

Refrigeration is the most common method of temperature control in fruit and vegetable preservation. Lowering the temperature slows down the respiration and ripening processes and inhibits the growth of microorganisms. This method is most effective for storing fruits and vegetables that are sensitive to heat and moisture, such as leafy greens, berries, and citrus fruits. The ideal temperature for most fruits and vegetables in refrigeration is between 0°C and 5°C.

Another method of temperature control is freezing. Freezing is an effective method of preserving fruits and vegetables for extended periods of time. Freezing slows down or stops the enzymatic and microbial processes, thereby extending the shelf life of fruits and vegetables. The ideal temperature for freezing fruits and vegetables is below -18°C.

On the other hand, some fruits and vegetables are sensitive to cold temperatures and can suffer from cold damage or chilling injury. These include tropical fruits such as bananas, avocados, and mangoes, and vegetables such as tomatoes and cucumbers. Chilling injury can cause the fruits and vegetables to develop brown spots, lose flavor, and become less crisp. To prevent chilling injury, these types of fruits and vegetables should be stored at temperatures above 10°C.

In addition to refrigeration and freezing, other temperature control methods include canning and pasteurization. Canning involves heating fruits and vegetables in sealed containers to high temperatures to kill microorganisms and stop the enzymatic reactions. Pasteurization is a heat treatment that is used to destroy microorganisms and enzymes in fruit and vegetable products such as juices and purees. The temperatures used in canning and pasteurization vary depending on the type of fruit or vegetable and the product being produced.

Temperature control is a critical principle in fruit and vegetable preservation. Proper temperature management can extend the shelf life of fruits and vegetables, maintain their quality, and prevent spoilage.

Dehydration

Dehydration is a method of preserving fruits and vegetables that involves removing the moisture from the produce. By removing the moisture, the growth of microorganisms that cause spoilage is prevented. Dehydrated fruits and vegetables have a longer shelf life and are easy to store, transport and use.

Dehydration can be achieved through several methods, including sun drying, air drying, and mechanical drying. Sun drying is the oldest and most traditional method of dehydrating fruits and vegetables. In this method, the produce is spread out in the sun and allowed to dry naturally. This method is only effective in areas with high temperatures and low humidity, and can take several days to complete.

Air drying is another method of dehydration that can be used in any climate. In this method, the produce is cut into small pieces and spread out in a well-ventilated area, such as a screen or wire mesh. Air drying can take several days to complete, depending on the climate and the type of produce being dehydrated.

Mechanical drying is a faster and more efficient method of dehydration. In this method, the produce is dried using specialized equipment such as a dehydrator, oven or microwave. A dehydrator uses low heat and a fan to circulate the air and remove moisture from the produce. An oven can also be used to dehydrate fruits and vegetables by setting it to a low temperature and leaving the door slightly ajar. A microwave can be used for small batches of produce by placing the slices on a microwave-safe plate and cooking them on a low power setting for several minutes.

Before dehydrating fruits and vegetables, it is important to properly prepare them by washing, peeling and slicing them into even-sized pieces. This ensures that the produce is dried evenly and thoroughly. It is also important to store dehydrated fruits and vegetables in an airtight container in a cool, dry place to prevent moisture from re-entering the produce and causing spoilage.

Dehydrated fruits and vegetables can be rehydrated by soaking them in water for several hours before use. They can be used in a variety of dishes, including soups, stews, salads and baked goods. Dehydrated fruits can also be used as a healthy snack or in trail mix.

Canning

Canning is a preservation method that involves sealing fruits and vegetables in airtight containers, such as jars or cans, and heating them to destroy microorganisms that cause spoilage. The method was first developed in the 18th century, and since then it has become one of the most popular methods of fruit and vegetable preservation.

The basic principles of canning are as follows:

1. **Preparation:** Before canning, fruits and vegetables are washed, peeled, and cut into suitable sizes. Vegetables are often blanched, which involves boiling them for a short period of time and then immediately cooling them in ice water. This helps to preserve their color, texture, and nutrient content.
2. **Filling:** The prepared fruits and vegetables are then packed into clean, sterilized jars or cans. The containers must be filled with enough liquid, such as water, syrup, or brine, to cover the produce and allow for heat penetration during processing.
3. **Sealing:** Once the containers are filled, they are sealed with a lid or cap. The sealing process is essential to prevent the entry of air and microorganisms that could cause spoilage.
4. **Processing:** The sealed containers are then processed by heating them to a specific temperature for a specific amount of time. This process, known as thermal processing, kills any bacteria, yeasts, or molds that may be present, and also inactivates enzymes that can cause deterioration of the product. The specific processing time and temperature vary depending on the type of produce being canned.
5. **Cooling:** After processing, the containers are removed from the heat source and allowed to cool. As they cool, a vacuum is created inside the container, which helps to ensure a tight seal and prevent the entry of air.

Canning is an effective method of fruit and vegetable preservation, as it can extend the shelf life of produce for up to several years. The method also retains the color, texture, and flavor of the produce, and can provide a convenient and easy way to store and use fruits and vegetables year-round.

Fermentation

Fermentation is a traditional method of food preservation that has been used for centuries to preserve fruits and vegetables. Fermentation involves the use of microorganisms, such as bacteria or yeast, to convert the natural sugars in fruits and vegetables into organic acids, alcohols, and gases. These organic acids and alcohols can inhibit the growth of spoilage-causing microorganisms and help to preserve the fruits and vegetables for long periods.

There are several types of fermentation methods that are commonly used for fruit and vegetable preservation, including lactic acid fermentation, acetic acid fermentation, and alcoholic fermentation. Lactic acid fermentation is the most common method of fermentation used for fruits and vegetables, and involves the use of lactic acid bacteria to convert the natural sugars in fruits and vegetables into lactic acid.

To carry out lactic acid fermentation, fruits and vegetables are first washed and then sliced, grated, or chopped into small pieces. Salt is then added to the fruits and vegetables to help draw out the natural juices and create an environment that is favorable for lactic acid bacteria. The fruits and vegetables are then packed into a fermentation vessel and left to ferment for several days to several weeks, depending on the type of fruits and vegetables and the desired degree of fermentation.

Acetic acid fermentation, also known as vinegar fermentation, involves the use of acetic acid bacteria to convert the natural sugars in fruits and vegetables into acetic acid. This method of fermentation is commonly used for the preservation of cucumbers, beets, and other vegetables.

Alcoholic fermentation involves the use of yeast to convert the natural sugars in fruits and vegetables into alcohol. This method of fermentation is commonly used for the preservation of fruits, such as grapes and apples, to make wine and cider.

Fermented fruits and vegetables are rich in probiotics, which are beneficial bacteria that can help to improve digestive health and boost the immune system. They are also a good source of vitamins, minerals, and antioxidants. Some common examples of fermented fruits and vegetables include sauerkraut, kimchi, pickles, and kefir.

Freezing

Freezing is a popular method of preserving fruits and vegetables, as it can retain the quality of the produce for an extended period. The principle behind freezing is that the low temperature inhibits or slows down the growth of microorganisms, which are responsible for spoilage. Freezing also helps to retain the natural color, flavor, and texture of the fruits and vegetables.

The process of freezing fruits and vegetables involves the following steps:

1. Selection of fresh and high-quality produce that is suitable for freezing.
2. Washing, trimming, and cutting the produce into the desired size and shape.
3. Blanching the produce in boiling water or steam for a short period, which helps to inactivate enzymes that cause loss of flavor, color, and texture.
4. Cooling the blanched produce immediately in ice water to stop the cooking process.
5. Draining the excess water and drying the produce.
6. Placing the produce in freezer bags or containers, and storing them at a temperature of –18°C or lower.

The duration of storage depends on the type of produce, as well as the temperature and conditions of storage. Generally, frozen fruits and vegetables can be stored for several months to a year. However, the quality of the produce may deteriorate over time due to factors such as freezer burn, which is caused by dehydration of the surface of the produce, and oxidation, which causes discoloration and loss of flavor.

To ensure the best quality of frozen fruits and vegetables, it is essential to follow proper freezing techniques and to use suitable packaging materials. The packaging should be airtight and moisture-resistant, and the size of the package should be appropriate for the amount of produce being frozen. It is also important to label the package with the type of produce, date of freezing, and storage instructions.

Freezing is an effective method of preserving fruits and vegetables, as it helps to retain the natural qualities of the produce and inhibit the growth of microorganisms. By following proper techniques for selection, preparation, blanching, packaging, and storage, frozen fruits and vegetables can be enjoyed for an extended period.

Vacuum Packing

Vacuum packing is a method of food preservation that involves removing air from a package to create a vacuum-sealed environment. This process helps to reduce the amount of oxygen in the package, which can slow down the growth of bacteria and fungi that can spoil food.

The vacuum packing process involves placing the food in a plastic bag or container and then using a vacuum sealer machine to remove the air from the package. The bag or container is then sealed, creating a tight seal that prevents air from re-entering the package.

One of the benefits of vacuum packing is that it can help to extend the shelf life of fruits and vegetables by slowing down the natural deterioration process. By reducing the amount of oxygen in the package, vacuum packing can help to slow down enzymatic reactions that can cause fruits and vegetables to become soft, mushy, or discolored.

Vacuum packing can also help to preserve the flavor and nutritional content of fruits and vegetables. By reducing the amount of exposure to oxygen, vacuum packing can help to reduce the oxidation of vitamins and other nutrients in the food.

Another benefit of vacuum packing is that it can help to reduce food waste. By extending the shelf life of fruits and vegetables, vacuum packing can help to prevent them from spoiling before they can be used, reducing the amount of food that goes to waste.

Vacuum packing is a useful method of fruit and vegetable preservation that can help to extend the shelf life of these perishable foods and reduce food waste.

Salting

Salting is a traditional method of preserving fruits and vegetables that involves adding salt to the produce to prevent spoilage. This method works by drawing out the water from the fruits and vegetables, which prevents the growth of bacteria and other microorganisms that cause decay. Salting is commonly used to preserve cucumbers, olives, and various types of cabbage.

The process of salting involves soaking the fruits or vegetables in a salt solution, also known as brine. The concentration of the brine and the length of time the produce is soaked in it depends on the type of produce being preserved and the desired level of saltiness. For example, cucumbers are typically soaked in a 5-10% brine solution for 1-3 weeks, while cabbage is soaked in a 2-3% brine solution for several weeks.

Once the produce has been soaked in the brine, it can be stored in airtight containers, such as jars or crocks, and kept in a cool, dark place. The salt acts as a natural preservative, extending the shelf life of the produce for several months or even years.

One advantage of salting is that it requires minimal equipment and can be done at home with relatively little effort. However, it is important to ensure that the produce is fully submerged in the brine to prevent spoilage. Additionally, some people may find the high salt content of salt-preserved produce to be undesirable from a health standpoint.

Salting is a simple and effective method of preserving fruits and vegetables that has been used for centuries.

The principles and methods of fruit and vegetable preservation are diverse and can be adapted to suit different types of produce and preservation goals. The choice of method depends on factors such as the type of produce, desired shelf life, and preservation method.

PREPARATION OF JELLIES, JAMS, KETCHUP, CHIPS AND THEIR PACKING

Preparation of jellies, jams, ketchup, chips, and their packing involve different processes and techniques. Here are some details on each:

Jellies

Preparation of jellies involves cooking fruit juice with sugar and pectin, which is a natural thickening agent found in many fruits. The process of making jellies involves the following steps:

1. **Fruit preparation:** Choose ripe, high-quality fruits that are free of blemishes and bruises. Wash and remove any stems, pits, or seeds, and chop or crush the fruit as needed.
2. **Mixing:** Combine the fruit with sugar and any other desired ingredients in a large pot or kettle. Pectin may be added to help the mixture set.
3. **Cooking:** Heat the mixture over medium heat, stirring frequently, until the sugar dissolves. Increase the heat to bring the mixture to a boil, and continue cooking until the mixture reaches the jelling point. This can be determined by using a thermometer or performing a plate test.
4. **Skimming:** Remove any foam or scum that forms on the surface of the jelly as it cooks.
5. **Filling and processing:** Pour the hot jelly mixture into sterilized jars, leaving a small amount of headspace at the top. Seal the jars with lids and bands, and process them in a water bath canner for the recommended time.
6. **Cooling and storage:** After processing, remove the jars from the canner and allow them to cool on a towel or rack. Check that the lids have sealed properly and store the jars in a cool, dry place.

Jellies can be made with a variety of fruits, and different flavorings and spices can be added for variety. Jellies can also be made without added pectin, by using fruits that are naturally high in pectin, such as apples or quince.

The packing of jellies is an essential step in the process of making jellies. Proper packing ensures that the jellies are protected from contamination and that they remain fresh and flavorful for a longer period of time.

The following are the steps involved in packing jellies:

1. **Sterilize the jars:** Before packing the jellies, it is important to sterilize the jars. This can be done by washing the jars and lids in hot, soapy water and then boiling them for 10 minutes.
2. **Fill the jars:** Once the jars are sterilized, fill them with the hot jelly mixture using a ladle, leaving about 1/4 inch of space at the top.
3. **Remove air bubbles:** To remove any air bubbles, run a plastic or wooden spatula around the inside of the jar.
4. **Wipe the rim:** Wipe the rim of the jar with a clean, damp cloth to remove any spills or drips.
5. **Place the lid:** Place the lid on the jar and screw the band tightly.
6. **Process the jars:** Process the jars in a boiling water bath for the recommended time based on the recipe.
7. **Cool and store:** Once processed, remove the jars from the water bath and allow them to cool on a wire rack. Check the seals of the jars to ensure they are properly sealed. Label the jars with the date and store them in a cool, dry place.

Proper packing of jellies helps to preserve the quality and shelf life of the product.

Jams

Preparation of jams involves the following steps:

1. **Selection of fruits:** The first step in preparing jams is the selection of ripe, fresh and high-quality fruits. The fruit should be free from any mold, bruises, or damage.
2. **Washing and preparation:** The fruits are washed thoroughly and then peeled, cored, and cut into small pieces. Some fruits, such as berries, can be mashed instead of cut.
3. **Cooking:** The prepared fruit is then cooked in a large pot along with sugar, pectin, and lemon juice. Pectin is a natural substance that helps the jam to set. The amount of pectin required depends on the type of fruit being used.
4. **Skimming:** As the fruit mixture cooks, it will produce foam or scum. This needs to be skimmed off regularly to ensure a smooth texture.
5. **Testing for set point:** Once the jam has cooked for a sufficient time, a spoonful is tested for its set point. To do this, a small amount of jam is placed on a cold plate and allowed to cool. If it is set and wrinkles when pushed with a finger, then the jam is ready.
6. **Jar preparation:** The jars and lids should be sterilized in boiling water and then dried. This ensures that the jam stays fresh and safe for consumption.
7. **Filling and sealing:** The hot jam is then poured into the sterilized jars, leaving about 1/4 inch of headspace. The jars are then sealed tightly with the sterilized lids.
8. **Cooling:** The jars are allowed to cool at room temperature, which helps to create a vacuum seal.
9. **Labeling and storage:** Once the jars are completely cool, they can be labeled with the date and type of jam. They can then be stored in a cool, dark place for up to a year.

The packing of jams is similar to that of jellies, where the jars are filled with the hot jam mixture and sealed with lids. The jars can then be labeled and stored in a cool, dark place. Some commercial jams are also packed in sachets or small plastic containers for easy and convenient use.

Packaging of jams is crucial to maintain their quality and shelf life. Here are some common packaging methods for jams:

1. **Glass jars:** Glass jars are a popular option for packing jams. They are non-reactive and do not affect the flavor or color of the jam. The jars should be sterilized before filling them with hot jam. The lids should also be sterilized and tightly sealed after filling.
2. **Plastic containers:** Plastic containers are a lightweight and convenient option for packing jams. They are available in different sizes and shapes. However, plastic containers may react with acidic foods and affect their flavor. It is recommended to use food-grade plastic containers for packing jams.
3. **Metal cans:** Metal cans are another option for packing jams. They provide a barrier to light and oxygen, which helps in preserving the quality of the jam. However, metal cans are not suitable for acidic foods as they may react with the metal and cause off-flavors.
4. **Flexible pouches:** Flexible pouches are becoming popular for packing jams. They are lightweight and convenient for storage and transportation. Flexible pouches are available in different sizes and shapes and can be custom printed with branding and nutritional information.

It is important to ensure that the packaging material is food-grade and suitable for the type of jam being packed. The packaging should be labeled with the name of the jam, ingredients, nutritional information, and any allergens. Proper labeling helps consumers make informed decisions and prevents any health issues.

Ketchup

Ketchup is a popular condiment made from tomatoes, vinegar, sugar, and various spices. Here is a step-by-step process for preparing ketchup:

1. **Selecting the tomatoes:** Choose ripe and firm tomatoes. Roma tomatoes are preferred for ketchup because they have less water content and more pulp.
2. **Cleaning and chopping:** Wash the tomatoes thoroughly and chop them into small pieces. Remove any stems or blemishes.
3. **Boiling the tomatoes:** Put the chopped tomatoes in a large pot and bring them to a boil. Reduce the heat and let the tomatoes simmer for about 30 minutes. Stir occasionally to prevent burning.
4. **Straining the tomatoes:** Once the tomatoes are soft and cooked, pass them through a strainer or a food mill to remove the seeds and skins. This will give you a smooth tomato puree.
5. **Adding the other ingredients:** Pour the tomato puree back into the pot and add vinegar, sugar, salt, and other spices such as onion powder, garlic powder, and paprika. Mix well and bring the mixture to a boil.
6. **Simmering and reducing:** Reduce the heat to low and let the ketchup simmer for about 1-2 hours until it thickens and reduces to a desired consistency. Stir occasionally.

7. **Blending and straining:** Once the ketchup has thickened, let it cool for a few minutes and then blend it with an immersion blender or a regular blender until smooth. Pass it through a strainer to remove any remaining solids.
8. **Bottling and storing:** Pour the ketchup into clean and sterilized bottles or jars. Seal them tightly and store them in a cool and dark place. Homemade ketchup can last up to 1 month in the refrigerator.

It is important to follow proper food safety measures when preparing and storing ketchup to prevent contamination and spoilage.

Ketchup can be packed in various containers such as glass bottles, plastic squeeze bottles, and sachets. The choice of packaging material depends on factors such as cost, convenience, and product shelf life.

Glass bottles are a popular choice for ketchup packaging as they are reusable and do not react with the acidic nature of the product. Plastic squeeze bottles are also commonly used as they are lightweight and unbreakable, making them ideal for outdoor events and picnics. Sachets are convenient for on-the-go consumption and are commonly used in fast-food restaurants.

Before packing, the ketchup is cooled and filtered to remove any impurities. It is then pumped into the packaging containers using a filling machine. The containers are sealed with an airtight cap or lid to prevent spoilage and contamination.

The packaging material may be labeled with information such as the ingredients, nutritional value, and manufacturing date. The label may also include branding and promotional messages to attract consumers.

Once the ketchup is packed, it is stored in a cool, dry place away from direct sunlight until it is ready to be distributed to retailers and consumers. Proper packaging and storage help to maintain the quality and freshness of the product, ensuring that it has a longer shelf life.

Chips

Chips, also known as crisps, are a popular snack made from sliced, fried or baked potatoes. The process of making chips involves several steps including selecting the right potatoes, slicing them into thin pieces, frying or baking them, and seasoning them.

A detailed explanation of the preparation process for chips:

1. **Selection of Potatoes:** The first step in preparing chips is selecting the right type of potatoes. Ideally, potatoes that are low in sugar and high in starch content should be used as they produce crispy chips. Popular varieties used for making chips include Russet, Yukon Gold, and Kennebec.
2. **Washing and Peeling:** The potatoes are washed thoroughly to remove any dirt or debris. They are then peeled using a potato peeler.
3. **Slicing:** The peeled potatoes are then sliced into thin, uniform pieces using a mandoline or a sharp knife. The thickness of the slices depends on personal preference, but they should be uniform to ensure even cooking.
4. **Drying:** The sliced potatoes are then placed on a clean kitchen towel or paper towels to dry out excess moisture. This is important to ensure that the chips become crispy when fried or baked.
5. **Frying or Baking:** The dried potato slices are then either fried in hot oil or baked in an oven until crispy and golden brown. For frying, a deep fryer or a heavy-bottomed pot is used with vegetable oil or other suitable frying oil. For baking, the potato slices are arranged in a single layer on a baking sheet and baked in a preheated oven until crispy.
6. **Seasoning:** Once the chips are cooked, they can be seasoned with salt or other seasonings such as garlic powder, paprika, or onion powder.
7. **Packaging:** The chips are then packaged in airtight bags or containers to keep them fresh and crispy. Nitrogen flushing is often used to remove oxygen and extend the shelf life of the chips.

The preparation of chips involves selecting the right type of potatoes, slicing them into thin pieces, drying, frying or baking them until crispy, seasoning, and packaging them in airtight bags or containers.

Packing of chips involves the use of various packaging materials to ensure that the chips are protected from contamination, moisture, and oxidation during storage and transportation. The most commonly used packaging materials for chips include plastic bags, aluminum foil bags, paper bags, and cans.

Plastic bags are the most common packaging material for chips. They are lightweight, easy to produce, and provide a good barrier against moisture and contamination. Plastic bags come in different sizes, shapes, and designs. The bags are usually printed with the brand name, product information, and nutritional facts.

Aluminum foil bags are another popular packaging material for chips. They offer a high level of protection against moisture, light, and oxygen. The bags are usually laminated with a layer of plastic film to provide a barrier against contamination. Aluminum foil bags are available in various sizes and shapes, and they can be printed with the brand name and product information.

Paper bags are an environmentally friendly alternative to plastic bags. They are made from renewable resources and are biodegradable. Paper bags are lightweight and can be printed with the brand name, product information, and nutritional facts. However, they provide less protection against moisture and contamination compared to plastic and aluminum foil bags.

Cans are also used for packing chips. They are durable, provide excellent protection against moisture and light, and are stackable, making them easy to store and transport. Cans can be printed with the brand name, product information, and nutritional facts. However, they are more expensive than other packaging materials, and they are not as convenient for consumers to carry around.

The packing of chips involves the use of various packaging materials such as plastic bags, aluminum foil bags, paper bags, and cans. The packaging material chosen depends on factors such as cost, level of protection required, and environmental concerns. The packaging is usually printed with the brand name, product information, and nutritional facts to help consumers make informed choices.

MULTIPLE CHOICE QUESTIONS

1. Arrange the steps of making cucumber pickle in the proper sequence.
(*a*) Washing and peeling.
(*b*) Cut into small pieces and mix with salt.
(*c*) Keep in sun for a week.
(*d*) Add spices and vinegar.
(*e*) Keep in a jar for 8 hours and remove excess water.

Choose the correct answer from the options given below
A. $(d) \to (a) \to (b) \to (e) \to (c)$
B. $(d) \to (b) \to (e) \to (a) \to (c)$
C. $(d) \to (e) \to (b) \to (a) \to (c)$
D. $(d) \to (a) \to (c) \to (b) \to (e)$

2. Identify the incorrect concepts with respect to traditional storage method of fruits and vegetables?
(*a*) Sand and coir storage
(*b*) High altitude storage
(*c*) Cold storage
(*d*) Pit storage
(*e*) Modified atmospheric storage

Choose the correct answer from the options given below:
A. (*c*) and (*e*) only B. (*a*) and (*c*) only
C. (*b*) and (*d*) only D. (*d*) and (*e*) only

3. The extent of food processing percentage in India is approximately:
A. 80% B. 20%
C. 40% D. 2%

4. The methods of preservation of fruit juices include:
(*a*) Carbonation
(*b*) Flash pasteurization
(*c*) Over flow method
(*d*) Holding pasteurization
(*e*) Fermentation

Choose the correct answer from the options given below:
A. (*a*), (*b*), (*c*) only B. (*b*), (*c*), (*d*) only
C. (*c*), (*e*) only D. (*a*), (*d*) only

5. Addition of sugar at minimum is required to pressure any food product. This also improves the taste and calorific value of the preserved products.
A. 50% B. 65%
C. 60% D. 75%

6. Which one of the following variety belongs to Rose flower?
A. Ruby red B. Gladiator
C. Cracker jack D. Butter scotch

7. Gerbera is commercially propagated through:
A. Suckers B. Cutting
C. Budding D. Layering

8. While preparing pickles, preservation is primarily achieved through the addition of:
A. Salt B. Colour
C. Water D. Pectin powder

9. Keeping micro-organisms out from entering into the food is termed as:
A. Spoilage B. Asepsis
C. Decomposition D. Deterioration

10. Rose is commercially propagated by:
A. Seed B. Layering
C. Grafting D. Budding

11. Desuckering and mattocking is practiced in which crop?
(*a*) Mango
(*b*) Citrus
(*c*) Banana
(*d*) Sugarcane
(*e*) Pomegranate

Choose the correct answer from the options given below:
A. (*a*) and (*c*) Only
B. (*b*) and (*e*) Only
C. (*c*) Only
D. (*c*) and (*d*) only

12. Lychee (Litchi chinensis) is typically propagated by which method?
A. Grafting
B. Cutting
C. Seed
D. Marcotting or gootee

13. Which is the regular bearing variety of mango?
A. Sindhu B. Neelam
C. Dudhpedha D. Kesar

14. Which of the following statements are incorrect with reference to the objective of storage of vegetables and fruits?
(*a*) Slow the biological activity and micro-organism growth
(*b*) Avoid glut and distress sale in the market
(*c*) Making the food available in on-season
(*d*) Regulate the market in an orderly manner
(*e*) Increasing ethylene production rate

Choose the correct answer from the options given below:
A. (*c*) and (*e*) only B. (*c*) and (*d*) only
C. (*a*) and (*b*) only D. (*a*) and (*e*) only

15. Identify the correct statements about horticulture.
(*a*) Fruits and vegetables yield large quantity of food per unit area as compared to cereals.
(*b*) Horticulture crops are not remunerative
(*c*) Fruits and vegetables are an important protective foods
(*d*) Horticultural products are not the raw materials for many industries
(*e*) Horticultural products are not contributing to national wealth

Choose the correct answer from the options given below:
A. (*d*) and (*e*) only B. (*a*) and (*b*) only
C. (*a*) and (*c*) only D. (*b*) and (*e*) only

16. In the system of planting, row to row and plant to plant distance is the same.
A. Triangular B. Rectangular
C. Contour D. Square

17. Mangifera indica is the botanical name of which crop?
A. Mango B. Guava
C. Papaya D. Anola

18. Rutaceae is the family of which crop?
A. Mango B. Orange
C. Papaya D. Banana

19. The branch of horticulture that refers to the study of vegetables is known as:
A. Pomology B. Floriculture
C. Plantation D. Olericulture

20. Which technique aims at the development of a strong framework of the plant?
A. Pruning B. Training
C. Bahar Treatment D. Ringing

21. What is the system of planting followed only on hills with high slopes?
A. Quincunx system
B. Hexagonal system
C. Rectangular system
D. Contour system

22. Which family does Mandarin orange (Santra) belong to?
A. Anacardiaceae B. Punicaceae
C. Rutaceae D. Gramineae

23. In which crop is denavelling practice followed?
A. Fig B. Orange
C. Grape D. Banana

24. Which pigment is responsible for the red color of tomatoes?
A. Capsanthin B. Lycopene
C. Anthocyanin D. Melanin

25. Which of the following is not a health benefit of consuming fruits and vegetables regularly?
A. Reduced risk of chronic diseases
B. Improved digestion and bowel movements
C. Enhanced immune system
D. Increased risk of heart disease

26. Which nutrient is commonly found in green leafy vegetables?
A. Vitamin C B. Calcium
C. Vitamin B12 D. Iron

27. What is the primary reason for including a variety of colorful fruits and vegetables in your diet?
A. They provide a range of essential vitamins and minerals
B. They enhance the flavor of meals
C. They are low in calories
D. They are easy to prepare and store

28. Which of the following is a root vegetable?
A. Broccoli B. Carrot
C. Spinach D. Tomato

29. Which vegetable is known for its high vitamin C content?
A. Spinach B. Carrots
C. Broccoli D. Bell peppers

30. Which of the following is an example of crop diversification?
A. Growing the same crop on the same field every year
B. Growing different crops on the same field in different seasons
C. Growing the same crop on different fields in different seasons
D. Growing only one type of crop on a farm

31. Which of the following is a benefit of crop diversification?
A. Increased soil erosion
B. Increased pesticide use
C. Increased risk of disease and pests
D. Reduced risk of crop failure

32. What is the primary goal of the processing industry in agriculture?
A. To reduce the amount of crops produced
B. To increase the amount of crops produced
C. To make crops easier to transport and store
D. To reduce the nutritional value of crops

33. Which of the following is an example of food processing?
A. Canning vegetables
B. Harvesting crops
C. Irrigating fields
D. Plowing fields

34. Which of the following is a challenge faced by the processing industry?
A. Lack of demand for processed foods
B. High costs of processing equipment
C. Difficulty in transporting processed foods
D. All of the above

35. What is the primary purpose of an orchard?
A. To grow ornamental plants
B. To grow vegetables
C. To grow fruits
D. To grow flowers

36. What is the ideal location for an orchard?
A. Low-lying areas with poor drainage
B. Areas with strong winds
C. Areas with heavy rainfall
D. Areas with well-drained soil and adequate sunlight

37. What is the purpose of a kitchen garden?
A. To grow vegetables for commercial purposes
B. To grow flowers for decoration
C. To grow herbs and vegetables for household consumption
D. To grow ornamental plants for display

38. Which of the following is a factor to consider when laying out an orchard?
A. The availability of ornamental plants
B. The amount of rainfall in the area
C. The amount of sunlight in the area
D. The availability of pesticides in the area

39. What is the purpose of ornamental gardening?
A. To grow fruits for commercial purposes
B. To grow flowers for decoration
C. To grow herbs and vegetables for household consumption
D. To grow ornamental plants for display

40. Which of the following is NOT a benefit of intercropping?
A. Reduced pest and disease incidence
B. Efficient use of land and other resources
C. Increased soil fertility
D. Decreased crop yields

41. What is the primary purpose of training and pruning in crop cultivation?
A. To increase yield
B. To control pests and diseases
C. To reduce water usage
D. To improve soil fertility

42. Which of the following is a common method of protection against frost?
A. Mulching
B. Irrigation
C. Fertilization
D. None of the above

43. What is the purpose of sunburn protection in crop cultivation?
A. To increase yield
B. To control pests and diseases
C. To reduce water usage
D. To prevent damage to plant tissues

44. Which of the following is NOT a planting system used in crop cultivation?
A. Quincunx B. Rectangular
C. Triangular D. Circular

45. Which of the following is not an example of a shrub?
A. Hibiscus B. Rose
C. Mango D. Camellia

46. What is the difference between an annual and a perennial plant?
A. Annuals are grown in pots while perennials are grown in the ground.
B. Annuals live for one growing season while perennials live for more than one season.
C. Annuals have woody stems while perennials have herbaceous stems.
D. Annuals are fruit-bearing while perennials are not.

47. Which of the following is not a method of plant propagation?
A. Tissue culture
B. Seed production
C. Fermentation
D. Grafting

48. What is the process of grafting?
A. Joining two plants together to create a new plant.
B. Separating a part of a plant to create a new plant.
C. Cutting off the top of a plant to encourage new growth.
D. Adding nutrients to the soil to improve plant growth.

49. Which of the following is not an example of a climber plant?
A. Grapes B. Jasmine
C. Bougainvillea D. Pansy

50. Which of the following fruits is a climacteric fruit?
A. Guava B. Citrus
C. Mango D. Papaya

51. Which of the following fruits requires a dry climate during ripening?
A. Banana B. Grapes
C. Mango D. Papaya

52. Which of the following fruits is a rich source of vitamin C?
A. Mango B. Papaya
C. Banana D. Citrus

53. Which of the following fruits requires ethylene treatment to induce ripening?
A. Grapes B. Citrus
C. Guava D. Banana

54. Which of the following fruits has the highest sugar content?
A. Mango B. Papaya
C. Banana D. Grapes

55. Which vegetable crop is considered as a good source of vitamin C?
A. Carrot B. Onion
C. Cabbage D. Tomato

56. Which of the following vegetable crops is not a root vegetable?
A. Radish B. Carrot
C. Onion D. Potato

57. Which vegetable crop is known for its high content of beta-carotene?
A. Cauliflower B. Spinach
C. Tomato D. Carrot

58. Which of the following vegetables is a good source of dietary fiber?
A. Radish B. Potato
C. Cabbage D. Spinach

59. Which vegetable crop is often used as a natural dye?
A. Radish B. Spinach
C. Onion D. Cabbage

60. Which of the following is a flower crop?
A. Mango B. Papaya
C. Marigold D. Guava

61. Which flower crop is commonly used for making garlands?
A. Gladiolus B. Canna
C. Chrysanthemums D. Roses

62. Which of the following vegetables is a root vegetable?
A. Tomato B. Onion
C. Cabbage D. Potato

63. Which vegetable crop is commonly used for making pickles?
A. Radish B. Carrot
C. Potato D. Onion

64. Which of the following is a leafy vegetable?
A. Radish B. Carrot
C. Spinach D. Cauliflower

65. Which method of fruit preservation involves heating the fruit in a sealed can or jar?
A. Dehydration B. Canning
C. Freezing D. Pickling

66. What is the process of removing air from packaging and sealing it to prevent spoilage?
A. Blanching
B. Canning
C. Vacuum packing
D. Fermentation

67. Which of the following is a chemical preservative commonly used in fruit preservation?
A. Salt B. Sugar
C. Vinegar D. Sulfur dioxide

68. What is the process of preserving food by exposing it to high pressure and temperature?
A. Dehydration B. Pasteurization
C. Irradiation D. Salting

69. Which method of vegetable preservation involves removing the water content through heat or air?
A. Canning B. Freezing
C. Dehydration D. Pickling

70. Which of the following is NOT a product prepared from fruits and vegetables?
A. Jellies B. Chips
C. Cheese D. Ketchup

71. Which preservation method involves removing water from the fruits and vegetables?
A. Canning
B. Pickling
C. Drying
D. Fermenting

72. Which of the following is NOT an ingredient used in preparing jams and jellies?
A. Sugar B. Pectin
C. Vinegar D. Fruit juice

73. Which of the following is a type of packaging used for preserving fruits and vegetables?
A. Aluminum foil
B. Plastic bags
C. Glass jars
D. All of the above

74. Which of the following is NOT a product made from potatoes?
A. Ketchup B. Chips
C. French fries D. Potato salad

ANSWERS

1	2	3	4	5	6	7	8	9	10
B	A	D	B	B	B	A	A	B	D
11	**12**	**13**	**14**	**15**	**16**	**17**	**18**	**19**	**20**
C	D	B	A	C	D	A	B	D	B
21	**22**	**23**	**24**	**25**	**26**	**27**	**28**	**29**	**30**
D	C	D	B	D	D	A	B	D	B
31	**32**	**33**	**34**	**35**	**36**	**37**	**38**	**39**	**40**
D	C	A	D	C	D	C	C	D	D
41	**42**	**43**	**44**	**45**	**46**	**47**	**48**	**49**	**50**
A	A	D	D	C	B	C	A	D	C
51	**52**	**53**	**54**	**55**	**56**	**57**	**58**	**59**	**60**
B	D	D	A	D	C	D	C	D	C
61	**62**	**63**	**64**	**65**	**66**	**67**	**68**	**69**	**70**
D	D	D	C	B	C	D	B	C	C
71	**72**	**73**	**74**						
C	C	D	A						

● ● ●

Passage Based Questions

PASSAGE 1

Weather and climate are critical factors that affect crop production. The elements of weather that are particularly important to crop growth and development include rainfall, temperature, humidity, wind velocity, and sunshine. These elements can either be beneficial or detrimental to crop production depending on their level and duration.

Rainfall is necessary for crop growth, but excessive or inadequate rainfall can cause problems. Temperature affects crop development, with both high and low temperatures posing potential issues. Humidity can cause diseases and pests, while wind velocity can damage crops and soil. Sunshine is essential for photosynthesis, but too much or too little can affect crop growth.

Weather forecasting can help farmers plan their agricultural activities accordingly. Forecasting can help farmers prepare for droughts, floods, and other weather events that can affect crop production. Climate change also affects crop production, with changes in temperature and rainfall patterns leading to reduced yields in some regions.

1. Which element of weather is necessary for crop growth?
A. Wind velocity B. Sunshine
C. Humidity D. Temperature

2. Which weather element can cause diseases and pests?
A. Rainfall B. Humidity
C. Wind velocity D. Temperature

3. Which weather element can damage crops and soil?
A. Rainfall B. Humidity
C. Wind velocity D. Sunshine

4. How can weather forecasting benefit farmers?
A. By helping them plan agricultural activities
B. By increasing rainfall
C. By reducing humidity
D. By decreasing wind velocity

5. What effect does climate change have on crop production?
A. It increases yields in all regions
B. It has no effect on crop production
C. It reduces yields in some regions
D. It reduces yields in all regions

PASSAGE 2

Cells are the building blocks of life and are the smallest unit of life that can perform all the functions necessary for survival. They are found in all living organisms, from simple bacteria to complex organisms like humans. The structure of a cell is composed of various organelles such as the nucleus, mitochondria, ribosomes, and many more. These organelles have specialized functions, and together they carry out the essential processes that keep the cell alive.

Cell division is the process by which cells divide to form new cells. There are two types of cell division: mitosis and meiosis. Mitosis is a type of cell division that occurs in all body cells except for the reproductive cells. It results in the formation of two identical daughter cells with the same number of chromosomes as the parent cell. Meiosis, on the other hand, is a type of cell division that occurs only in reproductive cells. It results in the formation of four non-identical daughter cells with half the number of chromosomes as the parent cell.

The significance of cell division lies in the fact that it is responsible for the growth and repair of tissues in the body. It also plays a critical role in the production of gametes (sperm and eggs) in sexually reproducing organisms.

1. What is the smallest unit of life?
A. Organelles B. Tissues
C. Cells D. Organisms

2. What are the organelles that make up the structure of a cell?
A. Cells
B. Tissues
C. Organs
D. Mitochondria, nucleus, ribosomes, etc.

3. What is the type of cell division that occurs in all body cells except for reproductive cells?
A. Meiosis B. Mitosis
C. Fertilization D. Gametogenesis

4. How many daughter cells are formed in meiosis?
A. Two identical daughter cells
B. Four non-identical daughter cells
C. One daughter cell
D. Three identical daughter cells

5. What is the significance of cell division?
   A. It has no significance
   B. It is responsible for the growth and repair of tissues
   C. It is responsible for the production of gametes
   D. It is responsible for the production of ATP

PASSAGE 3

Genetic information in living organisms is stored in the form of DNA (deoxyribonucleic acid) molecules. DNA is a long, double-stranded helix that consists of four types of nucleotides: adenine, thymine, cytosine, and guanine. The sequence of these nucleotides forms the genetic code that determines the traits and characteristics of an organism. The DNA molecule is organized into structures called chromosomes. Each chromosome contains a single, long DNA molecule wrapped around proteins called histones.

RNA (ribonucleic acid) is another type of nucleic acid that plays a critical role in the expression of genes. RNA is synthesized from DNA in a process called transcription. There are three types of RNA: messenger RNA (mRNA), transfer RNA (tRNA), and ribosomal RNA (rRNA). mRNA carries the genetic code from the DNA to the ribosomes where it is translated into proteins. tRNA carries amino acids to the ribosomes, where they are assembled into proteins. rRNA forms the structure of the ribosome.

1. Where is genetic information stored in living organisms?
   A. In proteins
   B. In carbohydrates
   C. In lipids
   D. In DNA
2. What is the structure of DNA?
   A. Single-stranded helix
   B. Double-stranded helix
   C. Triple-stranded helix
   D. Quadruple-stranded helix
3. What are chromosomes?
   A. Proteins that store genetic information
   B. Structures that store genetic information in the form of DNA molecules
   C. RNA molecules that carry genetic information
   D. Structures that carry amino acids to the ribosomes
4. What is the process by which RNA is synthesized from DNA?
   A. Translation
   B. Transcription
   C. Replication
   D. Mutation
5. What is the role of mRNA in protein synthesis?
   A. It carries amino acids to the ribosomes
   B. It forms the structure of the ribosome
   C. It carries the genetic code from the DNA to the ribosomes
   D. It breaks down proteins into amino acids

PASSAGE 4

Mendel's laws of inheritance are the fundamental principles of genetics that explain how traits are passed down from one generation to the next. In his experiments, Mendel studied pea plants and discovered two basic laws of inheritance: the law of segregation and the law of independent assortment. The law of segregation states that each individual has two copies of each gene, and these copies separate during gamete formation, with each gamete receiving only one copy. The law of independent assortment states that the inheritance of one gene does not affect the inheritance of another gene.

Mendel's success in his experiments can be attributed to his careful selection of traits, use of purebred plants, and rigorous statistical analysis of his results. He also made sure to control for environmental factors that could affect his results.

In his experiments, Mendel observed no linkage between traits, which means that the inheritance of one trait was not affected by the inheritance of another trait. This observation was later explained by the concept of genetic recombination, which occurs during meiosis when homologous chromosomes exchange genetic material.

1. What are the two basic laws of inheritance discovered by Mendel?
   A. The law of segregation and the law of independent assortment
   B. The law of dominance and the law of segregation
   C. The law of segregation and the law of linkage
   D. The law of independent assortment and the law of linkage
2. What did Mendel study in his experiments?
   A. Bacteria
   B. Pea plants
   C. Fish
   D. Humans
3. How did Mendel ensure the success of his experiments?
   A. By using impurebred plants
   B. By not controlling for environmental factors
   C. By using rigorous statistical analysis and controlling for environmental factors
   D. By not using careful selection of traits
4. What is the concept that explains the absence of linkage in Mendel's experiments?
   A. Genetic recombination
   B. Chromosomal crossover
   C. Genetic linkage
   D. Mitotic recombination
5. What does the law of independent assortment state?
   A. The inheritance of one gene affects the inheritance of another gene
   B. Each individual has two copies of each gene

C. The inheritance of one trait is not affected by the inheritance of another trait
D. The dominant allele masks the expression of the recessive allele

PASSAGE 5

pH is a measure of the acidity or basicity of a solution, with values ranging from 0 to 14. A pH of 7 is considered neutral, while values below 7 are acidic and values above 7 are basic. Buffers are solutions that can resist changes in pH when small amounts of acid or base are added. They are important in maintaining the pH of biological systems, such as blood, within a narrow range.

Carbohydrates, proteins, lipids, vitamins, and enzymes are all important biomolecules in living organisms. Carbohydrates are classified based on their size into monosaccharides, disaccharides, and polysaccharides. Proteins are composed of amino acids, and their functions include structural support, enzymatic catalysis, and regulation of gene expression. Lipids are hydrophobic molecules that include fats, oils, and steroids. Vitamins are essential organic compounds that cannot be synthesized by the body and must be obtained through diet. Enzymes are proteins that catalyze biochemical reactions, increasing the rate of chemical reactions in cells.

1. What is a pH?
   A. A measure of the acidity or basicity of a solution
   B. A measure of the concentration of protons in a solution
   C. A measure of the concentration of hydroxide ions in a solution
   D. A measure of the concentration of water in a solution
2. What are buffers?
   A. Solutions that can resist changes in pH when small amounts of acid or base are added
   B. Solutions that increase the pH of a solution
   C. Solutions that decrease the pH of a solution
   D. Solutions that are only found in acidic environments
3. What are lipids?
   A. Hydrophobic molecules that include fats, oils, and steroids
   B. Molecules composed of amino acids
   C. Essential organic compounds that cannot be synthesized by the body
   D. Proteins that catalyze biochemical reactions
4. What are enzymes?
   A. Proteins that catalyze biochemical reactions
   B. Carbohydrates that are important for energy storage
   C. Lipids that are important for membrane structure
   D. Vitamins that are important for bone growth
5. How are carbohydrates classified?
   A. Based on their color
   B. Based on their solubility in water
   C. Based on their size into monosaccharides, disaccharides, and polysaccharides
   D. Based on their ability to form double bonds

PASSAGE 6

Livestock plays a crucial role in agriculture and industry. They provide a variety of products such as meat, milk, eggs, wool, and leather. Livestock also provides non-food products like manure, which is an important source of nutrients for crops. In addition, livestock also play an important role in the cultural and social practices of many societies.

The livestock industry also provides employment opportunities for many people in different sectors, such as meat processing, veterinary medicine, and transportation. The livestock industry has a significant impact on the economy, both in terms of employment and the value of its products.

Livestock farming also has environmental impacts, such as greenhouse gas emissions and land use. Sustainable livestock management practices are important in reducing these impacts while still maintaining the production of livestock products.

1. What are some products provided by livestock?
   A. Vegetables and fruits
   B. Meat, milk, eggs, wool, and leather
   C. Fish and seafood
   D. Grains and cereals
2. What is the role of livestock in agriculture?
   A. Livestock provides an important source of nutrients for crops
   B. Livestock provides a source of renewable energy
   C. Livestock helps to control pests and weeds in fields
   D. Livestock is not important in agriculture
3. What is the economic impact of the livestock industry?
   A. It has no impact on the economy
   B. It provides employment opportunities for many people in different sectors
   C. It only benefits large corporations
   D. It is not a profitable industry
4. What are some environmental impacts of livestock farming?
   A. Reduced greenhouse gas emissions
   B. Reduced land use
   C. Increased air quality
   D. Increased greenhouse gas emissions and land use
5. Why is sustainable livestock management important?
   A. To increase greenhouse gas emissions
   B. To reduce the environmental impacts of livestock farming

C. To reduce the production of livestock products
D. To decrease employment opportunities in the livestock industry

PASSAGE 7

Since independence, India has made significant progress in foodgrain production. From a situation of food shortage and dependence on imports, India is now self-sufficient in foodgrains, producing enough to meet the needs of its population. The Green Revolution, which began in the 1960s, played a significant role in increasing foodgrain production, especially wheat and rice.

In recent years, there has been a focus on sustainable crop production, with an emphasis on reducing the use of chemical fertilizers and pesticides and promoting organic farming practices. This approach aims to improve soil health, reduce the environmental impact of agriculture, and promote the production of healthier food.

The commercialization of agriculture is also gaining importance in India. There is a growing demand for high-value crops, such as fruits and vegetables, and for processed food products. The growth of the food processing industry offers opportunities for farmers to add value to their products and increase their income.

1. What is the status of India's foodgrain production since independence?
   A. India is still dependent on food imports
   B. India is self-sufficient in foodgrains
   C. India produces enough food for export
   D. India's food production has remained stagnant
2. What was the Green Revolution in India?
   A. A movement to promote organic farming
   B. A campaign to reduce the use of chemical fertilizers
   C. A program to increase foodgrain production, especially wheat and rice
   D. A campaign to reduce the use of water in agriculture
3. What is sustainable crop production?
   A. A focus on reducing the use of chemical fertilizers and pesticides
   B. A focus on increasing foodgrain production at all costs
   C. A focus on using genetically modified crops
   D. A focus on maximizing profits for farmers
4. What is the commercialization of agriculture?
   A. A focus on promoting organic farming practices
   B. A focus on increasing the production of food for domestic consumption
   C. A focus on promoting the growth of the food processing industry
   D. A focus on reducing the use of water in agriculture
5. What are the benefits of sustainable crop production?
   A. Improved soil health and reduced environmental impact
   B. Increased use of chemical fertilizers and pesticides
   C. Reduced food production and increased food prices
   D. Increased profits for farmers

PASSAGE 8

Soil is a complex mixture of organic and inorganic materials that support plant growth. One important characteristic of soil is pH, which is a measure of the soil's acidity or alkalinity. Most plants grow best in soil with a pH between 6 and 7. Soil texture refers to the size of the mineral particles that make up the soil, which can affect water and nutrient retention.

Soil structure refers to how those particles are arranged, which can affect the soil's ability to hold water and air. Soil organisms, such as bacteria, fungi, and earthworms, play important roles in decomposing organic matter and making nutrients available to plants. Soil tilth refers to the physical condition of the soil, including its texture, structure, and water-holding capacity. Soil fertility is a measure of the soil's ability to provide essential nutrients to plants. Soil health refers to the overall condition of the soil, including its physical, chemical, and biological properties.

1. What is soil pH?
   A. A measure of the soil's acidity or alkalinity
   B. The size of the mineral particles in the soil
   C. The arrangement of the soil particles
   D. The physical condition of the soil
2. What is soil texture?
   A. The size of the mineral particles in the soil
   B. The arrangement of the soil particles
   C. The physical condition of the soil
   D. The measure of the soil's ability to provide essential nutrients to plants
3. What is soil structure?
   A. The size of the mineral particles in the soil
   B. The arrangement of the soil particles
   C. The measure of the soil's ability to provide essential nutrients to plants
   D. The measure of the soil's acidity or alkalinity
4. What are soil organisms?
   A. Plants that grow in soil
   B. Animals that live in soil
   C. Bacteria, fungi, and earthworms
   D. Rocks and minerals in the soil
5. What is soil health?
   A. The physical condition of the soil
   B. The measure of the soil's ability to provide essential nutrients to plants
   C. The overall condition of the soil, including its physical, chemical, and biological properties
   D. The size of the mineral particles in the soil

PASSAGE 9

Organic manure is a natural fertilizer that is made from decomposed plant and animal materials. It helps improve soil fertility, structure, and water-holding capacity. Common organic manures include compost, animal dung, and green manure. Straight fertilizers are those that contain only one nutrient, such as nitrogen, phosphorus, or potassium. Complex fertilizers contain two or more nutrients in each granule. Fertilizer mixtures are blends of straight and complex fertilizers to provide a balance of nutrients.

Biofertilizers are living organisms that are added to the soil to help improve soil fertility and nutrient uptake by plants. They include nitrogen-fixing bacteria, phosphate-solubilizing bacteria, and mycorrhizal fungi. Integrated nutrient management system is a strategy that combines the use of organic manure, fertilizers, and biofertilizers to optimize nutrient availability for plant growth while maintaining soil health and fertility.

1. What is organic manure?
A. A chemical fertilizer made from synthetic materials
B. A natural fertilizer made from decomposed plant and animal materials
C. A fertilizer that contains only one nutrient
D. A living organism that is added to the soil to improve fertility

2. What are straight fertilizers?
A. Fertilizers that contain only one nutrient
B. Fertilizers that contain two or more nutrients in each granule
C. Fertilizer blends of straight and complex fertilizers
D. Living organisms that are added to the soil to improve fertility

3. What are complex fertilizers?
A. Fertilizers that contain only one nutrient
B. Fertilizers that contain two or more nutrients in each granule
C. Fertilizer blends of straight and complex fertilizers
D. Living organisms that are added to the soil to improve fertility

4. What are biofertilizers?
A. Chemical fertilizers made from synthetic materials
B. Natural fertilizers made from decomposed plant and animal materials
C. Living organisms that are added to the soil to improve fertility
D. Fertilizer blends of straight and complex fertilizers

5. What is integrated nutrient management system?
A. A strategy that combines the use of organic manure, fertilizers, and biofertilizers
B. A fertilizer that contains only one nutrient
C. A fertilizer blend of straight and complex fertilizers
D. A living organism that is added to the soil to improve fertility

PASSAGE 10

Irrigation is an essential aspect of crop production, and scheduling it appropriately is crucial for optimal yield. The scheduling of irrigation is based on several factors, including the critical growth stages of the crop, time intervals, soil moisture content, and weather parameters.

The critical growth stages of a crop are the periods when the plant is most sensitive to water stress. At these stages, the plant requires more water to support its growth and development. Time intervals for irrigation depend on the type of soil and the crop being grown. For example, sandy soil requires more frequent irrigation than loamy soil.

Soil moisture content is an important factor in determining the need for irrigation. Soil moisture sensors can be used to measure soil moisture content and determine when irrigation is required. Weather parameters such as temperature, wind, and humidity also affect the amount of water that a crop requires.

1. What is irrigation scheduling?
A. The process of planting crops
B. The process of determining when to irrigate crops
C. The process of harvesting crops
D. The process of preparing the land for planting

2. What are critical growth stages of a crop?
A. The periods when the plant is most sensitive to water stress
B. The periods when the plant is most sensitive to pests
C. The periods when the plant is most sensitive to diseases
D. The periods when the plant is least sensitive to water stress

3. What factors determine time intervals for irrigation?
A. The type of soil and the crop being grown
B. The type of fertilizer used
C. The amount of sunlight the crop receives
D. The amount of rainfall in the area

4. How is soil moisture content measured?
A. By using a thermometer
B. By using a rain gauge
C. By using soil moisture sensors
D. By measuring the amount of dew on the plants

5. What weather parameters affect the amount of water a crop requires?
A. Temperature, wind, and humidity
B. Temperature, rainfall, and sunshine
C. Wind, rainfall, and humidity
D. Sunshine, rainfall, and wind

PASSAGE 11

Fruits and vegetables are essential components of a healthy human diet. They are excellent sources of vitamins, minerals, and fiber, which are necessary for maintaining good health. Fruits and vegetables contain phytochemicals, which are compounds that help protect against diseases such as cancer, heart disease, and diabetes.

Fruits and vegetables are also low in calories and fat, making them ideal for weight management. They also contain antioxidants, which can help reduce the risk of chronic diseases by protecting cells from damage caused by free radicals.

Consuming a variety of fruits and vegetables is recommended to ensure a well-balanced diet. The World Health Organization recommends consuming at least five servings of fruits and vegetables per day to reduce the risk of chronic diseases.

1. Why are fruits and vegetables important in human diet?
   A. They are high in calories
   B. They are low in calories and fat
   C. They contain harmful compounds
   D. They have no nutritional value
2. What are phytochemicals?
   A. Compounds that help protect against diseases
   B. Compounds that cause diseases
   C. Compounds that are toxic
   D. Compounds that have no effect on the body
3. How do fruits and vegetables help with weight management?
   A. They are high in calories and fat
   B. They are low in calories and fat
   C. They contain harmful compounds that reduce weight
   D. They have no effect on weight
4. What are antioxidants?
   A. Compounds that protect cells from damage caused by free radicals
   B. Compounds that cause damage to cells
   C. Compounds that have no effect on cells
   D. Compounds that are harmful to the body
5. How many servings of fruits and vegetables are recommended per day by the World Health Organization?
   A. Three servings B. Four servings
   C. Five servings D. Six servings

PASSAGE 12

Planting systems, training, pruning, intercropping, and protection from frost and sunburn are important techniques used in crop production to optimize yield and quality of crops.

Planting systems refer to the arrangement of plants in a field or plot. Different planting systems include monoculture, where only one crop is grown, and intercropping, where two or more crops are grown together in the same field. Intercropping can provide benefits such as increased yield, pest control, and soil fertility.

Training and pruning are techniques used to shape the plant and promote optimal growth. They involve removing unwanted branches, shoots, or leaves from the plant. This helps to improve the plant's structure, increase air circulation, and ensure proper distribution of nutrients.

Protection from frost and sunburn is crucial to ensure crop survival and yield. Frost protection methods include using frost blankets, heaters, and windbreaks, while sunburn protection methods include shading and use of reflective materials.

1. What is planting system?
   A. The arrangement of plants in a field or plot
   B. The method of watering plants
   C. The technique of pruning plants
   D. The type of fertilizer used in crop production
2. What is intercropping?
   A. Growing only one crop in a field
   B. Growing two or more crops together in the same field
   C. Growing crops in water
   D. Growing crops in a greenhouse
3. What is the purpose of training and pruning?
   A. To shape the plant and promote optimal growth
   B. To increase water uptake in the plant
   C. To increase nutrient content of the plant
   D. To reduce plant yield
4. What is a method of frost protection?
   A. Use of wind turbines
   B. Use of reflective materials
   C. Use of pesticides
   D. Use of loud noises
5. What is a method of sunburn protection?
   A. Use of frost blankets
   B. Use of heaters
   C. Use of shading
   D. Use of water

PASSAGE 13

Preservation of fruits and vegetables is important to extend their shelf life and prevent spoilage. The principles and methods of preservation vary depending on the type of fruit or vegetable and the desired end product.

One common method of preservation is canning, where fruits and vegetables are sealed in airtight containers and heated to high temperatures to kill microorganisms. Another

method is drying, where fruits and vegetables are dehydrated to remove moisture and inhibit bacterial growth. Freezing is also a popular preservation method that involves storing fruits and vegetables at very low temperatures to maintain their quality and freshness.

Other methods of preservation include pickling, where fruits and vegetables are soaked in vinegar or brine, and fermenting, where fruits and vegetables are soaked in a salt solution to encourage the growth of beneficial bacteria.

1. What is canning?
   A. Storing fruits and vegetables at low temperatures
   B. Sealing fruits and vegetables in airtight containers and heating to high temperatures
   C. Soaking fruits and vegetables in vinegar or brine
   D. Dehydrating fruits and vegetables
2. What is drying?
   A. Storing fruits and vegetables at low temperatures
   B. Sealing fruits and vegetables in airtight containers and heating to high temperatures
   C. Soaking fruits and vegetables in vinegar or brine
   D. Dehydrating fruits and vegetables
3. What is freezing?
   A. Storing fruits and vegetables at low temperatures
   B. Sealing fruits and vegetables in airtight containers and heating to high temperatures
   C. Soaking fruits and vegetables in vinegar or brine
   D. Dehydrating fruits and vegetables
4. What is pickling?
   A. Storing fruits and vegetables at low temperatures
   B. Sealing fruits and vegetables in airtight containers and heating to high temperatures
   C. Soaking fruits and vegetables in vinegar or brine
   D. Dehydrating fruits and vegetables
5. What is fermenting?
   A. Storing fruits and vegetables at low temperatures
   B. Sealing fruits and vegetables in airtight containers and heating to high temperatures
   C. Soaking fruits and vegetables in vinegar or brine
   D. Soaking fruits and vegetables in a salt solution

PASSAGE 14

Trees, shrubs, climbers, annuals, and perennials are all different types of plants based on their life cycles and growth habits. Trees are perennial woody plants that have a single stem or trunk with a well-defined crown. Shrubs are also woody plants, but they have multiple stems and usually grow to a shorter height than trees. Climbers are plants that climb on other plants or structures for support. Annuals complete their life cycle within a year, and their seeds need to be replanted each year for continuous growth. Perennials live for multiple years and regrow each season from the same roots.

Plants can be propagated by various methods, including seeds, cuttings, budding, layering, and grafting. Seeds are the most common method of propagation for annuals and some perennials. Cuttings are used to propagate shrubs and climbers, while budding and grafting are used to propagate fruit trees and other woody plants. Layering is a method of propagation where a branch is allowed to grow roots while still attached to the parent plant before being separated and replanted.

1. Which type of plant completes its life cycle within a year?
   A. Trees B. Shrubs
   C. Climbers D. Annuals
2. What is the primary method of propagation for annuals and some perennials?
   A. Seeds B. Cuttings
   C. Budding D. Grafting
3. Which method of propagation is used to propagate fruit trees and other woody plants?
   A. Seeds B. Cuttings
   C. Budding D. Grafting
4. Which type of plant regrows each season from the same roots?
   A. Trees B. Shrubs
   C. Climbers D. Perennials
5. Which method of propagation involves allowing a branch to grow roots while still attached to the parent plant before being separated and replanted?
   A. Seeds B. Cuttings
   C. Budding D. Layering

PASSAGE 15

Post-harvest technology plays a crucial role in maintaining the quality of agricultural produce and increasing the shelf life of crops. Storage, processing, and marketing of major field crops are essential to meet the food and nutritional requirements of a growing population.

Rice, wheat, maize, sorghum, pearl millet, groundnut, mustard, pigeon-pea, gram, sugarcane, cotton, and berseem are some of the major field crops in India. Proper storage techniques like fumigation, drying, and storage in airtight containers can prevent pest infestation and spoilage. Processing techniques like milling, threshing, and grading can improve the quality of the produce and increase its value.

Marketing of the crops involves the process of transportation, packaging, and selling to the consumers. Proper packaging techniques like vacuum packaging, modified atmosphere packaging, and use of preservatives can increase the shelf life of the crops and reduce wastage.

1. Which of the following is a major field crop in India?
   A. Mango B. Banana
   C. Wheat D. Papaya

2. Which of the following storage techniques can prevent pest infestation in crops?
A. Open storage B. Airtight containers
C. Direct sunlight D. High humidity

3. Which of the following processing techniques can improve the quality of the produce?
A. Over-ripening B. Milling
C. Delayed harvesting D. Improper grading

4. What is the process of transportation, packaging, and selling of crops called?
A. Cultivation B. Irrigation
C. Marketing D. Harvesting

5. Which of the following packaging techniques can increase the shelf life of crops?
A. Use of preservatives
B. Open packaging
C. Exposure to direct sunlight
D. Use of paper bags

PASSAGE 16

Weeds are unwanted plants that grow in crop fields and compete with crops for water, nutrients and sunlight. They reduce crop yield and quality. Effective weed control is essential for successful crop production. The principles of weed control include prevention, suppression and eradication of weeds.

Weed control can be achieved through cultural, mechanical, chemical, biological and integrated weed management methods. Cultural weed control involves practices like crop rotation, intercropping and use of cover crops to prevent weed growth. Mechanical weed control methods involve physical removal of weeds through hand weeding, hoeing, plowing, and use of weeders.

Chemical weed control involves the use of herbicides to kill weeds. Biological weed control involves the use of natural enemies of weeds like insects and pathogens to control weed growth. Integrated weed management involves the use of a combination of cultural, mechanical, chemical and biological weed control methods for effective weed control.

1. Which method of weed control involves the use of herbicides?
A. Cultural B. Mechanical
C. Chemical D. Biological

2. Which method of weed control involves physical removal of weeds?
A. Cultural B. Mechanical
C. Chemical D. Biological

3. Which method of weed control involves the use of natural enemies of weeds?
A. Cultural B. Mechanical
C. Chemical D. Biological

4. Which weed control method involves the use of crop rotation and intercropping?
A. Cultural B. Mechanical
C. Chemical D. Biological

5. Which method of weed control involves the use of a combination of cultural, mechanical, chemical and biological weed control methods?
A. Cultural
B. Mechanical
C. Chemical
D. Integrated weed management

PASSAGE 17

Plants require a variety of nutrients for their growth and development. There are 16 essential plant nutrients, including macronutrients and micronutrients. Macronutrients are required in large amounts, while micronutrients are needed in smaller quantities. The macronutrients include nitrogen, phosphorus, potassium, calcium, magnesium, and sulfur, while micronutrients include iron, manganese, zinc, copper, boron, molybdenum, chlorine, nickel, and cobalt.

Each nutrient has a specific function in the plant. Nitrogen is necessary for the growth of leaves and stems, phosphorus is important for root development and flower formation, potassium helps in the formation of strong stems and resistance to diseases, calcium is essential for cell wall formation, magnesium is required for chlorophyll synthesis, and sulfur is needed for protein synthesis.

Deficiency symptoms vary for each nutrient. Nitrogen deficiency leads to stunted growth and yellowing of leaves, while phosphorus deficiency causes slow growth and dark green leaves. Potassium deficiency results in yellowing and scorching of leaf margins, and calcium deficiency causes tip burn in fruits and leaves. Magnesium deficiency leads to yellowing of leaves between veins, and sulfur deficiency causes yellowing of young leaves.

1. How many essential plant nutrients are there?
A. 10 B. 12
C. 16 D. 20

2. Which nutrient is necessary for the growth of leaves and stems?
A. Nitrogen B. Phosphorus
C. Potassium D. Calcium

3. What does phosphorus deficiency cause in plants?
A. Yellowing of leaves
B. Stunted growth
C. Slow growth and dark green leaves
D. Yellowing and scorching of leaf margins

4. What does potassium deficiency cause in plants?
A. Yellowing of leaves
B. Stunted growth
C. Slow growth and dark green leaves
D. Yellowing and scorching of leaf margins

5. What does magnesium deficiency cause in plants?
A. Yellowing of leaves between veins
B. Stunted growth
C. Slow growth and dark green leaves
D. Tip burn in fruits and leaves

PASSAGE 18

Sources of irrigation play a crucial role in agriculture, as they ensure that crops receive adequate water for growth and development. The primary sources of irrigation include rain, canals, tanks, rivers, wells, and tubewells. Rain is the natural source of irrigation and is unpredictable, making it essential to store rainwater through the construction of tanks and reservoirs.

Canals are man-made channels that carry water from a river or a reservoir to the fields. Tanks are also used to store water, and they are typically constructed in areas with low rainfall. Rivers are another source of irrigation, with water being diverted from the river to the fields through canals. Wells and tubewells provide irrigation through groundwater, and they are essential in areas where there is a scarcity of surface water.

1. What is the primary source of irrigation?
A. Canals B. Tanks
C. Rain D. Rivers

2. Which source of irrigation involves the diversion of water from a river to the fields?
A. Wells B. Tanks
C. Canals D. Tubewells

3. In which areas are tanks typically constructed?
A. Areas with high rainfall
B. Areas with low rainfall
C. Areas with moderate rainfall
D. Areas with unpredictable rainfall

4. Which source of irrigation involves the use of groundwater?
A. Canals B. Tanks
C. Rain D. Wells

5. Which source of irrigation involves man-made channels?
A. Rain B. Wells
C. Canals D. Rivers

PASSAGE 19

Animal husbandry is a crucial aspect of agriculture that involves the breeding, feeding, and management of livestock. In India, livestock is a significant source of income for farmers, and it contributes significantly to the country's economy. Proper management of calves, bullocks, pregnant and milch animals, as well as chicks, crockrels, and layers in poultry, is essential to maintain their health and ensure optimum production.

The management of calves involves proper feeding, shelter, and regular health check-ups to ensure their growth and development. Bullocks are used in agriculture for plowing and transportation, and their management includes feeding, exercise, and regular veterinary check-ups. Pregnant and milch animals require proper nutrition, hygiene, and care to ensure their health and productivity. Chicks, cockerels and layers require proper housing, feed, and disease management for their growth and egg production.

1. Which of the following is NOT a crucial aspect of animal husbandry?
A. Breeding B. Management
C. Transportation D. Feeding

2. Which animal is used in agriculture for plowing and transportation?
A. Calves B. Layers
C. Bullocks D. Chicks

3. Which of the following is necessary for the management of pregnant and milch animals?
A. Regular exercise B. Proper nutrition
C. Housing D. Disease management

4. What is the primary requirement for the management of chicks, cockerels and layers in poultry?
A. Shelter
B. Disease management
C. Feed
D. Regular veterinary check-ups

5. Which animal requires regular health check-ups to ensure growth and development?
A. Calves B. Layers
C. Bullocks D. Chicks

PASSAGE 20

Plant biotechnology is the use of scientific methods and tools to modify plants for various purposes such as improving crop yields, developing resistance to pests and diseases, and creating plants with desirable traits. The scope of plant biotechnology is vast and includes genetic engineering, tissue culture, molecular biology, and bioinformatics.

With the advancement of technology, scientists can manipulate the genetic material of plants to produce crops with desirable traits, such as drought and salt tolerance, disease resistance, and improved nutritional value. This field also plays a vital role in sustainable agriculture and addressing global food security challenges. Plant biotechnology has the potential to revolutionize crop production, but it also raises ethical, environmental, and social concerns. Therefore, it is important to ensure that the development and use of plant biotechnology are ethical, safe, and sustainable.

1. What is plant biotechnology?
A. The study of plant growth
B. The use of scientific methods and tools to modify plants
C. The study of plant genetics
D. The study of plant diseases

2. What is the scope of plant biotechnology?
A. Genetic engineering only
B. Tissue culture only
C. Molecular biology only
D. Genetic engineering, tissue culture, molecular biology, and bioinformatics

3. What are the benefits of plant biotechnology?
A. Developing resistance to pests and diseases
B. Creating plants with desirable traits
C. Improving nutritional value of crops
D. All of the above

4. What are the ethical, environmental, and social concerns associated with plant biotechnology?
A. Overuse of pesticides
B. Genetic modification without proper regulation
C. Depletion of natural resources
D. All of the above

5. Why is it important to ensure the ethical, safe, and sustainable development and use of plant biotechnology?
A. To address global food security challenges
B. To reduce the cost of crop production
C. To increase the use of pesticides
D. None of the above

ANSWERS

PASSAGE 1

1	2	3	4	5
B	B	C	A	C

PASSAGE 2

1	2	3	4	5
C	D	B	B	B

PASSAGE 3

1	2	3	4	5
D	B	B	B	C

PASSAGE 4

1	2	3	4	5
A	B	C	A	C

PASSAGE 5

1	2	3	4	5
A	A	A	A	C

PASSAGE 6

1	2	3	4	5
B	A	B	D	B

PASSAGE 7

1	2	3	4	5
B	C	A	C	A

PASSAGE 8

1	2	3	4	5
A	A	B	C	C

PASSAGE 9

1	2	3	4	5
B	A	B	C	A

PASSAGE 10

1	2	3	4	5
B	A	A	C	A

PASSAGE 11

1	2	3	4	5
B	A	B	A	C

PASSAGE 12

1	2	3	4	5
A	B	A	B	C

PASSAGE 13

1	2	3	4	5
B	D	A	C	D

PASSAGE 14

1	2	3	4	5
D	A	D	D	D

PASSAGE 15

1	2	3	4	5
C	B	B	C	A

PASSAGE 16

1	2	3	4	5
C	B	D	A	D

PASSAGE 17

1	2	3	4	5
C	A	C	D	A

PASSAGE 18

1	2	3	4	5
C	C	B	D	C

PASSAGE 19

1	2	3	4	5
C	C	B	C	A

PASSAGE 20

1	2	3	4	5
B	D	D	B	A